SAS® Certified Specialist Prep Guide: Base Programming Using SAS® 9.4

SAS® Documentation

The correct bibliographic citation for this manual is as follows: SAS Institute Inc. 2019. *SAS® Certified Specialist Prep Guide: Base Programming Using SAS® 9.4*. Cary, NC: SAS Institute Inc.

SAS® Certified Specialist Prep Guide: Base Programming Using SAS® 9.4

ISBN 978-1-64295-179-0 (Hard copy)
ISBN 978-1-64295-176-9 (Epub)
ISBN 978-1-64295-177-6 (Mobi)
ISBN 978-1-64295-178-3 (PDF)

SAS Institute Inc., SAS Campus Drive, Cary, NC 27513-2414

February 2019

P1:certsppg

Contents

How to Prepare for the Exam

Requirements and Details

Requirements

To complete examples in this book, you must have access to SAS windowing environment, SAS Enterprise Guide, or SAS Studio.

Exam Objectives and Updates to This Book

The current exam objectives and a list of any updates to this book are available at www.sas.com/certify (https://www.sas.com/en_us/certification.html). Exam objectives are subject to change.

Take a Practice Exam

Practice exams are available for purchase through SAS and Pearson VUE. For more information about practice exams, see www.sas.com/base_programmer_cert (https://www.sas.com/en_us/certification/credentials/foundation-tools/base-programmer.html).

Registering for the Exam

To register for the SAS 9.4 Base Programming – Performance-Based Exam, see the SAS Global Certification website at www.sas.com/certify (https://www.sas.com/en_us/certification.html).

Additional Resources for Learning SAS Programming

From SAS Software	
Help	• SAS®9: Select **Help** ⇨ **SAS Help and Documentation**. • SAS Enterprise Guide: Select **Help** ⇨ **SAS Enterprise Guide Help**. • SAS Studio: Select the Help icon ⓘ.

From SAS Software	
Documentation	• SAS®9: Select **Help** ⇨ **SAS Help and Documentation**. • SAS Enterprise Guide: Access online documentation on the web. • SAS Studio: Select the Help icon ⓘ and then click **Help**.

On the Web	
Base SAS Glossary	support.sas.com/baseglossary (http://support.sas.com/baseglossary)
Bookstore	www.sas.com/books (http://www.sas.com/sas/books.html)
Certification	www.sas.com/certify (http://www.sas.com/certify)
Communities	communities.sas.com (http://communities.sas.com)
Knowledge Base	support.sas.com/notes (http://support.sas.com/notes/index.html)
Learning Center	www.sas.com (http://www.sas.com) and click **Learn**. Then select **Get Started with SAS**.
SAS Documentation	support.sas.com/documentation (http://support.sas.com/documentation/) documentation.sas.com (http://documentation.sas.com)
SAS Global Academic Program	www.sas.com (http://www.sas.com/en_us/learn.html) and click **Learn**. Then select **For Students and Educators**.
SAS OnDemand	support.sas.com/ondemand/ (http://support.sas.com/ondemand/)
Syntax Quick Reference Guide	support.sas.com/content/dam/SAS/support/en/books/data/base-syntax-ref.pdf (http://support.sas.com/content/dam/SAS/support/en/books/data/base-syntax-ref.pdf)
Training	www.sas.com/training (http://www.sas.com/training)
Technical Support	support.sas.com (http://support.sas.com/en/technical-support.html). Then select **Technical Support**.

Syntax Conventions

In this book, SAS syntax looks like this example:

DATA *output-SAS-data-set*
    (**DROP**=*variables(s)* | **KEEP**=*variables(s)*);
  SET *SAS-data-set <options>*;
  BY *variable(s)*;
RUN;

Here are the conventions that are used in the example:

- DATA, DROP=, KEEP=, SET, BY, and RUN are in uppercase bold because they must be spelled as shown.
- *output-SAS-data-set*, *variable(s)*, *SAS-data-set*, and *options* are in italics because each represents a value that you supply.
- *<options>* is enclosed in angle brackets because it is optional syntax.
- DROP= and KEEP= are separated by a vertical bar (|) to indicate that they are mutually exclusive.

The example syntax that is shown in this book includes only what you need to know in order to prepare for the certification exam. For complete syntax, see the appropriate SAS reference guide.

Accessibility Features of the Prep Guide

Overview

The *SAS Certified Specialist Prep Guide: Base Programming Using SAS 9.4* is a test preparation document that uses the following environments and products:

- SAS windowing environment
- SAS Enterprise Guide
- SAS Studio or SAS University Edition

Accessibility Documentation Help

The following table contains accessibility information for the listed products:

Accessibility Documentation Links

Product or Environment	Where to Find Accessibility Documentation
Base SAS (Microsoft Windows, UNIX, and z/OS)	support.sas.com/baseaccess (http://support.sas.com/baseaccess)
SAS Enterprise Guide	support.sas.com/documentation/onlinedoc/guide/index.html (http://support.sas.com/documentation/onlinedoc/guide/index.html)
SAS Studio	support.sas.com/studioaccess (http://support.sas.com/studioaccess)

Documentation Format

Contact accessibility@sas.com if you need this document in an alternative digital format.

Part 1

SAS Certified Specialist Prep Guide

Chapter 1

Setting Up Practice Data

Accessing Your Practice Data

Requirements

To complete examples in this book, you must have access to SAS Studio, SAS Enterprise Guide, or the SAS windowing environment.

Practice Data ZIP File

The ZIP file includes SAS data sets, Microsoft Excel workbooks (.xlsx), CSV files (.csv), and TXT files (.txt) that are used in examples in this book. To access these files and create your practice data, follow the instructions below.

Instructions

1. Navigate to support.sas.com/content/dam/SAS/support/en/books/data/base-guide-practice-data.zip (http://support.sas.com/content/dam/SAS/support/en/books/data/base-guide-practice-data.zip), download and save the practice data ZIP file.
2. Unzip the file and save it to a location that is accessible to SAS.
3. Open the `cre8data.sas` program in the SAS environment of your choice.
   - SAS Studio: In the Navigation pane, expand **Files and Folders** and then navigate to the `Cert` folder within the `practice-data` folder.
   - SAS Enterprise Guide: In the Servers list, expand **Servers** ⇨ **Local** ⇨ **Files**, and then navigate to the `Cert` folder in the `practice-data` folder.
   - SAS windowing environment: Click **File** ⇨ **Open Program**, and then navigate to the `Cert` folder in the `practice-data` folder.
4. In the Path macro variable, replace `/folders/myfolders` with the path to the `Cert` folder and run the program.

```
%let path=/folders/myfolders/cert;
```

Important: The location that you specify for the Path macro variable and the location of your downloaded SAS programs should be the same location. Otherwise, the **cre8data.sas** program cannot create the practice data.

Your practice data is now created and ready for you to use.

TIP When you end your SAS session, the Path macro variable in the **cre8data.sas** program is reset. To avoid having to rerun **cre8data.sas** every time, run the **libname.sas** program from the **Cert** folder to restore the libraries.

Chapter 2
Basic Concepts

Getting Started

In the SAS 9.4 Base Programming – Performance-Based exam, you are not tested on the details of running SAS software in the various environments. However, you might find such information useful when working with the practice data.

You can access a brief overview of the windows and menus in the SAS windowing environment, SAS Enterprise Guide, and SAS Studio at http://video.sas.com/ (https://video.sas.com//#category/videos/programming). From **Categories** select **How To Tutorials** ⇨ **Programming**. Select the video for your SAS environment. Other tutorials are available from the SAS website.

The Basics of the SAS Language

SAS Statements

A *SAS statement* is a type of SAS language element that is used to perform a particular operation in a SAS program or to provide information to a SAS program. SAS statements are free-format. This means that they can begin and end anywhere on a line, that one statement can continue over several lines, and that several statements can be on the same line. Blank or special characters separate words in a SAS statement.

TIP You can specify SAS statements in uppercase or lowercase. In most situations, text that is enclosed in quotation marks is case sensitive.

Here are two important rules for writing SAS programs:

- A SAS statement ends with a semicolon.
- A statement usually begins with a SAS keyword.

There are two types of SAS statements:

- statements that are used in DATA and PROC steps
- statements that are global in scope and can be used anywhere in a SAS program

Global Statements

Global statements are used anywhere in a SAS program and stay in effect until changed or canceled, or until the SAS session ends. Here are some common global statements: TITLE, LIBNAME, OPTIONS, and FOOTNOTE.

DATA Step

The *DATA step* creates or modifies data. Input for a DATA can include raw data or a SAS data set. Output from a DATA step can include a SAS data set or a report. A *SAS data set* is a data file that is formatted in a way that SAS can understand.

For example, you can use DATA steps to do the following:

- put your data into a SAS data set

- compute values
- check for and correct errors in your data
- produce new SAS data sets by subsetting, supersetting, merging, and updating existing data sets

PROC Step

The *PROC step* analyzes data, produces output, or manages SAS files. The input for a PROC (procedure) step is usually a SAS data set. Output from a PROC step can include a report or an updated SAS data set.

For example, you can use PROC steps to do the following:

- create a report that lists the data
- analyze data
- create a summary report
- produce plots and charts

SAS Program Structure

A SAS program consists of a sequence of steps. A program can be any combination of DATA or PROC steps. A step is a sequence of SAS statements.

Here is an example of a simple SAS program.

Example Code 1 *A Simple SAS Program*

```
title1 'June Billing';          /*#1*/
data work.junefee;              /*#2*/
  set cert.admitjune;
  where age>39;
run;                            /*#3*/
proc print data=work.junefee;   /*#4*/
run;
```

1 The TITLE statement is a global statement. Global statements are typically outside steps and do not require a RUN statement.

2 The DATA step creates a new SAS data set named Work.JuneFee. The SET statement reads in the data from Cert.AdmitJune. The new data set contains only those observations whose value for Age is greater than 39.

3 If a RUN or QUIT statement is not used at the end of a step, SAS assumes that the beginning of a new step implies the end of the previous step. If a RUN or QUIT statement is not used at the end of the last step in a program, SAS Studio and SAS Enterprise Guide automatically submit a RUN and QUIT statement after the submitted code.

4 The PROC PRINT step prints a listing of the new SAS data set. A PROC step begins with a PROC statement, which begins with the keyword PROC.

Output 2.1 *PRINT Procedure Output*

June Billing

Obs	ID	Name	Sex	Age	Date	Height	Weight	ActLevel	Fee
1	2575	Quigley, M	F	40	06/06/10	69	163	HIGH	124.80
2	2589	Wilcox, E	F	41	06/17/10	67	141	HIGH	149.75
3	2523	Johnson, R	F	43	06/17/10	63	137	MOD	149.75
4	2584	Takahashi, Y	F	43	06/18/10	65	123	MOD	124.80
5	2571	Nunnelly, A	F	44	06/19/10	66	140	HIGH	149.75
6	2578	Cameron, L	M	47	06/20/10	72	173	MOD	124.80
7	2568	Eberhardt, S	F	49	06/21/10	64	172	LOW	124.80
8	2539	LaMance, K	M	51	06/22/10	71	158	LOW	124.80
9	2595	Warren, C	M	54	06/15/10	71	183	MOD	149.75
10	2579	Underwood, K	M	60	06/11/10	71	191	LOW	149.75

Processing SAS Programs

When a SAS program is submitted for execution, SAS first validates the syntax and then compiles the statements. DATA and PROC statements signal the beginning of a new step. The beginning of a new step also implies the end of the previous step. At a step boundary, SAS executes any statement that has not been previously executed and ends the step.

Example Code 2 *Processing SAS Programs*

```
data work.admit2;                    /*#1*/
  set cert.admit;
  where age>39;
proc print data=work.admit2;         /*#2*/
run;                                 /*#3*/
```

1 The DATA step creates a new SAS data set named Work.Admit2 by reading Cert.Admit. The DATA statement is the beginning of the new step. The SET statement is used to read data. The WHERE statement conditionally reads only the observations where the value of the variable Age is greater than 39.

2 The PROC PRINT step prints the new SAS data set named Work.Admit2. The PROC PRINT statement serves as a step boundary in this example because a RUN statement was not used at the end of the DATA step. The PROC step also implies the end of the DATA step.

3 The RUN statement ends the PROC step.

TIP The RUN statement is not required between steps in a SAS program. However, it is a best practice to use a RUN statement because it can make the SAS program easier to read and the SAS log easier to understand when debugging.

Log Messages

The SAS log collects messages about the processing of SAS programs and about any errors that occur. Each time a step is executed, SAS generates a log of the processing activities and the results of the processing.

When SAS processes the sample program, it produces the log messages shown below. Notice that you get separate sets of messages for each step in the program.

Log 2.1 *SAS Log Messages for Each Program Step*

```
5    data work.admit2;
6        set cert.admit;
7        where age>39;
8    run;

NOTE: There were 10 observations read from the data set CERT.ADMIT.
      WHERE age>39;
NOTE: The data set WORK.ADMIT2 has 10 observations and 9 variables.
NOTE: DATA statement used (Total process time):
      real time           0.00 seconds
      cpu time            0.00 seconds

9    proc print data=work.admit2;
NOTE: Writing HTML Body file: sashtml.htm
10   run;

NOTE: There were 10 observations read from the data set WORK.ADMIT2.
NOTE: PROCEDURE PRINT used (Total process time):
      real time           0.35 seconds
      cpu time            0.24 seconds
```

Results of Processing

The DATA Step

Suppose you submit the sample program below:

```
data work.admit2;
  set cert.admit;
  where age>39;
run;
```

When the program is processed, it creates a new SAS data set, Work.Admit2, containing only those observations with age values greater than 39. The DATA step creates a new data set and produces messages in the SAS log, but it does not create a report or other output.

The PROC Step

If you add a PROC PRINT step to this same example, the program produces the same new data set as before, but it also creates the following report:

```
data work.admit2;
  set cert.admit;
  where age>39;
run;
```

```
proc print data=work.admit2;
run;
```

Figure 2.1 *PRINT Procedure Output*

The SAS System

Obs	ID	Name	Sex	Age	Date	Height	Weight	ActLevel	Fee
1	2523	Johnson, R	F	43	31	63	137	MOD	149.75
2	2539	LaMance, K	M	51	4	71	158	LOW	124.80
3	2568	Eberhardt, S	F	49	27	64	172	LOW	124.80
4	2571	Nunnelly, A	F	44	19	66	140	HIGH	149.75
5	2575	Quigley, M	F	40	8	69	163	HIGH	124.80
6	2578	Cameron, L	M	47	5	72	173	MOD	124.80
7	2579	Underwood, K	M	60	22	71	191	LOW	149.75
8	2584	Takahashi, Y	F	43	29	65	123	MOD	124.80
9	2589	Wilcox, E	F	41	16	67	141	HIGH	149.75
10	2595	Warren, C	M	54	7	71	183	MOD	149.75

Other Procedures

SAS programs often invoke procedures that create output in the form of a report, as is the case with the FREQ procedure:

```
proc freq data=sashelp.cars;
  table origin*DriveTrain;
run;
```

Figure 2.2 *FREQ Procedure Output*

The FREQ Procedure

Frequency Percent Row Pct Col Pct

Table of Origin by DriveTrain				
	DriveTrain			
Origin	All	Front	Rear	Total
Asia	34 7.94 21.52 36.96	99 23.13 62.66 43.81	25 5.84 15.82 22.73	158 36.92
Europe	36 8.41 29.27 39.13	37 8.64 30.08 16.37	50 11.68 40.65 45.45	123 28.74
USA	22 5.14 14.97 23.91	90 21.03 61.22 39.82	35 8.18 23.81 31.82	147 34.35
Total	92 21.50	226 52.80	110 25.70	428 100.00

Other SAS programs perform tasks such as sorting and managing data, which have no visible results except for messages in the log. (All SAS programs produce log messages, but some SAS programs produce only log messages.)

```
proc sort data=cert.admit;
  by sex;
run;
```

Log 2.2 *SAS Log: COPY Procedure Output*

```
11   proc sort data=cert.admit;
12       by sex;
13   run;

NOTE: There were 21 observations read from the data set
      CERT.ADMIT.
NOTE: The data set CERT.ADMIT has 21 observations and 9
      variables.
NOTE: PROCEDURE SORT used (Total process time):
      real time           0.01 seconds
      cpu time            0.00 seconds
```

SAS Libraries

Definition

A *SAS library* contains one or more files that are defined, recognized, and accessible by SAS, and that are referenced and stored as a unit. One special type of file is called a *catalog*. In SAS libraries, catalogs function much like subfolders for grouping other members.

Predefined SAS Libraries

By default, SAS defines several libraries for you:

Sashelp
: a permanent library that contains sample data and other files that control how SAS works at your site. This is a Read-Only library.

Sasuser
: a permanent library that contains SAS files in the Profile catalog and that stores your personal settings. This is also a convenient place to store your own files.

Work
: a temporary library for files that do not need to be saved from session to session.

You can also define additional libraries. When you define a library, you indicate the location of your SAS files to SAS. After you define a library, you can manage SAS files within it.

Note: If you are using SAS Studio, you might encounter the Webwork library. Webwork is the default output library in interactive mode. For more information about the Webwork library, see *SAS Studio: User's Guide*.

Defining Libraries

To define a library, you assign a library name to it and specify the location of the files, such as a directory path.

You can also specify an engine, which is a set of internal instructions that SAS uses for writing to and reading from files in a library.

You can define SAS libraries using programming statements. For information about how to write LIBNAME statements to define SAS libraries, see Assigning Librefs on page 25.

TIP Depending on your operating environment and the SAS/ACCESS products that you license, you can create libraries with various engines. Each engine enables you to read a different file format, including file formats from other software vendors.

When you delete a SAS library, the pointer to the library is deleted, and SAS no longer has access to the library. However, the contents of the library still exist in your operating environment.

How SAS Files Are Stored

A SAS library is the highest level of organization for information within SAS.

For example, in the Windows and UNIX environments, a library is typically a group of SAS files in the same folder or directory.

The table below summarizes the implementation of SAS libraries in various operating environments.

Table 2.1 *Environments and SAS Libraries*

Environment	Library Definition
Windows, UNIX	a group of SAS files that are stored in the same directory. Other files can be stored in the directory, but only the files that have SAS file extensions are recognized as part of the SAS library.
z/OS	a specially formatted host data set in which only SAS files are stored.

Storing Files Temporarily or Permanently

Depending on the library name that you use when you create a file, you can store SAS files temporarily or permanently.

Table 2.2 *Temporary and Permanent SAS Libraries*

Temporary SAS libraries last only for the current SAS session.	If you do not specify a library name when you create a file, the file is stored in the temporary SAS library, Work. If you specify the library name Work, then the file is stored in the temporary SAS library. When you end the session, the temporary library and all of its files are deleted.

Permanent SAS libraries are available to you during subsequent SAS sessions.	To store files permanently in a SAS library, specify a library name other than the default library name Work. In the example, when you specify the library name Cert when you create a file, you are specifying that the file is to be stored in a permanent SAS library.

Referencing SAS Files

Referencing Permanent SAS Data Sets

To reference a permanent SAS data set in your SAS programs, use a two-level name consisting of the library name and the data set name:

libref.dataset
: In the two-level name, *libref* is the name of the SAS library that contains the data set, and *data set* is the name of the SAS data set. A period separates the libref and data set name.

Figure 2.3 *Two-Level Permanent SAS Name*

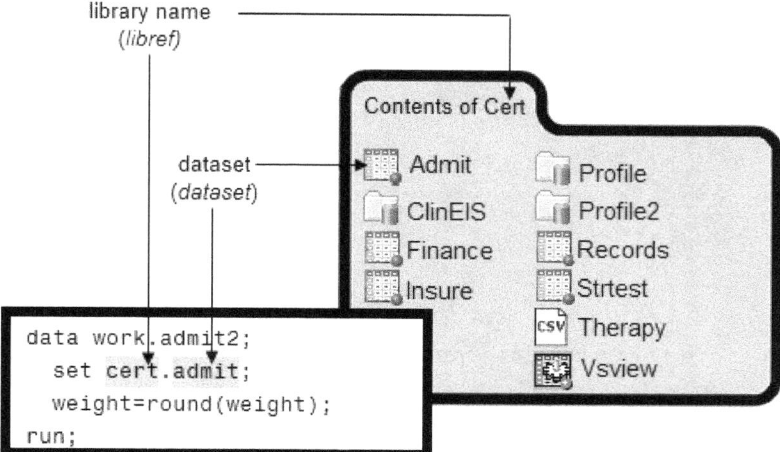

Referencing Temporary SAS Files

To reference temporary SAS files, you can specify the default libref Work, a period, and the data set name. For example, the two-level name, Work.Test, references the SAS data set named Test that is stored in the temporary SAS library Work.

Figure 2.4 Two-Level Temporary SAS Library Name

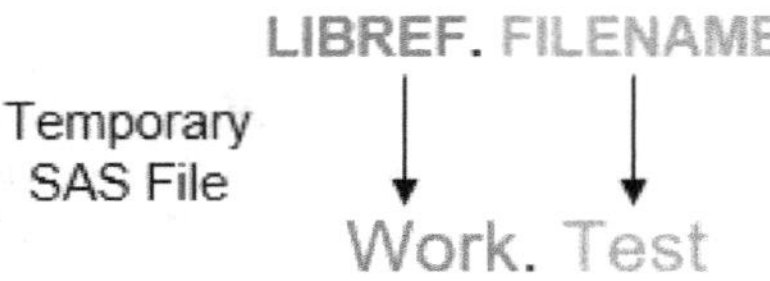

Alternatively, you can use a one-level name (the data set name only) to reference a file in a temporary SAS library. When you specify a one-level name, the default libref Work is assumed. For example, the one-level name Test references the SAS data set named Test that is stored in the temporary SAS library Work.

Figure 2.5 One-Level Temporary SAS Library Name

Rules for SAS Names

By default, the following rules apply to the names of SAS data sets, variables, and libraries:

- They must begin with a letter (A-Z, either uppercase or lowercase) or an underscore (_).
- They can continue with any combination of numbers, letters, or underscores.
- They can be 1 to 32 characters long.
- SAS library names (librefs) can be 1 to 8 characters long.

These are examples of valid data set names and variable names:

- Payroll
- LABDATA2015_2018
- _EstimatedTaxPayments3

VALIDVARNAME=System Option

SAS has various rules for variable names. You set these rules using the VALIDVARNAME= system option. VALIDVARNAME specifies the rules for valid SAS variable names that can be created and processed during a SAS session.

Syntax, VALIDVARNAME=

VALIDVARNAME= *V7|UPCASE|ANY*

V7 specifies that variable names must follow these rules:

- SAS variable names can be up to 32 characters long.
- The first character must begin with a letter of the Latin alphabet (A - Z, either uppercase or lowercase) or an underscore (_). Subsequent characters can be letters of the Latin alphabet, numerals, or underscores.
- Trailing blanks are ignored. The variable name alignment is left-justified.
- A variable name cannot contain blanks or special characters except for an underscore.
- A variable name can contain mixed-case letters. SAS stores and writes the variable name in the same case that is used in the first reference to the variable. However, when SAS processes a variable name, SAS internally converts it to uppercase. Therefore, you cannot use the same variable name with a different combination of uppercase and lowercase letters to represent different variables. For example, `cat`, `Cat`, and `CAT` all represent the same variable.
- Do not assign variables the names of special SAS automatic variables (such as _N_ and _ERROR_) or variable list names (such as _NUMERIC_, _CHARACTER_, and _ALL_) to variables.

UPCASE specifies that the variable name follows the same rules as V7, except that the variable name is uppercase, as in earlier versions of SAS.

ANY specifies that SAS variable names must follow these rules:

- The name can begin with or contain any characters, including blanks, national characters, special characters, and multi-byte characters.
- The name can be up to 32 bytes long.
- The name cannot contain any null bytes.
- Leading blanks are preserved, but trailing blanks are ignored.
- The name must contain at least one character. A name with all blanks is not permitted.
- A variable name can contain mixed-case letters. SAS stores and writes the variable name in the same case that is used in the first reference to the variable. However, when SAS processes a variable name, SAS internally converts it to uppercase. Therefore, you cannot use the same variable name with a different combination of uppercase and lowercase letters to represent different variables. For example, `cat`, `Cat`, and `CAT` all represent the same variable.

Note: If you use characters other than the ones that are valid when VALIDVARNAME=V7, then you must express the variable name as a name literal and set VALIDVARNAME=ANY. If the name includes either a percent sign (%) or an ampersand (&), then use single quotation marks in the name literal to avoid interaction with the SAS macro facility.

CAUTION:

Throughout SAS, using the name literal syntax with SAS member names that exceed the 32-byte limit or have excessive embedded quotation marks might cause unexpected results. The VALIDVARNAME=ANY system option enables compatibility with other DBMS variable (column) naming conventions, such as allowing embedded blanks and national characters.

VALIDMEMNAME=System Option

You can use the VALIDMEMNAME= system option to specify rules for naming SAS data sets.

Syntax, VALIDMEMNAME=

VALIDMEMNAME= COMPATIBLE | EXTEND

Important: COMPATIBLE is the default system option for VALIDMEMNAME=.

COMPATIBLE specifies that a SAS data set name must follow these rules:

- The length of the names can be up to 32 characters long.
- Names must begin with a letter of the Latin alphabet (A- Z, a - z) or an underscore. Subsequent characters can be letters of the Latin alphabet, numerals, or underscores.
- Names cannot contain blanks or special characters except for an underscore
- Names can contain mixed-case letters. SAS internally converts the member name to uppercase. Therefore, you cannot use the same member name with a different combination of uppercase and lowercase letters to represent different variables. For example, **`customer`**, **`Customer`**, and **`CUSTOMER`** all represent the same member name. How the name is saved on disk is determined by the operating environment.

EXTEND specifies that the data set name must follow these rules:

- Names can include national characters.
- The name can include special characters, except for the / \ * ? " < > |: - characters.
- The name must contain at least one character.
- The length of the name can be up to 32 bytes.
- Null bytes are not allowed.
- Names cannot begin with a blank or a '.' (period).
- Leading and trailing blanks are deleted when the member is created.
- Names can contain mixed-case letters. SAS internally converts the member name to uppercase. Therefore, you cannot use the same member name with a different combination of uppercase and lowercase letters to represent different variables. For example, **`customer`**, **`Customer`**, and **`CUSTOMER`** all represent the same member name. How the name appears is determined by the operating environment.

Note: If VALIDMEMNAME=EXTEND, SAS data set names must be written as a SAS name literal. If you use either a percent sign (%) or an ampersand (&), then you must use single quotation marks in the name literal in order to avoid interaction with the SAS macro facility.

CAUTION:

Throughout SAS, using the name literal syntax with SAS member names that exceed the 32-byte limit or that have excessive embedded quotation marks might cause unexpected results. The intent of the VALIDMEMNAME=EXTEND system option is to enable compatibility with other DBMS member naming conventions, such as allowing embedded blanks and national characters.

When to Use VALIDMEMNAME=System Option

Use VALIDMEMNAME= EXTEND system option when the characters in a SAS data set name contain one of the following:

- international characters
- characters supported by third-party databases
- characters that are commonly used in a filename

SAS Data Sets

Overview of Data Sets

A *SAS data set* is a file that consists of two parts: a descriptor portion and a data portion. Sometimes a SAS data set also points to one or more indexes, which enable SAS to locate rows in the data set more efficiently. (The data sets that are shown in this chapter do not contain indexes.) Extended attributes are user-defined attributes that further define a SAS data set.

Figure 2.6 *Parts of a SAS Data Set*

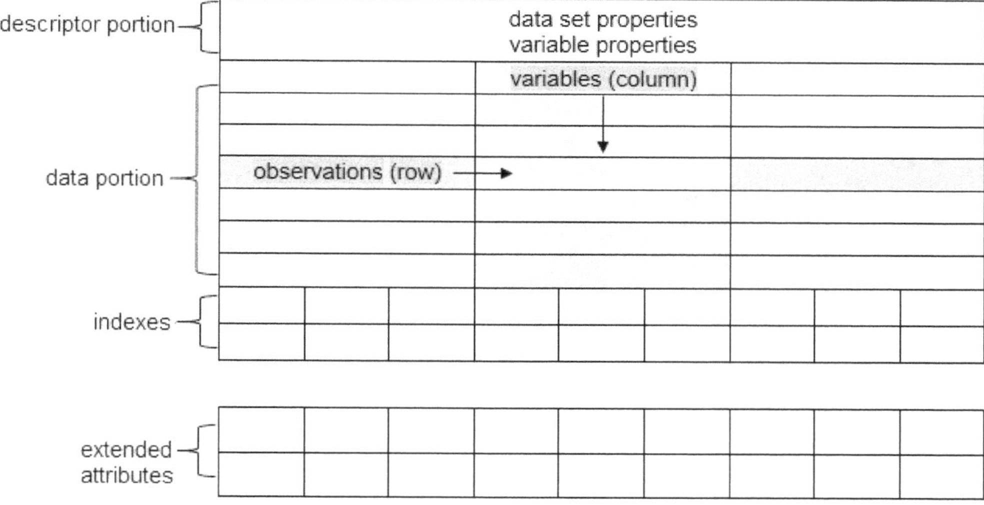

Descriptor Portion

The descriptor portion of a SAS data set contains information about the data set, including the following:

- the name of the data set
- the date and time that the data set was created
- the number of observations
- the number of variables

The table below lists part of the descriptor portion of the data set Cert.Insure, which contains insurance information for patients who are admitted to a wellness clinic.

Table 2.3 Descriptor Portion of Attributes in a SAS Data Set

Data Set Name:	CERT.INSURE
Member Type:	DATA
Engine:	V9
Created:	07/03/2018 10:53:05
Observations:	21
Variables:	7
Indexes:	0
Observation Length:	64

SAS Variable Attributes

The descriptor portion of a SAS data set contains information about the properties of each variable in the data set. The properties information includes the variable's name, type, length, format, informat, and label.

When you write SAS programs, it is important to understand the attributes of the variables that you use. For example, you might need to combine SAS data sets that contain same-named variables. In this case, the variables must be the same type (character or numeric). If the same-named variables are both character variables, you still need to check that the variable lengths are the same. Otherwise, some values might be truncated.

The following table uses Cert.Insure data and the VALIDVARNAME=ANY system option. The SAS variable has several attributes that are listed here:

Table 2.4 Variable Attributes

Variable Attribute	Definition	Example	Possible Values
Name	identifies a variable. A variable name must conform to SAS naming rules. See "Rules for SAS Names" for SAS names rules.	Policy Total Name	Any valid SAS name.

Variable Attribute	Definition	Example	Possible Values
Type	identifies a variable as numeric or character. Character variables can contain any values. Numeric variables can contain only numeric values (the numerals 0 through 9, +, -, ., and E for scientific notation).	Char Num Char	Numeric and character
Length	refers to the number of bytes used to store each of the variable's values in a SAS data set. Character variables can be up to 32,767 bytes long. All numeric variables have a default length of 8 bytes. Numeric values are stored as floating-point numbers in 8 bytes of storage.	5 8 14	2 to 8 bytes 1 to 32,767 bytes for character
Format	affects how data values are written. Formats do not change the stored value in any way; they merely control how that value is displayed. SAS offers a variety of character, numeric, and date and time formats.	$98.64	Any SAS format If no format is specified, the default format is **`BEST12.`** for a numeric variable, and **`$w.`** for a character variable.
Informat	reads data values in certain forms into standard SAS values. Informats determine how data values are read into a SAS data set. You must use informats to read numeric values that contain letters or other special characters.	99	Any SAS informat The default informat for numeric is **`w.d`** and for character is **`$w.`**
Label	refers to a descriptive label up to 256 characters long. A variable label, which can be printed by some SAS procedures, is useful in report writing.	Policy Number Total Balance Patient Name	Up to 256 characters

The following output is the descriptor portion of Cert.Insure.

Output 2.2 Descriptor Portion of Cert.Insure

Alphabetic List of Variables and Attributes						
#	Variable	Type	Len	Format	Informat	Label
7	BalanceDue	Num	8	6.2		
4	Company	Char	11			
1	ID	Char	4			
2	Name	Char	14			Patient Name
5	PctInsured	Num	8			
3	Policy	Char	5			Policy Number
6	Total	Num	8	DOLLAR8.2	COMMA10.	Total Balance

Data Portion

Data Portion Overview

The data portion of a SAS data set is a collection of data values that are arranged in a rectangular table. In the example below, the company **`MUTUALITY`** is a data value, Policy **`32668`** is a data value, and so on.

Figure 2.7 Parts of a SAS Data Set: Data Portion

ID	Patient Name	Policy Number	Company	PctInsured	Total Balance	BalanceDue
2458	Murray, W	32668	MUTUALITY	100	98.64	0.00
2462	Almers, C	95824	RELIABLE	80	780.23	156.05
2501	Bonaventure, T	87795	A&R	80	47.38	9.48
2523	Johnson, R	39022	ACME	50	122.07	61.04

Observations (Rows)

Observations (also called rows) in the data set are collections of data values that usually relate to a single object. The values **`2458`**, **`Murray W`**, **`32668`**, **`MUTALITY`**, **`100`**, **`98.64`**, and **`0.00`** are comprised in a single observation in the data set shown below.

Figure 2.8 Parts of a SAS Data Set: Observations

	ID	Patient Name	Policy Number	Company	PctInsured	Total Balance	BalanceDue
Observation	2458	Murray, W	32668	MUTUALITY	100	98.64	0.00
	2462	Almers, C	95824	RELIABLE	80	780.23	156.05
	2501	Bonaventure, T	87795	A&R	80	47.38	9.48
	2523	Johnson, R	39022	ACME	50	122.07	61.04

This data set has 21 observations, each containing information about an individual. To view the full descriptor portion of this data set, see Table 2.3 on page 18. A SAS data set can store any number of observations.

Variables (Columns)

Variables (also called columns) in the data set are collections of values that describe a particular characteristic. The values **2458**, **2462**, **2501**, and **2523** are comprised in the variable ID in the data set shown below.

Figure 2.9 *Parts of a SAS Data Set: Variables*

Variables

ID	Patient Name	Policy Number	Company	PctInsured	Total Balance	BalanceDue
2458	Murray, W	32668	MUTUALITY	100	98.64	0.00
2462	Almers, C	95824	RELIABLE	80	780.23	156.05
2501	Bonaventure, T	87795	A&R	80	47.38	9.48
2523	Johnson, R	39022	ACME	50	122.07	61.04

This data set contains seven variables: ID, Name, Policy, Company, PctInsured, Total, and BalanceDue. A SAS data set can store thousands of variables.

Missing Values

Every variable and observation in a SAS data set must have a value. If a data value is unknown for a particular observation, a missing value is recorded in the SAS data set. A period (.) is the default value for a missing numeric value, and a blank space is the default value for a missing character value.

Figure 2.10 *Parts of a SAS Data Set: Missing Data Values*

ID	Patient Name	Policy Number	Company	PctInsured	Total Balance	BalanceDue
2458	Murray, W	32668	MUTUALITY	100	98.64	0.00
2462	Almers, C	95824	RELIABLE	80	780.23	156.05
2501	Bonaventure, T	87795	A&R	.	47.38	9.48
2523	Johnson, R	39022	ACME	50	122.07	61.04

Missing Value

SAS Indexes

An index is a separate file that you can create for a SAS data file in order to provide direct access to a specific observation. The index file has the same name as its data file and a member type of INDEX. Indexes can provide faster access to specific observations, particularly when you have a large data set. The purpose of SAS indexes is to optimize WHERE expressions and to facilitate BY-group processing. For more information, see “Specifying WHERE Expressions” and see Chapter 8, “BY-Group Processing,”.

Extended Attributes

Extended attributes are user-defined metadata that is defined for a data set or for a variable (column). Extended attributes are represented as name-value pairs.

TIP You can use PROC CONTENTS to display data set and variable extended attributes.

Chapter Quiz

Select the best answer for each question. Check your answers using the answer key in the appendix.

1. How many observations and variables does the data set below contain?

Name	Sex	Age
Picker	M	32
Fletcher		28
Romano	F	.
Choi	M	42

   a. 3 observations, 4 variables

   b. 3 observations, 3 variables

   c. 4 observations, 3 variables

   d. cannot tell because some values are missing

2. How many program steps are executed when the program below is processed?

```
data user.tables;
  set work.jobs;run;
proc sort data=user.tables;
  by name;  run;
proc print data=user.tables;
run;
```

   a. three

   b. four

   c. five

   d. six

3. What type of variable is the variable AcctNum in the data set below?

AcctNum	Gender
3456_1	M
2451_2	
Romano	F
Choi	M

   a. numeric

   b. character

   c. can be either character or numeric

   d. cannot tell from the data shown

4. What type of variable is the variable Wear based on the justification of the text in the data set below?

Brand	Wear
Acme	43
Ajax	34
Atlas	.

   a. numeric
   b. character
   c. can be either character or numeric
   d. cannot tell from the data shown

5. With the system option VALIDVARNAME=ANY, which of the following variable names is valid?
   a. 4BirthDate
   b. $Cost
   c. Tax-Rate
   d. all of the above

6. Which of the following files is a permanent SAS file?
   a. Work.PrdSale
   b. Cert.MySales
   c. Certxl.Quarter1
   d. b and c only
   e. a, b, and c

7. In a DATA step, how can you reference a temporary SAS data set named Forecast?
   a. Forecast
   b. Work.Forecast
   c. Sales.Forecast (after assigning the libref Sales)
   d. a and b only

8. What is the default length for the numeric variable Balance?

Name	Balance
Adams	105.73
Geller	107.89
Martinez	97.45
Noble	182.50

   a. 5
   b. 6
   c. 7
   d. 8

9. How many statements does the following SAS program contain?

```
proc print data=cert.admit label double;
   var ID Name Sex Age; where Sex=F;
   label Sex='Gender'; run;
```

   a. three
   b. four
   c. five
   d. six

10. What is a SAS library?
   a. a collection of SAS files, such as SAS data sets and catalogs
   b. in some operating environments, a physical collection of SAS files
   c. a group of SAS files in the same folder or directory
   d. all of the above

Chapter 3
Accessing Your Data

SAS Libraries

A *SAS library* is a collection of one or more SAS files, including SAS data sets, that are referenced and stored as a unit. In a directory-based operating environment, a *SAS library* is a group of SAS files that are stored in the same directory. In z/OS, a *SAS library* is a group of SAS files that are stored in an operating environment file.

Assigning Librefs

Often the first step in setting up your SAS session is to define the libraries. You can use programming statements to assign library names.

To reference a permanent SAS file:

1. Assign a name (*libref*) to the SAS library in which the file is stored.
2. Use the libref as the first part of the two-level name (*libref.filename*) to reference the file within the library.

Figure 3.1 *Defining Libraries*

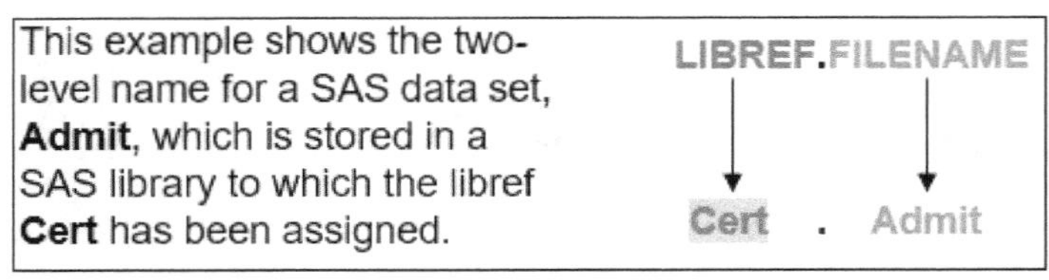

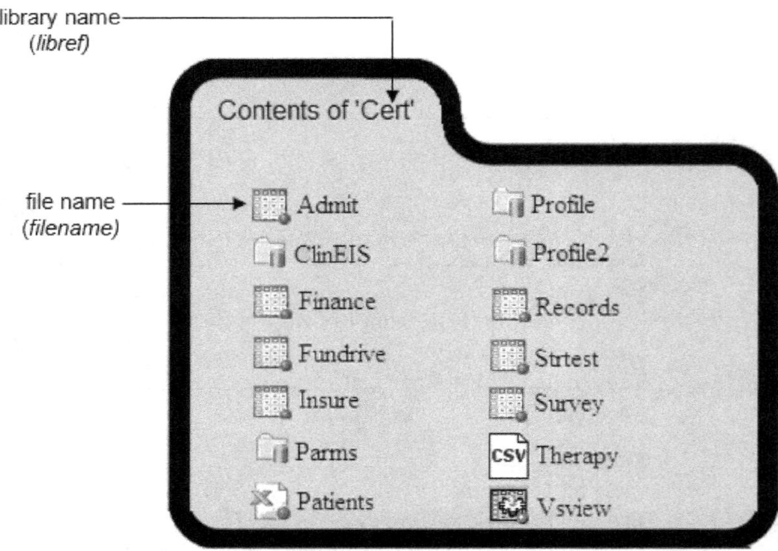

A logical name (libref) can be assigned to a SAS library using the LIBNAME statement. You can include the LIBNAME statement with any SAS program so that the SAS library is assigned each time the program is submitted. Using the user interface, you can set up LIBNAME statements to be automatically assigned when SAS starts.

Syntax, LIBNAME statement:

LIBNAME *libref engine 'SAS-data-library'*;

- *libref* is 1 to 8 characters long, begins with a letter or underscore, and contains only letters, numbers, or underscores.
- *engine* is the name of a library engine that is supported in your operating environment.

  Note: For SAS®9, the default engine is V9, which works in all operating environments.
- *SAS-data-library* is the name of a SAS library in which SAS data files are stored. The specification of the physical name of the library differs by operating environment.

The LIBNAME statement below assigns the libref Cert to the SAS library **`C:\Users\Student1\Cert`** in the Windows environment. When the default engine is used, you do not have to specify it in the LIBNAME statement.

```
libname cert 'C:\Users\Student1\Cert';
```

The table below gives examples of physical names for SAS libraries in various operating environments.

Table 3.1 Sample Physical Names for SAS Libraries

Environment	Sample Physical Name
Windows	c:\fitness\data
UNIX	/users/april/fitness/sasdata
z/OS)	april.fitness.sasdata

TIP You can use multiple LIBNAME statements to assign as many librefs as needed.

Verifying Librefs

After assigning a libref, it is a good idea to check the log to verify that the libref has been assigned successfully.

Log 3.1 Output for Cert Libref

```
1    libname cert 'C:\Users\Student1\Cert';
NOTE: Libref CERT was successfully assigned as follows:
      Engine:        V9
      Physical Name: C:\Users\Student1\Cert
```

How Long Librefs Remain in Effect

The LIBNAME statement is global, which means that the librefs remain in effect until changed or canceled, or until the SAS session ends.

By default, the LIBNAME statement assigns the libref for the current SAS session only. Each time you begin a SAS session, you must assign a libref to each permanent SAS library that contains files that you want to access in that session. (Remember that Work is the default libref for a temporary SAS library.)

Specifying Two-Level Names

After you assign a libref, you specify it as the first element in the two-level name for a SAS file.

In order for the PRINT procedure to read cert.admit, you specify the two-level name of the file as follows:

```
proc print data=cert.admit;
run;
```

Referencing Third-Party Data

You can use the LIBNAME statement to reference not only SAS files but also files that were created with other software products, such as database management systems.

A SAS engine is a set of internal instructions that SAS uses for writing to and reading from files in a SAS library or a third-party database. SAS can read or write these files by using the appropriate engine for that file type. For some file types, you need to tell SAS which engine to use. For others, SAS automatically chooses the appropriate engine.

An example of an engine that accesses third-party data is the XLSX engine, which processes Microsoft Excel workbooks.

Accessing Stored Data

If your site licenses SAS/ACCESS software, you can use the LIBNAME statement to access data that is stored in a database management system (DBMS) file. The types of data you can access depend on your operating environment and on which SAS/ACCESS products you have licensed. For more information about SAS/ACCESS engines, see the SAS documentation for your DBMS.

Viewing SAS Libraries

Viewing Libraries

Besides accessing library details with librefs, you can also see libraries in other environments. You can access a brief overview on the windows and menus for your environment at http://video.sas.com/ (https://video.sas.com//#category/videos/programming). From **Categories** select **How To Tutorials ⇨ Programming**. Select the video for your SAS environment. Other tutorials are available from the SAS website.

Viewing Libraries Using PROC CONTENTS

You can use the CONTENTS procedure to create SAS output that describes either of the following:

- the contents of a library
- the descriptor information for an individual SAS data set

The default library is either Work or User depending on your SAS solution or environment.

Syntax, PROC CONTENTS step:

PROC CONTENTS DATA=*SAS-file-specification* **NODS;**

RUN;

- *SAS-file-specification* specifies an entire library or a specific SAS data set within a library. *SAS-file-specification* can take one of the following forms:
  - *<libref.>SAS-data-set* names one SAS data set to process.
  - *<libref.>*_ALL_ requests a listing of all files in the library. (Use a period (.) to append _ALL_ to the libref.)
- NODS suppresses the printing of detailed information about each file when you specify _ALL_. (You can specify NODS *only* when you specify _ALL_.)

Example: View the Contents of an Entire Library

To view the contents of an entire library, specify the _ALL_ and NODS options in the PROC CONTENTS step. The _ALL_ option lists all files in the Cert library, and the NODS option suppresses the printing of detailed information about each specific file.

```
proc contents data=cert._all_ nods;
run;
```

The following output displays a partial output of the contents of the Cert library. The _ALL_ option lists all files including indexes, views, and catalogs.

Output 3.1 *PROC CONTENTS Output: the SAS Library Cert (partial output)*

The CONTENTS Procedure

Directory	
Libref	CERT
Engine	V9
Physical Name	C:\Users\Student1\cert
Filename	C:\Users\Student1\cert
Owner Name	Student1
File Size	32KB
File Size (bytes)	32768

#	Name	Member Type	File Size	Last Modified
1	ADMIT	DATA	128KB	12/03/2018 14:31:49
2	ADMITJUNE	DATA	128KB	11/26/2018 11:34:05
3	AGENCYEMP	DATA	128KB	11/26/2018 11:34:05
4	AMOUNTS	DATA	128KB	11/26/2018 11:34:05
5	APRBILLS	DATA	128KB	11/26/2018 11:34:05
6	BEFORE	DATA	128KB	11/26/2018 11:34:05
7	BOOKCASE	DATA	128KB	11/26/2018 11:34:05
8	CARS	DATA	128KB	11/26/2018 11:34:05
9	CHOICES	DATA	128KB	11/26/2018 11:34:06
10	CLASS	DATA	128KB	11/26/2018 11:34:06

Example: View Descriptor Information

To view the descriptor information for only a specific data set, use the PROC CONTENTS step. The following example lists the descriptor information for Cert.Amounts including an alphabetic list of the variables in the data set.

```
proc contents data=cert.amounts;
run;
```

The following output is the result from submitting the PROC CONTENTS step.

Output 3.2 *PROC CONTENTS Output*

Data Set Name	CERT.AMOUNTS	Observations	7
Member Type	DATA	Variables	4
Engine	V9	Indexes	0
Created	11/26/2018 11:34:05	Observation Length	40
Last Modified	11/26/2018 11:34:05	Deleted Observations	0
Protection		Compressed	NO
Data Set Type		Sorted	NO
Label			
Data Representation	WINDOWS_64		
Encoding	wlatin1 Western (Windows)		

Engine/Host Dependent Information	
Data Set Page Size	65536
Number of Data Set Pages	1
First Data Page	1
Max Obs per Page	1632
Obs in First Data Page	7
Number of Data Set Repairs	0
ExtendObsCounter	YES
Filename	C:\Users\Student1\cert\amounts.sas7bdat
Release Created	9.0401M4
Host Created	X64_10PRO
Owner Name	Student1
File Size	128KB
File Size (bytes)	131072

Alphabetic List of Variables and Attributes				
#	Variable	Type	Len	Format
4	Amount	Num	8	
3	Date	Num	8	DATE9.
2	EmpID	Num	8	
1	Name	Char	13	

Example: View Descriptor Information Using the Varnum Option

By default, PROC CONTENTS lists variables alphabetically. To list variable names in the order of their logical position (or creation order) in the data set, specify the VARNUM option in PROC CONTENTS.

```
proc contents data=cert.amounts varnum;
run;
```

Output 3.3 *View Descriptor Information for Cert.Amounts Using the VARNUM Option*

Variables in Creation Order			
#	Variable	Type	Len
1	Name	Char	13
2	EmplD	Num	8
3	Date	Num	8
4	Amount	Num	8

Chapter Quiz

Select the best answer for each question. Check your answers using the answer key in the appendix.

1. How long do librefs remain in effect?
   a. until the LIBNAME statement is changed
   b. until the LIBNAME statement is cleared
   c. until the SAS session ends
   d. all of the above
2. Which of the following statements are true?
   a. When using the default engine, you do not have to specify the libref in the LIBNAME statement.
   b. When using the default engine, you do not have to specify the engine name in the LIBNAME statement.
   c. When using the default engine, you do not have to specify the SAS library in the LIBNAME statement.
   d. When using the default engine, you have to specify the libref, engine name, and the SAS library in the LIBNAME statement.
3. When you specify an engine for a library, what are you specifying?
   a. the file format for files that are stored in the library
   b. the version of SAS that you are using
   c. permission to access to other software vendors' files
   d. instructions for creating temporary SAS files

4. Which statement prints a summary of all the files stored in the library named Area51?

   a. `proc contents data=area51._all_ nods;`

   b. `proc contents data=area51 _all_ nods;`

   c. `proc contents data=area51 _all_ noobs;`

   d. `proc contents data=area51 _all_.nods;`

5. Which of the following programs correctly references a SAS data set named SalesAnalysis that is stored in a permanent SAS library?

   a.
```
data saleslibrary.salesanalysis;
    set mydata.quarter1sales;
    if sales>100000;
run;
```

   b.
```
data mysales.totals;
    set sales_2017.salesanalysis;
    if totalsales>50000;
run;
```

   c.
```
proc print data=salesanalysis.quarter1;
    var sales salesrep month;
run;
```

   d.
```
proc freq data=2017data.salesanalysis;
    tables quarter*sales;
run;
```

   e. none of the above

6. What type of information does the CONTENTS procedure create?

   a. the contents of a library

   b. descriptor information for an individual SAS data set

   c. a and b only

   d. none of the above

7. Assuming you are using SAS code, which one of the following statements is false?

   a. LIBNAME statements can be stored with a SAS program to reference the SAS library automatically when you submit the program.

   b. When you delete a libref, SAS no longer has access to the files in the library. However, the contents of the library still exist on your operating system.

   c. Librefs can last from one SAS session to another.

   d. You can access files that were created with other vendors' software by submitting a LIBNAME statement.

8. What does the following statement do?

```
libname states 'c:\myfiles\sasdata\popstats';
```

   a. defines a library called States using the Popstats engine

   b. defines a library called Popstats using the States engine

   c. defines the default library using the default engines

   d. defines a library called States using the default engine

Chapter 4
Creating SAS Data Sets

Referencing an External Data File

Using a FILENAME Statement

Use the FILENAME statement to point to the location of the external file that contains the data.

Filerefs perform the same function as librefs: they temporarily point to a storage location for data. However, librefs reference SAS libraries, whereas filerefs reference external files.

Syntax, FILENAME statement:

FILENAME *fileref 'filename'*;

- *fileref* is a name that you associate with an external file. The name must be one to eight characters long, begin with a letter or underscore, and contain only letters, numbers, or underscores.
- *'filename'* is the fully qualified name or location of the file.

Defining a Fully Qualified Filename

The following FILENAME statement temporarily associates the fileref Exercise with the external file that contains the data from the exercise stress tests. The complete filename is specified as **C:\Users\Student1\cert\exercise.txt** in the Windows operating environment.

```
filename exercise 'C:\Users\Student1\cert\exercise.txt';
```

Referencing a Fully Qualified Filename

When you associate a fileref with an individual external file, you specify the fileref in subsequent SAS statements and commands.

Figure 4.1 Referencing a Fully Qualified Filename

```
filename exercise 'C:\Users\Student1\cert\exercise.txt';
proc import datafile=exercise
        dbms=dlm
        out=exstress
        replace;
     getnames=no;
run;
proc print data=exstress;
run;
```

The IMPORT Procedure

The Basics of PROC IMPORT

The IMPORT procedure reads data from an external data source and writes it to a SAS data set. You can import structured and unstructured data using PROC IMPORT. You can import delimited files (blank, comma, or tab) along with Microsoft Excel files. If you are using SAS 9.4, then you can import JMP 7 or later files as well.

When you run the IMPORT procedure, it reads the input file and writes the data to the specified SAS data set. By default, the IMPORT procedure expects the variable names to appear in the first row. The procedure scans the first 20 rows to count the variables, and it attempts to determine the correct informat and format for each variable. You can use the IMPORT procedure statements to do the following:

- indicate how many rows SAS scans for variables to determine the type and length (GUESSINGROWS=)
- modify whether SAS extracts the variable names from the first row of the data set (GETNAMES=)
- indicate at which row SAS begins to read the data (DATAROW=)

When the IMPORT procedure reads a delimited file, it generates a DATA step to import the data. You control the results with options and statements that are specific to the input data source.

The IMPORT procedure generates the specified output SAS data set and writes information about the import to the SAS log. The log displays the DATA step code that is generated by the IMPORT procedure.

PROC IMPORT Syntax

Syntax, PROC IMPORT statement:

PROC IMPORT
DATAFILE= "*filename*" | TABLE= "*tablename*"
OUT=<*libref. SAS-data-set*><*SAS-data-set-options*>
<DBMS=*identifier*><REPLACE>;

DATAFILE= "*filename*" | "*fileref*"
specifies the complete path and filename or fileref for the input PC file, spreadsheet, or delimited external file. A fileref is a SAS name that is associated with the physical location of the output file. To assign a fileref, use the FILENAME statement.

If you specify a fileref, complete path, and filename does not include special characters, then you can omit the quotation marks.

Restrictions The IMPORT procedure does not support device types or access methods for the FILENAME statement except for DISK. For example, the IMPORT procedure does not support the TEMP device type, which creates a temporary external file.

The IMPORT procedure can import data only if SAS supports the data type. SAS supports numeric and character types of data but not (for example) binary objects. If the data that you want to import is a type that SAS does not support, the IMPORT procedure might not be able to import it correctly. In many cases, the procedure attempts to convert the data to the best of its ability. However, conversion is not possible for some types.

Interactions: By default, the IMPORT procedure reads delimited files as varying record-length files. If your external file has a fixed-length format, use the FILENAME statement prior to PROC IMPORT to specify the input filename using the RECFM=F and LRECL= options.

When you use a fileref to specify a delimited file to import, the logical record length (LRECL) defaults to 256, unless you specify the LRECL= option in the FILENAME statement. The maximum LRECL value that the IMPORT procedure supports is 32,767.

For delimited files, the first 20 rows are scanned to determine the variable attributes. You can increase the number of rows that are scanned by using the GUESSINGROWS= statement. All values are read in as character strings. If a Date and Time format or a numeric informat can be applied to the data value, the type is declared as numeric. Otherwise, the type remains character.

OUT= ***<libref.> SAS-data-set***

identifies the output SAS data set with either a one or two-level SAS name (library and member name). If the specified SAS data set does not exist, the IMPORT procedure creates it. If you specify a one-level name, by default the IMPORT procedure uses either the USER library (if assigned) or the WORK library (if USER is not assigned).

A SAS data set name can contain a single quotation mark when the VALIDMEMNAME=EXTEND system option is also specified. Using VALIDMEMNAME= expands the rules for the names of certain SAS members, such as a SAS data set name.

If a SAS data set name contains national characters or special characters, use VALIDMEMNAME=EXTEND system option. The exceptions for special characters are: / \ * ? " < > | : —. Using VALIDMEMNAME= expands the rules for the name of certain SAS members, such as a SAS data set name. For more information, see "VALIDMEMNAME=System Option" on page 16.

TABLE= "*tablename*"

specifies the name of the input DBMS table. If the name does not include special characters (such as question marks), lowercase characters, or spaces, you can omit the quotation marks. Note that the DBMS table name might be case sensitive.

Requirement: When you import a DBMS table, you must specify the DBMS= option.

<DBMS=*identifier*>

specifies the type of data to import.

Here are the common DBMS identifiers that are included with Base SAS:

- CSV — comma-separated values. For a comma-separated file with a .CSV extension, DBMS= is optional.
- JMP — JMP files. Use JMP 7 or later. Use DBMS=JMP to specify importing JMP files. JMP variable names can be up to 255 characters long. SAS supports importing JMP files that have more than 32,767 variables.

- TAB — tab-delimited values. Specify DBMS=DLM to import any other delimited file that does not end in .CSV.

<REPLACE>
overwrites an existing SAS data set. If you omit REPLACE, the IMPORT procedure does not overwrite an existing data set.

Instead, use a SAS DATA step with the REPLACE= data set option to replace a permanent SAS data set.

<SAS-data-set-options>
specifies SAS data set options. For example, to assign a password to the resulting SAS data set, you can use the ALTER=, PW=, READ=, or WRITE= data set options. To import only data that meets a specified condition, you can use the WHERE= data set option.

Restriction You cannot specify data set options when importing delimited, comma-separated, or tab-delimited external files.

Example: Importing an Excel File with an XLSX Extension

This example imports an Excel file and creates a temporary SAS data set, Work.BootSales.

```
options validvarname=v7;                                       /*#1*/
proc import datafile='C:\Users\Student1\cert\boots.xlsx'   /*#2*/
  dbms=xlsx
  out=work.bootsales
  replace;
  sheet=boot;                                                  /*#3*/
  getnames=yes;                                                /*#4*/
run;
proc contents data=bootsales;                                  /*#5*/
run;
proc print data=bootsales;
run;
```

1 The VALIDVARNAME=V7 statement forces SAS to convert spaces to underscores when it converts column names to variable names. In SAS Studio, the _ (underscore) in Total_Sale would not be added without the VALIDVARNAME=V7 statement.

2 Specify the input file. DATAFILE= specifies the path for the input file. The DBMS= option specifies the type of data to import. When importing an Excel workbook, specify DBMS=XLSX. The REPLACE option overwrites an existing SAS data set. The OUT= option identifies the output SAS data set.

3 Use the SHEET option to import specific worksheets from an Excel workbook.

4 Set the GETNAMES= statement to YES to generate variable names from the first row of data.

5 Use the CONTENTS procedure to display the descriptor portion of the Work.BootSales data set.

The following is printed to the SAS log. The SAS log notes that the import was successful. It also notes that there is a variable name change from Total Sale (with a space between the two words) to Total_Sale. SAS converted the space to an underscore (_).

Log 4.1 *SAS Log*

```
75   options validvarname=v7;
76   proc import datafile='C:\Users\Student1\cert\boots.xlsx'
77      dbms=xlsx
78      out=work.bootsales replace;
79      sheet=boot;
80      getnames=yes;
81   run;

NOTE:    Variable Name Change.  Total Sale -> Total_Sale
NOTE: The import data set has 10 observations and 3 variables.
NOTE: WORK.BOOTSALES data set was successfully created.
```

Output 4.1 *PROC CONTENTS Descriptor Portion (partial output)*

Alphabetic List of Variables and Attributes						
#	Variable	Type	Len	Format	Informat	Label
2	City	Char	11	$11.	$11.	City
1	Region	Char	25	$25.	$25.	Region
3	Total_Sale	Num	8	DOLLAR15.2		Total Sale

Output 4.2 *PROC PRINT Output of the Work.BootSales Data Set*

Obs	Region	City	Total_Sale
1	Africa	Addis Ababa	$191,821.00
2	Asia	Bangkok	$9,576.00
3	Canada	Calgary	$63,280.00
4	Central America/Carribean	Kingston	$393,376.00
5	Eastern Europe	Budapest	$317,515.00
6	Middle East	Al-Khobar	$44,658.00
7	Pacific	Auckland	$97,919.00
8	South America	Bogota	$35,805.00
9	United States	Chicago	$305,061.00
10	Western Europe	Copenhagen	$4,657.00

For an alternate method of reading Microsoft Excel files in SAS, see "Reading Microsoft Excel Data with the XLSX Engine" on page 47.

Example: Importing a Delimited File with a TXT Extension

This example imports a delimited external file and creates a temporary SAS data set, Work.MyData. The delimiter is an ampersand (&).

```
options validvarname=v7;
proc import datafile='C:\Users\Student1\cert\delimiter.txt'     /*#1*/
  dbms=dlm                                                      /*#2*/
  out=mydata
  replace;
```

```
  delimiter='&';                                              /*#3*/
  getnames=yes;                                               /*#4*/
run;
proc print data=mydata;
run;
```

1 Specify the input file. DATAFILE= specifies the path for the input file. The DBMS= option specifies the type of data to import.

2 If the delimiter is a character other than TAB or CSV, then the DBMS= option is DLM. The REPLACE option overwrites an existing SAS data set. The OUT= option identifies the output SAS data set.

3 Specify an ampersand (&) for the DELIMITER statement.

4 Set the GETNAMES= statement to YES to generate variable names from the first row of data.

Output 4.3 *PROC PRINT Output: Work.MyData Data Set*

Obs	Region	State	Month	Expenses	Revenue
1	Southern	GA	JAN2001	2000	8000
2	Southern	GA	FEB2001	1200	6000
3	Southern	FL	FEB2001	8500	11000
4	Northern	NY	FEB2001	3000	4000
5	Northern	NY	MAR2001	6000	5000
6	Southern	FL	MAR2001	9800	13500
7	Northern	MA	MAR2001	1500	1000

Example: Importing a Space-Delimited File with a TXT Extension

This example imports a space-delimited file and creates a temporary SAS data set named Work.States.

The following input data illustrates enclosing values in quotation marks when you want to avoid separating their values by the space between the words.

```
Region State Capital Bird
South Georgia Atlanta 'Brown Thrasher'
South 'North Carolina' Raleigh Cardinal
North Connecticut Hartford Robin
West Washington Olympia 'American Goldfinch'
Midwest Illinois Springfield Cardinal
```

You can submit the following code to import the file.

```
options validvarname=v7;
filename stdata 'C:\Users\Student1\cert\state_data.txt' lrecl=100;  /*#1*/
proc import datafile=stdata                                          /*#2*/
  dbms=dlm
  out=states
  replace;
  delimiter=' ';                                                     /*#3*/
  getnames=yes;
run;
```

```
proc print data=states;
run;
```

1 Specify the fileref and the location of the file. Specify the LRECL= system option if the file has a fixed-length format. The LRECL= system option specifies the default logical record length to use when reading external files.

2 Specify the input file and specify that it is a delimited file. The DBMS= option specifies the type of data to import. If the delimiter type is a character other than TAB or CSV, then the DBMS= option is DLM. The REPLACE option overwrites an existing SAS data set. The OUT= option identifies the output SAS data set.

3 Specify a blank value for the DELIMITER statement. Set the GETNAMES= statement to YES to generate variable names from the first row of data.

Output 4.4 *PROC PRINT Output: Work.States Data Set*

Obs	Region	State	Capital	Bird
1	South	Georgia	Atlanta	Brown Thrasher
2	South	North Carolina	Raleigh	Cardinal
3	North	Connecticut	Hartford	Robin
4	West	Washington	Olympia	American Goldfinch
5	Midwest	Illinois	Springfield	Cardinal

Example: Importing a Comma-Delimited File with a CSV Extension

This example imports a comma-delimited file and creates a temporary SAS data set Work.Shoes. The input file Boot.csv is a comma-separated value file that is a delimited-text file and that uses a comma to separate values.

```
options validvarname=v7;
proc import datafile='C:\Users\Student1\cert\boot.csv'   /*#1*/
  dbms=csv
  out=shoes
  replace;
  getnames=no;                                            /*#2*/
run;
proc print data=work.shoes;
run;
```

1 Specify the input file. DATAFILE= specifies the input data file, and OUT= specifies the output data set. The DBMS= specifies the type of data to import. If the file type is CSV, then the DBMS= option is CSV. The REPLACE option overwrites an existing SAS data set.

2 Set the GETNAMES= statement to NO to not use the first row of data as variable names.

Output 4.5 *PROC PRINT Output: Work.Shoes Data Set*

Obs	VAR1	VAR2	VAR3	VAR4	VAR5	VAR6	VAR7
1	Africa	Boot	Addis Ababa	12	29761	191821	769
2	Asia	Boot	Bangkok	1	1996	9576	80
3	Canada	Boot	Calgary	8	17720	63280	472
4	Central America/Caribbean	Boot	Kingston	33	102372	393376	4454
5	Eastern Europe	Boot	Budapest	22	74102	317515	3341
6	Middle East	Boot	Al-Khobar	10	15062	44658	765
7	Pacific	Boot	Auckland	12	20141	97919	962
8	South America	Boot	Bogota	19	15312	35805	1229
9	United States	Boot	Chicago	16	82483	305061	3735
10	Western Europe	Boot	Copenhagen	2	1663	4657	129

Example: Importing a Tab-Delimited File

This example imports a tab-delimited file and creates a temporary SAS data set Work.Class.

```
proc import datafile='C:\Users\Student1\cert\class.txt'     /*#1*/
  dbms=tab
  out=class
  replace;
  delimiter='09'x;                                          /*#2*/
run;
proc print data=class;
run;
```

1 Specify the input file. DATAFILE= specifies the input data file, and OUT= specifies the output data set. DBMS= specifies the type of data to import. If the file type is TXT, then the DBMS= option is TAB. The REPLACE option overwrites an existing SAS data set. GETNAMES= statement defaults to YES.

2 Specify the delimiter. On an ASCII platform, the hexadecimal representation of a tab is '09'x. On an EBCDIC platform, the hexadecimal representation of a tab is a '05'x.

Output 4.6 *PROC PRINT Output of Work.Class*

Obs	Name	Gender	Age
1	Louise	F	12
2	James	M	12
3	John	M	12
4	Robert	M	12
5	Alice	F	13
6	Barbara	F	13
7	Jeffery	M	13
8	Carol	F	14
9	Judy	F	14
10	Alfred	M	14
11	Henry	M	14
12	Jenet	F	15
13	Mary	F	15
14	Ronald	M	15
15	William	M	15
16	Philip	M	16

Reading and Verifying Data

Verifying the Code That Reads the Data

Before you read a complete external file, you can verify the code that reads the data by limiting the number of observations that SAS reads. You can use the OPTIONS statement with the OBS= option before the IMPORT procedure to limit the number of observations that SAS reads from your external file.

The program below reads the first five records in the external data file that is referenced by PROC IMPORT.

```
options obs=5;
proc import datafile="C:\Users\Student1\cert\boot.csv"
  dbms=csv
  out=shoes
  replace;
  getnames=no;
run;
```

Checking DATA Step Processing

After PROC IMPORT runs the DATA step to read the data, messages in the log verify that the data was read correctly. The notes in the log indicate the following:

- Five records were read from the infile '**C:\Users\Student1\cert\boot.csv**'
- The SAS data set work.shoes was created with five observations and seven variables.

Log 4.2 *SAS Log*

```
NOTE: The infile 'C:\Users\Student1\cert\boot.csv' is:
      Filename=C:\Users\Student1\cert\boot.csv,
      RECFM=V,LRECL=32767,File Size (bytes)=657,
      Last Modified=25Jun2018:13:37:49,
      Create Time=25Jun2018:13:37:49

NOTE: 5 records were read from the infile
      'C:\Users\Student1\cert\boot.csv'.
      The minimum record length was 51.
      The maximum record length was 81.
NOTE: The data set WORK.SHOES has 5 observations and 7
      variables.
NOTE: DATA statement used (Total process time):
      real time           0.01 seconds
      cpu time            0.00 seconds


5 rows created in WORK.SHOES from
C:\Users\Student1\cert\boot.csv.



NOTE: WORK.SHOES data set was successfully created.
NOTE: The data set WORK.SHOES has 5 observations and 7
      variables.
NOTE: PROCEDURE IMPORT used (Total process time):
      real time           0.05 seconds
      cpu time            0.04 seconds
```

Printing the Data Set

The messages in the log indicate that the PROC IMPORT step correctly accessed the external data file. But it is a good idea to look at the five observations in the new data set before reading the entire external data file. The system option OBS=5 is still in effect, so you do not have to specify it again. You can submit a PROC PRINT step to view the data.

Data sets are assigned to the default Work library when the library reference is omitted. The example stored the Shoes data set in the temporary library, Work.

The following PROC PRINT step prints the Work.Shoes data set.

```
proc print data=work.shoes;
run;
```

The PROC PRINT output indicates that the variables in the Work.Shoes data set were read correctly for the first five records.

Figure 4.2 *PROC Print Output*

Obs	VAR1	VAR2	VAR3	VAR4	VAR5	VAR6	VAR7
1	Africa	Boot	Addis Ababa	12	29761	191821	769
2	Asia	Boot	Bangkok	1	1996	9576	80
3	Canada	Boot	Calgary	8	17720	63280	472
4	Central America/Caribbean	Boot	Kingston	33	102372	393376	4454
5	Eastern Europe	Boot	Budapest	22	74102	317515	3341

Reading the Entire External File

To modify the PROC step to read the entire external file, restore the default value to the OBS= system option. To do this, set OBS=MAX and then resubmit the program.

```
options obs=max;
proc import datafile="C:\Users\Student1\cert\boot.csv"
  dbms=csv
  out=shoes
  replace;
  getnames=no;
run;
```

Note: SAS Studio sets OBS=MAX before each code submission.

Using the Imported Data in a DATA Step

Naming the Data Set with the DATA Statement

The DATA statement indicates the beginning of the DATA step and names the SAS data set to be created.

Syntax, DATA statement:

DATA *SAS-data-set-1* <...*SAS-data-set-n*>;

SAS-data-set names (in the format *libref.filename*) the data set or data sets to be created.

Remember that a permanent SAS data set name is a two-level name. For example, the two-level name Clinic.Admit specifies that the data set Admit is stored in the permanent SAS library to which the libref Clinic has been assigned.

Specifying the Imported Data with the SET Statement

The SET statement specifies the SAS data set that you want to use as input data for your DATA step. When you import your external data using PROC IMPORT, you specify the name of the output data set using the OUT= option. Use the libref and data set name that you specified using the OUT= option as the SAS data set value for the SET statement.

SET Statement Syntax

Syntax, DATA step for reading a single data set:

DATA *SAS-data-set*;

SET *SAS-data-set*;

<*...more SAS statements...*>

RUN;

- *SAS-data-set* in the DATA statement is the name of the SAS data set to be created.
- *SAS-data-set* in the SET statement is the name of the SAS data set to be read.

Example: Using the SET Statement to Specify Imported Data

In this example, the DATA statement tells SAS to name the new data set, Boots, and store it in the temporary library Work. The SET statement in the DATA step specifies the output data set from the IMPORT procedure. You can use several statements in the DATA step to subset your data as needed. In this example, the WHERE statement is used with VAR1 to include only the observations where VAR1 is either South America or Canada.

```
proc import datafile="C:\certdata\boot.csv"
  out=shoes
  dbms=csv
  replace;
  getnames=no;
run;
data boots;
  set shoes;
  where var1='South America' OR var1='Canada';
run;
```

Output 4.7 *Results from the DATA Step Using the SET Statement*

Obs	VAR1	VAR2	VAR3	VAR4	VAR5	VAR6	VAR7
1	Canada	Boot	Calgary	8	17720	63280	472
2	South America	Boot	Bogota	19	15312	35805	1229

Reading a Single SAS Data Set to Create Another

Example: Reading a SAS Data Set

The data set Cert.Admit contains health information about patients in a clinic, their activity level, height, and weight. Suppose you want to create a subset of the data. Specifically, you want to create a small data set containing data about all the men in the group who are older than 50.

To create the data set, you must first reference the library in which Cert.Admit is stored. Then you must specify the name of the library in which you want to store the Males data set. Finally, you add statements to the DATA step to read your data and create a new data set.

The DATA step below reads all observations and variables from the existing data set Cert.Admit into the new data set Males. The DATA statement creates the permanent SAS data set Males, which is stored in the SAS library Men50. The SET statement reads the permanent SAS data set Cert.Admit and subsets the data using a WHERE statement. The new data set, Males, contains all males in Cert.Admit who are older than 50.

```
libname cert 'C:\Users\Student1\cert\';
libname Men50 'C:\Users\Student1\cert\Men50';
data Men50.males;
  set cert.admit;
  where sex='M' and age>50;
run;
```

When you submit this DATA step, the following messages appear in the log, confirming that the new data set was created:

Log 4.3 *SAS Log Output*

```
69205  data Men50.males;
69206    set cert.admit;
69207    where sex='M' and age>50;
69208  run;

NOTE: There were 3 observations read from the data set
      CERT.ADMIT.
      WHERE (sex='M') and (age>50);
NOTE: The data set MEN50.MALES has 3 observations and 9
      variables.
```

You can add a PROC PRINT statement to this same example to see the output of Men50.Males.

```
proc print data=Men50.males;
   title 'Men Over 50';
run;
```

Output 4.8 *PROC PRINT Output for the Data Set Males*

Men Over 50

Obs	ID	Name	Sex	Age	Date	Height	Weight	ActLevel	Fee
1	2539	LaMance, K	M	51	08/14/17	71	158	LOW	124.80
2	2579	Underwood, K	M	60	08/14/17	71	191	LOW	149.75
3	2595	Warren, C	M	54	08/17/17	71	183	MOD	149.75

Specifying DROP= and KEEP= Data Set Options

You can specify the DROP= and KEEP= data set options anywhere you name a SAS data set. You can specify DROP= and KEEP= in either the DATA statement or the SET statement. It depends on whether you want to drop variables from either the output data set or the source data set:

- If you never reference certain variables and you do not want them to appear in the new data set, use a DROP= option in the SET statement.

  In the DATA step shown below, the DROP= or KEEP= option in the SET statement prevents the variables *Triglyc* and *Uric* from being read. These variables do not appear in the Cert.Drug1h data set and are not available to be used by the DATA step.

- If you do need to reference a variable in the original data set (in a subsetting IF statement, for example), you can specify the variable in the DROP= or KEEP= option in the DATA statement. Otherwise, the statement that references the variable uses a missing value for that variable.

  This DATA step uses the variable Placebo to select observations. To drop Placebo from the new data set, the DROP= option must appear in the DATA statement.

  When used in the DATA statement, the DROP= option simply drops the variables from the new data set. However, they are still read from the original data set and are available within the DATA step.

```
data cert.drug1h(drop=placebo);
  set cert.cltrials(drop=triglyc uric);
  if placebo='YES';
run;
proc print data=cert.drug1h;
run;
```

Output 4.9 *PROC PRINT Output of Cert.Drug1h*

Obs	TestDate	Name	Sex	Cholesterol
1	09AUG2000	Johnson, R	F	200
2	01AUG2000	LaMance, K	M	250
3	22MAY2000	Nunnelly, A	F	210
4	22MAY2000	Cameron, L	M	198

Reading Microsoft Excel Data with the XLSX Engine

Running SAS with Microsoft Excel

The examples in this section are based on SAS 9.4 64-bit running with Microsoft Office 2016 64-bit on Microsoft Windows 10 64-bit.

This configuration does not require the SAS/ACCESS PC Files Server. If SAS runs in a UNIX environment and needs to access Excel files on Microsoft Windows, you must license the SAS/ACCESS PC Files Server.

Steps for Reading Excel Data

To read the Excel workbook file, SAS must receive the following information in the DATA step:

- a libref to reference the Excel workbook to be read
- the name of the Excel worksheet that is to be read

The table below outlines the basic statements that are used in a program that reads Excel data and creates a SAS data set from an Excel worksheet. The PROC CONTENTS and PROC PRINT statements are not requirements for reading Excel data and creating a SAS data set. However, these statements are useful for confirming that your Excel data has successfully been read into SAS.

Table 4.1 *Basic Steps for Reading Excel Data into a SAS Data Set*

Task	Statement	Example
Reference an Excel workbook file	SAS/ACCESS LIBNAME statement	LIBNAME cert `libname cert xlsx 'C:\Users\Student1\cert\exercise.xlsx';`
Write out the contents of the SAS Library	PROC CONTENTS	`proc contents data=cert._all_;`
Execute the PROC CONTENTS statement	RUN statement	`run;`
Name and create a new SAS data set	DATA statement	`data work.stress;`
Read in an Excel worksheet (as the input data for the new SAS data set)	SET statement	`set cert.ActLevel;`
Execute the DATA step	RUN statement	`run;`
View the contents of a particular data set	PROC PRINT	`proc print data=stress;`
Execute the PROC PRINT statement	RUN statement	`run;`

Here is the syntax for assigning a libref to an Excel workbook.

The LIBNAME Statement

To assign a libref to a database, use the LIBNAME statement. The SAS/ACCESS LIBNAME statement associates a SAS libref with a database, schema, server, or a group of tables and views.

Syntax, SAS/ACCESS LIBNAME statement:

LIBNAME *<libref>***XLSX** *<'physical-path-and-filename.xlsx'><options>*;

- *libref* is a name that you associate with an Excel workbook.
- *XLSX* is the SAS LIBNAME engine name for an XLSX file format. The SAS/ACCESS LIBNAME statement associates a libref with an XLSX engine that supports the connections to Microsoft Excel 2007, 2010, and later files.

  Important: The engine name XLSX is required.

  When reading XLSX data, the XLSX engine reads mixed data (columns containing numeric and character values) and converts it to character data values.

  The XLSX engine allows sequential reading of data only. It does not support random access. Therefore, it does not support certain tasks that require random access such as the RANK procedure, which requires the reading of rows in a random order.
- *'physical-path-and-filename.xlsx'* is the physical location of the Excel workbook.

Example:

libname results XLSX **`'C:\Users\Student1\cert\exercise.xlsx';`**

Note: The XLSX engine requires quotation marks for *physical-path-and-filename.xlsx*.

Referencing an Excel Workbook

Overview

This example uses data similar to the scenario used for the raw data in the previous section. The data shows the readings from exercise stress tests that have been performed on patients at a health clinic.

The stress test data is located in an Excel workbook named exercise.xlsx (shown below), which is stored in the location **`C:\Users\Student1\cert\`**.

Figure 4.3 *Excel Workbook*

ID	Name	RestHR	MaxHR	RecHR	TimeMin	TimeSec	Tolerance	TestDate
2458	Murray, W	72	185	128	12	38	D	8/25/2008
2462	Almers, C	68	171	133	10	5	I	6/26/2008
2501	Bonaventure, T	78	177	139	11	13	I	6/26/2008
2523	Johnson, R	69	162	114	9	42	S	7/4/2008
2539	LaMance, R	75	168	141	11	46	D	8/25/2008
2544	Jones, M	79	187	136	12	26	N	7/14/2008
2552	Reberson, P	69	158	139	15	41	D	8/25/2008
2555	King, E	70	167	122	13	13	I	7/14/2008
2563	Pitts, D	71	159	116	10	22	S	8/25/2008
2568	Eberhardt, S	72	182	122	16	49	N	6/26/2008
2571	Nunnelly, A	65	181	141	15	2	I	8/9/2008
2572	Oberon, M	74	177	138	12	11	D	8/8/2008
2574	Peterson, V	80	164	137	14	9	D	7/21/2008
2575	Quigley, M	74	152	.	11	26	I	7/13/2008
2578	Cameron, L	75	158	108	14	27	I	8/16/2008
2579	Underwood, K	72	165	127	13	19	S	6/27/2008
2584	Takahashi, Y	76	163	135	16	7	D	8/16/2008
2586	Derber, B	68	176	119	17	35	N	8/17/2008
2588	Ivan, H	70	182	126	15	41	N	6/18/2008
2589	Wilcox, E	78	189	138	14	57	I	7/19/2008
2595	Warren, C	77	170	136	12	10	S	7/20/2008

Worksheets

Cells formatted as dates

In the sample worksheet above, the date column is defined in Excel as dates. If you right-click the cells and select **Format Cells**, the cells have a category of Date. SAS reads this data just as it is stored in Excel. If the date had been stored as text in Excel, then SAS would have read it as a character string.

To read in this workbook, create a libref to point to the workbook's location:

```
libname certxl XLSX 'C:\Users\Student1\cert\exercise.xlsx';
```

The SAS/ACCESS LIBNAME statement creates the libref Certxl, which points to the Excel workbook exercise.xlsx. The workbook contains two worksheets, Tests and Adv, which are now available in the new SAS library (Results) as data sets.

Referencing an Excel Workbook in a DATA Step

SET Statement

Use the SET statement to indicate which worksheet in the Excel file you want to read.

```
data work.stress;
   set certxl.ActivityLevels;
run;
```

In this example, the DATA statement tells SAS to name the new data set, Stress, and store it in the temporary library Work. The SET statement specifies the libref (the reference to the Excel file) and the worksheet name as the input data.

You can use several statements in the DATA step to subset your data as needed. Here, the WHERE statement is used with a variable to include only those participants whose activity level is HIGH.

```
data work.stress;
   set certxl.ActivityLevels;
   where ActLevel='HIGH';
run;
```

The figure below shows the output for this DATA step in table format.

Figure 4.4 *DATA Step Output*

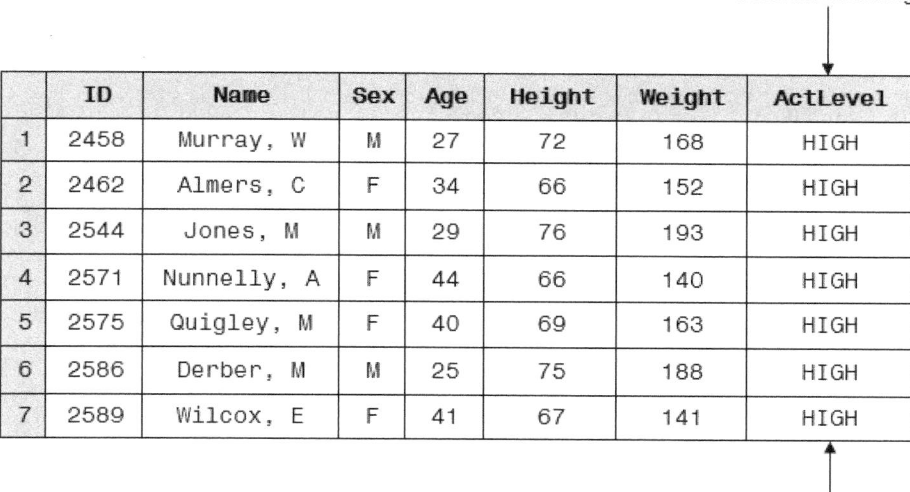

	ID	Name	Sex	Age	Height	Weight	ActLevel
1	2458	Murray, W	M	27	72	168	HIGH
2	2462	Almers, C	F	34	66	152	HIGH
3	2544	Jones, M	M	29	76	193	HIGH
4	2571	Nunnelly, A	F	44	66	140	HIGH
5	2575	Quigley, M	F	40	69	163	HIGH
6	2586	Derber, M	M	25	75	188	HIGH
7	2589	Wilcox, E	F	41	67	141	HIGH

Name Literals

The SAS/ACCESS LIBNAME statement created a permanent library, Certxl, which is the libref for the workbook file and its location. The new library contains two SAS data sets, which access the data from the Excel worksheets.

Name literals are required with the XLSX engine only when the worksheet name contains a special character or spaces. By default, SAS does not allow special characters in SAS data set names. A SAS *name literal* is a name token that is expressed as a string within quotation marks, followed by the uppercase or lowercase letter *n*. The name literal tells SAS to allow the special character ($) in the data set name.

The following example illustrates reading an Excel worksheet using a name literal. Specify the name of the worksheet in quotation marks with an n following the name. This syntax tells SAS that there are special characters or spaces in the data set name.

```
libname certxl xlsx 'C:\Users\Student1\cert\stock.xlsx';
data work.bstock;
  set certxl.'boots stock'n;
run;
```

Printing an Excel Worksheet as a SAS Data Set

After using the DATA step to read in the Excel data and create a SAS data set, you can use PROC PRINT to produce a report that displays the data set values. In the following example, the PROC PRINT statement displays all the data values for the new data set, Work.Bstock.

```
libname certxl xlsx 'C:\Users\Student1\cert\stock.xlsx';
data work.bstock;
  set certxl.'boots stock'n;
run;
proc print data=work.bstock;
run;
```

Output 4.10 *PROC PRINT Output of Work.Bstock*

Obs	Region	Item	City	Stock
1	Eastern Europe	Boot	Budapest	22
2	Middle East	Boot	Al-Khobar	10
3	Pacific	Boot	Auckland	12

In the following example, the PROC PRINT statement refers to the worksheet Boot Sales and prints the contents of the Excel worksheet that was referenced by the SAS/ACCESS LIBNAME statement.

```
libname certxl xlsx 'C:\Users\Student1\cert\stock.xlsx';
proc print data=cerxl.'boots stock'n;
run;
```

Output 4.11 *PROC PRINT Output Using Name Literals*

Obs	Region	Item	City	Stock
1	Eastern Europe	Boot	Budapest	22
2	Middle East	Boot	Al-Khobar	10
3	Pacific	Boot	Auckland	12

Creating Excel Worksheets

In addition to reading Microsoft Excel data, SAS can also create Excel worksheets from SAS data sets.

- If the Excel workbook does not exist, SAS creates it.
- If the Excel worksheet within the workbook does not exist, SAS creates it.
- If the Excel workbook and the worksheet already exist, then SAS overwrites the existing Excel workbook and worksheet.

In the following example, you use the SAS/ACCESS LIBNAME statement and the DATA step to create an Excel worksheet. The SAS/ACCESS LIBNAME statement specifies the name of the new Excel file as newExcel.xlsx. The DATA step reads in Cert.Stress and then creates the Excel worksheet HighStress in the newExcel.xlsx workbook.

```
libname excelout xlsx 'C:\Users\Student1\Cert\newExcel.xlsx';
data excelout.HighStress;
  set cert.stress;
run;
```

Output 4.12 *Excelout.HighStress Worksheet*

ID	Name	RestHR	MaxHR	RecHR	TimeMin	TimeSec	Tolerance
2458	Murray, W	72	185	128	12	38	D
2462	Almers, C	68	171	133	10	5	I
2501	Bonaventure, T	78	177	139	11	13	I
2523	Johnson, R	69	162	114	9	42	S
2539	LaMance, K	75	168	141	11	46	D
2544	Jones, M	79	187	136	12	26	N
2552	Reberson, P	69	158	139	15	41	D
2555	King, E	70	167	122	13	13	I
2563	Pitts, D	71	159	116	10	22	S
2568	Eberhardt, S	72	182	122	16	49	N
2571	Nunnelly, A	65	181	141	15	2	I
2572	Oberon, M	74	177	138	12	11	D
2574	Peterson, V	80	164	137	14	9	D
2575	Quigley, M	74	152	113	11	26	I
2578	Cameron, L	75	158	108	14	27	I
2579	Underwood, K	72	165	127	13	19	S
2584	Takahashi, Y	76	163	135	16	7	D
2586	Derber, B	68	176	119	17	35	N
2588	Ivan, H	70	182	126	15	41	N
2589	Wilcox, E	78	189	138	14	57	I
2595	Warren, C	77	170	136	12	10	S

Writing Observations Explicitly

To override the default way in which the DATA step writes observations to output, you can use an OUTPUT statement in the DATA step. Placing an explicit OUTPUT statement in a DATA step overrides the implicit output at the end of the DATA step. The observations are added to a data set only when the explicit OUTPUT statement is executed.

Syntax, OUTPUT statement:

OUTPUT <*SAS-data-set(s)*>;

SAS-data-set(s) names the data set or data sets to which the observation is written. All data set names that are specified in the OUTPUT statement must also appear in the DATA statement.

Using an OUTPUT statement without a following data set name causes the current observation to be written to all data sets that are specified in the DATA statement.

With an OUTPUT statement, your program now writes a single observation to output—observation 5. For more information on subsetting IF statements, see "Using a Subsetting IF Statement" on page 151.

```
data work.usa5;
  set cert.usa(keep=manager wagerate);
  if _n_=5 then output;
run;
proc print data=work.usa5;
run;
```

Figure 4.5 *Single Observation*

Obs	WageRate	Manager
1	4522.5	Coxe

Suppose your DATA statement contains two data set names, and you include an OUTPUT statement that references only one of the data sets. The DATA step creates both data sets, but only the data set that is specified in the OUTPUT statement contains output. For example, the program below creates two temporary data sets, Empty and Full. The result of this DATA step is that the data set Empty is created but contains no observations, and the data set Full contains all of the observations from Cert.Usa.

```
data empty full;
  set cert.usa;
  output full;
run;
```

Chapter Quiz

Select the best answer for each question. Check your answers using the answer key in the appendix.

1. Which SAS statement associates the fileref Crime with the raw data file **`C:\States\Data\crime.dat`**?

   a. `filename crime 'c:\states\data\crime.dat';`

   b. `filename crime c:\states\data\crime.dat;`

   c. `fileref crime 'c:\states\data\crime.dat';`

   d. `filename 'c:\states\data\crime' crime.dat;`

2. Which type of delimited file does PROC IMPORT read by default?

a. logical record-length files

b. varying record-length files

c. fixed record-length files

d. illogical record-length files

3. Which program correctly imports only the first seven lines from the external file that is delimited by a period (.) ? Hint: the first line in the external file contains variable names that you want to read in.

a.
```
options obs=7;
proc import data="C:\users\test.txt"
  out=exam
  dbms=dlm
  replace;
  getnames=yes;
run;
proc print data=exam;
run;
```

b.
```
options obs=7;
proc import datafile="c:\users\test.txt"
  out=exam
  dbms=dlm
  replace;
  delimiter='.';
  getnames=yes;
run;
proc print data=exam;
run;
```

c.
```
proc import datafile="c:\users\test.txt"
  out=exam
  dbms=dlm
  replace;
  delimiter=' ';
  getnames=no;
run;
proc print data=exam (obs=7);
run;
```

d.
```
proc import datafile="c:\users\test.txt"
  out=exam
  dbms=csv
  replace;
  delimiter=',';
  getnames=no;
run;
proc print data=exam;
  options obs=7;
run;
```

4. Which of the following pieces of information does SAS need in the DATA step in order to read an Excel workbook file and write it out to a SAS data set?

a. a libref to reference the Excel workbook to be read

b. the name and location (using another libref) of the new SAS data set

c. the name of the Excel worksheet that is to be read

d. all of the above

5. Which statement should you use if you want PROC IMPORT to generate SAS variable names from the values in the first row of an input file?

   a. `getnames=no;`

   b. `datarow=1;`

   c. `guessingrows=1;`

   d. `getnames=yes;`

6. Which SAS program correctly imports data from an external file?

   a.
   ```
   filename workbook 'C:\certdata\class1.csv';
   proc import datafile=workbook.class
     dbms=csv
     out=class1
     replace;
     getnames=yes;
   run;
   ```

   b.
   ```
   filename workbook 'C:\certdata\workbook.txt';
   proc import datafile=workbook
     dbms=dlm
     out=workbook
     replace;
     getnames=yes;
   run;
   ```

   c.
   ```
   filename workbook 'C:\certdata\workbook.txt';
   proc import datafile=class01
     dbms=dlm
     out=class01work
     replace;
     getnames=yes;
   run;
   ```

   d. all of the above.

7. Which delimited input file can be imported using PROC IMPORT?

   a.
   ```
   Region&State&Month&Expenses&Revenue
   Southern&GA&JAN2001&2000&8000
   Southern&GA&FEB2001&1200&6000
   Southern&FL&FEB2001&8500&11000
   Northern&NY&FEB2001&3000&4000
   Northern&NY&MAR2001&6000&5000
   Southern&FL&MAR2001&9800&13500
   Northern&MA&MAR2001&1500&1000
   ```

   b.
   ```
   "Africa","Boot","Addis Ababa","12","$29,761","$191,821","$769"
   "Asia","Boot","Bangkok","1","$1,996","$9,576","$80"
   "Canada","Boot","Calgary","8","$17,720","$63,280","$472"
   "Eastern Europe","Boot","Budapest","22","$74,102","$317,515","$3,341"
   "Middle East","Boot","Al-Khobar","10","$15,062","$44,658","$765"
   "Pacific","Boot","Auckland","12","$20,141","$97,919","$962"
   "South America","Boot","Bogota","19","$15,312","$35,805","$1,229"
   "United States","Boot","Chicago","16","$82,483","$305,061","$3,735"
   "Western Europe","Boot","Copenhagen","2","$1,663","$4,657","$129"
   ```

c.

```
Region State Capital Bird
South Georgia Atlanta 'Brown Thrasher'
South 'North Carolina' Raleigh Cardinal
North Connecticut Hartford Robin
West Washington Olympia 'American Goldfinch'
Midwest Illinois Springfield Cardinal
```

d. all of the above

8. To override the DATA step default behavior that writes observations to output, what should you use in a DATA step?

   a. DROP= and KEEP= data set options

   b. an OUTPUT statement

   c. an OUT= option

   d. a BY statement

Chapter 5
Identifying and Correcting SAS Language Errors

Error Messages

Types of Errors

SAS can detect several types of errors. Here are two common ones:

- syntax errors that occur when program statements do not conform to the rules of the SAS language
- semantic errors that occur when you specify a language element that is not valid for a particular usage

Syntax Errors

When you submit a program, SAS scans each statement for syntax errors, and then executes the step (if no syntax errors are found). SAS then goes to the next step and repeats the process. Syntax errors, such as misspelled keywords, generally prevent SAS from executing the step in which the error occurred.

Notes are written to the SAS log when the program finishes executing. When a program that contains an error is submitted, messages about the error appear in the SAS log. Here is what SAS does:

- displays the word ERROR
- identifies the possible location of the error
- gives an explanation of the error

Example: Syntax Error Messages

The following program contains a syntax error:

```
data work.admitfee;                /*#1*/
  set cert.admit;
run;
proc prin data=work.admitfee;      /*#2*/
  var id name actlevel fee;        /*#3*/
run;
```

1 The DATA step creates a new SAS data set named Work.Admitfee from the Cert.Admit data set.

2 The SAS keyword PRINT in PROC PRINT is spelled incorrectly. As a result, the PROC step fails.

3 The VAR statement prints the values for the following variables only: ID, Name, ActLevel, and Fee.

When the program is submitted, messages in the SAS log indicate that the procedure PRIN was not found and that SAS stopped processing the PROC step because of errors. No output is produced by the PRINT procedure, because the second step fails to execute.

Here is an explanation of the following log.

- The ERROR keyword is the notification of the error.
- The PRIN keyword in the SAS log is the possible location of the error in the statement.
- The error explanation is **`not found`**.

Log 5.1 *SAS Log*

```
265  proc prin data=work.admitfee;
ERROR: Procedure PRIN not found.
268     var id name actlevel fee;
267  run;
NOTE: The SAS System stopped processing this step because of errors.
```

TIP Errors in your statements or data might not be evident when you look at results in the Results viewer. Review the messages in the SAS log each time you submit a SAS program.

In addition to correcting spelling mistakes, you might need to resolve other common syntax errors such as these:

- missing RUN statement

- missing semicolon
- unbalanced quotation mark

You might also need to correct a semantic error such as this:

- invalid option

Correcting Common Errors

The Basics of Error Correction

To correct simple errors, such as the spelling error here, type over the incorrect text, delete text, or insert text. In the following program, the incorrect spelling of PRINT in the PROC step is corrected.

```
data work.admitfee;
  set cert.admit;
run;
proc print data=work.admitfee;
  var id name actlevel fee;
run;
```

Resubmitting a Revised Program

After correcting your program, you can resubmit it.

Figure 5.1 *Correct PRINT Procedure Output*

The SAS System

Obs	ID	Name	ActLevel	Fee
1	2458	Murray, W	HIGH	85.20
2	2462	Almers, C	HIGH	124.80
3	2501	Bonaventure, T	LOW	149.75
4	2523	Johnson, R	MOD	149.75
5	2539	LaMance, K	LOW	124.80
6	2544	Jones, M	HIGH	124.80
7	2552	Reberson, P	MOD	149.75
8	2555	King, E	MOD	149.75
9	2563	Pitts, D	LOW	124.80
10	2568	Eberhardt, S	LOW	124.80
11	2571	Nunnelly, A	HIGH	149.75
12	2572	Oberon, M	LOW	85.20
13	2574	Peterson, V	MOD	149.75
14	2575	Quigley, M	HIGH	124.80
15	2578	Cameron, L	MOD	124.80
16	2579	Underwood, K	LOW	149.75
17	2584	Takahashi, Y	MOD	124.80
18	2586	Derber, B	HIGH	85.20
19	2588	Ivan, H	LOW	85.20
20	2589	Wilcox, E	HIGH	149.75
21	2595	Warren, C	MOD	149.75

Remember to check the SAS log again to verify that your program ran correctly.

Log 5.2 *SAS Log: No Error Messages*

```
9231  data work.admitfee;
9232      set cert.admit;
9233  run;

NOTE: There were 21 observations read from the data set CERT.ADMIT.
NOTE: The data set WORK.ADMITFEE has 21 observations and 9 variables.
NOTE: DATA statement used (Total process time):
      real time           0.00 seconds
      cpu time            0.00 seconds


9234  proc print data=work.admitfee;
9235      var id name actlevel fee;
9236  run;

NOTE: There were 21 observations read from the data set WORK.ADMITFEE.
NOTE: PROCEDURE PRINT used (Total process time):
      real time           0.01 seconds
      cpu time            0.01 seconds
```

The Basics of Logic Errors

The PUTLOG Statement

A *logic error* occurs when the program statements execute, but produce incorrect results. Because no notes are written to the log, logic errors are often difficult to detect. Use the PUTLOG statement in the DATA step to write messages to the SAS log to help identify logic errors.

Syntax, PUTLOG statement

PUTLOG '*message*';

message specifies the message that you want to write to the SAS log. It can include character literals, variable names, formats, and pointer controls.

Note: You can precede your message text with WARNING, MESSAGE, or NOTE to better identify the output in the log.

The PUTLOG statement can be used to write to the SAS log in both batch and interactive modes. If an external file is open for output, use this statement to ensure that debugging messages are written to the SAS log and not to the external file.

Temporary Variables

The temporary variables _N_ and _ERROR_ can be helpful when you debug a DATA step.

Variable	Description	Debugging Use
_N_	The number of times the DATA step iterated	Displays debugging messages for a specified number of iterations of the DATA step
ERROR	Initialized to 0, set to 1 when an error occurs	Displays debugging messages when an error occurs

Example: The DATA Step Produces Wrong Results but There Are No Error Messages

The data set contains three test scores and homework grades for four students. The program below is designed to select students whose average score is below 70. Although the program produces incorrect results, there are no error messages in the log.

```
data work.grades;
  set cert.class;
  Homework=Homework*2;
  AverageScore=MEAN(Score1 + Score2 + Score3 + Homework);
    if AverageScore<70;
run;
```

A glance at the data set shows that there should be students whose mean scores are below 70. However, the data set Work.Grades has zero observations and six variables.

```
NOTE: There were 4 observations read from the data set
      CERT.CLASS.
NOTE: The data set WORK.GRADES has 0 observations and 6
      variables.
NOTE: DATA statement used (Total process time):
      real time           0.01 seconds
      cpu time            0.01 seconds
```

Use the PUTLOG statement to determine where the DATA step received incorrect instructions. Place the PUTLOG statement before the subsetting IF.

```
PUTLOG Name= Score1= Score2= Score3= Homework= AverageScore=;
```

```
data work.grades;
     set cert.class;
     Homework=Homework*2;
     AverageScore=MEAN(Score1 + Score2 + Score3 +
Homework);
     putlog Name= Score1= Score2= Score3= Homework=
AverageScore=;
     if AverageScore<70;
run;

Name=LINDA Score1=53 Score2=60 Score3=66 Homework=84
AverageScore=263
Name=DEREK Score1=72 Score2=64 Score3=56 Homework=64
AverageScore=256
Name=KATHY Score1=98 Score2=82 Score3=100 Homework=96
AverageScore=376
Name=MICHAEL Score1=80 Score2=55 Score3=95 Homework=100
AverageScore=330
NOTE: There were 4 observations read from the data set
      CERT.CLASS.
NOTE: The data set WORK.GRADES has 0 observations and 6
      variables.
NOTE: DATA statement used (Total process time):
      real time           0.01 seconds
      cpu time            0.01 seconds
```

Looking at the log, you can see the result of the PUTLOG statement. The data that is listed in the middle of the log shows that the variables were read in properly, and the variable Homework was adjusted to be weighted the same as Scores1–3. However, the values of AverageScore are incorrect. They are above the available maximum grade.

There is a syntax error in the line that computes AverageScore: Instead of commas separating the three score variables in the MEAN function, there are plus signs. Since functions can contain arithmetic expressions, SAS simply added the four variables together, as instructed, and computed the mean of a single number. That is why no observations had values of AverageScore below 70.

To fix the error, replace the plus signs in the MEAN function with commas. You can remove the PUTLOG statement and use a PROC PRINT statement to view your results.

```
data work.grades;
  set cert.class;
```

```
  Homework=Homework*2;
  AverageScore = MEAN(Score1, Score2, Score3, Homework);
    if AverageScore < 70;
run;
proc print data=work.grades;
run;
```

The figure below lists the names of students whose average score is below 70.

Figure 5.2 *Corrected Program Output*

Name	Score1	Score2	Score3	Homework	AverageScore
LINDA	53	60	66	84	65.75
DEREK	72	64	56	64	64.00

PUT Statement

Syntax

When the source of program errors is not apparent, you can use the PUT statement to examine variable values and to print your own message in the log. For diagnostic purposes, you can use IF-THEN/ELSE statements to conditionally check for values. For more information about IF-THEN/ELSE statements, see "Using a Subsetting IF Statement" on page 151.

Syntax, PUT statement:

PUT *specification(s)*;

specification specifies what is written, how it is written, and where it is written. Here are examples:

- a character string
- one or more data set variables
- the automatic variables _N_ and _ERROR_
- the automatic variable _ALL_

Example: Using the PUT Statement

The following example illustrates how to use the PUT statement to write messages to the SAS log.

```
data work.test;
  set cert.loan01;
  if code='1' then type='variable';                              /*#1*/
    else if code='2' then type='fixed';
    else type='unknown';
  if type='unknown' then put 'MY NOTE: invalid value: ' code=;   /*#2*/
run;
```

1 If the value of the variable Code equals **1**, then the program returns the value for Type as **variable**. If the value equals **2**, then the return value for Type is **fixed**. Otherwise, the value of Type is returned as **unknown**.

2 If Type contains the value **unknown**, then the PUT statement writes a message to the log.

Log 5.3 *SAS Log*

```
NOTE: Character values have been converted to numeric
      values at the places given by: (Line):(Column).
      148173:11   148174:18
MY NOTE: invalid value: Code=3
MY NOTE: invalid value: Code=3
MY NOTE: invalid value: Code=3
```

Example: Character Strings

You can use a PUT statement to specify a character string to identify your message in the log. The character string must be enclosed in quotation marks.

```
data work.loan01;
  set cert.loan;
  if code='1' then type='variable';
    else if code='2' then type='fixed';
    else type='unknown';
  put 'MY NOTE: The condition was met.';
run;
```

The following is printed to the SAS log.

Log 5.4 *SAS Log*

```
MY NOTE: The condition was met.
MY NOTE: The condition was met.
MY NOTE: The condition was met.
MY NOTE: The condition was met.
MY NOTE: The condition was met.
MY NOTE: The condition was met.
MY NOTE: The condition was met.
MY NOTE: The condition was met.
MY NOTE: The condition was met.
NOTE: There were 9 observations read from the data set
      CERT.LOAN.
NOTE: The data set WORK.LOAN01 has 9 observations and 6
      variables.
```

Example: Data Set Variables

You can use a PUT statement to specify one or more data set variables to be examined for that iteration of the DATA step.

Note: When you specify a variable in the PUT statement, only its value is written to the log. To write both the variable name and its value to the log, add an equal sign (=) to the variable name.

```
data work.loan01;
  set cert.loan;
  if code='1' then type='variable';
    else if code='2' then type='fixed';
    else type='unknown';
  put 'MY NOTE: Invalid Value: ' code= type= ;
```

```
run;
```

The following is printed to the SAS log.

Log 5.5 *SAS Log*

```
MY NOTE: Invalid Value: Code=1 type=variable
MY NOTE: Invalid Value: Code=1 type=variable
MY NOTE: Invalid Value: Code=1 type=variable
MY NOTE: Invalid Value: Code=2 type=fixed
MY NOTE: Invalid Value: Code=2 type=fixed
MY NOTE: Invalid Value: Code=2 type=fixed
MY NOTE: Invalid Value: Code=3 type=unknown
MY NOTE: Invalid Value: Code=3 type=unknown
MY NOTE: Invalid Value: Code=3 type=unknown
NOTE: There were 9 observations read from the data set
      CERT.LOAN.
NOTE: The data set WORK.LOAN01 has 9 observations and 6
      variables.
```

Example: Conditional Processing

You can use a PUT statement with conditional processing (that is, with IF-THEN/ELSE statements) to flag program errors or data that is out of range. In the example below, the PUT statement is used to flag any missing or zero values for the variable Rate.

```
data work.newcalc;
  set cert.loan;
  if rate>0 then Interest=amount*(rate/12);
    else put 'DATA ERROR: ' rate= _n_ = ;
run;
```

The following is printed to the SAS log:

Log 5.6 *SAS Log*

```
DATA ERROR: Rate=. _N_=7
NOTE: There were 10 observations read from the data set
      CERT.LOAN.
NOTE: The data set WORK.NEWCALC has 10 observations and 5
      variables.
```

Missing RUN Statement

Each step in a SAS program is compiled and executed independently from every other step. As a step is compiled, SAS recognizes the end of the current step when it encounters one of the following statements:

- a DATA or PROC statement, which indicates the beginning of a new step
- a RUN or QUIT statement, which indicates the end of the current step

  Note: The QUIT statement ends some SAS procedures.

```
data work.admitfee;                /* #1 */
  set cert.admit;
proc print data=work.admitfee;     /* #2 */
  var id name actlevel fee;
                                   /* #3 */
```

1 Even though there is no RUN statement after the DATA step, the DATA step executes because the PROC step acts as a step boundary.

2 The PROC step does not execute. There is no following RUN statement for the step, nor is there a DATA or PROC step following the PROC PRINT step. Therefore, there is no indication that the step has ended.

3 The RUN statement is necessary at the end of the last step. If the RUN statement is omitted from the last step, the program might not complete processing and might produce unexpected results.

If you are programming in Enterprise Guide or SAS Studio, the system submits a RUN statement after every program that you submit, so the above program would execute normally.

Note: Although omitting a RUN statement is not technically an error, it can produce unexpected results. A best practice is to always end a step with a RUN statement.

To correct the error, submit a RUN statement at the end of the PROC step.

```
run;
```

Missing Semicolon

One of the most common errors is a missing semicolon at the end of a statement. Here is an example:

```
data work.admitfee;
  set cert.admit;
run;
proc print data=work.admitfee
  var id name actlevel fee;
run;
```

When you omit a semicolon, SAS reads the statement that lacks the semicolon (along with the following statement) as one long statement.

Log 5.7 *SAS Log: Error Messages*

```
9240  proc print data=work.admitfee
9241       var id name actlevel fee;
           ---
           22
           76
ERROR 22-322: Syntax error, expecting one of the following: ;, (, BLANKLINE,
CONTENTS, DATA,
              DOUBLE, GRANDTOTAL_LABEL, GRANDTOT_LABEL, GRAND_LABEL,
GTOTAL_LABEL, GTOT_LABEL,
              HEADING, LABEL, N, NOOBS, NOSUMLABEL, OBS, ROUND, ROWS, SPLIT,
STYLE, SUMLABEL,
              UNIFORM, WIDTH.
ERROR 76-322: Syntax error, statement will be ignored.
9242  run
```

Correcting the Error: Missing Semicolon

1. Find the statement that lacks a semicolon. You can usually find it by looking at the underscored keywords in the error message and working backward.
2. Add a semicolon in the appropriate location.
3. Resubmit the corrected program.
4. Check the SAS log again to make sure there are no other errors.

Unbalanced Quotation Marks

Some syntax errors, such as the missing quotation mark after **HIGH** in the program below, cause SAS to misinterpret the statements in your program.

```
data work.admitfee;
  set cert.admit;
  where actlevel='HIGH;
run;
proc print data=work.admitfee;
  var id name actlevel fee;
run;
```

When the program is submitted, SAS is unable to resolve the DATA step, and a `DATA STEP running` message appears at the top of the active window.

TIP Both SAS Enterprise Guide and SAS Studio add a final line of code to stop unbalanced quotation marks.

Sometimes a warning appears in the SAS log that indicates the following:

- A quoted string has become too long.
- A statement that contains quotation marks (such as a TITLE or FOOTNOTE statement) is ambiguous because of invalid options or unquoted text.

When you have unbalanced quotation marks, SAS is often unable to detect the end of the statement in which it occurs. In Enterprise Guide or SAS Studio, simply add the balancing quotation mark and resubmit the program. However, in some environments, this technique usually does not correct the error. SAS still considers the quotation marks to be unbalanced.

Therefore, you need to resolve the unbalanced quotation mark by canceling the submitted statements (in the Windows and UNIX operating environments) or by submitting a line of SAS code (in the z/OS operating environment) before you recall, correct, and resubmit the program.

Correcting the Error in the Windows Operating Environment

1. Press the Ctrl and Break keys or click the Break Icon on the toolbar.
2. Select **1. Cancel Submitted Statements**, and then click **OK**.

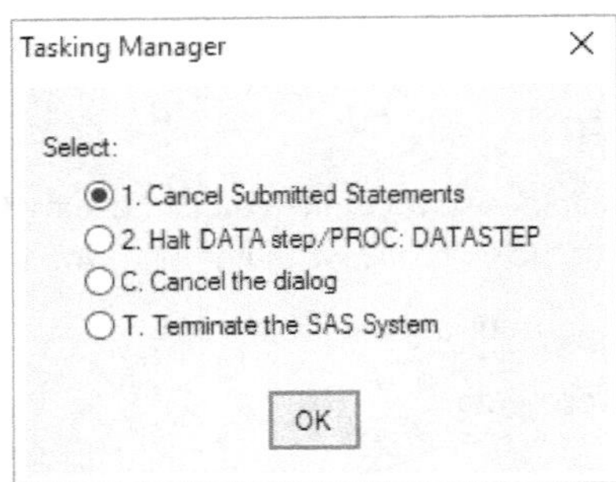

3. Select **Y to cancel submitted statements**, and then click **OK**.

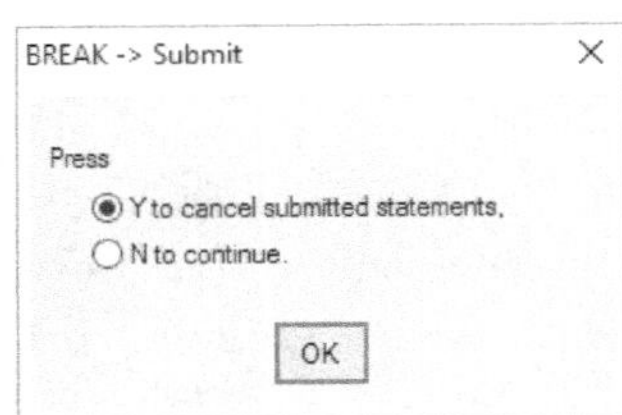

4. Correct the error and resubmit the program.

Correcting the Error in the UNIX Environment

1. Open the Session Management window and click **Interrupt**.

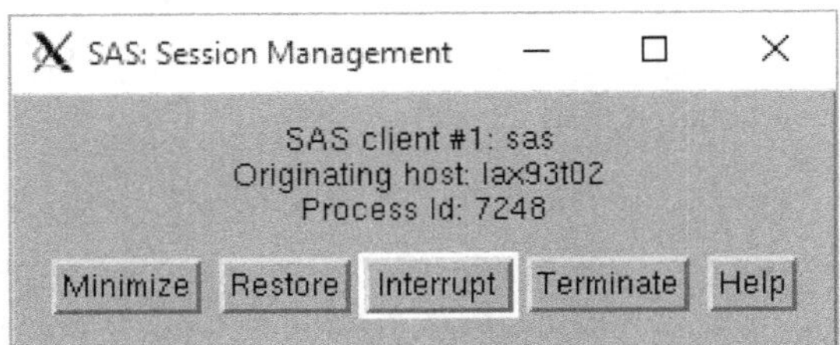

2. Select **1. Cancel Submitted Statements**, and then click **Y**.

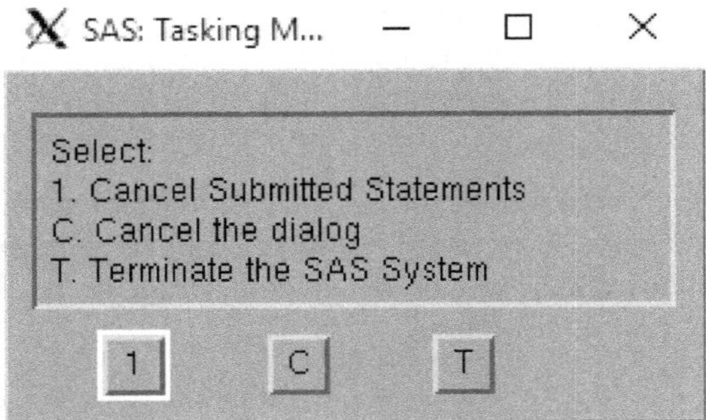

3. Correct the error and resubmit the program.

Correcting the Error in the z/OS Operating Environment

1. Submit an asterisk followed by a single quotation mark, a semicolon, and a RUN statement.

```
*'; run;
```

2. Delete the line that contains the asterisk followed by the single quotation mark, the semicolon, and the RUN statement.
3. Insert the missing quotation mark in the appropriate place.
4. Submit the corrected program.

TIP You can also use the above method in the Windows and UNIX operating environments.

Semantic Error: Invalid Option

An invalid option error occurs when you specify an option that is not valid in a particular statement. In the program below, the KEYLABEL option is not valid when it is used with the PROC PRINT statement.

```
data work.admitfee;
  set cert.admit;
  where weight>180 and (actlevel='MOD' or actlevel='LOW);
run;
proc print data=cert.admit keylabel;
  label actlevel='Activity Level';
run;
```

When a SAS statement that contains an invalid option is submitted, a message appears in the SAS log indicating that the option is not valid or not recognized.

Log 5.8 *SAS Log: Syntax Error Message*

```
9254  proc print data=cert.admit keylabel;
                                 --------
                                 22
                                 202
ERROR 22-322: Syntax error, expecting one of the following: ;, (, BLANKLINE,
CONTENTS, DATA,
              DOUBLE, GRANDTOTAL_LABEL, GRANDTOT_LABEL, GRAND_LABEL,
GTOTAL_LABEL, GTOT_LABEL,
              HEADING, LABEL, N, NOOBS, NOSUMLABEL, OBS, ROUND, ROWS, SPLIT,
STYLE, SUMLABEL,
              UNIFORM, WIDTH.
ERROR 202-322: The option or parameter is not recognized and will be ignored.
9255      label actlevel='Activity Level';
9256  run;

NOTE: The SAS System stopped processing this step because of errors.
```

Correcting the Error: Invalid Option

1. Remove or replace the invalid option, and check your statement syntax as needed.
2. Resubmit the corrected program.
3. Check the SAS log again to make sure there are no other errors.

Chapter Quiz

Select the best answer for each question. Check your answers using the answer key in the appendix.

1. Suppose you have submitted a SAS program that contains spelling errors. Which set of steps should you perform, in the order shown, to revise and resubmit the program?

   a. • Correct the errors.
      • Clear the SAS log.
      • Resubmit the program.
      • Check the Output window.
      • Check the SAS log.

   b. • Correct the errors.
      • Resubmit the program.
      • Check the Output window.

   c. • Correct the errors.
      • Clear the SAS log.
      • Resubmit the program.
      • Check the Output window.

   d. • Correct the errors.
      • Clear the Outputwindow.
      • Resubmit the program.
      • Check the Output window.

2. What happens if you submit the following program?

```
proc sort data=cert.stress out=maxrates;
   by maxhr;
run;
proc print data=maxrates label double noobs;
   label rechr='Recovery Heart Rate;
   var resthr maxhr rechr date;
   where toler='I' and resthr>90;
   sum fee;
run;
```

   a. SAS log messages indicate that the program ran successfully.

   b. A log message might indicate an error in a statement that seems to be valid.

   c. A SAS log message indicates that an option is not valid or not recognized.

   d. A SAS log message might indicate that a quoted string has become too long or that the statement is ambiguous.

3. What generally happens when a syntax error is detected?

   a. SAS continues processing the step.

   b. SAS continues to process the step, and the SAS log displays messages about the error.

   c. SAS stops processing the step in which the error occurred, and the SAS log displays messages about the error.

   d. SAS stops processing the step in which the error occurred, and the Output window displays messages about the error.

4. A syntax error occurs during the following actions:

   a. Some data values are not appropriate for the SAS statements that are specified in a program.

   b. The code executes successfully, but produces incorrect results.

   c. Program statements do not conform to the rules of the SAS language.

   d. none of the above

5. How can you tell whether you have specified an invalid option in a SAS program?

   a. A SAS log message indicates an error in a statement that seems to be valid.

   b. A SAS log message indicates that an option is not valid or not recognized.

   c. You cannot tell until you view the output from the program.

   d. none of the above

6. Which of the following programs contains a syntax error?

   a.
   ```
   proc sort data=cert.mysales;
     by region;
   run;
   ```

   b.
   ```
   data=work.mysales;
     set cert.sales17;
     where sales<5000;
   run;
   ```

   c.
   ```
   proc print data=work.mysales label;
     label region='Sales Region';
   run;
   ```

   d. none of the above

7. What are the temporary variables that can be helpful when debugging a DATA step?

   a. OBS

   b. _N_

   c. _ERROR_

   d. b and c only

8. When the source of the errors in the program is not apparent, which statement or statements can you use to examine errors and print messages to the log?

   a. PUTLOG statement

   b. PUT statement

   c. VAR statement

   d. a and b only

   e. none of the above

9. What types of errors can the PUTLOG statement help you resolve?
   a. syntax errors
   b. semantic errors
   c. logic errors
   d. all of the above

Chapter 6
Creating Reports

Creating a Basic Report

To produce a simple list report, you first reference the library where your SAS data set is stored. You can also set system options to control the appearance of your reports. Then you submit a PROC PRINT step.

Syntax, PROC PRINT step:

PROC PRINT DATA=*SAS-data-set***;**

RUN;

SAS-data-set is the name of the SAS data set to be printed.

In the program below, the PROC PRINT statement invokes the PRINT procedure and specifies the data set Therapy in the SAS library to which the libref Cert has been assigned.

```
libname cert 'C:\Users\Student1\Cert';
proc print data=cert.therapy;
run;
```

Notice the layout of the resulting report below. These are the default behaviors:

- All observations and variables in the data set are printed.
- A column for observation numbers appears on the far left.
- Variables and observations appear in the order in which they occur in the data set.

Figure 6.1 *Cert.Therapy Data Set (partial output)*

Obs	Date	AerClass	WalkJogRun	Swim
1	JAN2012	56	78	14
2	FEB2012	32	109	19
3	MAR2012	35	106	22
4	APR2012	47	115	24
5	MAY2012	55	121	31

Selecting Variables

The VAR Statement

By default, PROC PRINT lists all the variables in a data set. You can select variables and control the order in which they appear by using a VAR statement.

Syntax, VAR statement:

VAR *variable(s)*;

variable(s) is one or more variable names, separated by blanks.

For example, the following VAR statement specifies that only the variables Age, Height, Weight, and Fee be printed, in that order:

```
proc print data=cert.admit;
  var age height weight fee;
run;
```

The procedure output from the PROC PRINT step with the VAR statement lists only the values for those variables.

Figure 6.2 *PRINT Procedure Output*

The SAS System

Obs	Age	Height	Weight	Fee
1	27	72	168	85.20
2	34	66	152	124.80
3	31	61	123	149.75
4	43	63	137	149.75
5	51	71	158	124.80
6	29	76	193	124.80
7	32	67	151	149.75
8	35	70	173	149.75
9	34	73	154	124.80
10	49	64	172	124.80
11	44	66	140	149.75
12	28	62	118	85.20
13	30	69	147	149.75
14	40	69	163	124.80
15	47	72	173	124.80
16	60	71	191	149.75
17	43	65	123	124.80
18	25	75	188	85.20
19	22	63	139	85.20
20	41	67	141	149.75
21	54	71	183	149.75

Removing the OBS Column

In addition to selecting variables, you can suppress observation numbers.

To remove the Obs column, specify the NOOBS option in the PROC PRINT statement.

```
proc print data=work.example noobs;
  var age height weight fee;
run;
```

Figure 6.3 *PRINT Procedure Output with No Observation Numbers*

The SAS System

Age	Height	Weight	Fee
27	72	168	85.20
34	66	152	124.80
31	61	123	149.75
43	63	137	149.75
51	71	158	124.80
29	76	193	124.80
32	67	151	149.75
35	70	173	149.75
34	73	154	124.80
49	64	172	124.80
44	66	140	149.75
28	62	118	85.20
30	69	147	149.75
40	69	163	124.80
47	72	173	124.80
60	71	191	149.75
43	65	123	124.80
25	75	188	85.20
22	63	139	85.20
41	67	141	149.75
54	71	183	149.75

Identifying Observations

Using the ID Statement in PROC PRINT

The ID statement identifies observations using variable values, such as an identification number, instead of observation numbers.

Syntax, ID statement in the PRINT procedure:

ID *variable(s)*;

variable(s) specifies one or more variables to print whose value is used instead of the observation number at the beginning of each row of the report.

Example: ID Statement

In the following example, the OBS column in the output is replaced with the variable values for IDnum and LastName.

```
proc print data=cert.reps;
  id idnum lastname;
run;
```

Here is the output produced by PROC PRINT:

Figure 6.4 *PROC PRINT: ID Statement Output*

IDnum	LastName	FirstName	City	State	Sex	JobCode	Salary	Birth	Hired	HomePhone
1269	CASTON	FRANKLIN	STAMFORD	CT	M	NA1	41690.00	06MAY60	01DEC80	203/781-3335
1935	FERNANDEZ	KATRINA	BRIDGEPORT	CT		NA2	51081.00	31MAR42	19OCT69	203/675-2962
1417	NEWKIRK	WILLIAM	PATERSON	NJ	.	NA2	52270.00	30JUN52	10MAR77	201/732-6611
1839	NORRIS	DIANE	NEW YORK	YN	F	NA1	43433.00	02DEC58	06JUL81	718/384-1767
1111	RHODES	JEREMY	PRINCETON	NJ	M	NA1	40586.00	17JUL61	03NOV80	201/812-1837
1352	RIVERS	SIMON	NEW YORK	NY	M	NA2	5379.80	05DEC48	19OCT74	718/383-3345
1332	STEPHENSON	ADAM	BRIDGEPORT	CT	M	NA1	42178.00	20SEP58	07JUN79	203/675-1497
1443	WELLS	AGNES	STAMFORD	CT	F	NA1	422.74	20NOV56	01SEP79	203/781-5546

Example: ID and VAR Statement

You can use the ID and VAR statement together to control which variables are printed and in which order. If a variable in the ID statement also appears in the VAR statement, the output contains two columns for that variable.

```
proc print data=cert.reps;
  id idnum lastname;                /*#1*/
  var idnum sex jobcode salary;     /*#2*/
run;
```

1 The ID statement replaces the OBS column in the output with the IDnum and LastName variable values.

2 The VAR statement selects the variables that appear in the output and determines the order.

The variable IDnum appeared in both the ID statement and the VAR statement. Therefore, IDnum appears twice in the output.

Output 6.1 *PROC PRINT: ID and VAR Statement Output*

IDnum	LastName	IDnum	Sex	JobCode	Salary
1269	CASTON	1269	M	NA1	41690.00
1935	FERNANDEZ	1935		NA2	51081.00
1417	NEWKIRK	1417	.	NA2	52270.00
1839	NORRIS	1839	F	NA1	43433.00
1111	RHODES	1111	M	NA1	40586.00
1352	RIVERS	1352	M	NA2	5379.80
1332	STEPHENSON	1332	M	NA1	42178.00
1443	WELLS	1443	F	NA1	422.74

Selecting Observations

By default, a PROC PRINT step lists all the observations in a data set. You can control which observations are printed by adding a WHERE statement to your PROC PRINT step. There should be only one WHERE statement in a step. If multiple WHERE statements are issued, only the last statement is processed.

Syntax, WHERE statement:

WHERE *where-expression*;

where-expression specifies a condition for selecting observations. The *where-expression* can be any valid SAS expression.

Example Code 1 *Using the WHERE Statement in PROC PRINT*

```
proc print data=cert.admit;
  var age height weight fee;          /*#1*/
  where age>30;                       /*#2*/
run;
```

1 The VAR statement selects the variables Age, Height, Weight, and Fee and displays them in the output in that order.

2 The WHERE statement selects only the observations for which the value of Age is greater than 30 and prints them in the output.

The following output displays only the observations where the value of Age is greater than 30.

Figure 6.5 *PROC PRINT Output with a WHERE Statement*

Obs	Age	Height	Weight	Fee
2	34	66	152	124.80
3	31	61	123	149.75
4	43	63	137	149.75
5	51	71	158	124.80
7	32	67	151	149.75
8	35	70	173	149.75
9	34	73	154	124.80
10	49	64	172	124.80
11	44	66	140	149.75
14	40	69	163	124.80
15	47	72	173	124.80
16	60	71	191	149.75
17	43	65	123	124.80
20	41	67	141	149.75
21	54	71	183	149.75

VAR Statement

WHERE Statement

Specifying WHERE Expressions

In the WHERE statement, you can specify any variable in the SAS data set, not just the variables that are specified in the VAR statement. The WHERE statement works for both character and numeric variables. To specify a condition based on the value of a character variable, follow these rules:

- Enclose the value in quotation marks.
- Write the value with lowercase, uppercase, or mixed case letters exactly as it appears in the data set.

You use the following comparison operators to express a condition in the WHERE statement:

Table 6.1 *Comparison Operators in a WHERE Statement*

Symbol	**Meaning**	**Sample Program Code**
= or eq	equal to	`where name='Jones, C.';`
^= or ne	not equal to	`where temp ne 212;`
> or gt	greater than	`where income>20000;`
< or lt	less than	`where partno lt "BG05";`

Symbol	Meaning	Sample Program Code
>= or ge	greater than or equal to	`where id>='1543';`
<= or le	less than or equal to	`where pulse le 85;`

Using the CONTAINS Operator

The CONTAINS operator selects observations that include the specified substring. The symbol for the CONTAINS operator is **?**. You can use either the CONTAINS keyword or the symbol in your code, as shown below.

```
where firstname CONTAINS 'Jon';
where firstname ? 'Jon';
```

Specifying Compound WHERE Expressions

You can also use WHERE statements to select observations that meet multiple conditions. To link a sequence of expressions into compound expressions, you use logical operators, including the following:

Table 6.2 Compound WHERE Expression Operators

Operator, Symbol		Description
AND	&	and, both. If both expressions are true, then the compound expression is true.
OR	|	or, either. If either expression is true, then the compound expression is true.

Examples of WHERE Statements

- You can use compound expressions like these in your WHERE statements:

  ```
  where age<=55 and pulse>75;
  where area='A' or region='S';
  where ID>'1050' and state='NC';
  ```

- When you test for multiple values of the same variable, you specify the variable name in each expression:

  ```
  where actlevel='LOW' or actlevel='MOD';
  where fee=124.80 or fee=178.20;
  ```

- You can use the IN operator as a convenient alternative:

  ```
  where actlevel in ('LOW','MOD');
  where fee in (124.80,178.20);
  ```

- To control how compound expressions are evaluated, you can use parentheses (expressions in parentheses are evaluated first):

```
where (age<=55 and pulse>75) or area='A';
where age<=55 and (pulse>75 or area='A');
```

Using System Options to Specify Observations

SAS system options set the preferences for a SAS session. You can use the FIRSTOBS= and OBS= options in an OPTIONS statement to specify the observations to process from SAS data sets.

Specify either or both of these options as needed:

- FIRSTOBS= starts processing at a specific observation.
- OBS= stops processing after a specific observation.

Note: Using FIRSTOBS= and OBS= together processes a specific group of observations.

Syntax, FIRSTOBS=, and OBS= options in an OPTIONS statement:

FIRSTOBS=*n*

OBS=*n*

n is a positive integer. For FIRSTOBS=, *n* specifies the number of the *first* observation to process. For OBS=, *n* specifies the number of the *last* observation to process. By default, FIRSTOBS=1. The default value for OBS= is MAX, which is the largest signed, 8-byte integer that is representable in your operating environment. The number can vary depending on your operating system.

To reset the number of the last observation to process, you can specify OBS=MAX in the OPTIONS statement.

```
options obs=max;
```

This instructs any subsequent SAS programs in the SAS session to process through the last observation in the data set that is being read.

CAUTION:

Each of these options applies to every input data set that is used in a program or a SAS process because a system option sets the preference for the SAS session.

Examples: FIRSTOBS= and OBS= Options

The following examples use the data set Cert.Heart, which contains 20 observations and 8 variables.

Example Code 2 *Using the FIRSTOBS= Option*

```
options firstobs=10;          /*#1*/
proc print data=cert.heart;   /*#2*/
run;
```

1 Use the OPTIONS statement to specify the FIRSTOBS= option. In this example, the FIRSTOBS=10 option enables SAS to read the 10th observation of the data set first and read through the last observation.

2 A total of 11 observations are printed using the PROC PRINT step.

Here is the output:

Figure 6.6 PROC PRINT Output with FIRSTOBS=10

Obs	Patient	Sex	Survive	Shock	Arterial	Heart	Cardiac	Urinary
10	509	2	SURV	OTHER	79	84	256	90
11	742	1	DIED	HYPOVOL	100	54	135	0
12	609	2	DIED	NONSHOCK	93	101	260	90
13	318	2	DIED	OTHER	72	81	410	405
14	412	1	SURV	BACTER	61	87	296	44
15	601	1	DIED	BACTER	84	101	260	377
16	402	1	SURV	CARDIO	88	137	312	75
17	98	2	SURV	CARDIO	84	87	260	377
18	4	1	SURV	HYPOVOL	81	149	406	200
19	50	2	SURV	HYPOVOL	72	111	332	12
20	2	2	DIED	OTHER	101	114	424	97

You can specify the FIRSTOBS= and OBS= options together. In the following example, SAS reads only through the 10th observation.

Example Code 3 Using the FIRSTOBS= and OBS= Options

```
options firstobs=1 obs=10;        /*#1*/
proc print data=cert.heart;       /*#2*/
run;
```

1 The FIRSTOBS=1 option resets the FIRSTOBS= option to the default value. The default value reads the first observation in the data set. When you specify OBS=10 in the OPTIONS statement, SAS reads through the 10th observation.

2 A total of 10 observations are printed using the PROC PRINT step.

Here is the output:

Figure 6.7 PROC PRINT Output with FIRSTOBS=1 and Obs=10

Obs	Patient	Sex	Survive	Shock	Arterial	Heart	Cardiac	Urinary
1	203	1	SURV	NONSHOCK	88	95	66	110
2	54	1	DIED	HYPOVOL	83	183	95	0
3	664	2	SURV	CARDIO	72	111	332	12
4	210	2	DIED	BACTER	74	97	369	0
5	101	2	DIED	NEURO	80	130	291	0
6	102	2	SURV	OTHER	87	107	471	65
7	529	1	DIED	CARDIO	103	106	217	15
8	524	2	DIED	CARDIO	145	99	156	10
9	426	1	SURV	OTHER	68	77	410	75
10	509	2	SURV	OTHER	79	84	256	90

You can also combine FIRSTOBS= and OBS= to process observations in the middle of the data set.

Example Code 4 *Processing Middle Observations of a Data Set*

```
options firstobs=10 obs=15;      /* #1 */
proc print data=cert.heart;      /* #2 */
run;
```

1 When you set FIRSTOBS=10 and OBS=15, the program processes only observations 10 through 15.

2 A total of six observations are printed using the PROC PRINT step.

Here is the output:

Figure 6.8 *PROC PRINT Output with FIRSTOBS=10 and Obs=15*

Obs	Patient	Sex	Survive	Shock	Arterial	Heart	Cardiac	Urinary
10	509	2	SURV	OTHER	79	84	256	90
11	742	1	DIED	HYPOVOL	100	54	135	0
12	609	2	DIED	NONSHOCK	93	101	260	90
13	318	2	DIED	OTHER	72	81	410	405
14	412	1	SURV	BACTER	61	87	296	44
15	601	1	DIED	BACTER	84	101	260	377

Using FIRSTOBS= and OBS= for Specific Data Sets

Using the FIRSTOBS= or OBS= system options determines the first or last observation, respectively, that is read for all steps for the duration of your current SAS session or until you change the setting. However, you can still do the following:

- override these options for a given data set
- apply these options to a specific data set only

To affect any single file, use FIRSTOBS= or OBS= as data set options instead of using them as system options. You specify data set options in parentheses immediately following the input data set name.

TIP A FIRSTOBS= or OBS= specification from a data set option overrides the corresponding FIRSTOBS= or OBS= system option, but only for that DATA step.

Example: FIRSTOBS= and OBS= as Data Set Options

As shown in the following example, this program processes only observations 10 through 15, for a total of 6 observations:

```
options firstobs=10 obs=15;
proc print data=clinic.heart;
run;
```

You can create the same output by specifying FIRSTOBS= and OBS= as data set options, as follows. The data set options override the system options for this instance only.

```
options firstobs=10 obs=15;
proc print data=clinic.heart(firstobs=20 obs=30);
run;
```

To specify FIRSTOBS= or OBS= for this program only, you could omit the OPTIONS statement altogether and simply use the data set options.

Sorting Data

The SORT Procedure

By default, PROC PRINT lists observations in the order in which they appear in your data set. To sort your report based on values of a variable, you must use PROC SORT to sort your data before using the PRINT procedure to create reports from the data.

The SORT procedure does the following:

- rearranges the observations in a SAS data set
- creates a new SAS data set that contains the rearranged observations
- replaces the original SAS data set by default
- can sort on multiple variables
- can sort in ascending or descending order
- treats missing values as the smallest possible values

Note: PROC SORT does not generate printed output.

Syntax, PROC SORT step:

PROC SORT DATA=*SAS-data-set* <OUT=*SAS-data-set*>;

  BY <DESCENDING> *BY-variable(s)*;

RUN;

- The DATA= option specifies the data set to be read.
- The OUT= option creates an output data set that contains the data in sorted order.
- *BY-variable(s)* in the required BY statement specifies one or more variables whose values are used to sort the data.
- The DESCENDING option in the BY statement sorts observations in descending order. If you have more that one variable in the BY statement, DESCENDING applies only to the variable that immediately follows it.

CAUTION:

If you do not use the OUT= option, PROC SORT overwrites the data set that is specified in the DATA= option.

Example: PROC SORT

```
proc sort data=cert.admit out=work.wgtadmit;      /*#1*/
  by weight age;
run;
proc print data=work.wgtadmit;                    /*#2*/
  var weight age height fee;                      /*#3*/
  where age>30;                                   /*#4*/
run;
```

1 The PROC SORT step sorts the permanent SAS data set Cert.Admit by the values of the variable Age within the values of the variable Weight. The OUT= option creates the temporary SAS data set Wgtadmit.

2 The PROC PRINT step prints a subset of the Wgtadmit data set.

3 The VAR statement selects only the variables Weight, Age, Height, and Fee to be printed in the output.

4 The WHERE statement subsets the data by printing only those observations where the values of Age are greater than 30.

The report displays observations in ascending order of Age within Weight.

Figure 6.9 *Observations Displayed in Ascending Order of Age within Weight*

The SAS System

Obs	Weight	Age	Height	Fee
2	123	31	61	149.75
3	123	43	65	124.80
4	137	43	63	149.75
6	140	44	66	149.75
7	141	41	67	149.75
9	151	32	67	149.75
10	152	34	66	124.80
11	154	34	73	124.80
12	158	51	71	124.80
13	163	40	69	124.80
15	172	49	64	124.80
16	173	35	70	149.75
17	173	47	72	124.80
18	183	54	71	149.75
20	191	60	71	149.75

Adding the DESCENDING option to the BY statement sorts observations in ascending order of age within descending order of weight. Notice that DESCENDING applies only to the variable Weight.

```
proc sort data=cert.admit out=work.wgtadmit;
   by descending weight age;
run;
proc print data=work.wgtadmit;
   var weight age height fee;
   where age>30;
run;
```

Figure 6.10 *Observations Displayed in Descending Order by Weight and Age*

The SAS System

Obs	Weight	Age	Height	Fee
2	191	60	71	149.75
4	183	54	71	149.75
5	173	35	70	149.75
6	173	47	72	124.80
7	172	49	64	124.80
9	163	40	69	124.80
10	158	51	71	124.80
11	154	34	73	124.80
12	152	34	66	124.80
13	151	32	67	149.75
15	141	41	67	149.75
16	140	44	66	149.75
18	137	43	63	149.75
19	123	31	61	149.75
20	123	43	65	124.80

Generating Column Totals

The SUM Statement

To produce column totals for numeric variables, you can list the variables to be summed in a SUM statement in your PROC PRINT step.

Syntax, SUM statement:

SUM *variable(s)***;**

variable(s) is one or more numeric variable names, separated by blanks.

The SUM statement in the following PROC PRINT step requests column totals for the variable BalanceDue:

```
proc print data=cert.insure;
  var name policy balancedue;
  where pctinsured < 100;
  sum balancedue;
run;
```

Column totals appear at the end of the report in the same format as the values of the variables.

Figure 6.11 Column Totals

The SAS System

Obs	Name	Policy	BalanceDue
2	Almers, C	95824	156.05
3	Bonaventure, T	87795	9.48
4	Johnson, R	39022	61.04
5	LaMance, K	63265	43.68
6	Jones, M	92478	52.42
7	Reberson, P	25530	207.41
8	King, E	18744	27.19
9	Pitts, D	60976	310.82
10	Eberhardt, S	81589	173.17
13	Peterson, V	75986	228.00
14	Quigley, M	97048	99.01
15	Cameron, L	42351	111.41
17	Takahashi, Y	54219	186.58
18	Derber, B	74653	236.11
20	Wilcox, E	94034	212.20
21	Warren, C	20347	164.44
			2279.0

Note: If you specify the same variable in the VAR statement and the SUM statement, you can omit the variable name in the VAR statement. If a SUM variable is not specified in the VAR statement, the variable to be summed is added to the output in the order in which it appears in the SUM statement.

Creating Subtotals for Variable Groups

You might also want to group and subtotal numeric variables. You group variables using the BY statement. SAS calls these groups BY groups. You can use the SUM statement to create a subtotal value for variables in the group.

Syntax, BY statement in the PRINT procedure:

BY <DESCENDING> *BY-variable-1*

<...<DESCENDING> <*BY-variable-n*>>

<NOTSORTED>**;**

- *BY-variable* specifies a variable that the procedure uses to form BY groups. You can specify more than one variable, separated by blanks.
- The DESCENDING option specifies that the data set is sorted in descending order by the variable that immediately follows.
- The NOTSORTED option specifies that the observations in the data set that have the same BY values are grouped together, but are not necessarily sorted in alphabetical or numeric order. For example, the observations might be sorted in chronological order using a date format such as DDMMYY. If observations that have the same values for the BY variables are not contiguous, the procedure treats each contiguous set as a separate BY group.

Note: The NOTSORTED option applies to all of the variables in the BY statement. You can specify the NOTSORTED option anywhere within the BY statement. The requirement for ordering or indexing observations according to the values of BY variables is suspended when you use the NOTSORTED option.

When you sort the data set, you must use the same BY variable in PROC SORT as you do in PROC PRINT.

Example: SUM Statement

The following example uses the SUM statement and the BY statement to generate subtotals for each BY group and a sum of all of the subtotals of the Fee variable.

```
proc sort data=cert.admit out=work.activity;      /*#1*/
  by actlevel;
run;
proc print data=work.activity;
  var age height weight fee;
  where age>30;
  sum fee;                                        /*#2*/
  by actlevel;                                    /*#3*/
run;
```

1 The PROC SORT step sorts the permanent SAS data set Cert.Admit by the values of the variable ActLevel. The OUT= option creates the temporary SAS data set Activity.

2 The SUM statement produces column totals for the numeric variable Fee.

3 The BY statement specifies ActLevel as the variable that PROC PRINT uses to form BY groups.

In the output, the BY variable name and value appear before each BY group. The BY variable name and the subtotal appear at the end of each BY group.

Figure 6.12 *BY-Group Output: High*

ActLevel=HIGH

Obs	Age	Height	Weight	Fee
2	34	66	152	124.80
4	44	66	140	149.75
5	40	69	163	124.80
7	41	67	141	149.75
ActLevel				549.10

Figure 6.13 *BY-Group Output: Low*

ActLevel=LOW

Obs	Age	Height	Weight	Fee
8	31	61	123	149.75
9	51	71	158	124.80
10	34	73	154	124.80
11	49	64	172	124.80
13	60	71	191	149.75
ActLevel				673.90

Figure 6.14 BY-Group Output: Mod

ActLevel=MOD

Obs	Age	Height	Weight	Fee
15	43	63	137	149.75
16	32	67	151	149.75
17	35	70	173	149.75
19	47	72	173	124.80
20	43	65	123	124.80
21	54	71	183	149.75
ActLevel				**848.60**
				2071.60

Creating a Customized Layout with BY Groups and ID Variables

In the previous example, you might have noticed the redundant information for the BY variable. For example, in the PROC PRINT output below, the BY variable ActLevel is identified both before the BY group and for the subtotal.

Figure 6.15 Creating a Customized Layout with BY Groups and ID Variables

ActLevel=HIGH

Obs	Age	Height	Weight	Fee
2	34	66	152	124.80
4	44	66	140	149.75
5	40	69	163	124.80
7	41	67	141	149.75
ActLevel				**549.10**

To show the BY variable heading only once, use an ID statement and a BY statement together with the SUM statement. Here are the results when an ID statement specifies the same variable as the BY statement:

- The Obs column is suppressed.
- The ID or BY variable is printed in the left-most column.
- Each ID or BY value is printed only at the start of each BY group and on the line that contains that group's subtotal.

Example: ID, BY, and SUM Statements

The ID, BY, and SUM statements work together to create the output shown below.

```
proc sort data=cert.admit out=work.activity;     /*#1*/
  by actlevel;
run;
proc print data=work.activity;
  var age height weight fee;
  where age>30;
  sum fee;                                        /*#2*/
  by actlevel;                                    /*#3*/
```

```
  id actlevel;                                /* #4 */
run;
```

1 The PROC SORT step sorts the permanent SAS data set Cert.Admit by the values of the variable ActLevel. The OUT= option creates the temporary SAS data set Activity.

2 The SUM statement produces column totals for the numeric variable Fee.

3 The BY statement specifies ActLevel as the variable that PROC PRINT uses to form BY groups.

4 The ID statement specifies ActLevel as the variable that replaces the Obs column and listed only once for each BY group and once for each sum. The BY lines are suppressed, and the values of the ID statement variable ActLevel identify each BY group.

Output 6.2 *Creating Custom Output Example Output*

The SAS System

ActLevel	Age	Height	Weight	Fee
HIGH	34	66	152	124.80
	44	66	140	149.75
	40	69	163	124.80
	41	67	141	149.75
HIGH				**549.10**

ActLevel	Age	Height	Weight	Fee
LOW	31	61	123	149.75
	51	71	158	124.80
	34	73	154	124.80
	49	64	172	124.80
	60	71	191	149.75
LOW				**673.90**

ActLevel	Age	Height	Weight	Fee
MOD	43	63	137	149.75
	32	67	151	149.75
	35	70	173	149.75
	47	72	173	124.80
	43	65	123	124.80
	54	71	183	149.75
MOD				**848.60**
				2071.60

Creating Subtotals on Separate Pages

As another enhancement to your PROC PRINT report, you can request that each BY group be printed on a separate page by using the PAGEBY statement.

Syntax, PAGEBY statement:

PAGEBY *BY-variable*;

BY-variable identifies a variable that appears in the BY statement in the PROC PRINT step. PROC PRINT begins printing a new page if the value of the BY variable changes, or if the value of any BY variable that precedes it in the BY statement changes.

Note: The variable specified in the PAGEBY statement must also be specified in the BY statement in the PROC PRINT step.

Example: PAGEBY Statement

The PAGEBY statement prints each BY group on a separate page. The following example uses the PAGEBY statement to print the BY groups for the variable ActLevel on separate pages. The BY groups are separated by horizontal lines in the HTML output.

```
proc sort data=cert.admit out=work.activity;
  by actlevel;
run;
proc print data=work.activity;
  var age height weight fee;
  where age>30;
  sum fee;
  by actlevel;
  id actlevel;
  pageby actlevel;
run;
```

Output 6.3 *PAGEBY Example Output*

ActLevel	Age	Height	Weight	Fee
HIGH	34	66	152	124.80
	44	66	140	149.75
	40	69	163	124.80
	41	67	141	149.75
HIGH				**549.10**

The SAS System

ActLevel	Age	Height	Weight	Fee
LOW	31	61	123	149.75
	51	71	158	124.80
	34	73	154	124.80
	49	64	172	124.80
	60	71	191	149.75
LOW				**673.90**

The SAS System

ActLevel	Age	Height	Weight	Fee
MOD	43	63	137	149.75
	32	67	151	149.75
	35	70	173	149.75
	47	72	173	124.80
	43	65	123	124.80
	54	71	183	149.75
MOD				**848.60**
				2071.60

Specifying Titles and Footnotes in Procedure Output

TITLE and FOOTNOTE Statements

To make your report more meaningful and self-explanatory, you can assign up to 10 titles with procedure output by using TITLE statements before the PROC step. Likewise, you can specify up to 10 footnotes by using FOOTNOTE statements before the PROC step.

TIP Because TITLE and FOOTNOTE statements are global statements, place them anywhere within or before the PRINT procedure. Titles and footnotes are assigned as soon as TITLE or FOOTNOTE statements are read; they apply to all subsequent output.

Syntax, TITLE, and FOOTNOTE statements:

TITLE<*n*> *'text'*;

FOOTNOTE<*n*> *'text'*;

n is a number from 1 to 10 that specifies the title or footnote line, and *'text'* is the actual title or footnote to be displayed. The maximum title or footnote length depends on your operating environment and on the value of the LINESIZE= option.

The keyword TITLE is equivalent to TITLE1. Likewise, FOOTNOTE is equivalent to FOOTNOTE1. If you do not specify a title, the default title is The SAS System. No footnote is printed unless you specify one.

As a best practice be sure to match quotation marks that enclose the title or footnote text.

Example: Creating Titles

In the following example, the two TITLE statements are specified for lines 1 and 3. These two TITLE statements define titles for the PROC PRINT output. You can create a blank line between two titles by skipping a number in the TITLE statement.

```
title1 'Heart Rates for Patients with:';
title3 'Increased Stress Tolerance Levels';
proc print data=cert.stress;
  var resthr maxhr rechr;
  where tolerance='I';
run;
```

Output 6.4 *PROC PRINT Output with Titles*

Heart Rates for Patients with:

Increased Stress Tolerance Levels

Obs	RestHR	MaxHR	RecHR
2	68	171	133
3	78	177	139
8	70	167	122
11	65	181	141
14	74	152	113
15	75	158	108
20	78	189	138

Example: Creating Footnotes

In the following example, the two FOOTNOTE statements are specified for lines 1 and 3. These two FOOTNOTE statements define footnotes for the PROC PRINT output. Since there is no FOOTNOTE2, a blank line is inserted between FOOTNOTE1 and FOOTNOTE3 in the output.

```
footnote1 'Data from Treadmill Tests';
footnote3 '1st Quarter Admissions';
proc print data=cert.stress;
  var resthr maxhr rechr;
  where tolerance='I';
run;
```

Footnotes appear at the bottom of each page of procedure output. Notice that footnote lines are pushed up from the bottom. The FOOTNOTE statement that has the largest number appears on the bottom line.

Output 6.5 *PROC PRINT Output with Footnotes*

Heart Rates for Patients with

Increased Stress Tolerance Levels

Obs	RestHR	MaxHR	RecHR
2	68	171	133
3	78	177	139
8	70	167	122
11	65	181	141
14	74	152	113
15	75	158	108
20	78	189	138

Data from Treadmill Tests

1st Quarter Admissions

Modifying and Canceling Titles and Footnotes

As global statements, the TITLE and FOOTNOTE statements remain in effect until you modify the statements, cancel the statements, or end your SAS session. In the following example, the titles and footnotes that are assigned in the PROC PRINT step also appear in the output for the PROC MEANS step.

```
title1 'Heart Rates for Patients with';
title3 'Increased Stress Tolerance Levels';
footnote1 'Data from Treadmill Tests';
footnote3 '1st Quarter Admissions';
proc print data=cert.stress;
  var resthr maxhr rechr;
  where tolerance='I';
run;
proc means data=cert.stress;
  where tolerance='I';
  var resthr maxhr;
run;
```

Output 6.6 *PROC PRINT Output with Titles and Footnotes*

Heart Rates for Patients with

Increased Stress Tolerance Levels

Obs	RestHR	MaxHR	RecHR
2	68	171	133
3	78	177	139
8	70	167	122
11	65	181	141
14	74	152	113
15	75	158	108
20	78	189	138

Data from Treadmill Tests

1st Quarter Admissions

Output 6.7 *PROC MEANS Output with Titles and Footnotes*

Heart Rates for Patients with

Increased Stress Tolerance Levels

The MEANS Procedure

Variable	N	Mean	Std Dev	Minimum	Maximum
RestHR	7	72.5714286	5.0284903	65.0000000	78.0000000
MaxHR	7	170.7142857	12.9449383	152.0000000	189.0000000

Data from Treadmill Tests

1st Quarter Admissions

Redefining a title or footnote line cancels any higher numbered title or footnote lines, respectively. In the example below, defining a title for line 2 in the second report automatically cancels title line 3.

```
title1 'Heart Rates for Patients with';
title3 'Participation in Exercise Therapy';
footnote1 'Data from Treadmill Tests';
footnote3 '1st Quarter Admissions';
proc print data=cert.therapy;
  var swim walkjogrun aerclass;
run;
title2 'Report for March';
proc print data=cert.therapy;
run;
```

Output 6.8 *PROC PRINT Output of Cert.Therapy with Title 1 and Title 3 (partial output)*

Heart Rates for Patients with

Participation in Exercise Therapy

Obs	Swim	WalkJogRun	AerClass
1	14	78	56
2	19	109	32
...more observations...			
20	53	65	63
21	68	49	60
22	41	70	78
23	58	44	82
24	47	57	93

Data from Treadmill Tests

1st Quarter Admissions

Output 6.9 *PROC PRINT Output of Cert.Therapy with Title 1 and Title 2 (partial output)*

Heart Rates for Patients with
Report for March

Obs	Date	AerClass	WalkJogRun	Swim
1	JAN2012	56	78	14
2	FEB2012	32	109	19
. . . more observations. . .				
20	AUG2013	63	65	53
21	SEP2013	60	49	68
22	OCT2013	78	70	41
23	NOV2013	82	44	58
24	DEC2013	93	57	47

Data from Treadmill Tests

1st Quarter Admissions

To cancel all previous titles or footnotes, specify a null TITLE or FOOTNOTE statement. A null TITLE or FOOTNOTE statement does not contain any number or text and cancels all footnotes and titles that are in effect.

```
title1;                                     /*#1*/
footnote1 'Data from Treadmill Tests';      /*#2*/
footnote3 '1st Quarter Admissions';
proc print data=cert.stress;
  var resthr maxhr rechr;
  where tolerance='I';
run;
footnote;                                   /*#3*/
proc means data=cert.stress;
```

```
    where tolerance='I';
    var resthr maxhr;
  run;
```

1 Specifying the TITLE1 statement cancels all previous titles and cancels the default title **The SAS System**. The PRINT procedure and the MEANS procedure do not contain any titles in the output.

2 Specifying the FOOTNOTE1 and FOOTNOTE3 statements before the PRINT procedure results in footnotes in the PROC PRINT output.

3 Specifying a null FOOTNOTE statement cancels the previously defined footnotes that are in effect.

Output 6.10 *PROC PRINT Output with Footnotes and No Titles*

Obs	RestHR	MaxHR	RecHR
2	68	171	133
3	78	177	139
8	70	167	122
11	65	181	141
14	74	152	113
15	75	158	108
20	78	189	138

Data from Treadmill Tests

1st Quarter Admissions

Output 6.11 *PROC MEANS Output with No Footnotes and No Titles*

The MEANS Procedure

Variable	N	Mean	Std Dev	Minimum	Maximum
RestHR	7	72.5714286	5.0284903	65.0000000	78.0000000
MaxHR	7	170.7142857	12.9449383	152.0000000	189.0000000

Assigning Descriptive Labels

Temporarily Assigning Labels to Variables

To enhance your PROC PRINT by labeling columns:

- Use the LABEL statement to assign a descriptive label to a variable.
- Use the LABEL option in the PROC PRINT statement to specify that the labels be displayed.

Syntax, LABEL statement:

LABEL *variable1='label1'*
variable2='label2'
... ;

Labels can be up to 256 characters long. Enclose the label in quotation marks.

Tip: The LABEL statement applies only to the PROC step in which it appears.

Example: Using the LABEL Option in the PROC PRINT Statement

In the PROC PRINT step below, the variable name WalkJogRun is displayed with the label Walk/Jog/Run. Note that the LABEL option is in the PROC PRINT statement.

```
proc print data=cert.therapy label;
  label walkjogrun='Walk/Jog/Run';
run;
```

Output 6.12 *PROC PRINT Output with LABEL Option (partial output)*

Obs	Date	AerClass	Walk/Jog/Run	Swim
1	JAN2012	56	78	14
2	FEB2012	32	109	19
. . . more observations. . .				
20	AUG2013	63	65	53
21	SEP2013	60	49	68
22	OCT2013	78	70	41
23	NOV2013	82	44	58
24	DEC2013	93	57	47

If you omit the LABEL option in the PROC PRINT statement, PROC PRINT uses the name of the column heading, **`walkjogrun`**, even though you specified a value for the variable.

Example: Using Multiple LABEL Statements

The following example illustrates the use of multiple LABEL statements.

```
proc print data=cert.admit label;          /*#1*/
  var age height;
  label age='Age of Patient';              /*#2*/
  label height='Height in Inches';         /*#3*/
run;
```

1 Use the LABEL option with the PROC PRINT statement. If you omit the LABEL option in the PROC PRINT statement, PROC PRINT uses the variable name.

2 You can assign labels in separate LABEL statements. In this example, label the variable Age as Age of Patients.

3 This is the second LABEL statement in this example. Label the variable Height as Height in Inches.

Output 6.13 *PROC PRINT Output with Multiple LABEL Statements (partial output)*

Obs	Age of Patient	Height in Inches
1	27	72
2	34	66
...*more observations*...		
17	43	65
18	25	75
19	22	63
20	41	67
21	54	71

Example: Using a Single LABEL Statement to Assign Multiple Labels

You can also assign multiple labels using a single LABEL statement.

```
proc print data=cert.admit label;              /*#1*/
  var actlevel height weight;
  label actlevel='Activity Level'              /*#2*/
        height='Height in Inches'
        weight='Weight in Pounds';
run;
```

1 Use the LABEL option with the PROC PRINT statement.

2 A single LABEL statement assigns three labels to three different variables. Note that you do not need a semicolon at the end of your label until you are ready to close your LABEL statement. In this example, the semicolon is at the end of the label for Weight.

Output 6.14 *PROC PRINT Output with a Single LABEL Statement (partial output)*

Obs	Activity Level	Height in Inches	Weight in Pounds
1	HIGH	72	168
2	HIGH	66	152
. . . *more observations*. . .			
17	MOD	65	123
18	HIGH	75	188
19	LOW	63	139
20	HIGH	67	141
21	MOD	71	183

Using Permanently Assigned Labels

When you use a LABEL statement within a PROC step, the label applies only to the output from that step.

However, in PROC steps, you can also use permanently assigned labels. Permanent labels can be assigned in the DATA step. These labels are saved with the data set, and they can be reused by procedures that reference the data set.

For example, the DATA step below creates the data set Cert.Paris and defines the label for the variable Date. Because the LABEL statement is inside the DATA step, the labels are written to the Cert.Paris data set and are available to the subsequent PRINT procedure.

```
data cert.paris;
  set cert.laguardia;
  where dest='PAR' and (boarded=155 or boarded=146);
  label date='Departure Date';
run;
proc print data=cert.paris label;
  var date dest boarded;
run;
```

Output 6.15 *Using Permanent Labels*

Obs	Departure Date	Dest	Boarded
1	04MAR2012	PAR	146
2	07MAR2012	PAR	155
3	04MAR2012	PAR	146
4	07MAR2012	PAR	155

Notice that the PROC PRINT statement still requires the LABEL option in order to display the permanent labels. Other SAS procedures display permanently assigned labels without additional statements or options.

For more information about permanently assigning labels, see "Assigning Descriptive Labels" on page 100.

Chapter Quiz

Select the best answer for each question. Check your answers using the answer key in the appendix.

1. Which PROC PRINT step below creates the sample output with the labels and variables being displayed? Hint: PROC CONTENTS output is shown first to assist you.

Alphabetic List of Variables and Attributes					
#	Variable	Type	Len	Format	Label
6	Boarded	Num	8		On
2	Date	Num	8	DATE7.	
3	Depart	Num	8	TIME5.	
8	Deplaned	Num	8		
5	Dest	Char	3		
1	Flight	Char	3		
4	Orig	Char	3		
9	Revenue	Num	8		
7	Transferred	Num	8		Changed

Date	On	Changed	Flight
04MAR12	232	18	219
05MAR12	160	4	219
06MAR12	163	14	219
07MAR12	241	9	219
08MAR12	183	11	219
09MAR12	211	18	219
10MAR12	167	7	219

a.
```
proc print data=cert.laguardia noobs;
   var on changed flight;
   where on>=160;
run;
```

b.
```
proc print data=cert.laguardia;
   var date on changed flight;
   where changed>3;
run;
```

c.
```
proc print data=cert.laguardia label;
   id date;
   var boarded transferred flight;
   label boarded='On' transferred='Changed';
   where flight='219';
run;
```

d.
```
proc print cert.laguardia noobs;
   id date;
   var date on changed flight;
   where flight='219';
run;
```

2. Which of the following PROC PRINT steps is correct if labels are not stored with the data set?

a.
```
proc print data=cert.totals label;
   label region8='Region 8 Yearly Totals';
```

```
run;
```

b.
```
proc print data=cert.totals;
   label region8='Region 8 Yearly Totals';
run;
```

c.
```
proc print data cert.totals label noobs;
run;
```

d.
```
proc print cert.totals label;
run;
```

3. Which of the following statements selects from a data set only those observations for which the value of the variable Style is **RANCH**, **SPLIT**, or **TWOSTORY**?

   a. `where style='RANCH' or 'SPLIT' or 'TWOSTORY';`

   b. `where style in 'RANCH' or 'SPLIT' or 'TWOSTORY';`

   c. `where style in (RANCH, SPLIT, TWOSTORY);`

   d. `where style in ('RANCH','SPLIT','TWOSTORY');`

4. If you want to sort your data and create a temporary data set named Calc to store the sorted data, which of the following steps should you submit?

   a.
   ```
   proc sort data=work.calc out=finance.dividend;
   run;
   ```

   b.
   ```
   proc sort dividend out=calc;
      by account;
   run;
   ```

   c.
   ```
   proc sort data=finance.dividend out=work.calc;
      by account;
   run;
   ```

   d.
   ```
   proc sort from finance.dividend to calc;
      by account;
   run;
   ```

5. Which of the following statements can you use in a PROC PRINT step to create this output?

Month	Instructors	AerClass	WalkJogRun	Swim
1	1	37	91	83
2	2	41	102	27
3	1	52	98	19
4	1	61	118	22
5	3	49	88	29
6	2	24	101	54
7	1	45	91	69
8	2	63	65	53
9	1	60	49	68
10	1	78	70	41
11	3	82	44	58
12	2	93	57	47
	20	**685**	**974**	**570**

a.
```
var month instructors;
sum instructors aerclass walkjogrun swim;
```

b.
```
var month;
sum instructors aerclass walkjogrun swim;
```

c.
```
var month instructors aerclass;
sum instructors aerclass walkjogrun swim;
```

d. all of the above

6. What happens if you submit the following program?

```
proc sort data=cert.diabetes;
run;
proc print data=cert.diabetes;
   var age height weight pulse;
   where sex='F';
run;
```

a. The PROC PRINT step runs successfully, printing observations in their sorted order.

b. The PROC SORT step permanently sorts the input data set.

c. The PROC SORT step generates errors and stops processing, but the PROC PRINT step runs successfully, printing observations in their original (unsorted) order.

d. The PROC SORT step runs successfully, but the PROC PRINT step generates errors and stops processing.

7. If you submit the following program, which output does it create?

```
proc sort data=cert.loans out=work.loans;
   by months amount;
run;
```

```
proc print data=work.loans noobs;
   var months amount payment;
   sum amount payment;
   where months<360;
run;
```

a.

Months	Amount	Payment
12	$3,500	$308.52
24	$8,700	$403.47
36	$10,000	$325.02
48	$5,000	$128.02
60	$18,500	$393.07
60	$22,000	$467.43
	$67,700	**$2,025.53**

b.

Months	Amount	Payment
12	$3,500	$308.52
24	$8,700	$403.47
36	$10,000	$325.02
48	$5,000	$128.02
60	$18,500	$393.07
60	$22,000	$467.43
	67,700	

c.

Months	Amount	Payment
12	$3,500	$308.52
48	$5,000	$128.02
60	$18,500	$393.07
24	$8,700	$403.47
360	$10,000	$325.02
600	$22,000	$467.43
	$67,700	**$2,025.53**

d.

Months	Amount	Payment
12	$3,500	$308.52
24	$8,700	$403.47
36	$10,000	$325.02
48	$5,000	$128.02
60	$18,500	$393.07
60	$22,000	$467.43
		$2,025.53

8. Which statement below selects rows that satisfy both these conditions?

   - The amount is less than or equal to $5000.
   - The account is 101-1092 or the rate equals 0.095.

   a. `where amount <= 5000 and`

```
account='101-1092' or rate = 0.095;
```

b.
```
where (amount le 5000 and account='101-1092')
      or rate = 0.095;
```

c.
```
where amount <= 5000 and
      (account='101-1092' or rate eq 0.095);
```

d.
```
where amount <= 5000 or account='101-1092'
      and rate = 0.095;
```

9. What does PROC PRINT display by default?

   a. PROC PRINT does not create a default report; you must specify the rows and columns to be displayed.

   b. PROC PRINT displays all observations and variables in the data set. If you want an additional column for observation numbers, you can request it.

   c. PROC PRINT displays columns in the following order: a column for observation numbers, all character variables, and all numeric variables.

   d. PROC PRINT displays all observations and variables in the data set, a column for observation numbers on the far left, and variables in the order in which they occur in the data set.

Chapter 7
Understanding DATA Step Processing

How SAS Processes Programs

When you submit a DATA step, SAS processes the DATA step and creates a new SAS data set. A SAS DATA step is processed in two phases:

Figure 7.1 *DATA Step Process*

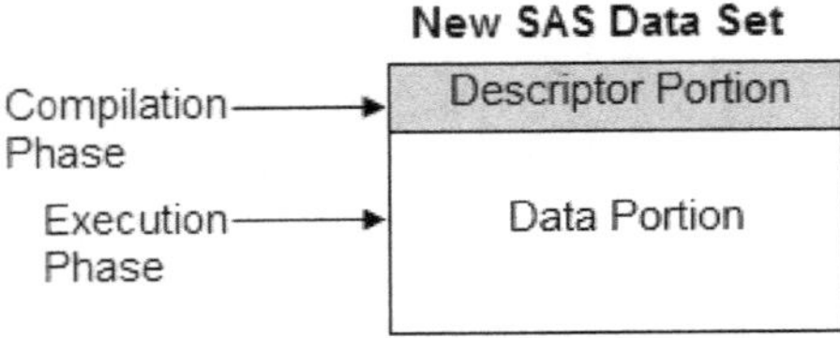

When you submit a DATA step for execution, SAS checks the syntax of the SAS statements and compiles them. In this phase, SAS identifies the type and length of each new variable, and determines whether a variable type conversion is necessary for each subsequent reference to a variable. During the compilation phase, SAS creates the following items:

- program data vector (PDV)
- descriptor information

When the compilation phase is complete, the descriptor portion of the new data set is created.

By default, a simple DATA step iterates once for each observation that is being created. The flow of action in the execution phase of a simple DATA step is described as follows:

1. The DATA step begins with a DATA statement. Each time the DATA statement executes, a new iteration of the DATA step begins, and the _N_ automatic variable is incremented by 1. The _N_ automatic variable represents the number of times the DATA step has iterated.
2. SAS sets the newly created program variables to missing in the program data vector (PDV).
3. SAS reads an observation from a SAS data set directly into the PDV. You can use MERGE, SET, MODIFY, or UPDATE statement to read a record.
4. SAS executes any subsequent programming statements sequentially and updates the PDV.
5. When SAS executes the last statement in the DATA step, all values (except temporary variables and those marked to be dropped) are written as a single observation to the data set. Note that variables that you read with a SET, MERGE, MODIFY, or UPDATE statement are not reset to missing here.
6. SAS counts another iteration, reads the next observation, and executes the subsequent programming statements for the current observation.
7. The DATA step terminates when SAS encounters the end-of-file in a SAS data set.

Figure 7.2 shows the general flow of DATA step processing for reading raw data.

Figure 7.2 *Compilation and Execution Phases of DATA Step Processing*

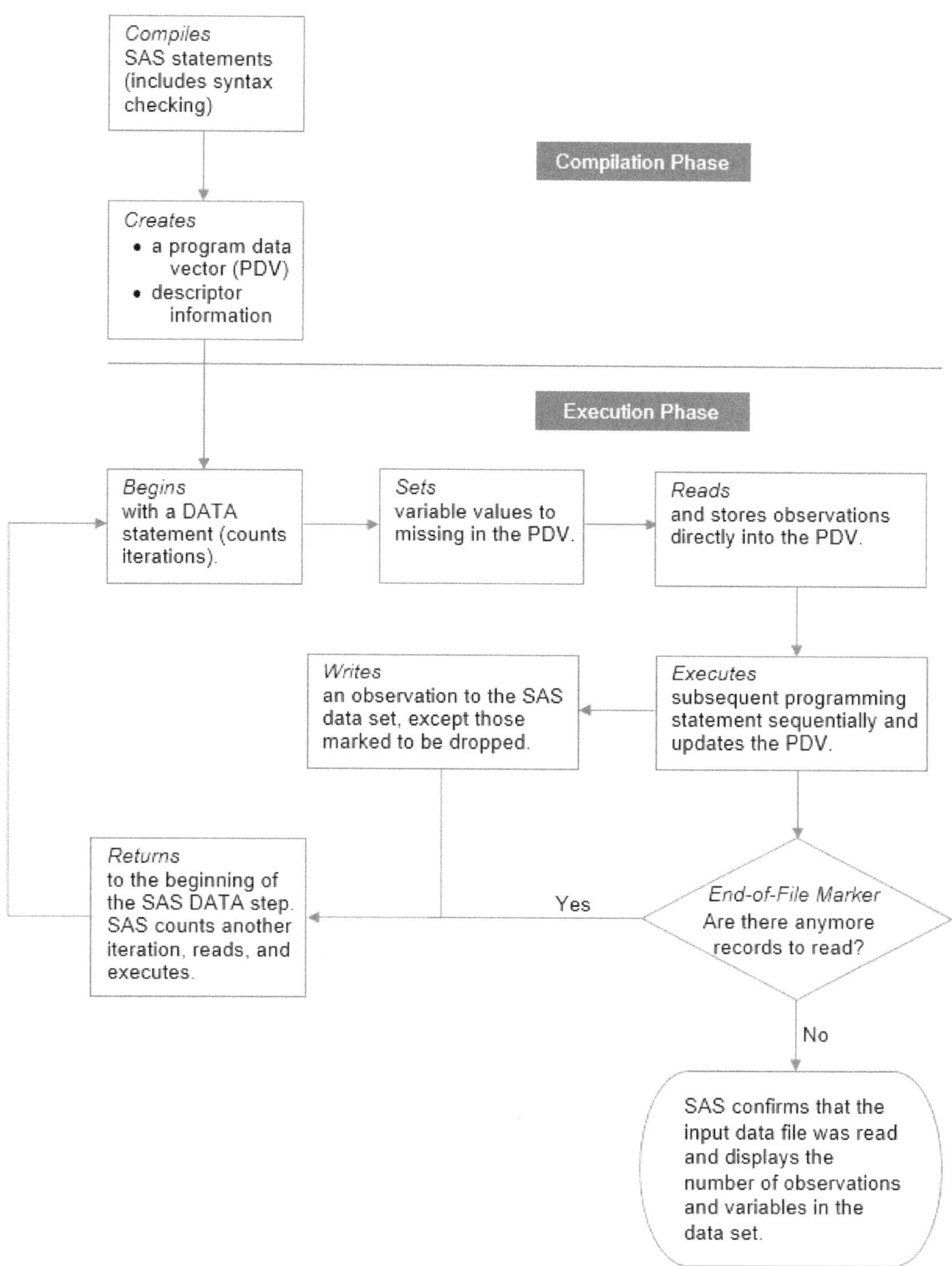

Compilation Phase

Program Data Vector (PDV)

The PDV is a logical area in memory where SAS builds a data set, one observation at a time. When a program executes, SAS reads data values or creates them by executing SAS language statements. The data values are assigned to the appropriate variables in the PDV. From here, SAS writes the values to a SAS data set as a single observation.

Along with data set variables and computed variables, the PDV contains these automatic variables:

- the _N_ variable, which counts the number of times the DATA step iterates.
- the _ERROR_ variable, which signals the occurrence of an error caused by the data during execution. The value of _ERROR_ is 0 when there are no errors. When an error occurs, whether one error or multiple errors, the value is set to 1. The default value is 0.

Note: SAS does not write these variables to the output data set.

Syntax Checking

During the compilation phase, SAS scans each statement in the DATA step, looking for syntax errors. Here are examples:

- missing or misspelled keywords
- invalid variable names
- missing or invalid punctuation
- invalid options

Data Set Variables

As the SET statement compiles, a slot is added to the PDV for each variable in the new data set. Generally, variable attributes such as length and type are determined the first time a variable is encountered.

```
data work.update;
  set cert.invent;
  Total=instock+backord;
  SalePrice=(CostPerUnit*0.65)+CostPerUnit;
  format CostPerUnit SalePrice dollar6.2;
run;
```

Figure 7.3 *Program Data Vector*

Program Data Vector

Item	IDnum	InStock	BackOrd	CostPerUnit			_N_	_ERROR_

Any variables that are created with an assignment statement in the DATA step are also added to the PDV. For example, the assignment statement below creates two variables, Total and SalePrice. As the statement is compiled, the variable is added to the PDV. The attributes of the variable are determined by the expression in the statement. Because the expression contains an arithmetic operator and produces a numeric value, Total and SalePrice are defined as numeric variables and are assigned the default length of 8.

```
data work.update;
  set cert.invent;
  Total=instock+backord;
  SalePrice=(CostPerUnit*0.65)+CostPerUnit;
  format CostPerUnit SalePrice dollar6.2;
run;
```

Figure 7.4 *Program Data Vector*

Program Data Vector

Item	IDnum	InStock	BackOrd	CostPerUnit	Total	SalePrice	_N_	_ERROR_

Descriptor Portion of the SAS Data Set

The descriptor portion is information that SAS creates and maintains about each SAS data set, including data set attributes and variable attributes. Here are examples:

- the name of the data set and its member type
- the date and time that the data set was created
- the names, data types (character or numeric), and lengths of the variables

Extended attribute descriptor information is defined by the user and includes the name of the attribute, the name of the variable, and the value of the attribute. The descriptor information also contains information about extended attributes (if defined in a data set). You can use the CONTENTS procedure to display descriptor information.

```
proc contents data=work.update;
run;
```

Figure 7.5 *CONTENTS Procedure Output: Data Set Descriptor Specifics*

Data Set Name	WORK.UPDATE	Observations	9
Member Type	DATA	Variables	7
Engine	V9	Indexes	0
Created	07/25/2018 15:13:34	Observation Length	64
Last Modified	07/25/2018 15:13:34	Deleted Observations	0
Protection		Compressed	NO
Data Set Type		Sorted	NO
Label			
Data Representation	WINDOWS_64		
Encoding	wlatin1 Western (Windows)		

Engine/Host Dependent Information	
Data Set Page Size	65536
Number of Data Set Pages	1
First Data Page	1
Max Obs per Page	1021
Obs in First Data Page	9
Number of Data Set Repairs	0
ExtendObsCounter	YES
Filename	C:\Users\Student1\SAS Temporary Files_TD18132_D7C049_\update.sas7bdat
Release Created	9.0401M4
Host Created	X64_10PRO
Owner Name	Student1
File Size	128KB
File Size (bytes)	131072

Alphabetic List of Variables and Attributes				
#	Variable	Type	Len	Format
4	BackOrd	Num	8	
5	CostPerUnit	Num	8	DOLLAR6.2
2	IDnum	Char	5	
3	InStock	Num	8	
1	Item	Char	13	
7	SalePrice	Num	8	DOLLAR6.2
6	Total	Num	8	

At this point, the data set contains the six variables that are defined in the input data set and in the assignment statement. _N_ and _ERROR_ are not written to the data set. There are no observations because the DATA step has not yet executed. During execution, each raw data record is processed and is then written to the data set as an observation.

Execution Phase

Initializing Variables

At the beginning of the execution phase, the value of _N_ is 1. Because there are no data errors, the value of _ERROR_ is 0.

```
data work.update;
  set cert.invent;
  Total=instock+backord;
  SalePrice=(CostPerUnit*0.65)+CostPerUnit;
  format CostPerUnit SalePrice dollar6.2;
run;
```

Figure 7.6 *Program Data Vector: Initializing Variables*

Program Data Vector

Item	IDnum	InStock	BackOrd	CostPerUnit	Total	SalePrice	_N_	_ERROR_
		•	•	•	•	•	1	0

The remaining variables are initialized to missing. Missing numeric values are represented by periods, and missing character values are represented by blanks.

SET Statement

The SET statement identifies the location of the input data set. Columns are added to the PDV in the order in which they appear in the input table. Attributes are inherited from the input table.

```
data work.update;
  set cert.invent;
  Total=instock+backord;
  SalePrice=(CostPerUnit*0.65)+CostPerUnit;
  format CostPerUnit SalePrice dollar6.2;
run;
```

Sequentially Process Statements

After the SET statement, SAS executes the remaining statements sequentially and updates the values in the PDV.

```
data work.update;
  set cert.invent;
  Total=instock+backord;                          /*#1*/
  SalePrice=(CostPerUnit*0.65)+CostPerUnit;       /*#2*/
  format CostPerUnit SalePrice dollar6.2;
run;
```

1 SAS processes the first assignment statement to create the new variable, Total. The values of InStock and BackOrd are added together to create a value for Total. See Figure 7.7 below for a visual representation of how the PDV processes the first assignment statement.

2 SAS processes the second assignment statement to create the new variable, SalePrice. The value of CostPerUnit is multiplied by 0.65, and the resulting value is added to the value of CostPerUnit to create a value for SalePrice. See Figure 7.8 below for a visual representation of how the PDV processes the second assignment statement.

Figure 7.7 *PDV: Create a New Variable, Total*

Program Data Vector

Item	IDnum	InStock	BackOrd	CostPerUnit	Total	SalePrice	_N_	_ERROR_
Bird Feeder	LG088	3	20	$5.00	23	•	1	0

Figure 7.8 *PDV: Create a New Variable, SalePrice*

Program Data Vector

Item	IDnum	InStock	BackOrd	CostPerUnit	Total	SalePrice	_N_	_ERROR_
Bird Feeder	LG088	3	20	$5.00	23	$8.25	1	0

The formats for each variable are applied before SAS adds the values to the PDV.

End of the DATA Step

At the end of the DATA step, several actions occur. First, the values in the PDV are written to the output data set as the first observation.

```
data work.update;
  set cert.invent;
  Total=instock+backord;
  SalePrice=(CostPerUnit*0.65)+CostPerUnit;
  format CostPerUnit SalePrice dollar6.2;
run;
```

Figure 7.9 *Program Data Vector and Output Data Set*

Program Data Vector

Item	IDnum	InStock	BackOrd	CostPerUnit	Total	SalePrice	_N_	_ERROR_
Bird Feeder	LG088	3	20	$5.00	23	$8.25	1	0

SAS Data Set Work.Update Output

Obs	Item	IDnum	InStock	BackOrd	CostPerUnit	Total	SalePrice
1	Bird Feeder	LG088	3	20	$5.00	23	$8.25

Next, control returns to the top of the DATA step, and the value of _N_ increments from 1 to 2. Finally, the variable values in the PDV are reset to missing. Notice that the automatic variable _ERROR_ is reset to 0 if necessary.

```
data work.update;
  set cert.invent;
  Total=instock+backord;
  SalePrice=(CostPerUnit*0.65)+CostPerUnit;
  format CostPerUnit SalePrice dollar6.2;
run;
```

Figure 7.10 *Program Data Vector and Output Data Set*

Program Data Vector

Item	IDnum	InStock	BackOrd	CostPerUnit	Total	SalePrice	_N_	_ERROR_
Bird Feeder	LG088	3	20	$5.00	•	•	2	0

SAS Data Set Work.Update Output

Obs	Item	IDnum	InStock	BackOrd	CostPerUnit	Total	SalePrice
1	Bird Feeder	LG088	3	20	$5.00	23	$8.25

Iterations of the DATA Step

You can see that the DATA step works like a loop, repetitively executing statements to read data values and create observations one by one. At the beginning of the second iteration, the value of _N_ is 2, and _ERROR_ is still 0. Each loop (or cycle of execution) is called an *iteration.*

Figure 7.11 *Iterations of the DATA Step*

```
data work.update;
     set cert.invent;
     Total=instock+backord;
     SalePrice=(CostPerUnit*0.65)+CostPerUnit;
     format CostPerUnit SalePrice dollar6.2;
run;
```

As the SET statement executes for the second time, the values from the second record are read from the input table into the PDV.

Figure 7.12 *Program Data Vector and Output Data Set*

Program Data Vector

Item	IDnum	InStock	BackOrd	CostPerUnit	Total	SalePrice	_N_	_ERROR_
6 Glass Mugs	SB082	6	12	$1.50	•	•	2	0

SAS Data Set Work.Update Output

Obs	Item	IDnum	InStock	BackOrd	CostPerUnit	Total	SalePrice
2	6 Glass Mugs	SB082	6	12	$1.50	18	$2.48

Next, the value for Total is calculated based on the current values for InStock and BackOrd.

```
data work.update;
  set cert.invent;
  Total=instock+backord;
  SalePrice=(CostPerUnit*0.65)+CostPerUnit;
  format CostPerUnit SalePrice dollar6.2;
run;
```

Figure 7.13 Program Data Vector and Output Data Set

Program Data Vector

Item	IDnum	InStock	BackOrd	CostPerUnit	Total	SalePrice	_N_	_ERROR_
6 Glass Mugs	SB082	6	12	$1.50	18	•	2	0

+ =

SAS Data Set Work.Update Output

Obs	Item	IDnum	InStock	BackOrd	CostPerUnit	Total	SalePrice
2	6 Glass Mugs	SB082	6	12	$1.50	18	$2.48

Next, the value for SalePrice is calculated based on the values for CostPerUnit, multiplied by 0.65, and added to the value of CostPerUnit.

```
data work.update;
  set cert.invent;
  Total=instock+backord;
  SalePrice=(CostPerUnit*0.65)+CostPerUnit;
  format CostPerUnit SalePrice dollar6.2;
run;
```

Figure 7.14 Program Data Vector and Output Data Set

Program Data Vector

Item	IDnum	InStock	BackOrd	CostPerUnit	Total	SalePrice	_N_	_ERROR_
6 Glass Mugs	SB082	6	12	$1.50	18	$2.48	2	0

+(CostPerUnit X 0.65) =

SAS Data Set Work.Update Output

Obs	Item	IDnum	InStock	BackOrd	CostPerUnit	Total	SalePrice
2	6 Glass Mugs	SB082	6	12	$1.50	18	$2.48

The RUN statement indicates the end of the DATA step loop. At the bottom of the DATA step, the values in the PDV are written to the data set as the second observation.

```
data work.update;
  set cert.invent;
  Total=instock+backord;
  SalePrice=(CostPerUnit*0.65)+CostPerUnit;
  format CostPerUnit SalePrice dollar6.2;
run;
```

Next, the value of _N_ increments from 2 to 3, control returns to the top of the DATA step, and the values for Item, IDnum, InStock, BackOrd, CostPerUnit, Total, and SalePrice are reset to missing.

```
data work.update;
  set cert.invent;
  Total=instock+backord;
  SalePrice=(CostPerUnit*0.65)+CostPerUnit;
  format CostPerUnit SalePrice dollar6.2;
run;
```

Figure 7.15 Program Data Vector and Output Data

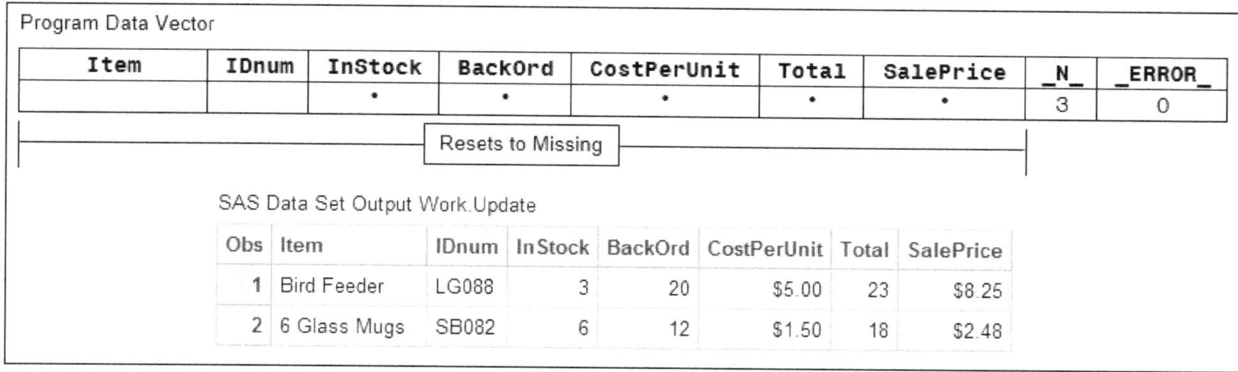

Program Data Vector

Item	IDnum	InStock	BackOrd	CostPerUnit	Total	SalePrice	_N_	_ERROR_
		•	•	•	•	•	3	0

SAS Data Set Output Work.Update

Obs	Item	IDnum	InStock	BackOrd	CostPerUnit	Total	SalePrice
1	Bird Feeder	LG088	3	20	$5.00	23	$8.25
2	6 Glass Mugs	SB082	6	12	$1.50	18	$2.48

When PROC IMPORT reads raw data, SAS sets the value of each variable in the DATA step to missing at the beginning of each cycle of execution, with these exceptions:

- variables that are named in a RETAIN statement
- variables that are created in a sum statement
- automatic variables

In contrast, when reading variables from a SAS data set, SAS sets the values to missing only before the first cycle of execution of the DATA step. Therefore, the variables retain their values until new values become available (for example, through an assignment statement or through the next execution of a SET or MERGE statement). Variables that are created with options in a SET or MERGE statement also retain their values from one cycle of execution to the next.

End-of-File Marker

The execution phase continues in this manner until the end-of-file marker is reached in the input data file. When there are no more records in the input data file to be read, the data portion of the new data set is complete and the DATA step stops.

This is the output data set that SAS creates:

Figure 7.16 SAS Data Set Work.Update

	Item	IDnum	InStock	BackOrd	CostPerUnit	Total	SalePrice
1	Bird Feeder	LG088	3	20	$5.00	23	$8.25
2	6 Glass Mugs	SB082	6	12	$1.50	18	$2.48
3	Glass Tray	BQ049	12	6	$2.50	18	$4.13
4	Padded Hangrs	MN256	15	6	$2.00	21	$3.30
5	Jewelry Box	AJ498	23	0	$6.50	23	$10.73
6	Red Apron	AQ072	9	12	$1.00	21	$1.65
7	Crystal Vase	AQ672	27	0	$7.00	27	$11.55
8	Picnic Basket	LS930	21	0	$3.50	21	$5.78
9	Brass Clock	AN910	2	10	$11.50	12	$18.98

End of the Execution Phase

At the end of the execution phase, the SAS log confirms that the input data file was read, and it displays the number of observations and variables in the data set.

Log 7.1 *SAS Log*

```
NOTE: There were 9 observations read from the data set
      CERT.INVENT.
NOTE: The data set WORK.UPDATE has 9 observations and 7
      variables.
```

Recall that you can display the data set with the PRINT procedure.

```
proc print data=work.update;
run;
```

Output 7.1 *Output from the PRINT Procedure*

Obs	Item	IDnum	InStock	BackOrd	CostPerUnit	Total	SalePrice
1	Bird Feeder	LG088	3	20	$5.00	23	$8.25
2	6 Glass Mugs	SB082	6	12	$1.50	18	$2.48
3	Glass Tray	BQ049	12	6	$2.50	18	$4.13
4	Padded Hangrs	MN256	15	6	$2.00	21	$3.30
5	Jewelry Box	AJ498	23	0	$6.50	23	$10.73
6	Red Apron	AQ072	9	12	$1.00	21	$1.65
7	Crystal Vase	AQ672	27	0	$7.00	27	$11.55
8	Picnic Basket	LS930	21	0	$3.50	21	$5.78
9	Brass Clock	AN910	2	10	$11.50	12	$18.98

Debugging a DATA Step

Diagnosing Errors in the Compilation Phase

Errors that are detected during the compilation phase include these:

- misspelled keywords and data set names
- unbalanced quotation marks
- invalid options

During the compilation phase, SAS can interpret some syntax errors (such as the keyword DATA misspelled as DAAT). If it cannot interpret the error, SAS does the following:

- prints the word ERROR followed by an error message in the SAS log
- compiles but does not execute the step where the error occurred, and prints the following message:

  ```
  NOTE: The SAS System stopped processing this step because of errors.
  ```

Some errors are explained fully by the message that SAS prints; other error messages are not as easy to interpret. For example, because SAS statements are free-format, when you fail to end a SAS statement with a semicolon, SAS cannot detect the error.

Diagnosing Errors in the Execution Phase

When SAS detects an error in the execution phase, the following can occur, depending on the type of error:

- A note, warning, or error message is displayed in the SAS log.
- The values that are stored in the PDV are displayed in the SAS log.
- The processing of the step either continues or stops.

Debugging Data Errors

Recall that data errors occur when data values are not appropriate for the SAS statements that are specified in a program. SAS detects data errors during program execution. When a data error is detected, SAS continues to execute the program.

In general, SAS procedures analyze data, produce output, or manage SAS files. In addition, SAS procedures can be used to detect invalid data. In addition to the PRINT procedure showing missing values, the following procedures can be used to detect invalid data:

- PROC FREQ
- PROC MEANS

The FREQ procedure detects invalid character and numeric values by looking at distinct values. You can use PROC FREQ to identify any variables that were not given an expected value.

Syntax, FREQ procedure:

PROC FREQ DATA=*SAS-data-set <NLEVELS>*;

    TABLES *variable(s);*

RUN;

- The NLEVELS option displays a table that provides the number of distinct values for each variable that is named in the TABLES statement.
- The TABLES statement specifies the frequency tables to produce based on the number of variables that are specified.

In the following example, the data set contains invalid characters for the variables Gender and Age. PROC FREQ displays the distinct values of variables and is therefore useful for finding invalid values in data. You can use PROC FREQ with the TABLES statement to produce a frequency table for specific variables.

```
proc freq data=cert.pats;
     tables Gender Age;
run;
```

In the following figures, notice the valid (M and F) and invalid (G) values for Gender, and the valid and invalid (202) values for Age. In both the Gender and Age FREQ tables, data in one observation needs to be cleaned.

Output 7.2 *FREQ Procedure Output*

Gender	Frequency	Percent	Cumulative Frequency	Cumulative Percent
F	10	66.67	10	66.67
G	2	13.33	12	80.00
M	3	20.00	15	100.00

Age	Frequency	Percent	Cumulative Frequency	Cumulative Percent
16	1	6.67	1	6.67
18	1	6.67	2	13.33
39	2	13.33	4	26.67
40	1	6.67	5	33.33
42	1	6.67	6	40.00
48	1	6.67	7	46.67
56	1	6.67	8	53.33
57	1	6.67	9	60.00
59	1	6.67	10	66.67
60	1	6.67	11	73.33
63	1	6.67	12	80.00
64	1	6.67	13	86.67
116	1	6.67	14	93.33
202	1	6.67	15	100.00

The MEANS procedure can also be used to validate data because it produces summary reports that display descriptive statistics. For example, PROC MEANS can show whether the values for a particular variable are within their expected range.

Syntax, MEANS procedure:

PROC MEANS DATA=*SAS-data-set <statistics>*;

VAR *variable(s)*;

RUN;

- The statistics to display can be specified as an option in the PROC MEANS statement.
- The VAR statement specifies the analysis variables and their order in the results.

Using the same data set as in the previous example, you can submit PROC MEANS to determine whether the age of all test subjects is within a reasonable range. Notice that the VAR statement is specified with that particular variable (Age) to get the statistical information, or range, of the data values.

```
proc means data=cert.pats;
  var Age;
run;
```

The following figure shows the output for the MEANS procedure. It displays a range of 16 to 202, which clearly indicates that there is invalid data somewhere in the Age column.

Output 7.3 *MEANS Procedure Output*

Analysis Variable : Age				
N	Mean	Std Dev	Minimum	Maximum
15	61.2666667	45.3375698	16.0000000	202.0000000

Using an Assignment Statement to Clean Invalid Data

You can use an assignment statement or a conditional clause to programmatically clean invalid data when it is identified.

For example, if your input data contains a field and that field contains an invalid value, you can use an assignment statement to clean your data. To avoid overwriting your original data set, you can use the DATA statement to create a new data set. The new data set contains all of the data from your original data set, along with the correct values for invalid data.

The following example assumes that Gender has an invalid value of **G** in the input data. This error might be the result of a data entry error. If **G** should actually be **M**, it is possible to correct the invalid data for Gender by using an assignment statement along with an IF-THEN statement:

```
data work.pats_clean;
  set cert.pats;
  gender=upcase(Gender);
  if Gender='G' then Gender='M';
run;
proc print data=work.pats_clean;
run;
```

Notice that two observations contain invalid values for Age. These values exceed a maximum value of 100. It is possible to uniquely identify each of the observations by specifying the variable ID. After checking the date of birth in each of the observations and determining the correct value for Age, you can change the data by inserting an IF-THEN-ELSE statement:

```
data work.clean_data;
  set cert.pats;
  gender=upcase(Gender);
  if Gender='G' then Gender='M';
  if id=1147 then age=65;
  else if id=5277 then age=75;
run;
proc print data=work.clean_data;
run;
```

Output 7.4 *PROC PRINT Output of Work.Clean_Data Data Set*

Obs	ID	Gender	Age
1	1129	F	48
2	1147	M	65
3	1387	F	57
4	2304	F	16
5	2486	F	63
6	4759	F	60
7	5277	F	75
8	5438	F	42
9	6745	M	18
10	6488	F	59
11	8045	M	40
12	8125	M	39
13	9012	F	39
14	9125	F	56
15	9968	M	64

Another way of ensuring that your output data set contains valid data is to programmatically identify invalid data and delete the associated observations from your output data set:

```
data work.clean_data;
  set cert.pats;
  gender=upcase(Gender);
  if Gender='G' then Gender='M';
  if Age>110 then delete;
run;
proc print data=work.clean_data;
run;
```

Output 7.5 *PROC PRINT Output of Work.Clean_Data Data Set with Deleted Observations*

Obs	ID	Gender	Age
1	1129	F	48
2	1387	F	57
3	2304	F	16
4	2486	F	63
5	4759	F	60
6	5438	F	42
7	6745	M	18
8	6488	F	59
9	8045	M	40
10	8125	M	39
11	9012	F	39
12	9125	F	56
13	9968	M	64

Testing Your Programs

Limiting Observations

Remember that you can use the OBS= option in the SET statement to limit the number of observations that are read or created during the execution of the DATA step.

```
data work.limitobs;
  set cert.invent (obs=10);
  total=instock+backord;
run;
```

When processed, this DATA step creates the Work.LimitObs data set with variables but with only 10 observations.

Example: Viewing Execution in the SAS Log

You can view the execution process in the SAS log. Use the PUTLOG statement to print the PDV in the SAS log. This enables you to view the execution process as the control goes from one record to the next. You can also place the PUTLOG statement before the FORMAT statement to see how the variables are being populated.

```
data work.update;
  set cert.invent;
  putlog 'PDV After SET Statement';
  putlog _all_;
  Total=instock+backord;
  SalePrice=(CostPerUnit*0.65)+CostPerUnit;
  format CostPerUnit SalePrice dollar 6.2;
run;
```

***Log 7.2** SAS Log*

```
PDV After SET Statement
Item=Bird Feeder IDnum=LG088 InStock=3 BackOrd=20
CostPerUnit=$5.00 Total=. SalePrice=. _ERROR_=0 _N_=1

PDV After SET Statement
Item=6 Glass Mugs IDnum=SB082 InStock=6 BackOrd=12
CostPerUnit=$1.50 Total=. SalePrice=. _ERROR_=0 _N_=2

PDV After SET Statement
Item=Glass Tray IDnum=BQ049 InStock=12 BackOrd=6
CostPerUnit=$2.50 Total=. SalePrice=. _ERROR_=0 _N_=3
PDV After SET Statement
Item=Padded Hangrs IDnum=MN256 InStock=15 BackOrd=6
CostPerUnit=$2.00 Total=. SalePrice=. _ERROR_=0 _N_=4

PDV After SET Statement
Item=Jewelry Box IDnum=AJ498 InStock=23 BackOrd=0
CostPerUnit=$6.50 Total=. SalePrice=. _ERROR_=0 _N_=5

PDV After SET Statement
Item=Red Apron IDnum=AQ072 InStock=9 BackOrd=12
CostPerUnit=$1.00 Total=. SalePrice=. _ERROR_=0 _N_=6

PDV After SET Statement
Item=Crystal Vase IDnum=AQ672 InStock=27 BackOrd=0
CostPerUnit=$7.00 Total=. SalePrice=. _ERROR_=0 _N_=7

PDV After SET Statement
Item=Picnic Basket IDnum=LS930 InStock=21 BackOrd=0
CostPerUnit=$3.50 Total=. SalePrice=. _ERROR_=0 _N_=8

PDV After SET Statement
Item=Brass Clock IDnum=AN910 InStock=2 BackOrd=10
CostPerUnit=$11.50 Total=. SalePrice=. _ERROR_=0 _N_=9
```

Chapter Quiz

Select the best answer for each question. Check your answers using the answer key in the appendix.

1. Which of the following is not written to the output during the compilation phase?
   a. the data set descriptor
   b. the first observation
   c. the program data vector
   d. the _N_ and _ERROR_ automatic variables
2. During the compilation phase, SAS scans each statement in the DATA step, looking for syntax errors. Which of the following is not considered a syntax error?
   a. incorrect values and formats
   b. invalid options or variable names
   c. missing or invalid punctuation

d. missing or misspelled keywords

3. Unless otherwise directed, how does the DATA step execute?

   a. once for each compilation phase

   b. once for each DATA step statement

   c. once for each record in the input file

   d. once for each variable in the input file

4. At the beginning of the execution phase, the value of _N_ is 1, the value of _ERROR_ is 0, and the values of the remaining variables are set to the following:

   a. 0

   b. 1

   c. undefined

   d. missing

5. Suppose you run a program that causes three DATA step errors. What is the value of the automatic variable _ERROR_ when the observation that contains the third error is processed?

   a. 0

   b. 1

   c. 2

   d. 3

6. Which of the following actions occurs at the beginning of an iteration of the DATA step?

   a. The automatic variables _N_ and _ERROR_ are incremental by one.

   b. The DATA step stops execution.

   c. The descriptor portion of the data set is written.

   d. The values of variables created in programming statements are reset to missing in the program data vector.

7. Consider the following DATA step. Based on the sample input file below, in what order are the variables stored in the new SAS data set?

```
data work.fin2;
  set cert.finance;
  if Salary>25000 then Raise=0.03;
  else Raise=0.05;
  NewSalary=(Salary*Raise)+Salary;
run;
```

	SSN	Name	Salary	Date
1	029-46-9261	Rudelich	35000	02JAN17
2	074-53-9892	Vincent	35000	02JAN17
3	228-88-9649	Benito	28000	16JAN17
4	442-21-8075	Sirignano	5000	06FEB17
5	446-93-2122	Harbinger	33900	06FEB17
6	776-84-5391	Phillipon	29750	06JUN16
7	929-75-0218	Gunter	27500	06JUN16

   a. `SSN Name Salary Date Raise NewSalary`

b. `Raise NewSalary SSN Name Salary Date`

c. `NewSalary Raise SSN Name Salary Date`

d. `SSN Name Date Salary Raise NewSalary`

8. What happens when SAS cannot interpret syntax errors?

   a. Data set variables contain missing values.

   b. The DATA step does not compile.

   c. The DATA step still compiles, but it does not execute.

   d. The DATA step still compiles and executes.

9. What is wrong with this program?

```
data work.fin2;
  set cert.finance;
  length Raise $9;
  if Salary>25000 then Raise='3 Percent';
    else Raise='5 Percent';
  if Salary>25000 then NewSalary=(25000*0.03)+Salary;
    else NewSalary=(Salary*0.05)+Salary;
  length Bonus $5;
  Bonus=Raise*0.02;
run;
```

   a. There is a missing semicolon on the second line.

   b. There is a missing semicolon on the third line.

   c. The variables Bonus and Raise have the incorrect length.

   d. The variable type for Bonus is incorrect.

10. Which procedure produces distinct values of variables and can be used to clean your data?

    a. PROC CONTENTS

    b. PROC MEANS

    c. PROC FREQ

    d. PROC PRINT

11. At the start of DATA step processing, during the compilation phase, variables are created in the program data vector (PDV), and observations are set to which of the following:

    a. blank.

    b. missing.

    c. 0.

    d. there are no observations.

Chapter 8
BY-Group Processing

Definitions

BY-group processing
: is a method of processing observations from one or more SAS data sets that are grouped or ordered by values of one or more common variables.

BY variable
: names a variable or variables by which the data set is sorted. All data sets must be ordered by the values of the BY variable.

BY value
: is the value of the BY variable.

BY group
: includes all observations with the same BY value. If you use more than one variable in a BY statement, a BY group is a group of observations with the same combination of values for these variables. Each BY group has a unique combination of values for the variables.

FIRST.*variable* and LAST.*variable*
: are variables that SAS creates for each BY variable. SAS sets FIRST.*variable* when it is processing the first observation in a BY group, and sets LAST.*variable* when it is processing the last observation in a BY group. These assignments enable you to take different actions, based on whether processing is starting for a new BY group or ending for a BY group.

Preprocessing Data

Determine Whether the Data Requires Preprocessing

Before you perform BY-group processing on one or more data sets using the SET, MERGE, and UPDATE statements, you must check the data to determine whether it requires preprocessing. The data requires no preprocessing if the observations in all of the data sets occur in one of the following patterns:

- ascending or descending numeric order
- ascending or descending character order
- not alphabetical or numerical order, but grouped in some way, such as by calendar month

If the observations are not in the order that you want, sort the data set before using BY-group processing.

Example: Sorting Observations for BY-Group Processing

You can use the SORT procedure to change the physical order of the observations in the data set. You can either replace the original data set, or create a new, sorted data set by using the OUT= option of the SORT procedure. In this example, PROC SORT rearranges the observations in the data set Cert.Usa in ascending order based on the values of the variable Manager. Then, the sorted data is created as a new, sorted data set Work.Usa.

Note: The default sort order for the SORT procedure is ascending.

```
proc sort data=cert.usa out=work.usa;
  by manager;
run;
proc print data=work.usa;
run;
```

Specify the variables in the PROC SORT BY statement in the same order that you intend to specify them in subsequent DATA or PROC steps.

The following output shows the Work.Usa data set sorted by the variable Manager in ascending order.

Output 8.1 *Sorted Work.Usa Data Set*

Obs	Dept	WageCat	WageRate	Manager	JobType
1	ADM10	S	3392.50	Coxe	3
2	ADM10	S	3420.00	Coxe	50
3	ADM10	S	6862.50	Coxe	50
4	ADM10	H	13.65	Coxe	240
5	ADM20	S	4522.50	Coxe	240
6	ADM20	S	2960.00	Delgado	240
7	ADM20	S	5260.00	Delgado	240
8	ADM20	S	1572.50	Delgado	420
9	ADM30	S	3819.20	Delgado	420
10	ADM30	S	1813.30	Delgado	440
11	CAM10	S	6855.90	Overby	1
12	CAM10	S	4045.80	Overby	5
13	CAM20	S	4480.50	Overby	10
14	ADM10	S	5910.80	Overby	20
15	CAM10	S	9073.80	Overby	20

FIRST. and LAST. DATA Step Variables

How the DATA Step Identifies BY Groups

In the DATA step, SAS identifies the beginning and end of each BY group by creating the following two temporary variables:

- FIRST.*variable*
- LAST.*variable*

The temporary variables are available for DATA step programming, but they are not added to the output data set. Their values indicate whether an observation is one of the following positions:

- the first one in a BY group
- the last one in a BY group
- neither the first nor the last one in a BY group
- both first and last, as is the case when there is only one observation in a BY group

How SAS Determines FIRST.variable and LAST.variable

- When an observation is the first in a BY group, SAS sets the value of the FIRST.*variable* to 1. This happens when the value of the variable changed from the previous observation.
- For all other observations in the BY group, the value of FIRST.*variable* is 0.
- When an observation is the last in a BY group, SAS sets the value of LAST.*variable* to 1. This happens when the value of the variable changes in the next observation.
- For all other observations in the BY group, the value of LAST.*variable* is 0.
- For the last observation in a data set, the value of all LAST.*variable* variables are set to 1.

Example: Grouping Observations Using One BY Variable

In this example, the Cert.Usa data set contains payroll information for individual employees. Suppose you want to compute the annual payroll by department. Assume 2,000 work hours per year for hourly employees.

Before computing the annual payroll, you need to group observations by the values of the variable Dept.

Output 8.2 *Sample Data Set: Cert.Usa*

Obs	Dept	WageCat	WageRate	Manager	JobType
1	ADM10	S	3392.50	Coxe	3
2	ADM10	S	3420.00	Coxe	50
3	ADM10	S	6862.50	Coxe	50
4	ADM10	H	13.65	Coxe	240
5	ADM20	S	4522.50	Coxe	240
6	ADM20	S	2960.00	Delgado	240
7	ADM20	S	5260.00	Delgado	240
8	ADM20	S	1572.50	Delgado	420
9	ADM30	S	3819.20	Delgado	420
10	ADM30	S	1813.30	Delgado	440
11	CAM10	S	6855.90	Overby	1
12	CAM10	S	4045.80	Overby	5
13	CAM20	S	4480.50	Overby	10
14	ADM10	S	5910.80	Overby	20
15	CAM10	S	9073.80	Overby	20

The following program computes the annual payroll by department. Notice that the variable name Dept has been appended to FIRST. and LAST.

```
proc sort data=cert.usa out=work.temp;                  /*#1*/
  by dept;
```

```
run;
data work.budget(keep=dept payroll);                    /* #2 */
  set work.temp;
  by dept;                                              /* #3 */
  if wagecat='S' then Yearly=wagerate*12;               /* #4 */
    else if wagecat='H' then Yearly=wagerate*2000;
  if first.dept then Payroll=0;                         /* #5 */
  payroll+yearly;                                       /* #6 */
  if last.dept;                                         /* #7 */
run;
```

1 The SORT procedure sorts the data in Cert.Usa by the variable Dept. The results of the SORT procedure are stored in Work.Temp.

2 The KEEP= data set option keeps the variables Dept and Payroll in the output data set, Work.Budget.

3 The BY statement in a DATA step applies only to the SET statement. The data set Work.Temp must be sorted by the Dept variable for the BY statement to set up grouping variables. By specifying Dept as the variable, you can identify the first and last observations for each Dept group. The Dept groups are **ADM10**, **ADM20**, **ADM30**, **CAM10**, and **CAM20**.

4 The IF statement executes the statements conditionally. If the value for WageCat is **S**, then the variable Yearly contains the value of WageRate multiplied by 12. If the value of WageCat is **H**, then the variable Yearly contains the value of WageRate multiplied by 2000.

5 If the observation is the first observation for the variable Dept, initialize Payroll to **0**.

Note: FIRST.Dept variable is not written to the data set and does not appear in the output.

6 Add the value of Yearly to the value of Payroll.

7 If this observation is the last in the variable, Dept, then end. If not, then read the next observation.

Note: LAST.Dept variable is not written to the data set and does not appear in the output.

The following figure illustrates how SAS processes FIRST.Dept and LAST.Dept. Notice that the values of FIRST.Dept and LAST.Dept change as the value for Dept changes.

Figure 8.1 *BY Group for Dept*

_N_	Dept	Yearly	Payroll	FIRST.Dept	LAST.Dept
1	ADM10	40710.0	40710.0	1	0
2	ADM10	41040.0	81750.0	0	0
3	ADM10	82350.0	164100.0	0	0
4	ADM10	27300.0	191400.0	0	0
5	ADM10	70929.6	262329.6	0	1
6	ADM20	54270.0	54270.0	1	0
7	ADM20	35520.0	89790.0	0	0
8	ADM20	63120.0	152910.0	0	0
9	ADM20	18870.0	171780.0	0	1
10	ADM30	45830.4	45830.4	1	0
11	ADM30	21759.6	67590.0	0	1
12	CAM10	82270.8	82270.8	1	0
13	CAM10	48549.6	130820.4	0	0
14	CAM10	108885.6	239706.0	0	1
15	CAM20	53766.0	53766.0	1	1

When you print the new data set, you can now list and sum the annual payroll by department.

```
proc print data=work.budget noobs;
  sum payroll;
  format payroll dollar12.2;
run;
```

Output 8.3 *PROC PRINT Output of Work.Budget: Sum of Payroll*

The SAS System

Dept	Payroll
ADM10	$262,329.60
ADM20	$171,780.00
ADM30	$67,590.00
CAM10	$239,706.00
CAM20	$53,766.00
	$795,171.60

Example: Grouping Observations Using Multiple BY Variables

Suppose you now want to compute the annual payroll by job type for each manager. In the following example, you specify two BY variables, Manager and JobType, creating two groups. The Manager group contains three subgroups: **Coxe**, **Delgado**, and **Overby**. The JobType subgroup contains nine subgroups: **1**, **3**, **5**, **10**, **20**, **50**, **240**, **420**, and **440**. Within these subgroups, you can identify the first and last observations for each of these subgroups.

```
proc sort data=cert.usa out=work.temp2;                    /*#1*/
  by manager jobtype;
run;
data work.budget2 (keep=manager jobtype payroll);          /*#2*/
  set work.temp2;
  by manager jobtype;                                      /*#3*/
  if wagecat='S' then Yearly=wagerate*12;                  /*#4*/
    else if wagecat='H' then Yearly=wagerate*2000;
  if first.jobtype then Payroll=0;                         /*#5*/
  payroll+yearly;                                          /*#6*/
  if last.jobtype;                                         /*#7*/
run;
```

1 The SORT procedure sorts the data in Cert.Usa by the variables Manager and JobType. The results of the SORT procedure are stored in Work.Temp2.

2 The KEEP= data set option specifies the variables Manager, JobType, and Payroll and writes the variables to the new data set, Work.Budget.

3 The BY statement in a DATA step applies only to the SET statement. The data set Work.Temp2 must be sorted by the Manager and JobType variables in order for the BY statement to set up grouping variables. The data set is sorted by the variable Manager first and then by JobType.

4 The IF statement executes the statements conditionally. If the value for WageCat is **S**, then the variable Yearly contains the value of WageRate multiplied by 12. If the value of WageCat is **H**, then the variable Yearly contains the value of WageRate multiplied by 2000.

5 If the observation is the first for JobType, then initialize Payroll to 0.

6 Add the value of Yearly to the value of Payroll.

7 If this observation is the last in the variable, JobType, then end. If not, then read the next observation.

The following figure illustrates how SAS processes FIRST.Manager, FIRST.JobType, LAST.Manager, and LAST.JobType. Notice how the values of FIRST.Manager and LAST.Manager change only when the Manager value changes. However, the values for FIRST.JobType and LAST.JobType values change multiple times even when the Manager value remains the same.

Figure 8.2 *Multiple BY Group Variables: Manager and JobType*

_N_	Manager	JobType	WageRate	Yearly	Payroll	FIRST.Manager	LAST.Manager	FIRST.JobType	LAST.JobType
1	Coxe	3	3392.50	40710.00	40710.00	1	0	1	1
2	Coxe	50	3420.00	41040.00	41040.00	0	0	1	0
3	Coxe	50	6862.50	82350.00	123390.00	0	0	0	1
4	Coxe	240	13.65	27300.00	27300.00	0	0	1	0
5	Coxe	240	4522.50	54270.00	81570.00	0	1	0	1
6	Delgado	240	2960.00	35520.00	35520.00	1	0	1	0
7	Delgado	240	5260.00	63120.00	98640.00	0	0	0	1
8	Delgado	420	1572.50	18870.00	18870.00	0	0	1	0
9	Delgado	420	3819.20	45830.40	64700.40	0	0	0	1
10	Delgado	440	1813.30	21759.60	21759.60	0	1	1	1
11	Overby	1	6855.90	82270.80	82270.80	1	0	1	1
12	Overby	5	4045.80	48549.60	48549.60	0	0	1	1
13	Overby	10	4480.50	53766.00	53766.00	0	0	1	1
14	Overby	20	5910.80	70929.60	70929.60	0	0	1	0
15	Overby	20	9073.80	108885.60	179815.20	0	1	0	1

You can generate a sum for the annual payroll by job type for each manager. The example below shows the payroll sum for only two managers, Coxe and Delgado.

```
proc print data=work.budget2 noobs;
  by manager;
  var jobtype;
  sum payroll;
  where manager in ('Coxe', 'Delgado');
  format payroll dollar12.2;
run;
```

Figure 8.3 *Payroll Sum by Job Type and Manager*

Manager=Coxe

JobType	Payroll
3	$40,710.00
50	$123,390.00
240	$81,570.00
Manager	**$245,670.00**

Manager=Delgado

JobType	Payroll
240	$98,640.00
420	$64,700.40
440	$21,759.60
Manager	**$185,100.00**
	$430,770.00

Chapter Quiz

Select the best answer for each question. Check your answers using the answer key in the appendix.

1. Which of the following statements is false when you use the BY statement with the SET statement?

   a. The data sets listed in the SET statement must be indexed or sorted by the values of the BY variable or variables.

   b. The DATA step automatically creates two variables, FIRST. and LAST., for each variable in the BY statement.

   c. FIRST. and LAST. identify the first and last observation in each BY group, respectively.

   d. FIRST. and LAST. are stored in the data set.

2. Your data does not require any preprocessing if the observations in all of the data sets occur in which of the following patterns?

   a. Ascending or descending character order.

   b. Ascending or descending numeric order.

   c. The data must be grouped in some way.

   d. all of the above

3. Which temporary variables are available for DATA step programming during BY-group processing only, but are not added to the data set?

   a. FIRST.*variable* and LAST.*variable*.

   b. _N_ and _ERROR variables.

   c. Both a and b.

   d. none of the above

4. Which program below creates the following output?

Obs	Account	Name	Type	Transaction
1	7821	MICHELLE STANTON	A	304.45
2	1086	KATHERINE MORRY	A	64.98
3	6201	MARY WATERS	C	45.00
4	6621	WALTER LUND	C	234.76
5	7821	ELIZABETH WESTIN	C	188.23
6	0265	JEFFREY DONALDSON	C	78.90
7	1118	ART CONTUCK	D	57.69
8	2287	MICHAEL WINSTONE	D	145.89
9	0556	LEE McDONALD	D	70.82
10	1010	MARTIN LYNN	D	150.55

a.
```
proc print data=cert.credit;
  by type;
run;
```

b.
```
proc sort data=cert.credit;
  by type ascending;
run;
```

c.
```
proc sort data=cert.credit;
  by type;
run;
```

d.
```
proc sort data=cert.credit;
  by type descending;
run;
```

5. What statement correctly describes a BY group?

   a. It contains temporary variables that SAS creates for each BY variable.

   b. It includes all observations with the same BY value.

   c. It names a variable or variables by which the data set is sorted.

   d. It is a method of processing observations from one or more SAS data sets that are group or ordered by one or more common variables.

6. How does SAS determine FIRST.*variable*?

   a. When an observation is the first in a BY group, SAS sets the value of the FIRST.*variable* to 1. This happens when the value of the variable changed from the previous observation.

   b. For all other observations in the BY group, the value of FIRST.*variable* is 0.

   c. Both a and b.

   d. When an observation is the last in a BY group, SAS sets the value of FIRST.*variable* to 1.

7. Which program creates the following output?

Obs	Day	Flavor
1	01	CHOCOLATE
2	01	RASPBERRY
3	01	VANILLA
4	02	PEACH
5	02	VANILLA
6	03	CHOCOLATE
7	04	CHOCOLATE
8	04	PEACH
9	04	RASPBERRY
10	05	CHOCOLATE
11	05	STRAWBERRY
12	05	VANILLA

a.
```
proc sort data=cert.choices out=work.choices;
```

```
   by day flavor;
run;
proc print data=work.choices;
run;
```

b.
```
proc sort data=cert.choices out=work.choices;
   by day;
run;
proc print data=work.choices;
run;
```

c.
```
proc print data=cert.choices out=work.choices;
   by day;
run;
```

d.
```
proc sort data=cert.choices out=work.choices;
   by flavor;
run;
proc print data=work.choices;
run;
```

Chapter 9
Creating and Managing Variables

Creating Variables

Assignment Statements

Use an assignment statement in any DATA step in order to modify existing values or create new variables.

Syntax, assignment statement:

variable=expression;

- *variable* names a new or existing variable
- *expression* is any valid SAS expression

Tip: The assignment statement is one of the few SAS statements that do not begin with a keyword.

For example, here is an assignment statement that assigns the character value **`Toby Witherspoon`** to the variable Name:

```
Name='Toby Witherspoon';
```

SAS Expressions

You use SAS expressions in assignment statements and many other SAS programming statements to do the following:

- transform variables
- create new variables
- conditionally process variables
- calculate new values
- assign new values

An expression is a sequence of operands and operators that form a set of instructions.

- Operands are variable names or constants. They can be numeric, character, or both.
- Operators are special-character operators, grouping parentheses, or functions.

Using Operators in SAS Expressions

Use the following arithmetic operators to perform a calculation.

Table 9.1 *Arithmetic Operators*

Operator	Action	Example	Priority
-	negative prefix	`negative=-x;`	1
**	exponentiation	`raise=x**y;`	1
*	multiplication	`mult=x*y;`	2
/	division	`divide=x/y;`	2
+	addition	`sum=x+y;`	3
-	subtraction	`diff=x-y;`	3

The order of operation is determined by the following conditions:

- Operations of priority 1 are performed before operations of priority 2, and so on.
- Consecutive operations that have the same priority are performed in this order:
  - from right to left within priority 1
  - from left to right within priority 2 and 3
- You can use parentheses to control the order of operations.

Note: When a value that is used with an arithmetic operator is missing, the result of the expression is missing. The assignment statement assigns a missing value to a variable if the result of the expression is missing.

Use the following comparison operators to express a condition.

Table 9.2 *Comparison Operators*

Operator	Meaning	Example
= or eq	equal to	`name='Jones, C.'`
^= or ne	not equal to	`temp ne 212`
> or gt	greater than	`income>20000`
< or lt	less than	`x=5000` `x<8000`
>= or ge	greater than or equal to	`x=5000` `x>=2000`
<= or le	less than or equal to	`pulse le 85`

Use logical operators to link a sequence of expressions into compound expressions.

Table 9.3 Logical Operators

Operator, symbol	Description
AND or &	and, both. If both expressions are true, then the compound expression is true.
OR or |	or, either. If either expression is true, then the compound expression is true.

Note: In SAS, any numeric value other than 0 or missing is true, and a value of 0 or missing is false. Therefore, a numeric variable or expression can stand alone in a condition.

- 0 = False
- . = False
- 1 = True

Examples: Assign Variables

Example 1: Create a New Variable

The assignment statement in the DATA step below creates a new variable, TotalTime, by multiplying the values of TimeMin by 60 and then adding the values of TimeSec.

```
data work.stresstest;
  set cert.tests;
  TotalTime=(timemin*60)+timesec;
run;
proc print data=work.stresstest;
run;
```

Output 9.1 Assignment Statement Output (partial output)

Obs	ID	Name	RestHR	MaxHR	RecHR	TimeMin	TimeSec	Tolerance	TotalTime
1	2458	Murray, W	72	185	128	12	38	D	758
2	2462	Almers, C	68	171	133	10	5	I	605
3	2501	Bonaventure, T	78	177	139	11	13	I	673
4	2523	Johnson, R	69	162	114	9	42	S	582
5	2539	LaMance, K	75	168	141	11	46	D	706

. . . more observations. . .

Obs	ID	Name	RestHR	MaxHR	RecHR	TimeMin	TimeSec	Tolerance	TotalTime
16	2579	Underwood, K	72	165	127	13	19	S	799
17	2584	Takahashi, Y	76	163	135	16	7	D	967
18	2586	Derber, B	68	176	119	17	35	N	1055
19	2588	Ivan, H	70	182	126	15	41	N	941
20	2589	Wilcox, E	78	189	138	14	57	I	897
21	2595	Warren, C	77	170	136	12	10	S	730

Example 2: Re-evaluating Variables

In the following example, the assignment statement contains the variable RestHR, which appears on both sides of the equal sign. This assignment statement evaluates each observation to redefine each RestHR observation as 10% higher. When a variable name appears on both sides of the equal sign, the original value on the right side is used to evaluate the expression. The result is assigned to the variable on the left side of the equal sign.

```
data work.stresstest;
  set cert.tests;
  resthr=resthr+(resthr*.10);
run;
proc print data=work.stresstest;
run;
```

Output 9.2 *PROC PRINT Output of Work.StressTest (partial output)*

Obs	ID	Name	RestHR	MaxHR	RecHR	TimeMin	TimeSec	Tolerance
1	2458	Murray, W	79.2	185	128	12	38	D
2	2462	Almers, C	74.8	171	133	10	5	I
3	2501	Bonaventure, T	85.8	177	139	11	13	I
4	2523	Johnson, R	75.9	162	114	9	42	S
5	2539	LaMance, K	82.5	168	141	11	46	D
6	2544	Jones, M	86.9	187	136	12	26	N
		. . . more	observations. . .					
17	2584	Takahashi, Y	83.6	163	135	16	7	D
18	2586	Derber, B	74.8	176	119	17	35	N
19	2588	Ivan, H	77.0	182	126	15	41	N
20	2589	Wilcox, E	85.8	189	138	14	57	I
21	2595	Warren, C	84.7	170	136	12	10	S

Date Constants

You can assign date values to variables in assignment statements by using date constants. SAS converts a date constant to a SAS date. To represent a constant in SAS date form, specify the date as *'ddmmmyy'* or *'ddmmmyyyy'*, immediately followed by a D.

Syntax, date constant:

'ddmmmyy'd

or

'ddmmmyy'd

- *dd* is a one- or two-digit value for the day.
- *mmm* is a three-letter abbreviation for the month (JAN, FEB, and so on).
- *yy* or *yyyy* is a two- or four-digit value for the year, respectively.

Tip: Be sure to enclose the date in quotation marks.

TIP You can also use SAS time constants and SAS datetime constants in assignment statements.

```
Time='9:25't;
DateTime='18jan2018:9:27:05'dt;
```

Example: Assignment Statements and Date Values

In the following program, the second assignment statement assigns a date value to the variable TestDate.

```
data work.stresstest;
  set cert.tests;
  TotalTime=(timemin*60)+timesec;
  TestDate='01jan2015'd;
run;
proc print data=work.stresstest;
run;
```

Notice how the values for TestDate in the PROC PRINT output are displayed as SAS date values.

Output 9.3 *PROC PRINT Output of Work.StressTest with SAS Date Values (partial output)*

Obs	ID	Name	RestHR	MaxHR	RecHR	TimeMin	TimeSec	Tolerance	TotalTime	TestDate
1	2458	Murray, W	72	185	128	12	38	D	758	21185
2	2462	Almers, C	68	171	133	10	5	I	605	21185
3	2501	Bonaventure, T	78	177	139	11	13	I	673	21185
4	2523	Johnson, R	69	162	114	9	42	S	582	21185
5	2539	LaMance, K	75	168	141	11	46	D	706	21185
. . . more observations. . .										
17	2584	Takahashi, Y	76	163	135	16	7	D	967	21185
18	2586	Derber, B	68	176	119	17	35	N	1055	21185
19	2588	Ivan, H	70	182	126	15	41	N	941	21185
20	2589	Wilcox, E	78	189	138	14	57	I	897	21185
21	2595	Warren, C	77	170	136	12	10	S	730	21185

You can use a FORMAT statement in the PROC PRINT step to modify the TestDate values and change them to another format. To apply formats to your output, see Chapter 12, “SAS Formats and Informats,” on page 225.

Modifying Variables

Selected Useful Statements

Here are examples of statements that accomplish specific data-manipulation tasks.

Table 9.4 *Manipulating Data Using the DATA Step*

Task	Example Code
Subset data	`if resthr<70 then delete;` `if tolerance='D';`
Drop unwanted variables	`drop timemin timesec;`
Create or modify a variable	`TotalTime=(timemin*60)+timesec;`
Initialize and retain a variable	`retain SumSec 5400;`
Accumulate totals	`sumsec+totaltime;`
Specify a variable's length	`length TestLength $ 6;`
Execute statements conditionally	`if totaltime>800 then TestLength='Long'; else if 750<=totaltime<=800 then TestLength='Normal'; else if totaltime<750 then TestLength='Short';`

The following topics discuss these tasks.

Accumulating Totals

To add the result of an expression to an accumulator variable, you can use a sum statement in your DATA step.

Syntax, sum statement:

variable+expression;

- *variable* specifies the name of the accumulator variable. This variable must be numeric. The variable is automatically set to 0 before the first observation is read. The variable's value is retained from one DATA step execution to the next.
- *expression* is any valid SAS expression.

Note: If the expression produces a missing value, the sum statement ignores it.

The sum statement is one of the few SAS statements that do not begin with a keyword.

The sum statement adds the result of the expression that is on the right side of the plus sign (+) to the numeric variable that is on the left side of the plus sign. The value of the accumulator variable is initialized to 0 instead of missing before the first iteration of the DATA step. Subsequently, the variable's value is retained from one iteration to the next.

Example: Accumulating Totals

To find the total number of elapsed seconds in treadmill stress tests, you need the variable SumSec, whose value begins at 0 and increases by the amount of the total seconds in each observation. To calculate the total number of elapsed seconds in treadmill stress tests, use the sum statement shown below:

```
data work.stresstest;
  set cert.tests;
  TotalTime=(timemin*60)+timesec;
  SumSec+totaltime;
run;
```

The value of the variable on the left side of the plus sign, SumSec, begins at 0 and increases by the value of TotalTime with each observation.

SumSec	=	TotalTime	+	Previous total
0				
758	=	758	+	0
1363	=	605	+	758
2036	=	673	+	1363
2618	=	582	+	2036
3324	=	706	+	2618

Initializing Sum Variables

In the previous example, the sum variable SumSec was initialized to 0 before the first observation was read. However, you can initialize SumSec to a different number than 0.

Use the RETAIN statement to assign an initial value, other than 0, to an accumulator variable in a sum statement.

The RETAIN statement has several purposes:

- It assigns an initial value to a retained variable.
- It prevents variables from being initialized each time the DATA step executes.

Syntax, RETAIN statement for initializing sum variables:

RETAIN *variable* <*initial-value*>;

- *variable* is a variable whose values you want to retain.
- *initial-value* specifies an initial value (numeric or character) for the preceding variable.

Note: The following statements are true about the RETAIN statement:

- It is a compile-time-only statement that creates variables if they do not already exist.
- It initializes the retained variable to missing before the first execution of the DATA step if you do not supply an initial value.
- It has no effect on variables that are read with SET, MERGE, or UPDATE statements.

Example: RETAIN Statement

Suppose you want to add 5400 seconds (the accumulated total seconds from a previous treadmill stress test) to the variable SumSec in the StressTest data set when you create the data set. To initialize SumSec with the value 5400, use the RETAIN statement shown below. Now the value of SumSec begins at 5400 and increases by the value of TotalTime with each observation.

```
data work.stresstest;
  set cert.tests;
  TotalTime=(timemin*60)+timesec;
  retain SumSec 5400;
  sumsec+totaltime;
run;
proc print data=work.stresstest;
run;
```

SumSec	=	TotalTime	+	Previous Total
5400				
6158	=	758	+	5400
6763	=	605	+	6158
7436	=	673	+	6763
8018	=	582	+	7436
8724	=	706	+	8018

Specifying Lengths for Variables

Avoiding Truncated Variable Values

During the compilation phase, use an assignment statement to create a new character variable. SAS allocates as many bytes of storage space as there are characters in the first value that it encounters for that variable.

In the following figure, the variable TestLength has a length of four bytes. The word Short is truncated because the word Norm uses four bytes.

Figure 9.1 *Truncated Variable Values (partial output)*

TestLength
Norm
Shor
Shor
Shor
Shor
Shor
Long

When you assign a character constant as the value of the new variable, use the LENGTH statement to specify a length to avoid truncation of your values.

Syntax, LENGTH statement:

LENGTH *variable(s)* <$> *length***;**

- *variable(s)* names the variable or variables to be assigned a length.
- $ is specified if the variable is a character variable.
- *length* is an integer that specifies the length of the variable.

Here is a variable list in which all three variables are assigned a length of $200.

```
length Address1 Address2 Address3 $200;
```

Example: LENGTH Statement

Within the program, a LENGTH statement is included to assign a length to accommodate the longest value of the variable TestLength. The longest value is **Normal**, which has six characters. Because TestLength is a character variable, you must follow the variable name with a dollar sign ($).

Make sure the LENGTH statement appears before any other reference to the variable in the DATA step.

```
data stress;
  set cert.stress;
  TotalTime=(timemin*60)+timesec;
  retain SumSec 5400;
  sumsec+totaltime;
  length TestLength $ 6;
  if totaltime>800 then testlength='Long';
  else if 750<=totaltime<=800 then testlength='Normal';
  else if totaltime<750 then TestLength='Short';
run;
```

Note: If the variable has been created by another statement, then a later use of the LENGTH statement does not change its length.

Now that the LENGTH statement has been added to the program, the values of TestLength are no longer truncated.

Figure 9.2 *Variable Values That Are Not Truncated (partial output)*

TestLength
Normal
Short
Short
Short
Short
Short
Long

Subsetting Data

Using a Subsetting IF Statement

The subsetting IF statement causes the DATA step to continue processing only those observations that meet the condition of the expression specified in the IF statement. The resulting SAS data set or data sets contain a subset of the original external file or SAS data set.

Syntax, subsetting IF statement:

IF *expression*;

expression is any valid SAS expression.

- If the expression is true, the DATA step continues to process that observation.
- If the expression is false, no further statements are processed for that observation, and control returns to the top of the DATA step.

Example: Subsetting IF Statement

The subsetting IF statement below selects only observations whose values for Tolerance are `D`. It is positioned in the DATA step for efficiency: other statements do not need to process unwanted observations.

```
data work.stresstest;
  set cert.tests;
  if tolerance='D';
    TotalTime=(timemin*60)+timesec;
run;
proc print data=work.stresstest;
run;
```

Because Tolerance is a character variable, the value `D` must be enclosed in quotation marks, and it must be the same case as in the data set.

Notice that, in the output below, only the values where Tolerance contains the value of `D` are displayed and TotalTime was calculated.

Output 9.4 *Subsetted Data of Work.StressTest*

Obs	ID	Name	RestHR	MaxHR	RecHR	TimeMin	TimeSec	Tolerance	TotalTime
1	2458	Murray, W	72	185	128	12	38	D	758
2	2539	LaMance, K	75	168	141	11	46	D	706
3	2552	Reberson, P	69	158	139	15	41	D	941
4	2572	Oberon, M	74	177	138	12	11	D	731
5	2574	Peterson, V	80	164	137	14	9	D	849
6	2584	Takahashi, Y	76	163	135	16	7	D	967

Categorizing Values

Suppose you want to create a variable that categorizes the length of time that a subject spends on the treadmill during a stress test. This new variable, TestLength, is based on the value of the existing variable TotalTime. The value of TestLength is assigned conditionally:

Value for TotalTime	Resulting Value for TestLength
greater than 800	Long
750 - 800	Normal
less than 750	Short

To perform an action conditionally, use an IF-THEN statement. The IF-THEN statement executes a SAS statement when the condition in the IF clause is true.

Syntax, IF-THEN statement:

IF *expression* **THEN** *statement*;

- *expression* is any valid SAS expression.
- *statement* is any executable SAS statement.

Example: IF-THEN Statement

To assign the value **Long** to the variable TestLength when the value of TotalTime is greater than 800, add the following IF-THEN statement to your DATA step:

```
data work.stresstest;
  set cert.tests;
  TotalTime=(timemin*60)+timesec;
  retain SumSec 5400;
  sumsec+totaltime;
  if totaltime>800 then TestLength='Long';
run;
```

SAS executes the assignment statement only when the condition (TotalTime>800) is true. If the condition is false, the value of TestLength is missing.

Examples: Logical Operators

The following examples use IF-THEN statements with logical operators:

- Use the AND operator to execute the THEN statement if both expressions that are linked by AND are true.

```
if status='OK' and type=3
   then Count+1;
if (age^=agecheck | time^=3)
   & error=1 then Test=1;
```

- Use the OR operator to execute the THEN statement if either expression that is linked by OR is true.

```
if (age^=agecheck | time^=3)
   & error=1 then Test=1;
if status='S' or cond='E'
   then Control='Stop';
```

- Use the NOT operator with other operators to reverse the logic of a comparison.

```
if not(loghours<7500)
   then Schedule='Quarterly';
if region not in ('NE','SE')
   then Bonus=200;
```

- Character values must be specified in the same case in which they appear in the data set and must be enclosed in quotation marks.

```
if status='OK' and type=3
   then Count+1;
if status='S' or cond='E'
   then Control='Stop';
if not(loghours<7500)
   then Schedule='Quarterly';
if region not in ('NE','SE')
   then Bonus=200;
```

Logical comparisons that are enclosed in parentheses are evaluated as true or false before they are compared to other expressions. In the example below, the OR comparison in parenthesis is evaluated before the first expression and the AND operator are evaluated.

Figure 9.3 *Example of a Logical Comparison*


```
if test>=95 and (theme='A' or project='A')
   then grade='A+';
```

Therefore, be careful when using the OR operator with a series of comparisons. Remember that only one comparison in a series of OR comparisons must be true to make a condition true, and any nonzero, not missing constant is always evaluated as true. Therefore, the following subsetting IF statement is always true:

```
if x=1 or 2;
```

SAS first evaluates x=1, and the result can be either true or false. However, since the 2 is evaluated as nonzero and not missing (true), the entire expression is true. In this statement, however, the condition is not necessarily true because either comparison can be evaluated as true or false:

```
if x=1 or x=2;
```

Note: Both sides of the OR must contain complete expressions.

Providing an Alternative Action

Suppose you want to assign a value to TestLength based on the other possible values of TotalTime. One way to do this is to add IF-THEN statements for the other two conditions.

```
if totaltime>800 then TestLength='Long';
if 750<=totaltime<=800 then TestLength='Normal';
if totaltime<750 then TestLength='Short';
```

However, when the DATA step executes, each IF statement is evaluated in order, even if the first condition is true. This wastes system resources and slows the processing of your program.

Instead of using a series of IF-THEN statements, you can use the ELSE statement to specify an alternative action to be performed when the condition in an IF-THEN statement is false. As shown below, you can write multiple IF-THEN/ELSE statements to specify a series of mutually exclusive conditions.

```
if totaltime>800 then TestLength='Long';
  else if 750<=totaltime<=800 then TestLength='Normal';
  else if totaltime<750 then TestLength='Short';
```

The ELSE statement must immediately follow the IF-THEN statement in your program. An ELSE statement executes only if the previous IF-THEN/ELSE statement is false.

Syntax, ELSE statement:

ELSE *statement***;**

statement is any executable SAS statement, including another IF-THEN statement.

To assign a value to TestLength when the condition in your IF-THEN statement is false, you can add the ELSE statement to your DATA step:

```
data work.stresstest;
  set cert.tests;
  TotalTime=(timemin*60)+timesec;
  retain SumSec 5400;
  sumsec+totaltime;
  length TestLength $6;
  if totaltime>800 then TestLength='Long';
      else if 750<=totaltime<=800 then TestLength='Normal';
      else if totaltime<750 then TestLength='Short';
run;
proc print data=work.stresstest;
run;
```

For greater efficiency, construct your IF-THEN/ELSE statements with conditions of decreasing probability.

TIP You can use PUT statements to test your conditional logic.

```
if totaltime>800 then TestLength='Long';
   else if 750<=totaltime<=800 then TestLength='Normal';
      else put 'NOTE: Check this Length: ' totaltime=;
run;
```

Deleting Unwanted Observations

You can specify any executable SAS statement in an IF-THEN statement. For example, you can use an IF-THEN statement with a DELETE statement to determine which observations to omit as you read data.

Syntax, DELETE statement:

DELETE;

To conditionally execute a DELETE statement, use the following syntax for an IF statement:

IF *expression* **THEN DELETE;**

The expression is evaluated as follows:

- If it is true, execution stops for that observation. The DELETE statement deletes the observation from the output data set, and control returns to the top of the DATA step.
- If it is false, the DELETE statement does not execute, and processing continues with the next statement in the DATA step.

Example: IF-THEN and DELETE Statements

In the following example, the IF-THEN and DELETE statements omit any observations whose values for RestHR are below 70.

```
data work.stresstest;
  set cert.tests;
  if resthr<70 then delete;
  TotalTime=(timemin*60)+timesec;
  retain SumSec 5400;
  sumsec+totaltime;
  length TestLength $6;
  if totaltime>800 then TestLength='Long';
    else if 750<=totaltime<=800 then TestLength='Normal';
    else if totaltime<750 then TestLength='Short';
run;
proc print data=work.stresstest;
run;
```

Output 9.5 *Values for RestHR Less Than 70 Are Not in the Output (partial output)*

Obs	ID	Name	RestHR	MaxHR	RecHR	TimeMin	TimeSec	Tolerance	TotalTime	SumSec	TestLength
1	2458	Murray, W	72	185	128	12	38	D	758	6158	Normal
2	2501	Bonaventure, T	78	177	139	11	13	I	673	6831	Short
3	2539	LaMance, K	75	168	141	11	46	D	706	7537	Short
4	2544	Jones, M	79	187	136	12	26	N	746	8283	Short
5	2555	King, E	70	167	122	13	13	I	793	9076	Normal
					. . . more observations. . .						
12	2579	Underwood, K	72	165	127	13	19	S	799	14639	Normal
13	2584	Takahashi, Y	76	163	135	16	7	D	967	15606	Long
14	2588	Ivan, H	70	182	126	15	41	N	941	16547	Long
15	2589	Wilcox, E	78	189	138	14	57	I	897	17444	Long
16	2595	Warren, C	77	170	136	12	10	S	730	18174	Short

Selecting Variables

You might want to read and process variables that you do not want to keep in your output data set. In this case, use the DROP= and KEEP= data set options to specify the variables to drop or keep.

Use the KEEP= option instead of the DROP= option if more variables are dropped than kept.

Syntax, DROP=, and KEEP= data set options:

(DROP=*variable(s)*)

(KEEP=*variable(s)*)

- The DROP= or KEEP= options, in parentheses, follow the names of the data sets that contain the variables to be dropped or kept.
- *variable(s)* identifies the variables to drop or keep.

Example: DROP Data Set Option

Suppose you want to use theTimeMin and TimeSec variables to calculate the total time in the TotalTime variable, but you do not want to keep them in the output data set. You want to keep only the TotalTime variable. When you use the DROP data set option, the TimeMin and TimeSec variables are not written to the output data set:

```
data work.stresstest (drop=timemin timesec);
  set cert.tests;
  if resthr<70 then delete;
  TotalTime=(timemin*60)+timesec;
  retain SumSec 5400;
  sumsec+totaltime;
  length TestLength $6;
  if totaltime>800 then TestLength='Long';
    else if 750<=totaltime<=800 then TestLength='Normal';
```

```
        else if totaltime<750 then TestLength='Short';
run;
proc print data=work.stresstest;
run;
```

Output 9.6 *StressTest Data Set with Dropped Variables (partial output)*

Obs	ID	Name	RestHR	MaxHR	RecHR	Tolerance	TotalTime	SumSec	TestLength
1	2458	Murray, W	72	185	128	D	758	6158	Normal
2	2501	Bonaventure, T	78	177	139	I	673	6831	Short
3	2539	LaMance, K	75	168	141	D	706	7537	Short
4	2544	Jones, M	79	187	136	N	746	8283	Short
5	2555	King, E	70	167	122	I	793	9076	Normal
			. . . more observations. . .						
12	2579	Underwood, K	72	165	127	S	799	14639	Normal
13	2584	Takahashi, Y	76	163	135	D	967	15606	Long
14	2588	Ivan, H	70	182	126	N	941	16547	Long
15	2589	Wilcox, E	78	189	138	I	897	17444	Long
16	2595	Warren, C	77	170	136	S	730	18174	Short

Another way to exclude variables from a data set is to use the DROP statement or the KEEP statement. Like the DROP= and KEEP= data set options, these statements drop or keep variables. However, the DROP and KEEP statements differ from the DROP= and KEEP= data set options in the following ways:

- You cannot use the DROP and KEEP statements in SAS procedure steps.
- The DROP and KEEP statements apply to all output data sets that are named in the DATA statement. To exclude variables from some data sets but not from others, use the DROP= and KEEP= data set options in the DATA statement.

The KEEP statement is similar to the DROP statement, except that the KEEP statement specifies a list of variables to write to output data sets. Use the KEEP statement instead of the DROP statement if the number of variables to keep is smaller than the number to drop.

Syntax, DROP, and KEEP statements:

DROP *variable(s);*

KEEP *variable(s);*

variable(s) identifies the variables to drop or keep.

Example: Using the DROP Statement

The following example uses the DROP statement to drop unwanted variables.

```
data work.stresstest;
  set cert.tests;
  if tolerance='D';
  drop timemin timesec;
```

```
   TotalTime=(timemin*60)+timesec;
   retain SumSec 5400;
   sumsec+totaltime;
   length TestLength $6;
   if totaltime>800 then TestLength='Long';
     else if 750<=totaltime<=800 then TestLength='Normal';
     else if totaltime<750 then TestLength='Short';
run;
proc print data=work.stresstest;
run;
```

Transposing Variables into Observations

The TRANSPOSE Procedure

The Basics of PROC TRANSPOSE

The TRANSPOSE procedure creates an output data set by restructuring the values in a SAS data set, transposing selected variables into observations. By using PROC TRANSPOSE, you can often avoid writing a lengthy DATA step to achieve the same result. Further, the output data set can be used in subsequent DATA or PROC steps for analysis, reporting, or further data manipulation.

PROC TRANSPOSE does not produce printed output. To print the output data set from the PROC TRANSPOSE step, use PROC PRINT.

PROC TRANSPOSE Syntax

To create a transposed variable, the procedure transposes the values of an observation in the input data set into values of a variable in the output data set.

Syntax, PROC TRANSPOSE statement:

PROC TRANSPOSE<DATA=*input-data-set*> <OUT=*output-data-set*> <PREFIX=*prefix*>**;**

BY <DESCENDING> *variable-1*
<NOTSORTED>;

ID *variable(s)***;**

VAR *variable(s)***;**

- *input-data-set* names the SAS data set to transpose.
- *output-data-set* names the output data set. If *output-data-set* does not exist, then PROC TRANSPOSE creates it by using the DATA*n* naming convention. The default is DATA*n*.
- *prefix* specifies a prefix to use in constructing names for transposed variables in the output data set. For example, if PREFIX=VAR, then the names of the variables are VAR1, VAR2, ..., VAR*n*. The default variable name is COL*n*.

Note: When you use PREFIX= with an ID statement, the variable name begins with the prefix value followed by the ID value.

Tip: You can use name literals (n-literals) for the value of PREFIX. Name literals are helpful when specifying typographical or foreign characters, especially when VALIDVARNAME=ANY. To recall how VALIDVARNAME=ANY interacts with name literals, see "VALIDVARNAME=System Option" on page 14.

PROC TRANSPOSE Results

Output Data Set Variables

The TRANSPOSE procedure always produces an output data set, regardless of whether you specify the OUT= option in the PROC TRANSPOSE statement.

The output data set contains the following variables:

- variables that result from transposing the values of each variable into an observation.
- a variable whose values identify the source of the values in each observation in the output data set. This variable is a character variable whose values are the names of the variables that are transposed from the input data set. By default, PROC TRANSPOSE names this variable _NAME_. To override the default name, use the NAME= option. The label for the _NAME_ variable is NAME OF FORMER VARIABLE.
- a character variable whose values are the variable labels of the variables that are being transposed (if any of the variables that the procedure is transposing have labels). Specify the name of the variable by using the LABEL= option. The default is _LABEL_.
- variables that PROC TRANSPOSE copies from the input data set when you use either the BY or COPY statement. These variables have the same names and values as they do in the input data set. These variables also have the same attributes (for example: type, length, label, informat, and format).

Note: If the value of the LABEL= option or the NAME= option is the same as a variable that appears in a BY or COPY statement, then the output data set does not contain a variable whose values are the names or labels of the transposed variables. See Output 9.7 on page 160 for a sample transposed data set.

Attributes of Transposed Variables

Transposed variables contain the following attributes:

- All transposed variables are the same type and length.
- If all variables that the procedure is transposing are numeric, then the transposed variables are numeric. Thus, if the numeric variable has a character string as a formatted value, then its unformatted numeric value is transposed.
- If any variable that the procedure is transposing is character, then all transposed variables are character. If you are transposing a numeric variable that has a character string as a formatted value, then the formatted value is transposed.
- The length of the transposed variables is equal to the length of the longest variable that is being transposed.

Example: Performing a Simple Transposition

Here is the Cert.Class data set before any transposition.

Figure 9.4 *Cert.Class Data Set*

Obs	Name	Score1	Score2	Score3	Homework
1	LINDA	53	60	66	42
2	DEREK	72	64	56	32
3	KATHY	98	82	100	48
4	MICHAEL	80	55	95	50

This example performs a default transposition and uses no subordinate statements.

```
proc transpose data=cert.class out=score_transposed;       /*#1*/
run;
proc print data=score_transposed noobs;                    /*#2*/
  title 'Scores for the Year';
run;
```

1 PROC TRANSPOSE transposes only the numeric variables Score1, Score2, Score3, and Homework. OUT= puts the result of the transposition in the data set Score_Transposed.

2 PROC PRINT prints the Score_Transposed data set. The NOOBS option suppresses the printing of observation numbers.

In the output data set Score_Transposed, the variables COL1 through COL4 contain the values of Score 1, Score 2, Score 3, and Homework for the year for each student. The variable _NAME_ contains the names of the variables from the input data set that were transposed.

Output 9.7 *Student Test Scores in Variables*

Scores for the Year

NAME	COL1	COL2	COL3	COL4
Score1	53	72	98	80
Score2	60	64	82	55
Score3	66	56	100	95
Homework	42	32	48	50

Transposing Specific Variables

Use the VAR statement to list the variables to transpose. If you omit the VAR statement, then the TRANSPOSE procedure transposes all numeric variables in the input data set that are not listed in another statement. You must list character variables in a VAR statement if you want to transpose them.

Note: If the procedure is transposing any character variable, then all transposed variables are character variables.

Syntax, VAR statement:

VAR *variable(s)*;

- *variable(s)* names one or more variables to transpose.

Here is the Cert.Trials data set:

Figure 9.5 *Cert.Trials Data Set*

Obs	Name	TestDate	Sex	Placebo	Cholesterol	Triglyc	Uric
1	Johnson	22MAY2000	F	YES	200	180	3.7
2	Eberhardt	22MAY2000	F	NO	244	320	4.6
3	Nunnelly	22MAY2000	F	YES	210	300	4.0
4	Johnson	01AUG2000	F	YES	205	185	3.8
5	Eberhardt	01AUG2000	F	NO	249	325	4.7
6	Nunnelly	01AUG2000	F	YES	215	305	4.1
7	Johnson	09AUG2000	F	YES	215	190	3.9
8	Eberhardt	09AUG2000	F	NO	254	330	4.8
9	Nunnelly	09AUG2000	F	YES	220	310	4.2

```
proc transpose data=cert.trials out=transtrials1;     /*#1*/
   var Cholesterol Triglyc Uric;                      /*#2*/
run;
proc print data=transtrials1;                         /*#3*/
run;
```

1 Transpose the data set Cert.Trials and put the results of the transposition in the Transtrials1 data set.

2 The VAR statement specifies the Cholesterol, Triglyc, and Uric variables as the only variables to be transposed.

3 Use the PROC PRINT statement to print the Transtrials1 data set.

In the following output, the variables in the Transtrials1 data set, Cholesterol, Triglyc, and Uric, are the only variables that are transposed. The procedure uses the default variable name COL*n*.

Output 9.8 *PROC PRINT Results: Transtrials1 Data Set*

Obs	_NAME_	COL1	COL2	COL3	COL4	COL5	COL6	COL7	COL8	COL9
1	Cholesterol	200.0	244.0	210	205.0	249.0	215.0	215.0	254.0	220.0
2	Triglyc	180.0	320.0	300	185.0	325.0	305.0	190.0	330.0	310.0
3	Uric	3.7	4.6	4	3.8	4.7	4.1	3.9	4.8	4.2

Naming Transposed Variables

Use the ID statement to create variable names in the output data set that are based on one or more variables from the input data set.

When a variable name is formed in the transposed data set, the formatted values of all listed ID variables are concatenated in the same order that the variables are listed in the ID statement. The PREFIX= option specifies a common character or character string to appear at the beginning of the formed variable names.

Syntax, ID statement:

ID *variable(s)*;

- *variable(s)* names one or more variables whose formatted values are used to form the names of the variables in the output data set.

TIP If the value of any ID variable is missing, then PROC TRANSPOSE writes a warning message to the log. The procedure does not transpose observations that have a missing value for any ID variable.

The following example uses the values of a variable and a user-supplied value to name transposed variables.

```
proc transpose data=cert.trials out=transtrials2;   /*#1*/
   var cholesterol triglyc uric;                    /*#2*/
   id name testdate;                                /*#3*/
run;
proc print data=transtrials2;                       /*#4*/
run;
```

1 Transpose the data set Cert.Trials and put the results of the transposition in the Transtrials2 data set.

2 The VAR statement specifies the Cholesterol, Triglyc, and Uric variables as the only variables to be transposed.

3 The ID statement specifies Name and TestDate as the variables whose nonmissing formatted values name the transposed variables in the output data set, Transtrials2. Because the ID statement specifies two variables, the values of those variables are concatenated to create the new variable names.

4 Use the PROC PRINT statement to print the Transtrials2 data set.

Output 9.9 *PROC PRINT Results: Transtrials2 Data Set*

Obs	_NAME_	Johnson22MAY2000	Eberhardt22MAY2000	Nunnelly22MAY2000	Johnson01AUG2000
1	Cholesterol	200.0	244.0	210	205.0
2	Triglyc	180.0	320.0	300	185.0
3	Uric	3.7	4.6	4	3.8

Eberhardt01AUG2000	Nunnelly01AUG2000	Johnson09AUG2000	Eberhardt09AUG2000	Nunnelly09AUG2000
249.0	215.0	215.0	254.0	220.0
325.0	305.0	190.0	330.0	310.0
4.7	4.1	3.9	4.8	4.2

Transposing BY Groups

Use the BY statement in the PROC TRANSPOSE step to define and transpose BY groups.

Syntax, BY statement:

BY <DESCENDING> *variable-1*
<NOTSORTED>**;**

- *variable* specifies the variable that PROC TRANSPOSE uses to form BY groups. You can specify more than one variable. If you do not use the NOTSORTED option in the BY statement, then either the observations must be sorted by all the variables that you specify, or they must be indexed appropriately. Variables in a BY statement are called *BY variables.*
- DESCENDING specifies that the input data set is sorted in descending order by the variable that immediately follows the word DESCENDING in the BY statement.
- NOTSORTED specifies that observations are not necessarily sorted in alphabetic or numeric order.

  The requirement for ordering or indexing observations according to the values of BY variables is suspended for BY-group processing when you use the NOTSORTED option. The procedure does not use an index if you specify NOTSORTED. The procedure defines a BY group as a set of contiguous observations that have the same values for all BY variables. If observations with the same values for the BY variables are not contiguous, then the procedure treats each contiguous set as a separate BY group.

```
proc transpose data=cert.trials out=transtrials3;     /*#1*/
   var cholesterol triglyc uric;                       /*#2*/
   id name;                                            /*#3*/
   by testdate;                                        /*#4*/
run;
proc print data=transtrials3;                           /*#5*/
run;
```

1 Transpose the data set. The OUT= option puts the results of the transposition in the Transtrials3 data set.

2 The VAR statement specifies the Cholesterol, Triglyc, and Uric variables as the only variables to be transposed.

3 The ID statement specifies Name as the variable whose nonmissing formatted values name the transposed variables in the output data set, Transtrials3.

4 The BY statement creates BY groups for each unique TestDate. The procedure does not transpose the BY variables.

5 Use the PROC PRINT statement to print the Transtrials3 data set.

The following data set is the output data set, Transtrials3. For each BY group in the original data set, PROC TRANSPOSE creates three observations, one for each variable that it is transposing.

Output 9.10 *PROC PRINT Results: Transtrials3 Data*

Obs	TestDate	_NAME_	Johnson	Eberhardt	Nunnelly
1	22MAY2000	Cholesterol	200.0	244.0	210.0
2	22MAY2000	Triglyc	180.0	320.0	300.0
3	22MAY2000	Uric	3.7	4.6	4.0
4	01AUG2000	Cholesterol	205.0	249.0	215.0
5	01AUG2000	Triglyc	185.0	325.0	305.0
6	01AUG2000	Uric	3.8	4.7	4.1
7	09AUG2000	Cholesterol	215.0	254.0	220.0
8	09AUG2000	Triglyc	190.0	330.0	310.0
9	09AUG2000	Uric	3.9	4.8	4.2

Using SAS Macro Variables

%LET Statement

The SAS macro language enables you to design dynamic programs that you can easily update or modify.

A macro variable can be defined to represent a string of text that appears in your program. For example, if you reference a specific variable value in multiple places in a program, you can substitute a macro variable in its place. Then, if you want to update the value of the variable, you need to update the macro variable definition only once, rather than searching through your code to find the value in multiple places. It is common to place macro variable assignments at the top of SAS programs.

Use the %LET statement to create a macro variable and assign it a value.

Syntax, %LET statement:

%LET*macro-variable*=<*value*>**;**

- *macro-variable* is either the name of a macro variable or a text expression that produces a macro variable name. The name can refer to a new or existing macro variable.
- *value* is a character string or a text expression. Omitting *value* produces a null value (0 characters). Leading and trailing blanks in *value* are ignored.

You reference the macro variable that you created by using the name of the macro variable with an ampersand (&). An example is ¯o-variable.

Note: If the macro variable has already been previously defined in the program, the value is replaced with the most current value.

Example: Using SAS Macro Variables with Numeric Values

When referencing a SAS macro variable with numeric values, use the name of the macro variable with a preceding ampersand (&) and no quotation marks.

```
%let Cyl_Count=5;                          /*#1*/
proc print data=sashelp.cars;
   where Cylinders=&Cyl_Count;             /*#2*/
   var Type Make Model Cylinders MSRP;
run;
proc freq data=sashelp.cars;
   where Cylinders=&Cyl_Count;
   tables Type;
run;
```

1 Use the %LET statement to create a macro variable named Cyl_Count that stores the value 5.

2 To reference the macro variable Cyl_Count in your code, use an ampersand (&) and then the macro variable name. Doing so enables you to reference the value of Cyl_Count without having to repeatedly write out the full value.

Seven observations are printed.

Output 9.11 *PROC PRINT Results*

Obs	Type	Make	Model	Cylinders	MSRP
419	Sedan	Volvo	S60 2.5 4dr	5	$31,745
420	Sedan	Volvo	S60 T5 4dr	5	$34,845
421	Sedan	Volvo	S60 R 4dr	5	$37,560
423	Sedan	Volvo	S80 2.5T 4dr	5	$37,885
424	Sedan	Volvo	C70 LPT convertible 2dr	5	$40,565
425	Sedan	Volvo	C70 HPT convertible 2dr	5	$42,565
428	Wagon	Volvo	XC70	5	$35,145

Output 9.12 *PROC FREQ Results*

Type	Frequency	Percent	Cumulative Frequency	Cumulative Percent
Sedan	6	85.71	6	85.71
Wagon	1	14.29	7	100.00

When you want to run the code for a different cylinder count, you change only the value of Cyl_Count at the top of the program.

Example: Using SAS Macro Variables with Character Values

When referencing a SAS macro variable with character values, enclose the ampersand (&) and the macro variable in double quotation marks.

In the following example, the macro variable is "Wagon", and the WHERE statement would be **where Type = "Wagon"**. The macro variable is simply taking the place of Wagon, so the macro variable goes inside the quotation marks. Although constants can be enclosed in single quotation marks, macro variables with character variables must always be enclosed in double quotation marks.

```
%let CarType=Wagon;                  /*#1*/
proc print data=sashelp.cars;
  where Type="&CarType";             /*#2*/
  var Type Make Model MSRP;
run;
proc means data=sashelp.cars;
  where Type="&CarType";
  var MSRP MPG_Highway;
run;
proc freq data=sashelp.cars;
  where Type="&CarType";
  tables Origin Make;
run;
```

1 Use the %LET statement to create a macro variable named CarType that stores the text Wagon.

   Note: It is recommended that you do not include quotation marks when you define the macro variable value. Use quotation marks when necessary after the macro variable is resolved.

2 To reference the macro variable CarType in your code, use an ampersand (&) and then the macro variable name.

   If you want to run reports later on a different type of car, such as an SUV, then update the value of the macro variable to SUV and rerun the program. If you did not use a macro variable, then you would have to replace the value throughout the code.

The following PRINT, MEANS, and FREQ output shows results where the value for Type is Wagon.

Output 9.13 *PROC PRINT Results*

Obs	Type	Make	Model	MSRP
25	Wagon	Audi	A6 3.0 Avant Quattro	$40,840
26	Wagon	Audi	S4 Avant Quattro	$49,090
46	Wagon	BMW	325xi Sport	$32,845
90	Wagon	Chevrolet	Malibu Maxx LS	$22,225
105	Wagon	Chrysler	Pacifica	$31,230
140	Wagon	Ford	Focus ZTW	$17,475
141	Wagon	Ford	Taurus SE	$22,290
186	Wagon	Infiniti	FX35	$34,895
187	Wagon	Infiniti	FX45	$36,395
215	Wagon	Kia	Rio Cinco	$11,905
229	Wagon	Lexus	IS 300 SportCross	$32,455
275	Wagon	Mercedes-Benz	C240	$33,780
276	Wagon	Mercedes-Benz	E320	$50,670
277	Wagon	Mercedes-Benz	E500	$60,670
286	Wagon	Mercury	Sable GS	$22,595
299	Wagon	Mitsubishi	Lancer Sportback LS	$17,495
316	Wagon	Nissan	Murano SL	$28,739
330	Wagon	Pontiac	Vibe	$17,045
344	Wagon	Saab	9-5 Aero	$40,845
352	Wagon	Saturn	L300 2	$23,560
354	Wagon	Scion	xB	$14,165
364	Wagon	Subaru	Forester X	$21,445
365	Wagon	Subaru	Outback	$23,895
373	Wagon	Suzuki	Aerio SX	$16,497
401	Wagon	Toyota	Matrix XR	$16,695
414	Wagon	Volkswagen	Jetta GL	$19,005
415	Wagon	Volkswagen	Passat GLS 1.8T	$24,955
416	Wagon	Volkswagen	Passat W8	$40,235
427	Wagon	Volvo	V40	$26,135
428	Wagon	Volvo	XC70	$35,145

Output 9.14 *PROC MEANS Results*

The MEANS Procedure

Variable	Label	N	Mean	Std Dev	Minimum	Maximum
MSRP MPG_Highway	 MPG (Highway)	30 30	28840.53 27.9000000	11834.00 4.4127558	11905.00 19.0000000	60670.00 36.0000000

Output 9.15 *PROC FREQ Results*

The FREQ Procedure

Origin	Frequency	Percent	Cumulative Frequency	Cumulative Percent
Asia	11	36.67	11	36.67
Europe	12	40.00	23	76.67
USA	7	23.33	30	100.00

Make	Frequency	Percent	Cumulative Frequency	Cumulative Percent
Audi	2	6.67	2	6.67
BMW	1	3.33	3	10.00
Chevrolet	1	3.33	4	13.33
Chrysler	1	3.33	5	16.67
Ford	2	6.67	7	23.33
Infiniti	2	6.67	9	30.00
Kia	1	3.33	10	33.33
Lexus	1	3.33	11	36.67
Mercedes-Benz	3	10.00	14	46.67
Mercury	1	3.33	15	50.00
Mitsubishi	1	3.33	16	53.33
Nissan	1	3.33	17	56.67
Pontiac	1	3.33	18	60.00
Saab	1	3.33	19	63.33
Saturn	1	3.33	20	66.67
Scion	1	3.33	21	70.00
Subaru	2	6.67	23	76.67
Suzuki	1	3.33	24	80.00
Toyota	1	3.33	25	83.33
Volkswagen	3	10.00	28	93.33
Volvo	2	6.67	30	100.00

Example: Using Macro Variables in TITLE Statements

The following example uses multiple macro variables with character and numeric values. There are two %LET statements that are used to define two different macro variables. The first is a TITLE statement that contains character values. The other %LET statement contains numeric values. Notice that when you are referencing macro variables with character values, the ampersand (&) and the macro variable name are enclosed in double quotation marks, but the macro variables with numeric values are not.

```
%let TitleX=PROC PRINT Of Only &Cyl_Count Cylinder Vehicles;
%let Cyl_Count=5;
Title "&TitleX";
proc print data=sashelp.cars;
   where Cylinders=&Cyl_Count;
   var Type Make Model Cylinders MSRP;
run;
```

Output 9.16 *PROC PRINT Results: 5-Cylinder Vehicles*

PROC PRINT Of Only 5 Cylinder Vehicles

Obs	MSRP
419	$31,745
420	$34,845
421	$37,560
423	$37,885
424	$40,565
425	$42,565
428	$35,145

If you want to rerun the code to find 12–cylinder vehicles and want to run PROC MEANS instead, simply update your macro variables and rerun the code.

```
%let TitleX=PROC MEANS Of Only &Cyl_Count Cylinder Vehicles;
%let Cyl_Count=12;
Title "&TitleX";
proc means data=sashelp.cars;
   where Cylinders=&Cyl_Count;
   var MSRP;
run;
```

Output 9.17 *PROC MEANS Results: 12–Cylinder Vehicles*

PROC MEANS Of Only 12 Cylinder Vehicles

The MEANS Procedure

Analysis Variable : MSRP				
N	Mean	Std Dev	Minimum	Maximum
3	110030.00	30349.49	75000.00	128420.00

Chapter Quiz

Select the best answer for each question. Check your answers using the answer key in the appendix.

1. Given the following data set, which program creates the output shown below?

	StockNum	Finish	Style	Item	Price
1	310	oak	pedestal	table	229.99
2	311	maple	pedestal	table	369.99
3	312	brass	floor	lamp	79.99
4	313	glass	table	lamp	59.99
5	314	oak	rocking	chair	153.99
6	315	oak	pedestal	table	178.99
7	316	glass	table	lamp	49.99
8	317	maple	pedestal	table	169.99
9	318	maple	rocking	chair	199.99

StockNum	Finish	Style	Item	TotalPrice
310	oak	pedestal	table	229.99
311	maple	pedestal	table	599.98
312	brass	floor	lamp	679.97
313	glass	table	lamp	739.96
316	glass	table	lamp	789.95
317	maple	pedestal	table	959.94
318	maple	rocking	chair	1159.93

a.
```
data test2;
  set cert.furnture;
  if finish='oak';
  if price<100 then delete;
  TotalPrice+price;
  drop price;
run;
proc print data=test2 noobs;
run;
```

b.
```
data test2;
  set cert.furnture;
```

```
  if finish='oak' and price<200;
  TotalPrice+price;
  drop price;
run;
proc print data=test2 noobs;
run;
```

c.
```
data test2;
  set cert.furnture;
  if finish='oak' and price<200 then delete;
  TotalPrice+price;
  drop price;
    run;
proc print data=test2 noobs;
run;
```

d.
```
data test2;
  set cert.furnture;
  if finish='oak' and price<100 then do;
    TotalPrice+price;
      drop price;
  end;
run;
proc print data=test2 noobs;
run;
```

2. Consider the IF-THEN statement shown below. When the statement is executed, which expression is evaluated first?

```
if finlexam>=95
   and (research='A' or
       (project='A' and present='A'))
   then Grade='A+';
```

a. `finlexam>=95`

b. `research='A'`

c. `project='A' and present='A'`

d. `research='A' or (project='A' and present='A')`

3. For the observation shown below, what is the result of the IF-THEN statements?

Status	Type	Count	Action	Control
OK	3	12	E	Go

```
if status='OK' and type=3
   then Count+1;
if status='S' or action='E'
   then Control='Stop';
```

a. `Count = 12    Control = Go`

b. `Count = 13    Control =Stop`

c. `Count = 12    Control =Stop`

d. `Count = 13    Control = Go`

4. Which of the following can determine the length of a new variable?

   a. the length of the variable's first reference in the DATA step

   b. the assignment statement

   c. the LENGTH statement

   d. all of the above

5. Which set of statements is equivalent to the code shown below?

```
if code='1' then Type='Fixed';
if code='2' then Type='Variable';
if code^='1' and code^='2' then Type='Unknown';
```

   a.
```
if code='1' then Type='Fixed';
else if code='2' then Type='Variable';
  else Type='Unknown';
```

   b.
```
 if code='1' then Type='Fixed';
if code='2' then Type='Variable';
else Type='Unknown';
```

   c.
```
if code='1' then type='Fixed';
else code='2' and type='Variable';
else type='Unknown';
```

   d.
```
if code='1' and type='Fixed';
then code='2' and type='Variable';
else type='Unknown';
```

6. What is the length of the variable Type, as created in the DATA step below?

```
data work.newloan;
  set cert.records;
  TotLoan+payment;
  if code='1' then Type='Fixed';
  else Type='Variable';
  length type $ 10;
run;
```

   a. 5

   b. 8

   c. 10

   d. It depends on the first value of Type.

7. Which program contains an error?

   a.
```
data stresstest(drop=timemin timesec);
  set cert.tests;
  TotalTime=(timemin*60)+timesec;
  SumSec+totaltime;
run;
```

   b.
```
proc print data=stresstest;
  label totaltime='Total Duration of Test';
  drop sumsec;
run;
```

   c.
```
proc print data=stresstest(keep=totaltime timemin);
   label totaltime='Total Duration of Test';
run;
```

d.
```
data stresstest;
   set cert.tests;
   TotalTime=(timemin*60)+timesec;
   keep id totaltime tolerance;
run;
```

8. If you submit the following program, which variables appear in the new data set?

```
data work.cardiac(drop=age group);
  set cert.fitness(keep=age weight group);
  if group=2 and age>40;
run;
```

   a. none
   b. Weight
   c. Age, Group
   d. Age, Weight, Group

9. Which of the following programs correctly reads the data set Orders and creates the data set FastOrdr?

a.
```
data cert.fastordr(drop=ordrtime);
   set cert.orders(keep=product units price);
   if ordrtime<4;
   Total=units*price;
run;
```

b.
```
data cert.orders(drop=ordrtime);
   set cert.fastordr(keep=product units price);
   if ordrtime<4;
   Total=units*price;
run;
```

c.
```
data cert.fastordr(drop=ordrtime);
    set cert.orders(keep=product units price
                    ordrtime);
    if ordrtime<4;
    Total=units*price;
run;
```

d. none of the above

Chapter 10

Combining SAS Data Sets

How to Prepare Your Data Sets

Determining the Structure and Contents of Data Sets

Typically, data comes from multiple sources and might be in different formats. Many applications require input data to be in a specific format before the data can be processed. Although application requirements vary, there are common factors for all applications that access, combine, and process data. You can identify these common factors for your data. Here are tasks to help you start:

- Determine how the input data is related.
- Ensure that the data is properly sorted or indexed, if necessary.
- Select the appropriate access method to process the input data.
- Select the appropriate SAS tools to complete the task.

You can use the CONTENTS, DATASETS, and PRINT procedures to review the structure of your data.

Relationships among multiple sources of input data exist when each of the sources contains common data, either at the physical or logical level. For example, employee data and department data could be related through an employee ID variable that shares common values. Another data set could contain numeric sequence numbers whose partial values logically relate it to a separate data set by observation number.

You must be able to identify the existing relationships in your data. This knowledge is crucial for understanding how to process input data in order to produce desired results. All related data falls into one of these four categories, characterized by how observations relate among the data sets:

- one-to-one
- one-to-many
- many-to-one
- many-to-many

Finally, to obtain the desired results, you should understand how each of these methods combines observations and how each treats duplicate, missing, or unmatched values of common variables. Some of the methods require that you preprocess your data sets by sorting or creating indexes. Testing is a good first step.

Testing Your Program

Create small temporary data sets that contain a sample of rows that test all of your program's logic. If your logic is faulty and you get unexpected output, you can debug your program.

Looking at Sources of Common Problems

If your program does not run correctly, review your input data for the following errors:

- columns that have the same name but that represent different data

To correct the error, you can rename columns before you combine the data sets by using the RENAME= table option in the SET or MERGE statement. As an alternative, use the DATASETS procedure to display all library management functions for all member types (except catalogs).

- common columns that have the same data but different attributes

Methods of Combining SAS Data Sets: The Basics

A common task in SAS programming is to combine observations from two or more data sets into a new data set. Using the DATA step, you can combine data sets in several ways.

Table 10.1 Quick-Reference Overview of Data-Combining Methods

Method of Combining	Illustration
One-to-one reading Creates observations that contain all of the variables from each contributing data set. Combines observations based on their relative position in each data set. Statement: SET	See illustration below
Concatenating Appends the observations from one data set to another. Statement: SET	See illustration below

One-to-one reading — Illustration

SAS Data Set C

Num	VarA
1	A1
3	A2
5	A3

SAS Data Set D

Num	VarB
2	B1
4	B2

Merge

Combined SAS Data Set

Num	VarA	VarB
2	A1	B1
4	A2	B2

Concatenating — Illustration

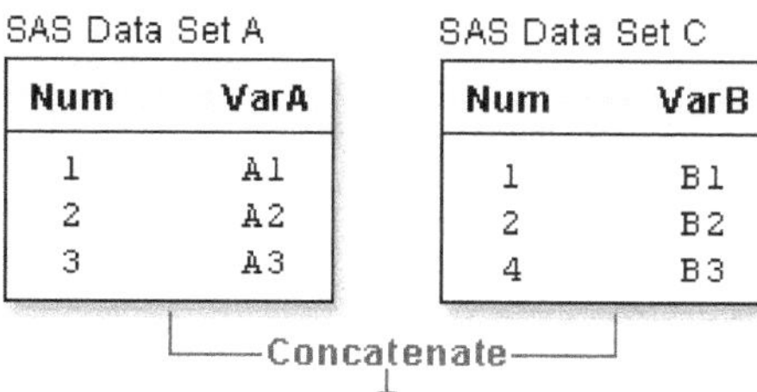

Concatenate

Combined SAS Data Set

Num	VarA	VarB
1	A1	
2	A2	
3	A3	
1		B1
2		B2
4		B3

Method of Combining	Illustration
Match-merging Matches observations from two or more data sets into a single observation in a new data set according to the values of a common variable. Statements: MERGE, BY	SAS Data Set A Num VarA 1 A1 2 A2 3 A3 SAS Data Set B Num VarB 1 B1 2 B2 4 B3 Match-Merge Combined SAS Data Set Num VarA VarB 1 A1 B1 2 A2 B2 3 A3 4 B3

TIP You can also use PROC SQL to join data sets according to common values.

One-to-One Reading: Details

One-to-One Reading Syntax

Use multiple SET statements in a DATA step to combine data sets. One-to-one reading combines rows from two or more data sets by creating rows that contain all of the columns from each contributing data set. Rows are combined based on their relative position in each data set. That is, the first row in one data set is combined with the first in the other, and so on. The data program stops after it has read the last row from the smallest data set.

Syntax, DATA step for one-to-one reading:

DATA *output-SAS-data-set*;

SET *SAS-data-set-1*;

SET *SAS-data-set-2*;

RUN;

- *output-SAS-data-set* names the data set to be created.
- *SAS-data-set-1* and *SAS-data-set-2* specify the data sets to be read.

How One-to-One Reading Selects Data

The following statements are true when you perform one-to-one reading:

- The new data set contains all the variables from all the input data sets. If the data sets contain variables that have the same names, the values that are read from the last data set overwrite the values that were read from earlier data sets.
- The number of observations in the new data set is the number of observations in the smallest original data set. Observations are combined based on their relative position in each data set. That is, the first observation in one data set is joined with the first

observation in the other, and so on. The DATA step stops after it has read the last observation from the smallest data set.

```
data one2one;
  set a;
  set b;
run;
```

Figure 10.1 *One-to-One Reading*

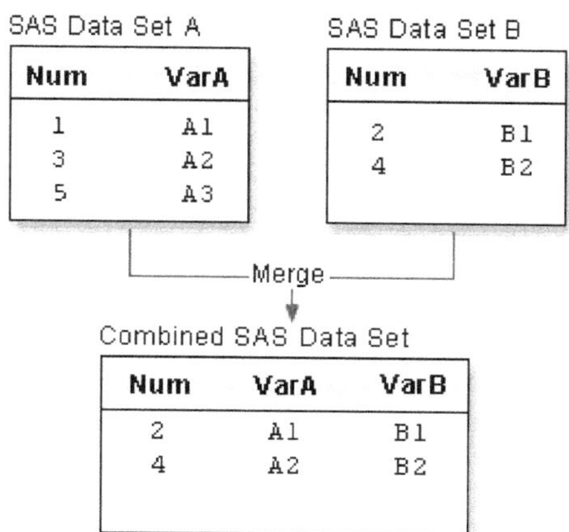

How One-to-One Reading Works

Here is a simple example of one-to-one reading.

```
data one2one;
  set a;
  set b;
run;
```

1. The first SET statement reads the first observation from data set A into the PDV.

Program Data Vector

Num	VarA
1	A1

2. The second SET statement reads the first observation from data set B into the PDV, and SAS writes the contents of the PDV to the new data set. The value for Num from data set B overwrites the value for Num from data set A.

Program Data Vector

Num	VarA	VarB
2	A1	B1

SAS Data Set

Num	VarA	VarB
2	A1	B1

3. The first SET statement reads from data set A into the PDV.

Program Data Vector

Num	VarA	VarB
3	A2	

4. The second SET statement reads the second observation from data set B, and SAS writes the contents of the PDV to the new data set. The value for Num from data set B overwrites the value for Num from data set A.

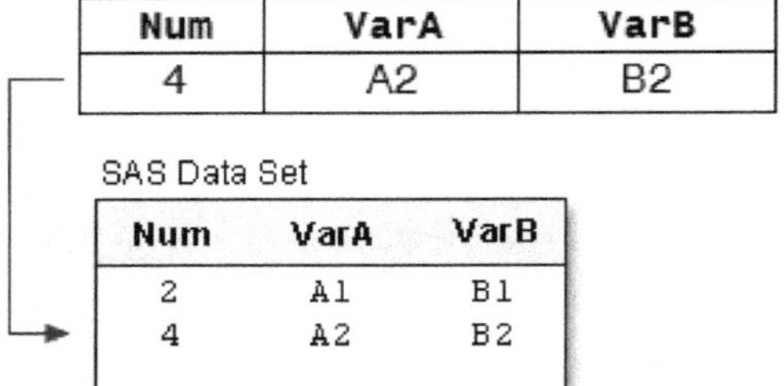

Program Data Vector

Num	VarA	VarB
4	A2	B2

SAS Data Set

Num	VarA	VarB
2	A1	B1
4	A2	B2

5. The first SET statement reads the third observation from data set A into the PDV.

Program Data Vector

Num	VarA	VarB
5	A3	

6. The second SET statement reads the end of file in data set B, which stops the DATA step processing with no further output written to the data set. The last observation in data set A is read into the PDV, but it is not written to the output data set.

Num	VarA	VarB
2	A1	B1
4	A2	B2

Example: Using One-to-One Reading to Combine Data Sets

In the following example, you have basic patient data in Cert.Patients that you want to combine with other patient data that is stored in Cert.Measure. The height and weight data is stored in the data set Cert.Measure. Both data sets are sorted by the variable ID.

Notice that Cert.Patients contains nine out of eleven observations in which the patient age is less than 60.

Figure 10.2 *Example: One-to-One Reading*

SAS Data Set Cert.Patients

	ID	Sex	Age
1	1129	F	48
2	1387	F	57
3	2304	F	16
4	2486	F	63
5	4759	F	60
6	5438	F	42
7	6488	F	59
8	9012	F	39
9	9125	F	56
10	8045	M	40
11	8125	M	39

SAS Data Set Cert.Measure

	ID	Height	Weight
1	1129	61	137
2	1387	64	142
3	2304	61	102
4	5438	62	168
5	6488	64	154
6	8045	72	200
7	8125	70	176
8	9012	63	157
9	9125	65	148

To subset observations from the first data set and combine them with observations from the second data set, you can submit the following program:

```
data work.one2one;
  set cert.patients;
  if age<60;
  set cert.measure;
run;
```

The resulting data set, Work.One2one, contains six observations (the number of observations read from the smallest data set, which is Cert.Measure). The last observation in Cert.Patients is not written to the data set because the second SET statement reaches an end-of-file, which stops the DATA step processing.

Figure 10.3 *The Resulting Data Set for One-to-One Reading Example*

	ID	Sex	Age	Height	Weight
1	1129	F	48	61	137
2	1387	F	57	64	142
3	2304	F	16	61	102
4	5438	F	42	62	168
5	6488	F	59	64	154
6	8045	M	40	72	200
7	8125	M	39	70	176
8	9012	F	39	63	157
9	9125	F	56	65	148

Concatenating: Details

Concatenating Syntax

Another way to combine SAS data sets with the SET statement is concatenating, which appends the observations from one data set to another data set. To concatenate SAS data sets, you specify a list of data set names in the SET statement.

Syntax, DATA step for concatenating:

DATA *output-SAS-data-set*;

SET *SAS-data-set-1 SAS-data-set-2*;

RUN;

- *output-SAS-data-set* names the data set to be created.
- *SAS-data-set-1* and *SAS-data-set-2* specify the data sets to concatenate.

How Concatenating Selects Data

When a program concatenates data sets, all of the observations are read from the first data set listed in the SET statement. Then all of the observations are read from the second data set listed, and so on, until all of the listed data sets have been read. The new data set contains all of the variables and observations from all of the input data sets.

```
data concat;
  set a c;
run;
```

Figure 10.4 *How Concatenating Selects*

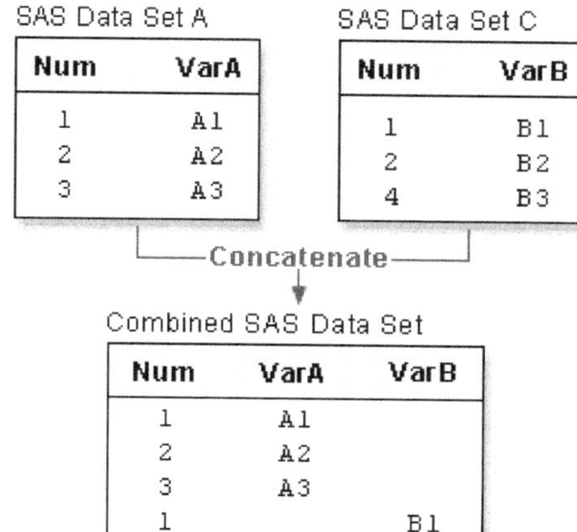

Notice that A and C contain a common variable named Num:

- Both instances of Num (or any common variable) must have the same type attribute, or SAS stops processing the DATA step and issues an error message stating that the variables are incompatible.
- However, if the length attribute is different, SAS takes the length from the first data set that contains the variable. In this case, the length of Num in A determines the length of Num in Concat.
- The same is true for the label, format, and informat attributes: If any of these attributes are different, SAS takes the attribute from the first data set that contains the variable with that attribute.

Example: Using Concatenating to Combine Data Sets

The following DATA step creates Work.Concat by concatenating Cert.Therapy2012 and Cert.Therapy2013. Each data set contains 12 observations.

```
data work.concat;
  set cert.therapy2012 cert.therapy2013;
run;
proc print data=work.concat;
run;
```

The first 12 observations in the new output data set Work.Concat were read from Cert.Therapy2012, and the last 12 observations were read from Cert.Therapy2013.

Figure 10.5 *Example: Concatenating (partial output)*

Obs	Month	Year	AerClass	WalkJogRun	Swim
1	1	2012	26	78	14
2	2	2012	32	109	19
3	3	2012	15	106	22
4	4	2012	47	115	24
5	5	2012	95	121	31
. . . *more observations* . . .					
20	8	2013	63	65	53
21	9	2013	60	49	68
22	10	2013	78	70	41
23	11	2013	82	44	58
24	12	2013	93	57	47

Match-Merging: Details

Match-Merging Syntax

Match-merging combines observations from two or more data sets into a single observation in a new data set according to the values of a common variable.

When match-merging, use the MERGE statement rather than the SET statement to combine data sets.

Syntax, DATA step for match-merging:

DATA *output-SAS-data-set*;

  MERGE *SAS-data-set-1 SAS-data-set-2*;

  BY <DESCENDING> *variable(s)*;

RUN;

- *output-SAS-data-set* names the data set to be created.
- *SAS-data-set-1* and *SAS-data-set-2* specify the data sets to be read.
- *variable(s)* in the BY statement specifies one or more variables whose values are used to match observations.
- DESCENDING indicates that the input data sets are sorted in descending order (largest to smallest numerically, or reverse alphabetical for character variables) by the variable that is specified. If you have more that one variable in the BY statement, DESCENDING applies only to the variable that immediately follows it. The default sort order is ASCENDING.

TIP Each input data set in the MERGE statement must be sorted in order of the values of the BY variable or variables, or it must have an appropriate index. Each BY variable must have the same type in all data sets to be merged.

How Match-Merging Selects Data

During match-merging SAS sequentially checks each observation of each data set to see whether the BY values match and then writes the combined observation to the new data set.

```
data merged;
  merge a b;
  by num;
run;
```

Figure 10.6 *How Match-Merging Selects Data*

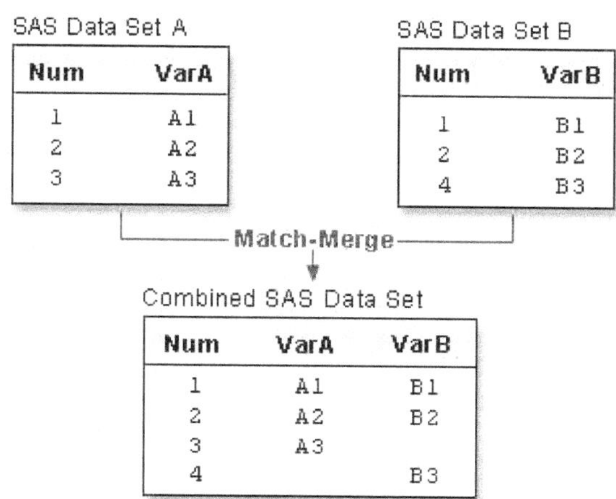

Basic DATA step match-merging produces an output data set that contains values from all observations in all input data sets. You can add statements and options to select only matching observations.

If your input data set does not have any observations for a value of the BY variable, then the observations in the output data set will contain missing values. The missing values are for the variables that are unique to the input data set.

TIP In match-merging, often one data set contains unique values for the BY variable and other data sets contain multiple values for the BY variable.

Example: Using Match-Merging to Combine Data Sets

The data sets Cert.Demog and Cert.Visit have been sorted as follows:

```
proc sort data=cert.demog;
  by id;
run;
proc print data=cert.demog;
run;
```

Figure 10.7 *HTML Output: Sorting Cert.Demog*

Obs	ID	Age	Sex	Date
1	A001	21	M	05/22/2007
2	A002	32	M	06/15/2006
3	A003	24	F	08/17/2007
4	A004	.		01/27/2006
5	A005	44	F	02/24/2005
6	A007	39	M	01/11/2005

```
proc sort data=cert.visit;
  by id;
run;
proc print data=cert.visit;
run;
```

Figure 10.8 *HTML Output: Sorting Cert.Visit*

Obs	ID	Visit	SysBP	DiasBP	Weight	Date
1	A001	1	140	85	195	11/05/2009
2	A001	2	138	90	198	10/13/2009
3	A001	3	145	95	200	07/04/2009
4	A002	1	121	75	168	04/14/2009
5	A003	1	118	68	125	08/12/2009
6	A003	2	112	65	123	08/21/2009
7	A004	1	143	86	204	03/30/2009
8	A005	1	132	76	174	02/27/2009
9	A005	2	132	78	175	07/11/2009
10	A005	3	134	78	176	04/16/2009
11	A008	1	126	80	182	05/22/2009

You can then submit this DATA step to create Work.Merged by merging Cert.Demog and Cert.Visit according to values of the variable ID.

```
data work.merged;
  merge cert.demog cert.visit;
  by id;
run;
proc print data=work.merged;
run;
```

Note: All observations, including unmatched observations and observations that have missing data, are written to the output data set.

Figure 10.9 *HTML Output: Match-Merging Output*

Obs	ID	Age	Sex	Date	Visit	SysBP	DiasBP	Weight
1	A001	21	M	11/05/2009	1	140	85	195
2	A001	21	M	10/13/2009	2	138	90	198
3	A001	21	M	07/04/2009	3	145	95	200
4	A002	32	M	04/14/2009	1	121	75	168
5	A003	24	F	08/12/2009	1	118	68	125
6	A003	24	F	08/21/2009	2	112	65	123
7	A004	.		03/30/2009	1	143	86	204
8	A005	44	F	02/27/2009	1	132	76	174
9	A005	44	F	07/11/2009	2	132	78	175
10	A005	44	F	04/16/2009	3	134	78	176
11	A007	39	M	01/11/2005	.	.	.	.
12	A008	.		05/22/2009	1	126	80	182

Example: Merge in Descending Order

The example above illustrates merging two data sets that are sorted in ascending order of the BY variable ID. To sort the data sets in descending order and then merge them, you can submit the following program.

```
proc sort data=cert.demog;
  by descending id;
run;
proc sort data=cert.visit;
  by descending id;
run;
data work.merged;
  merge cert.demog cert.visit;
  by descending id;
run;
proc print data=work.merged;
run;
```

Note: Specify the DESCENDING option in the BY statements in both the PROC SORT steps and the DATA step. If you omit the DESCENDING option in the DATA step, you generate error messages about improperly sorted BY variables.

Figure 10.10 *HTML Output: Merge in Descending Order*

Obs	ID	Age	Sex	Date	Visit	SysBP	DiasBP	Weight
1	A008	.		05/22/2009	1	126	80	182
2	A007	39	M	01/11/2005	.	.	.	.
3	A005	44	F	02/27/2009	1	132	76	174
4	A005	44	F	07/11/2009	2	132	78	175
5	A005	44	F	04/16/2009	3	134	78	176
6	A004	.		03/30/2009	1	143	86	204
7	A003	24	F	08/12/2009	1	118	68	125
8	A003	24	F	08/21/2009	2	112	65	123
9	A002	32	M	04/14/2009	1	121	75	168
10	A001	21	M	11/05/2009	1	140	85	195
11	A001	21	M	10/13/2009	2	138	90	198
12	A001	21	M	07/04/2009	3	145	95	200

Match-Merge Processing

The Basics of Match-Merge Processing

The match-merging examples in this book are straightforward. However, match-merging can be more complex, depending on your data and on the output data set that you want to create. To predict the results of match-merges correctly, you need to understand how the DATA step performs match-merges.

When you submit a DATA step, it is processed in two phases:

- the compilation phase, in which SAS checks the syntax of the SAS statements and compiles them (translates them into machine code). During this phase, SAS also sets up descriptor information for the output data set and creates the PDV.
- the execution phase in which the DATA step reads data and executes any subsequent programming statements. When the DATA step executes, data values are read into the appropriate variables in the PDV. From here, the variables are written to the output data set as a single observation.

The Compilation Phase: Setting Up a New Data Set

To prepare to merge data sets, SAS does the following:

- reads the descriptor portions of the data sets that are listed in the MERGE statement
- reads the rest of the DATA step program
- creates the PDV for the merged data set
- assigns a tracking pointer to each data set that is listed in the MERGE statement

If there are variables with the same name in more than one data set, then the variable from the first data set (the order in which the data sets are listed in the MERGE statement) determines the length of the variable.

Figure 10.11 *The Compilation Phase: Setting Up the New Data Set*

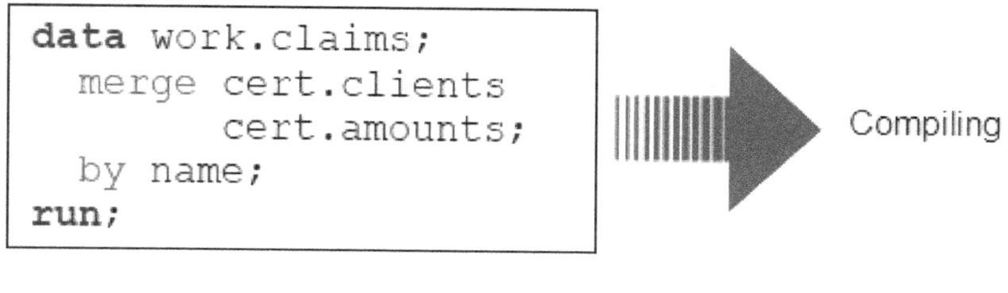

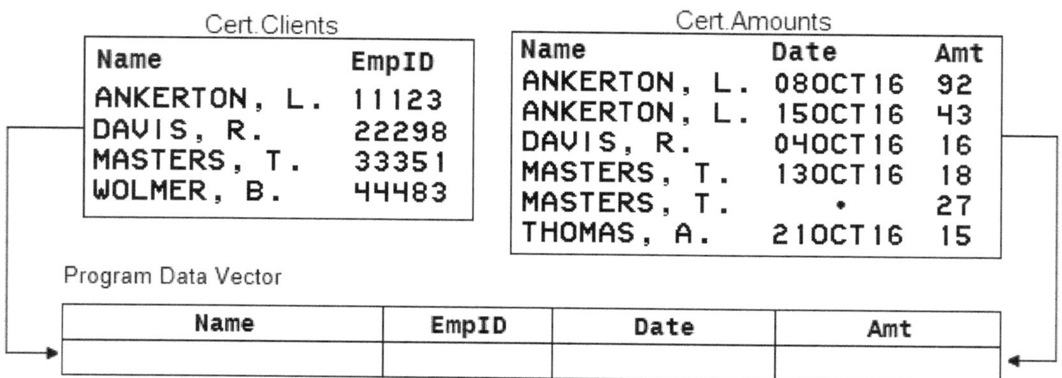

Cert.Clients

Name	EmpID
ANKERTON, L.	11123
DAVIS, R.	22298
MASTERS, T.	33351
WOLMER, B.	44483

Cert.Amounts

Name	Date	Amt
ANKERTON, L.	08OCT16	92
ANKERTON, L.	15OCT16	43
DAVIS, R.	04OCT16	16
MASTERS, T.	13OCT16	18
MASTERS, T.	•	27
THOMAS, A.	21OCT16	15

Program Data Vector

Name	EmpID	Date	Amt

After reading the descriptor portions of the data sets Clients and Amounts, SAS does the following:

1. creates a PDV for the new Claims data set. The PDV contains all variables from the two data sets. Note that although Name appears in both input data sets, it appears in the PDV only once.
2. assigns tracking pointers to Clients and Amounts.

The Execution Phase: Match-Merging Observations

After compiling the DATA step, SAS sequentially match-merges observations by moving the pointers down each observation of each data set and checking to see whether the BY values match.

- If the BY values match, the observations are read into the PDV in the order in which the data sets appear in the MERGE statement. Values of any same-named variable are overwritten by values of the same-named variable in subsequent observations. SAS writes the combined observation to the new data set and retains the values in the PDV until the BY value changes in all the data sets.

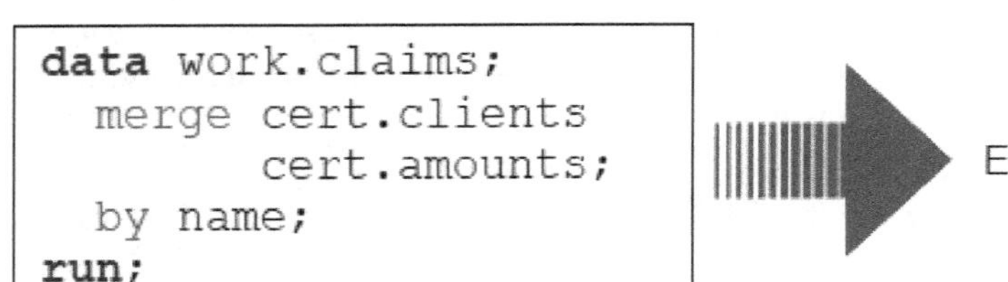

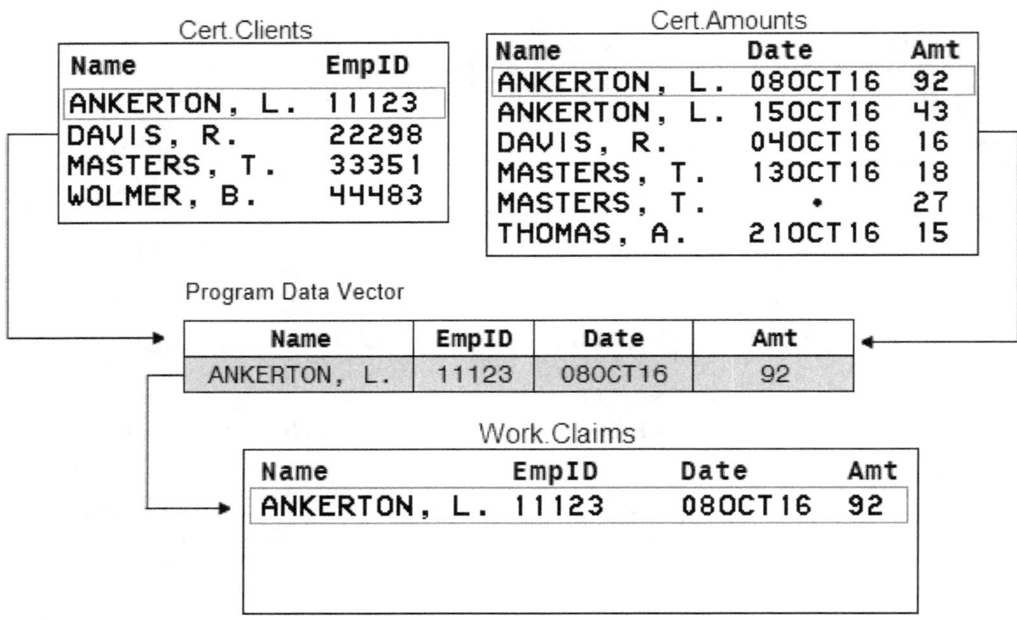

Cert.Clients

Name	EmpID
ANKERTON, L.	11123
DAVIS, R.	22298
MASTERS, T.	33351
WOLMER, B.	44483

Cert.Amounts

Name	Date	Amt
ANKERTON, L.	08OCT16	92
ANKERTON, L.	15OCT16	43
DAVIS, R.	04OCT16	16
MASTERS, T.	13OCT16	18
MASTERS, T.	•	27
THOMAS, A.	21OCT16	15

Program Data Vector

Name	EmpID	Date	Amt
ANKERTON, L.	11123	08OCT16	92

Work.Claims

Name	EmpID	Date	Amt
ANKERTON, L.	11123	08OCT16	92

- If the BY values do not match, SAS determines which BY value comes first and reads the observation that contains this value into the PDV. Then the contents of the PDV are written.

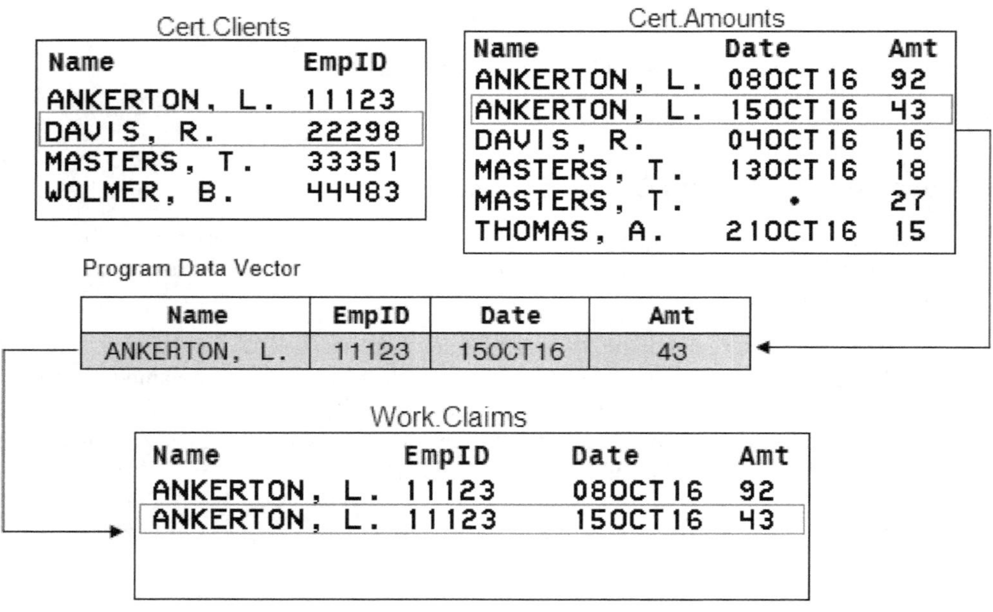

Cert.Clients

Name	EmpID
ANKERTON, L.	11123
DAVIS, R.	22298
MASTERS, T.	33351
WOLMER, B.	44483

Cert.Amounts

Name	Date	Amt
ANKERTON, L.	08OCT16	92
ANKERTON, L.	15OCT16	43
DAVIS, R.	04OCT16	16
MASTERS, T.	13OCT16	18
MASTERS, T.	•	27
THOMAS, A.	21OCT16	15

Program Data Vector

Name	EmpID	Date	Amt
ANKERTON, L.	11123	15OCT16	43

Work.Claims

Name	EmpID	Date	Amt
ANKERTON, L.	11123	08OCT16	92
ANKERTON, L.	11123	15OCT16	43

- When the BY value changes in all the input data sets, the PDV is initialized to missing.

Cert.Clients

Name	EmpID
ANKERTON, L.	11123
DAVIS, R.	22298
MASTERS, T.	33351
WOLMER, B.	44483

Cert.Amounts

Name	Date	Amt
ANKERTON. L.	08OCT16	92
ANKERTON. L.	15OCT16	43
DAVIS, R.	04OCT16	16
MASTERS, T.	13OCT16	18
MASTERS, T.	•	27
THOMAS, A.	21OCT16	15

Program Data Vector

Name	EmpID	Date	Amt
		•	

Work.Claims

Name	EmpID	Date	Amt
ANKERTON. L.	11123	08OCT16	92
ANKERTON. L.	11123	15OCT16	43

The DATA step merge continues to process every observation in each data set until it has processed all observations in all data sets.

Handling Unmatched Observations and Missing Values

By default, all observations that are read into the PDV, including observations that have missing data and no matching BY values, are written to the output data set. If you specify a subsetting IF statement to select observations, then only those that meet the IF condition are written.

- If an observation contains missing values for a variable, then the observation in the output data set contains the missing values as well. Observations that have missing values for the BY variable appear at the top of the output data set because missing values sort first in ascending order.

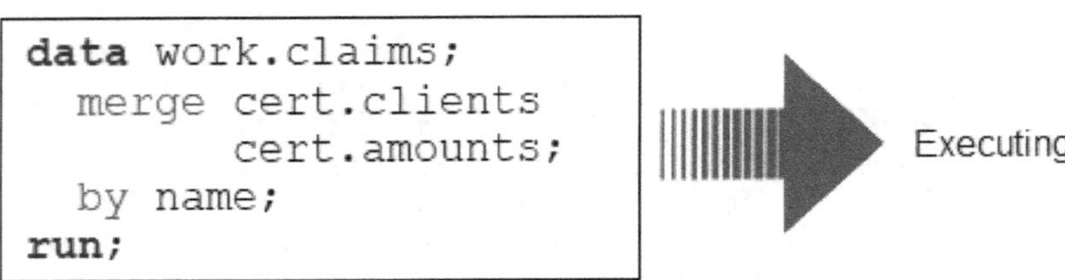

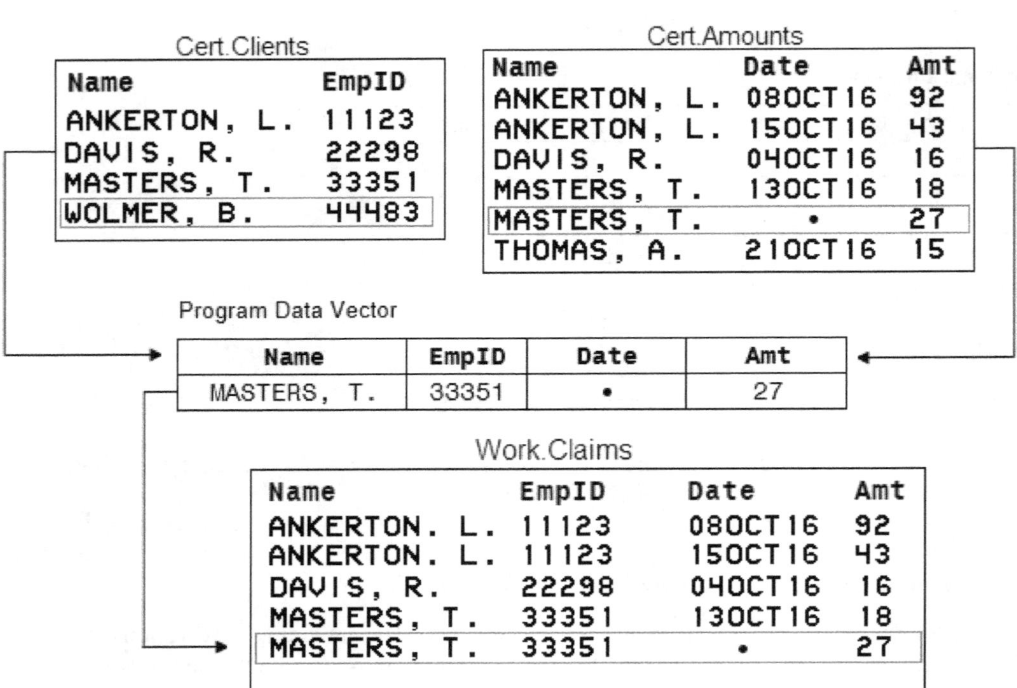

- If an input data set does not have a matching BY value, then the observation in the output data set contains missing values for the variables that are unique to that input data set.

Cert.Clients

Name	EmpID
ANKERTON, L.	11123
DAVIS, R.	22298
MASTERS, T.	33351
WOLMER, B.	44483

Cert.Amounts

Name	Date	Amt
ANKERTON, L.	08OCT16	92
ANKERTON, L.	15OCT16	43
DAVIS, R.	04OCT16	16
MASTERS, T.	13OCT16	18
MASTERS, T.	•	27
THOMAS, A.	21OCT16	15

Program Data Vector

Name	EmpID	Date	Amt
THOMAS, A		21OCT16	15

Work.Claims

Name	EmpID	Date	Amt
ANKERTON. L.	11123	08OCT16	92
ANKERTON. L.	11123	15OCT16	43
DAVIS, R.	22298	04OCT16	16
MASTERS, T.	33351	13OCT16	18
MASTERS, T.	33351	•	27
THOMAS, A.	•	21OCT16	15

- The last observation in Cert.Clients would be added after the last observation in Cert.Amounts.

Cert.Clients

Name	EmpID
ANKERTON, L.	11123
DAVIS, R.	22298
MASTERS, T.	33351
WOLMER, B.	44483

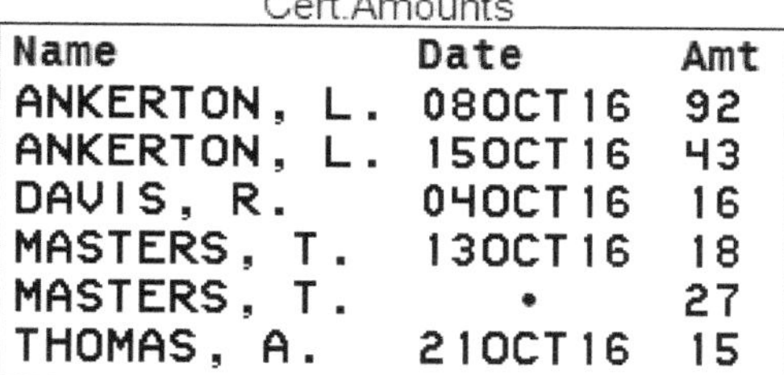

Cert.Amounts

Name	Date	Amt
ANKERTON, L.	08OCT16	92
ANKERTON, L.	15OCT16	43
DAVIS, R.	04OCT16	16
MASTERS, T.	13OCT16	18
MASTERS, T.	•	27
THOMAS, A.	21OCT16	15

Program Data Vector

Name	EmpID	Date	Amt
WOLMER, B.	44483	•	•

Work.Claims

Name	EmpID	Date	Amt
ANKERTON. L.	11123	08OCT16	92
ANKERTON. L.	11123	15OCT16	43
DAVIS, R.	22298	04OCT16	16
MASTERS, T.	33351	13OCT16	18
MASTERS, T.	33351	•	27
THOMAS, A.	•	21OCT16	15
WOLMER, B.	44483	•	•

The PROC PRINT output is displayed below. Use the FORMAT statement for the date variable in the PRINT procedure. To learn how to apply a format, see "Applying SAS Formats and Informats" on page 225.

```
proc print data=work.claims noobs;
  format date date9.;
```

```
run;
```

Figure 10.12 *PROC PRINT Output of Merged Data*

Obs	Name	EmpID	Date	Amount
1	ANKERTON, L.	11123	08OCT2016	92
2	ANKERTON, L.	11123	15OCT2016	43
3	DAVIS, R.	22298	04OCT2016	16
4	MASTERS, T.	33351	13OCT2016	18
5	MASTERS, T.	33351	.	27
6	THOMAS, A.	.	21OCT2016	15
7	WOLMER, B.	44483	.	.

Renaming Variables

The Basics of Renaming Variables

DATA step match-merging overwrites values of the like-named variable in the first data set in which it appears with values of the like-named variable in subsequent data sets.

Consider Cert.Patdat, which contains the variable Date (date of birth), and Cert.Visit, which also contains Date (date of the clinic visit in 2009). The DATA step below overwrites the date of birth with the date of the clinic visit.

```
data work.merged;
  merge cert.patdat cert.visit;
  by id;
run;
proc print data=work.merged;
run;
```

The following output shows the effects of overwriting the values of a variable in the Work.Merged data set. In most observations, the date is now the date of the clinic visit. In observation 11, the date is still the birthdate because Cert.Visit did not contain a matching ID value and did not contribute to the observation.

Figure 10.13 *Renaming Variables*

Obs	ID	Age	Sex	Date	Visit	SysBP	DiasBP	Weight
1	A001	21	M	11/05/2009	1	140	85	195
2	A001	21	M	10/13/2009	2	138	90	198
3	A001	21	M	07/04/2009	3	145	95	200
4	A002	32	M	04/14/2009	1	121	75	168
5	A003	24	F	08/12/2009	1	118	68	125
6	A003	24	F	08/21/2009	2	112	65	123
7	A004	28	M	03/30/2009	1	143	86	204
8	A005	44	F	02/27/2009	1	132	76	174
9	A005	44	F	07/11/2009	2	132	78	175
10	A005	44	F	04/16/2009	3	134	78	176
11	A007	39	M	07/10/1979	.	.	.	.
12	A008	30	F	05/22/2009	1	126	80	182

RENAME Statement Syntax

To prevent overwriting, you can rename variables by using the RENAME= data set option in the MERGE statement.

Syntax, RENAME= data set option:

(RENAME=(*old-variable-name*=*new-variable-name***))**

- the RENAME= option, in parentheses, follows the name of each data set that contains one or more variables to be renamed
- *old-variable-name* specifies the variable to be renamed.
- *new-variable-name* specifies the new name for the variable.

TIP Use RENAME= to rename variables in the SET statement or in the output data set that is specified in the DATA statement.

Example: Renaming Variables

In the following example, the RENAME= option renames the variable Date in Cert.Patdat to BirthDate, and it renames the variable Date in Cert.Visit to VisitDate.

```
data work.merged;
  merge cert.patdat (rename=(date=BirthDate))
    cert.visit (rename=(date=VisitDate));
    by id;
run;
proc print data=work.merged;
run;
```

The following output shows the effect of the RENAME= option.

Figure 10.14 *Output for RENAME= Option*

Obs	ID	Age	Sex	BirthDate	Visit	SysBP	DiasBP	Weight	VisitDate
1	A001	21	M	08/17/1997	1	140	85	195	11/05/2009
2	A001	21	M	08/17/1997	2	138	90	198	10/13/2009
3	A001	21	M	08/17/1997	3	145	95	200	07/04/2009
4	A002	32	M	02/18/1986	1	121	75	168	04/14/2009
5	A003	24	F	06/07/1994	1	118	68	125	08/12/2009
6	A003	24	F	06/07/1994	2	112	65	123	08/21/2009
7	A004	28	M	01/27/1990	1	143	86	204	03/30/2009
8	A005	44	F	04/24/1974	1	132	76	174	02/27/2009
9	A005	44	F	04/24/1974	2	132	78	175	07/11/2009
10	A005	44	F	04/24/1974	3	134	78	176	04/16/2009
11	A007	39	M	07/10/1979	.	.	.	.	.
12	A008	30	F	09/16/1988	1	126	80	182	05/22/2009

Excluding Unmatched Observations

Overview

By default, DATA step match-merging combines all observations in all input data sets.

To exclude unmatched observations from your output data set, use the following in your DATA step:

- Use the IN= data set option to create and name a variable that indicates whether the data set contributed data to the current observation.
- Use the subsetting IF statement to check the IN= values and write to the merged data set only matching observations

Identifying Observation in Both Data Sets

To match-merge the data sets Cert.Patdat and Cert.Visit and select only observations that appear in both data sets, use IN= to create two temporary variables, Inpat and Invisit. The IN= variable is a temporary variable that is available to program statements during the DATA step, but it is not included in the output SAS data set.

Syntax, IN= data set option:

(IN= *variable***)**

- The IN= option, in parentheses, follows the data set name.
- *variable* names the variable to be created.

Within the DATA step, the value of the variable is 1 if the data set contributed data to the current observation. Otherwise, its value is 0.

The DATA step that contains the IN= options appears below. The first IN= creates the temporary variable, Inpat, which is set to 1 when an observation from Cert.Patdat contributes to the current observation. Otherwise, it is set to 0. Likewise, the value of Invisit depends on whether Cert.Visit contributes to an observation or not.

```
data work.merged;
  merge cert.patdat(in=inpat)
    cert.visit(in=invisit
    rename=(date=BirthDate));
   by id;
run;
```

TIP To specify multiple data set options for a given data set, enclose the options in a single set of parentheses.

Selecting Matching Observations

To select only observations that appear in both Cert.Patdat and Cert.Visit, specify a subsetting IF statement in the DATA step.

The subsetting IF statement checks the values of Inpat and Invisit and continues processing only those observations that meet the condition of the expression. The condition is that both Cert.Patdat and Cert.Visit contribute to the observation. If the condition is met, the new observation is written to Work.Merged. Otherwise, the observation is deleted.

```
data work.merged;
  merge cert.patdat(in=inpat
    rename=(date=BirthDate))
    cert.visit(in=invisit
    rename=(date=VisitDate));
   by id;
   if inpat=1 and invisit=1;
run;
proc print data=work.merged;
run;
```

In previous examples, Work.Merged contained 12 observations. In the output below, notice that only 10 observations met the condition in the IF expression.

Figure 10.15 Selecting Matching Observations

Obs	ID	Age	Sex	BirthDate	Visit	SysBP	DiasBP	Weight	VisitDate
1	A001	21	M	08/17/1997	1	140	85	195	11/05/2009
2	A001	21	M	08/17/1997	2	138	90	198	10/13/2009
3	A001	21	M	08/17/1997	3	145	95	200	07/04/2009
4	A002	32	M	02/18/1986	1	121	75	168	04/14/2009
5	A003	24	F	06/07/1994	1	118	68	125	08/12/2009
6	A003	24	F	06/07/1994	2	112	65	123	08/21/2009
7	A004	28	M	01/27/1990	1	143	86	204	03/30/2009
8	A005	44	F	04/24/1974	1	132	76	174	02/27/2009
9	A005	44	F	04/24/1974	2	132	78	175	07/11/2009
10	A005	44	F	04/24/1974	3	134	78	176	04/16/2009
11	A008	30	F	09/16/1988	1	126	80	182	05/22/2009

SAS evaluates the expression within an IF statement to produce a result that is either nonzero, zero, or missing. A nonzero and nonmissing result causes the expression to be true; a zero or missing result causes the expression to be false.

It is possible to specify the subsetting IF statement from the previous example in either of the following ways. The first IF statement checks specifically for a value of 1. The second IF statement checks for a value that is neither missing nor 0 (which for IN= variables is always 1).

```
if inpat=1 and invisit=1;
```

```
if inpat and invisit;
```

Chapter Quiz

Select the best answer for each question. Check your answers using the answer key in the appendix.

1. Which program combines Work.One and Work.Two to produce Work.Three?

Work.One

VarX	VarY
1	Groucho
3	Harpo
5	Karl

\+

Work.Two

VarX	VarZ
2	Chico
4	Zeppo

=

Work.Three

VarX	VarY	VarZ
2	Groucho	Chico
4	Harpo	Zeppo

a.
```
data work.three;
   set work.one;
   set work.two;
run;
```

b.
```
data work.three;
   set work.one work.two;
run;
```

c.
```
data work.three;
   set work.one work.two;
   by varx;
run;
```

d.
```
data work.three;
   merge work.one work.two;
   by varx;
run;
```

2. Which program combines Cert.Props1 and Cert.Props2 to produce Work.Props3?

Cert.Props1

Actor	Prop
Curly	Anvil
Larry	Ladder
Moe	Poker

\+

Cert.Props2

Actor	Prop
Curly	Ladder
Moe	Pliers

=

Work.Props3

Actor	Prop
Curly	Anvil
Larry	Ladder
Moe	Poker
Curly	Ladder
Moe	Pliers

a.
```
data work.props3;
   set cert.props1;
   set cert.props2;
run;
```

b.
```
data work.props3;
   set cert.props1 cert.props2;
run;
```

c.
```
data work.props3;
   set cert.props1 cert.props2;
   by actor;
run;
```

d.
```
data work.props3;
   merge cert.props1 cert.props2;
   by actor;
run;
```

3. If you submit the following program, which new data set is created?

Work.Dataone

Career	Supervis	Finance
72	26	9
63	76	7
96	31	7
96	98	6
84	94	6

Work.Datatwo

Variety	Feedback	Autonomy
10	11	70
85	22	93
83	63	73
82	75	97
36	77	97

```
data work.jobsatis;
   set work.dataone work.datatwo;
run;
proc print data=work.jobsatis noobs;
run;
```

a.

Career	Supervis	Finance	Variety	Feedback	Autonomy
72	26	9	.	.	.
63	76	7	.	.	.
96	31	7	.	.	.
96	98	6	.	.	.
84	94	6	.	.	.
.	.	.	10	11	70
.	.	.	85	22	93
.	.	.	83	63	73
.	.	.	82	75	97
.	.	.	36	77	97

b.

Career	Supervis	Finance	Variety	Feedback	Autonomy
72	26	9	10	11	70
63	76	7	85	22	93
96	31	7	83	63	73
96	98	6	82	75	97
84	94	6	36	77	97

c.

Career	Supervis	Finance
72	26	9
63	76	7
96	31	7
96	98	6
84	94	6
10	11	70
85	22	93
83	63	73
82	75	97
36	77	97

d. none of the above

4. If you concatenate the data sets below in the order shown, what is the value of Sale in observation 2 of the new data set?

Work.Reps

ID	Name
1	Nay Rong
2	Kelly Windsor
3	Julio Meraz
4	Richard Krabill

Work.Close

ID	Sale
1	$28,000
2	$30,000
2	$40,000
3	$15,000
3	$20,000
3	$25,000
4	$35,000

Work.Bonus

ID	Bonus
1	$2,000
2	$4,000
3	$3,000
4	$2,500

a. missing

b. $30,000

c. $40,000

d. You cannot concatenate these data sets.

5. What happens if you merge the following data sets by the variable SSN?

1st

SSN	Age
029-46-9261	39
074-53-9892	34
228-88-9649	32
442-21-8075	12
446-93-2122	36
776-84-5391	28
929-75-0218	27

2nd

SSN	Age	Date
029-46-9261	37	02/15/95
074-53-9892	32	05/22/97
228-88-9649	30	03/04/96
442-21-8075	10	11/22/95
446-93-2122	34	07/08/96
776-84-5391	26	12/15/96
929-75-0218	25	04/30/97

a. The values of Age in the data set 1st overwrite the values of Age in the data set 2nd.

b. The values of Age in the data set 2nd overwrite the values of Age in the data set 1st.

c. The DATA step fails because the two data sets contain same-named variables that have different values.

d. The values of Age in the data set 2nd are set to missing.

6. Suppose you merge data sets Cert.Set1 and Cert.Set2 below:

Cert.Set1

ID	Sex	Age
1128	F	48
1274	F	50
1387	F	57
2304	F	16
2486	F	63
4425	F	48
4759	F	60
5438	F	42
6488	F	59
9012	F	39
9125	F	56

Cert.Set2

ID	Height	Weight
1129	61	137
1387	64	142
2304	61	102
5438	62	168
6488	64	154
9012	63	157
9125	64	159

Which output does the following program create?

```
data work.merged;
   merge cert.set1(in=in1) cert.set2(in=in2);
   by id;
   if in1 and in2;
run;
proc print data=work.merged;
run;
```

a.

Obs	ID	Sex	Age	Height	Weight
1	1387	F	57	64	142
2	2304	F	16	61	102
3	5438	F	42	62	168
4	6488	F	59	64	154
5	9012	F	39	63	157
6	9125	F	56	64	159

b.

Obs	ID	Sex	Age	Height	Weight
1	1128	F	48	.	.
2	1129		.	61	137
3	1274	F	50	.	.
4	1387	F	57	.	.
5	1387		.	64	142
6	2304	F	16	.	.
7	2304		.	61	102
8	2486	F	63	.	.
9	4425	F	48	.	.
10	4759	F	60	.	.
11	5438	F	42	.	.
12	5438		.	62	168
13	6488	F	59	.	.
14	6488		.	64	154
15	9012	F	39	.	.
16	9012		.	63	157
17	9125	F	56	.	.
18	9125		.	64	159

c.

Obs	ID	Sex	Age	Height	Weight
1	1129	F	48	61	137
2	1387	F	50	64	142
3	2304	F	57	61	102
4	5438	F	16	62	168
5	6488	F	63	64	154
6	9012	F	48	63	157
7	9125	F	60	64	159

d. none of the above

7. The data sets Cert.Spring and Cert.Sum both contain a variable named Blue. How do you prevent the values of the variable Blue from being overwritten when you merge the two data sets?

a.
```
data work.merged;
   merge cert.spring(in=blue)
         cert.summer;
   by fabric;
run;
```

b.
```
data work.merged;
   merge cert.spring(out=blue)
         cert.summer;
```

```
   by fabric;
run;
```

c.
```
data work.merged;
   merge cert.spring(blue=navy)
         cert.summer;
   by fabric;
run;
```

d.
```
data work.merged;
   merge cert.spring(rename=(blue=navy))
         cert.summer;
   by fabric;
run;
```

8. What happens if you submit the following program to merge Cert.Donors1 and Cert.Donors2, shown below?

```
data work.merged;
   merge cert.donors1 cert.donors2;
   by id;
run;
```

Cert.Donors1

ID	Type	Units
2304	O	16
1129	A	48
1129	A	50
1129	A	57
2486	B	63

Cert.Donors2

ID	Code	Units
6488	65	27
1129	63	32
5438	62	39
2304	61	45
1387	64	67

a. The merged data set contains some missing values because not all observations have matching observations in the other data set.

b. The merged data set contains eight observations.

c. The DATA step produces errors.

d. Values for Units in Cert.Donors2 overwrite values of Units in Cert.Donors1.

9. If you merge Cert.Staff1 and Cert.Staff2 below by ID, how many observations does the new data set contain?

Cert.Staff1

ID	Name	Dept	Project
000	Miguel	A12	Document
111	Fred	B45	Survey
222	Diane	B45	Document
888	Monique	A12	Document
999	Vien	D03	Survey

Cert.Staff2

ID	Name	Hours
111	Fred	35
222	Diana	40
777	Steve	0
888	Monique	37

a. 4

b. 5

c. 6

d. 9

10. If you merge data sets Work.Reps, Work.Close, and Work.Bonus by ID, what is the value of Bonus in the third observation in the new data set?

Work.Reps

ID	Name
1	Nay Rong
2	Kelly Windsor
3	Julio Meraz
4	Richard Krabill

Work.Close

ID	Sale
1	$28,000
2	$30,000
2	$40,000
3	$15,000
3	$20,000
3	$25,000
4	$35,000

Work.Bonus

ID	Bonus
1	$2,000
2	$4,000
3	$3,000
4	$2,500

a. $4,000

b. $3,000

c. missing

d. You cannot tell from the information given.

Chapter 11
Processing Data with DO Loops

The Basics of DO Loops

The Basics of Using Grouping Statements and DO Groups

You can execute a group of statements as a unit by using DO groups.

To construct a DO group, you use the DO and END statements along with other SAS statements.

Syntax, DO group:

DO;

SAS statements

END;

- The DO statement begins DO-group processing.
- *SAS statements* between the DO and END statements are called a DO group and are executed as a unit.
- The END statement terminates DO-group processing.

Tip: You can nest DO statements within DO groups.

You can use DO groups in IF-THEN/ELSE statements and SELECT groups to execute many statements as part of the conditional action.

Example: DO and END Statements

In this simple DO group, the statements between DO and END are performed only when TotalTime is greater than 800. If TotalTime is less than or equal to 800, statements in the DO group are not executed, and the program continues with the assignment statement that follows the appropriate ELSE statement.

```
data work.stresstest;
  set cert.tests;
  TotalTime=(timemin*60)+timesec;
  retain SumSec 5400;
  sumsec+totaltime;
  length TestLength $6 Message $20;
  if totaltime>800 then
    do;
        TestLength='Long';
        message='Run blood panel';
    end;
    else if 750<=totaltime<=800 then TestLength='Normal';
    else if totaltime<750 then TestLength='Short';
run;
proc print data=work.stresstest;
run;
```

Output 11.1 *PROC PRINT Output Work.StressTest (partial output)*

Obs	ID	Name	TimeSec	Tolerance	TotalTime	SumSec	TestLength	Message
1	2458	Murray, W	38	D	758	6158	Normal	
			. . . *more observations.* . .					
7	2552	Reberson, P	41	D	941	10411	Long	Run blood panel
			. . . *more observations.* . .					
10	2568	Eberhardt, S	49	N	1009	12835	Long	Run blood panel
11	2571	Nunnelly, A	2	I	902	13737	Long	Run blood panel
			. . . *more observations.* . .					
13	2574	Peterson, V	9	D	849	15317	Long	Run blood panel
			. . . *more observations.* . .					
15	2578	Cameron, L	27	I	867	16870	Long	Run blood panel
			. . . *more observations.* . .					
17	2584	Takahashi, Y	7	D	967	18636	Long	Run blood panel
18	2586	Derber, B	35	N	1055	19691	Long	Run blood panel
19	2588	Ivan, H	41	N	941	20632	Long	Run blood panel
20	2589	Wilcox, E	57	I	897	21529	Long	Run blood panel

DO Statement, Iterative Syntax

The *iterative DO statement* executes statements between the DO and END statements repetitively, based on the value of an index variable.

Syntax, DO statement, iterative:

DO *index-variable=specification-1* <, *...specification-n*>;

...more SAS statements...

END;

- *index-variable* names a variable whose value governs execution of the DO group.

  CAUTION:
  Avoid changing the index variable within the DO group. If you modify the index variable within the iterative DO group, you might cause infinite looping.

  Note: Unless you specify to drop it, the index variable is included in the data set that is being created.

- *specification* denotes an expression or series of expressions such as these:

start <TO *stop*> <BY *increment*> <WHILE(*expression*) | UNTIL(*expression*)>

The DO group is executed first with *index-variable* equal to *start*. The value of *start* is evaluated before the first execution of the loop.

- *start* specifies the initial value of the index variable.
- TO *stop* specifies the ending value of the index variable.

  TIP Any changes to stop made within the DO group do not affect the number of iterations. To stop iteration of a loop before it finishes processing, change the value of *index-variable*, or use a LEAVE statement to go to a statement outside the loop.

- BY *increment* specifies a positive or negative number (or an expression that yields a number) to control the incrementing of *index-variable*.

  The value of *increment* is evaluated before the execution of the loop. If no increment is specified, the index variable is increased by 1. When *increment* is positive, *start* must be the lower bound, and *stop*, if present, must be the upper bound for the loop. If *increment* is negative, *start* must be the upper bound, and *stop*, if present, must be the lower bound for the loop.

- WHILE(*expression*) | UNTIL(*expression*) evaluates, either before or after execution of the DO group, any SAS expression that you specify. Enclose the expression in parentheses.

  A WHILE expression is evaluated before each execution of the loop, so that the statements inside the group are executed repetitively while the expression is true. An UNTIL expression is evaluated after each execution of the loop, so that the statements inside the group are executed repetitively until the expression is true.

Note: The order of the optional TO and BY clauses can be reversed.

Note: When you use more than one specification, each one is evaluated before its execution.

Example: Processing Iterative DO Loops

DO loops process a group of statements repeatedly rather than once. This can greatly reduce the number of statements required for a repetitive calculation. For example, these 12 sum statements compute a company's annual earnings from investments. Notice that all 12 statements are identical.

```
data work.earn (drop=month);
  set cert.master;
```

```
    Earned=0;
    earned+(amount+earned)*(rate/12);
    earned+(amount+earned)*(rate/12);
    earned+(amount+earned)*(rate/12);
    earned+(amount+earned)*(rate/12);
    earned+(amount+earned)*(rate/12);
    earned+(amount+earned)*(rate/12);
    earned+(amount+earned)*(rate/12);
    earned+(amount+earned)*(rate/12);
    earned+(amount+earned)*(rate/12);
    earned+(amount+earned)*(rate/12);
    earned+(amount+earned)*(rate/12);
    earned+(amount+earned)*(rate/12);
  run;
```

In this program, each sum statement accumulates the calculated interest that is earned for an investment for one month. The variable Earned is created in the DATA step to store the earned interest. The investment is compounded monthly, meaning that the value of the earned interest is cumulative.

By contrast, a DO loop enables you to achieve the same results with fewer statements. In this case, the sum statement executes 12 times within the DO loop during each iteration of the DATA step. In this example, the DO group Month is the index variable, 1 is the start-variable, and 12 is the stop variable.

```
data work.earnings (drop=month);
  set cert.master;
  Earned=0;
  do month=1 to 12;
    earned+(amount+earned)*(rate/12);
  end;
  Balance=Amount+Earned;
run;
proc print data=work.earnings;
run;
```

Output 11.2 *PROC PRINT Output of Work.Earnings*

Obs	Account	Amount	Rate	Earned	Balance
1	1025	9600	0.07	693.985	10293.98
2	1026	1500	0.05	76.743	1576.74
3	1027	2500	0.05	127.905	2627.90
4	1028	5000	0.08	414.998	5415.00
5	1029	6500	0.07	469.886	6969.89
6	1030	5000	0.07	361.450	5361.45
7	1031	4000	0.06	246.711	4246.71
8	1032	3000	0.01	30.138	3030.14
9	1033	2500	0.04	101.854	2601.85
10	1034	3500	0.04	142.595	3642.60
11	1035	1000	0.02	20.184	1020.18

Constructing DO Loops

DO Loop Execution

Here is how the DO loop executes in the DATA step. This example sums the interest that was earned each month for a one-year investment.

```
data work.earnings;
  Amount=1000;
  Rate=0.75/12;
  do month=1 to 12;
    Earned+(amount+earned)*rate;
  end;
run;
```

This DATA step does not read data from an external source. When submitted, it compiles and then executes only once to generate data. During compilation, the program data vector is created for the Work.Earnings data set.

Program Data Vector

_N_	Amount	Rate	month	Earned
•	•	•	•	•

When the DATA step executes, the values of Amount and Rate are assigned.

Program Data Vector

_N_	Amount	Rate	month	Earned
1	1000	0.0625	•	0

Next, the DO loop executes. During each execution of the DO loop, the value of Earned is calculated and is added to its previous value. Then the value of Month is incremented. On the 12th execution of the DO loop, the value of Month is incremented to 12 and the value of Earned is 1069.839.

Program Data Vector

_N_	Amount	Rate	month	Earned
1	1000	0.0625	12	1069.83

After the 12th execution of the DO loop, the value of Month is incremented to 13. Because 13 exceeds the stop value of the iterative DO statement, the DO loop stops executing, and processing continues to the next DATA step statement. The end of the DATA step is reached, the values are written to the Work.Earnings data set, and in this example, the DATA step ends. Only one observation is written to the data set.

Figure 11.1 *SAS Data Set Work.Earnings*

	Amount	Rate	month	Earned
1	1000	0.0625	13	1069.8899918

Notice that the index variable Month is also stored in the data set. In most cases, the index variable is needed only for processing the DO loop and can be dropped from the data set.

Using Explicit OUTPUT Statements

To create an observation for each iteration of the DO loop, place an OUTPUT statement inside the loop. By default, every DATA step contains an implicit OUTPUT statement at the end of the step. But placing an explicit OUTPUT statement in a DATA step overrides automatic output, causing SAS to add an observation to the data set only when the explicit OUTPUT statement is executed.

The previous example created one observation because it used automatic output at the end of the DATA step. In the following example, the OUTPUT statement overrides automatic output, so the DATA step writes 20 observations.

```
data work.earn;
  Value=2000;
  do Year=1 to 20;
    Interest=value*.075;
    value+interest;
    output;
  end;
run;
proc print data=work.earn;
run;
```

Figure 11.2 *HTML Output: OUTPUT Statement inside Each DO Loop (partial output)*

Obs	Value	Interest
1	2150.00	150.000
2	2311.25	161.250
3	2484.59	173.344
4	2670.94	186.345
5	2871.26	200.320
...more observations...		
15	5917.75	412.867
16	6361.59	443.832
17	6838.71	477.119
18	7351.61	512.903
19	7902.98	551.371
20	8495.70	592.723

Decrementing DO Loops

You can decrement a DO loop's index variable by specifying a negative value for the BY clause. For example, the specification in this iterative DO statement decreases the index variable by **1**, resulting in values of **5**, **4**, **3**, **2**, and **1**. The following brief examples show you the syntax.

```
DO index-variable=5 to 1 by -1;
   ...more SAS statements...
END;
```

When you use a negative BY clause value, the start value must always be greater than the stop value in order to decrease the index variable during each iteration.

```
DO index-variable=5 to 1 by -1;
   ...more SAS statements...
END;
```

Specifying a Series of Items

You can also specify how many times a DO loop executes by listing items in a series.

Syntax, DO loop with a variable list:

DO *index-variable=value1, value2, value3...* ;

...more SAS statements...

END;

values can be character or numeric.

When the DO loop executes, it executes once for each item in the series. The index variable equals the value of the current item. You must use commas to separate items in the series.

To list items in a series, you must specify one of the following, as shown in the syntax:

- all numeric values.

  ```
  DO index-variable=2,5,9,13,27;
     ...more SAS statements...
  END;
  ```

- all character values, which are enclosed in quotation marks.

  ```
  DO index-variable='MON','TUE','WED','THR','FRI';
     ...more SAS statements...
  END;
  ```

- all variable names. The index variable takes on the values of the specified variables.

  ```
  DO index-variable=win,place,show;
     ...more SAS statements...
  END;
  ```

Variable names must represent either all numeric or all character values. Do not enclose variable names in quotation marks.

Nesting DO Loops

Indenting and Nesting DO Groups

You can nest DO groups to any level, just like you nest IF-THEN/ELSE statements.

Note: The memory capabilities of your system might limit the number of nested DO statements that you can use.

Here is an example structure of nested DO groups:

```
do;
    ...more SAS statements...;
        do;
            ...more SAS statements...;
                do;
                    ...more SAS statements...;
                end;
        end;
end;
```

TIP It is good practice to indent the statements in DO groups, as shown in the preceding statements, so that their position indicates the levels of nesting.

Examples: Nesting DO Loops

Iterative DO statements can be executed within a DO loop. Putting a DO loop within a DO loop is called nesting.

```
do i=1 to 20;
   ...more SAS statements...
   do j=1 to 10;
      ...more SAS statements...
   end;
   ...more SAS statements...
end;
```

The DATA step below computes the value of a one-year investment that earns 7.5% annual interest, compounded monthly.

```
data work.earn;
  Capital=2000;
  do month=1 to 12;
    Interest=capital*(.075/12);
    capital+interest;
  end;
run;
```

Assume that the same amount of capital is to be added to the investment each year for 20 years. The new program must perform the calculation for each month during each of the 20 years. To do this, you can include the monthly calculations within another DO loop that executes 20 times.

```
data work.earn;
```

```
  do year=1 to 20;
    Capital+2000;
      do month=1 to 12;
        Interest=capital*(.075/12);
        capital+interest;
      end;
  end;
run;
```

During each iteration of the outside DO loop, an additional 2,000 is added to the capital, and the nested DO loop executes 12 times.

```
data work.earn;
  do year=1 to 20;
    Capital+2000;
      do month=1 to 12;
        Interest=capital*(.075/12);
        capital+interest;
      end;
  end;
run;
```

Remember, in order for nested DO loops to execute correctly, you must do the following:

- Assign a unique index-variable name in each iterative DO statement.

```
data work.earn;
  do year=1 to 20;
    Capital+2000;
      do month=1 to 12;
        Interest=capital*(.075/12);
        capital+interest;
      end;
  end;
run;
```

- End each DO loop with an END statement.

```
data work.earn;
  do year=1 to 20;
    Capital+2000;
      do month=1 to 12;
        Interest=capital*(.075/12);
        capital+interest;
      end;
  end;
run;
```

It is easier to manage nested DO loops if you indent the statements in each DO loop as shown above.

Iteratively Processing Observations from a Data Set

Previous examples of DATA steps used DO loops to generate one or more observations from one iteration of the DATA step. It is also possible to write a DATA step that reads a data set and uses variables in the input data set to compute the value of a new variable.

The SAS data set Work.CDRates contains interest rates for certificates of deposit (CDs) that are available from several institutions.

Suppose you want to compare how much each CD earns at maturity with an investment of $5,000. The DATA step below creates a new data set, Work.Compare, that contains the added variable, Investment.

```
data work.compare(drop=i);
  set work.cdrates;
  Investment=5000;
  do i=1 to years;
    investment+rate*investment;
  end;
run;
proc print data=work.compare;
run;
```

The index variable is used only to execute the DO loop, so it is dropped from the new data set. Notice that the data set variable Years is used as the stop value in the iterative DO statement. As a result, the DO loop executes the number of times specified by the current value of Years.

Here is what happens during each iteration of the DATA step:

- An observation is read from Work.CDRates.
- The value 5000 is assigned to the variable Investment.
- The DO loop executes, based on the current value of Years.
- The value of Investment is incremented (each time that the DO loop executes), using the current value of Rate.

At the end of the first iteration of the DATA step, the first observation is written to the Work.Compare data set. Control returns to the top of the DATA step, and the next observation is read from Work.CDRates. These steps are repeated for each observation in Work.CDRates. The resulting data set contains the computed values of Investment for all observations that have been read from Work.CDRates.

Figure 11.3 *HTML Output: Work.Compare Data Set*

Obs	Institution	Rate	Years	Investment
1	MBNA America	0.0817	5	7404.64
2	Metropolitan Bank	0.0814	3	6323.09
3	Standard Pacific	0.0806	4	6817.57

Conditionally Executing DO Loops

Overview

The iterative DO statement specifies a fixed number of iterations for the DO loop. However, there are times when you want to execute a DO loop until a condition is reached or while a condition exists, but you do not know how many iterations are needed.

Suppose you want to calculate the number of years required for an investment to reach $50,000. In the DATA step below, using an iterative DO statement is inappropriate because you are trying to determine the number of iterations required for Capital to reach $50,000.

```
data work.invest;
  do year=1 to ? ;
    Capital+2000;
    capital+capital*.10;
  end;
run;
```

The DO WHILE and DO UNTIL statements enable you to execute DO loops based on whether a condition is true or false.

Using the DO UNTIL Statement

The DO UNTIL statement executes a DO loop until the expression becomes true.

Syntax, DO UNTIL statement:

DO UNTIL(*expression***);**

...more SAS statements...

END;

expression is a valid SAS expression enclosed in parentheses.

The expression is not evaluated until the bottom of the loop. Therefore, a DO UNTIL loop always executes at least once. When the expression is evaluated as true, the DO loop stops.

Assume you want to know how many years it takes to earn $50,000 if you deposit $2,000 each year into an account that earns 10% interest. The DATA step below uses a DO UNTIL statement to perform the calculation until $50,000 is reached. Each iteration of the DO loop represents one year.

```
data work.invest;
  do until(Capital>=50000);
    capital+2000;
    capital+capital*.10;
    Year+1;
  end;
run;
```

Here is what happens during each iteration of the DO loop:

- 2000 is added to the value of Capital to reflect the annual deposit of $2,000.
- 10% interest is added to Capital.
- The value of Year is incremented by 1.

Because there is no index variable in the DO UNTIL statement, the variable Year is created in a sum statement to count the number of iterations of the DO loop. This program produces a data set that contains the single observation shown below. To accumulate more than $50,000 in capital requires 13 years (and 13 iterations of the DO loop).

Figure 11.4 *SAS Data Set Work.Invest: Accumulation of More Than $50,000*

	Capital	Year
1	53949.97	13

Using the DO WHILE Statement

Like the DO UNTIL statement, the DO WHILE statement executes DO loops conditionally. You can use the DO WHILE statement to execute a DO loop while the expression is true.

Syntax, DO WHILE statement:

DO WHILE(*expression*)**;**

...more SAS statements...

END;

expression is a valid SAS expression enclosed in parentheses.

An important difference between the DO UNTIL and DO WHILE statements is that the DO WHILE expression is evaluated at the top of the DO loop. If the expression is false the first time it is evaluated, the DO loop never executes. For example, in the following program the DO loop does not execute because the value of Capital is initially zero, which is less than 50,000.

```
data work.invest;
  do while(Capital>=50000);
    capital+2000;
    capital+capital*.10;
    Year+1;
  end;
run;
```

Suppose you also want to limit the number of years you invest your capital to 10 years. You can add the UNTIL or WHILE expression to an iterative DO statement to further control the number of iterations. This iterative DO statement enables you to execute the DO loop until Capital is greater than or equal to 50000 or until the DO loop executes 10 times, whichever occurs first.

```
data work.invest;
  do year=1 to 10 until (Capital>=50000);
    capital+2000;
    capital+capital*.10;
  end;
run;
```

Figure 11.5 *SAS Data Set Work.Invest: Executing DO Loop until Capital >=$50,000*

	Year	Capital
1	10	35062.33

In this case, the DO loop stops executing after 10 iterations, and the value of Capital never reaches 50000. If you increase the amount added to Capital each year to 4000, the DO loop stops executing after the eighth iteration when the value of Capital exceeds 50000.

```
data work.invest;
  do year=1 to 10 until (Capital>=50000);
    capital+4000;
    capital+capital*.10;
  end;
run;
```

Figure 11.6 *SAS Data Set Work.Invest: Increase Amount Added to Capital Using a DO Loop*

	year	Capital
1	8	50317.91

The UNTIL and WHILE expressions in an iterative DO statement function similarly to the DO UNTIL and DO WHILE statements. As shown in the following syntax, both statements require a valid SAS expression that is enclosed in parentheses.

DO *index-variable=start* TO *stop* BY *increment* UNTIL(*expression*);

DO *index-variable=start* TO *stop* BY *increment* WHILE(*expression*);

The UNTIL expression is evaluated at the bottom of the DO loop. Therefore, the DO loop always executes at least once. The WHILE expression is evaluated before the execution of the DO loop. As a result, if the condition is initially false, the DO loop never executes.

Chapter Quiz

Select the best answer for each question. Check your answers using the answer key in the appendix.

1. Which statement is false regarding the use of DO loops?
   a. They can contain conditional clauses.
   b. They can generate multiple observations.
   c. They can be used to combine DATA and PROC steps.
   d. They can be used to read data.
2. During each execution of the following DO loop, the value of Earned is calculated and is added to its previous value. How many times does this DO loop execute?

```
data work.earnings;
  Amount=1000;
  Rate=.075/12;
  do month=1 to 12;
    Earned+(amount+earned)*rate;
  end;
```

```
run;
```

a. 0

b. 1

c. 12

d. 13

3. On January 1 of each year, $5,000 is invested in an account. Complete the DATA step below to determine the value of the account after 15 years if a constant interest rate of 10% is expected.

```
data work.invest;
  ...
    Capital+5000;
    capital+(capital*.10);
  end;
run;
```

a. `do count=1 to 15;`

b. `do count=1 to 15 by 10%;`

c. `do count=1 to capital;`

d. `do count=capital to (capital*.10);`

4. In the data set Work.Invest, what would be the stored value for Year?

```
data work.invest;
  do year=1990 to 2004;
    Capital+5000;
    capital+(capital*.10);
  end;
run;
```

a. missing

b. 1990

c. 2004

d. 2005

5. Which of the following statements is false regarding the program shown below?

```
data work.invest;
  do year=1990 to 2004;
    Capital+5000;
    capital+(capital*.10);
    output;
  end;
run;
```

a. The OUTPUT statement writes current values to the data set immediately.

b. The last value for Year in the new data set is 2005.

c. The OUTPUT statement overrides the automatic output at the end of the DATA step.

d. The DO loop performs 15 iterations.

6. How many observations will the data set Work.Earn contain?

```
data work.earn;
```

```
  Value=2000;
  do year=1 to 20;
    Interest=value*.075;
    value+interest;
    output;
  end;
run;
```

a. 0

b. 1

c. 19

d. 20

7. Which of the following would you use to compare the result of investing $4,000 a year for five years in three different banks that compound interest monthly? Assume a fixed rate for the five-year period.

   a. DO WHILE statement

   b. nested DO loops

   c. DO UNTIL statement

   d. a DO group

8. Which statement is false regarding DO UNTIL statements?

   a. The condition is evaluated at the top of the loop, before the enclosed statements are executed.

   b. The enclosed statements are always executed at least once.

   c. SAS statements in the DO loop are executed until the specified condition is true.

   d. The DO loop must have a closing END statement.

9. Select the DO WHILE statement that would generate the same result as the program below.

```
data work.invest;
  capital=100000;
  do until(Capital gt 500000);
    Year+1;
    capital+(capital*.10);
  end;
run;
```

   a. `do while(Capital ge 500000);`

   b. `do while(Capital=500000);`

   c. `do while(Capital le 500000);`

   d. `do while(Capital>500000);`

10. In the following program, complete the statement so that the program stops generating observations when Distance reaches 250 miles or when 10 gallons of fuel have been used.

```
data work.go250;
  set cert.cars;
  do gallons=1 to 10 ... ;
    Distance=gallons*mpg;
    output;
```

```
  end;
run;
```

a. `while(Distance<=250)`

b. `when(Distance>250)`

c. `over(Distance le 250)`

d. `until(Distance=250)`

Chapter 12
SAS Formats and Informats

Applying SAS Formats and Informats

Temporarily Assigning Formats to Variables

In your SAS reports, formats control how the data values are displayed. To make data values more understandable when they are displayed in your procedure output, you can use the FORMAT statement, which associates formats with variables.

Formats affect only how the data values appear in output, not the actual data values as they are stored in the SAS data set.

Syntax, FORMAT statement:

FORMAT *variable(s) format-name*;

- *variable(s)* is the name of one or more variables whose values are to be written according to a particular pattern
- *format-name* specifies a SAS format or a user-defined format that is used to write out the values.

Tip: The FORMAT statement applies only to the PROC step in which it appears.

You can use a separate FORMAT statement for each variable, or you can format several variables (using either the same format or different formats) in a single FORMAT statement.

Table 12.1 *Formats That Are Used to Format Data*

FORMAT Statement	Description	Example
`format date mmddyy8.;`	associates the format MMDDYY8. with the variable Date	01/06/17
`format net comma5.0` `gross comma8.2;`	associates the format COMMA5.0 with the variable Net and the format COMMA8.2 with the variable Gross	1,234 5,678.90
`format net gross dollar9.2;`	associates the format DOLLAR9.2 with both variables, Net, and Gross	$1,234.00 $5,678.90

For example, the FORMAT statement below writes values of the variable Fee using dollar signs, commas, and no decimal places.

```
proc print data=cert.admit;
  var actlevel fee;
  where actlevel='HIGH';
  format fee dollar4.;
run;
```

Figure 12.1 *FORMAT Statement Output*

Obs	ActLevel	Fee
1	HIGH	$85
2	HIGH	$125
6	HIGH	$125
11	HIGH	$150
14	HIGH	$125
18	HIGH	$85
20	HIGH	$150

Specifying SAS Formats

The table below describes some SAS formats that are commonly used in reports.

Table 12.2 *Commonly Used SAS Formats*

Format	**Description**	**Example**
COMMA*w.d*	specifies values that contain commas and decimal places	comma8.2
DOLLAR*w.d*	specifies values that contain dollar signs, commas, and decimal places	dollar6.2
MMDDYY*w*.	specifies values as date values of the form 09/12/17 (MMDDYY8.) or 09/12/2017 (MMDDYY10.)	mmddyy10.
w.	specifies values that are rounded to the nearest integer in *w* spaces	7.
w.d	specifies values that are rounded to *d* decimal places in *w* spaces	8.2
$*w*.	specifies values as character values in *w* spaces	$12.
DATE*w*.	specifies values as date values of the form 16OCT17 (DATE7.) or 16OCT2017 (DATE9.)	date9.

Field Widths

All SAS formats specify the total field width (*w*) that is used for displaying the values in the output. For example, suppose the longest value for the variable Net is a four-digit number, such as 5400. To specify the COMMA*w.d* format for Net, you specify a field width of 5 or more. You must count the comma, because it occupies a position in the output.

Note: When you use a SAS format, specify a field width (*w*) that is wide enough for the largest possible value. Otherwise, values might not be displayed properly.

Figure 12.2 *Specifying a Field Width (w) with the FORMAT Statement*

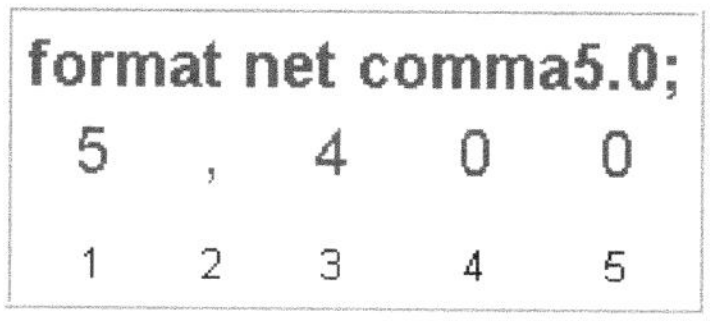

```
format net comma5.0;
5 , 4 0 0
1 2 3 4 5
```

Decimal Places

For numeric variables, you can also specify the number of decimal places (*d*), if any, to be displayed in the output. Numbers are rounded to the specified number of decimal places. In the example above, no decimal places are displayed.

Writing the whole number 2030 as 2,030.00 requires eight print positions, including two decimal places and the decimal point.

Figure 12.3 *Whole Number Decimal Places*

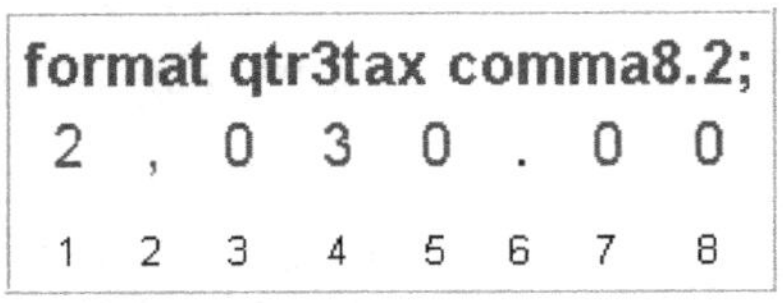

format qtr3tax comma8.2;							
2	,	0	3	0	.	0	0
1	2	3	4	5	6	7	8

Formatting 15374 with a dollar sign, commas, and two decimal places requires 10 print positions.

Figure 12.4 *Specifying 10 Decimal Places*

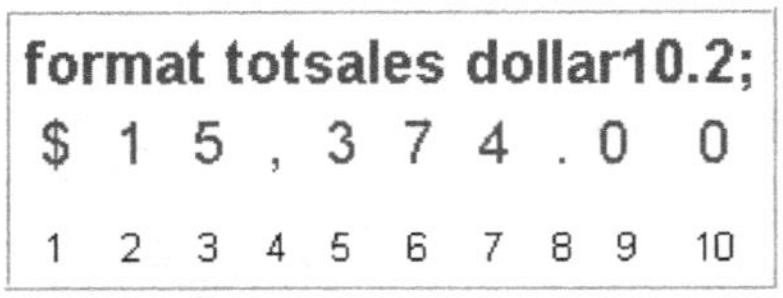

format totsales dollar10.2;									
$	1	5	,	3	7	4	.	0	0
1	2	3	4	5	6	7	8	9	10

Examples: Data Values and Formats

This table shows you how data values are displayed when different format, field width, and decimal place specifications are used.

Table 12.3 *Displaying Data Values with Formats*

Stored Value	Format	Displayed Value
38245.3975	COMMA9.2	38,245.40
38245.3975	8.2	38245.40
38245.3975	DOLLAR10.2	$38,245.40
38245.3975	DOLLAR9.2	$38245.40
38245.3975	DOLLAR8.2	38245.40
0	MMDDYY8.	01/01/60
0	MMDDYY10.	01/01/1960

Stored Value	Format	Displayed Value
0	DATE7.	01JAN60
0	DATE9.	01JAN1960

TIP If a format is too small, the following message is written to the SAS log:

```
NOTE: At least one W.D format was too small for the number to be
printed. The decimal might be shifted by the 'BEST' format.
```

The FORMAT Procedure

Definitions

SAS format
determines how variable values are printed according to the data type: numeric, character, date, time, or timestamp.

SAS informat
determines how data values are read and stored according to the data type: numeric, character, date, time, or timestamp.

A Word about PROC FORMAT

SAS provides you with formats and informats that you can use to read and write your data. However, if the SAS formats or informats do not meet your needs, you can use the FORMAT procedure to define your own formats and informats. PROC FORMAT stores user-defined formats and informats as entries in a SAS catalog.

The following output of Work.Carsurvey has a value of `1` or `2` for Sex, and values of `B`, `G`, `W`, and `Y` for Color. SAS does not provide formats to make the values for Sex and Color easier to read. You can create your own formats to format the values. You can also apply a format to the values of Income.

Figure 12.5 *Work.Carsurvey Data Set*

Obs	Age	Sex	Income	Color
1	19	1	14000	Y
2	45	1	65000	G
3	62	2	35000	W
4	31	1	44000	Y
5	58	2	83000	W
6	68	1	44000	B
7	17	2	15000	G
8	70	2	33000	B

The PROC FORMAT Statement

To begin a PROC FORMAT step, you use a PROC FORMAT statement.

Syntax, PROC FORMAT statement:

PROC FORMAT *<options>***;**

options includes the following:

- LIBRARY=*libref* specifies the libref for a SAS library to store a permanent catalog of user-defined formats
- FMTLIB displays a list of all of the formats in your catalog, along with descriptions of their values.

Anytime you use PROC FORMAT to create a format, the format is stored in a format catalog. If the SAS library does not already contain a format catalog, SAS automatically creates one. If you do not specify the LIBRARY= option, the formats are stored in a default format catalog named Work.Formats.

The libref Work signifies that any format that is stored in Work.Formats is a temporary format; it exists only for the current SAS session.

Permanently Storing Your Formats

To store formats in a permanent format catalog named Formtlib.Formats:

- Specify a LIBNAME statement that associates the libref with the permanent SAS library in which the format catalog is to be stored.

  ```
  libname formtlib 'c:\sas\formats\lib';
  ```

- Specify the LIBRARY= option in the PROC FORMAT statement and specify the libref formtlib.

  ```
  PROC FORMAT LIBRARY=formtlib;
  ```

  The LIBRARY= option accepts a libref and a catalog in the format *library.format*. When the LIBRARY= option specifies a libref and not a catalog, PROC FORMAT uses the catalog Formats.

When you associate a user-defined format with a variable in a subsequent DATA or PROC step, use the Library libref to reference the location of the format catalog.

Any format that you create in this PROC FORMAT step is now stored in a permanent format catalog called Formtlib.Formats.

```
libname formtlib 'C:\Users\Student1\formats\lib';
proc format library=formtlib;
   ...more SAS statements...
run;
```

In the program above, the catalog Formtlib.Formats is located in the SAS library **C:\Users\Student1\formats\lib**, which is referenced by the libref Formtlib.

Notice that LIB= is an acceptable abbreviation for the LIBRARY= option.

```
proc format lib=formtlib;
```

Defining a Unique Format

The VALUE Statement

Use the VALUE statement to define a format for displaying one or more values.

Syntax, VALUE statement:

VALUE *format-name*
range1='label1'
range2='label2'
...more format-names...;

The following are true about *format-name*:

- A format name must begin with a dollar sign ($) if the format applies to character data.
- A format name must be a valid SAS name.
- A format name cannot be the name of an existing SAS format.
- A format name cannot end in a number.
- A format name does not end in a period when specified in a VALUE statement.
- A numeric format name can be up to 32 characters long.
- A character format name can be up to 31 characters long.

Tip: If you are running a version of SAS prior to SAS®9, the format name must be a SAS name up to eight characters long and cannot end in a number.

Notice that the statement begins with the keyword VALUE and ends with a semicolon after all the labels have been defined. The following VALUE statements create the GENDER, AGEGROUP, and $COL formats to specify descriptive labels that are later assigned to the variables Sex, Age, and Color respectively:

```
proc format;
   value gender
             1 = 'Male'
             2 = 'Female';
   value agegroup
            13 -< 20  = 'Teen'
            20 -< 65  = 'Adult'
            65 - HIGH = 'Senior';
   value $col
            'W' = 'Moon White'
            'B' = 'Sky Blue'
            'Y' = 'Sunburst Yellow'
            'G' = 'Rain Cloud Gray';
run;
```

The VALUE range specifies the following types of values:

- a single value, such as 24 or **'S'**
- a range of numeric values, such as 0-1500
- a range of character values enclosed in quotation marks, such as **'A'-'M'**

- a list of unique values separated by commas, such as 90,180,270 or 'B', 'D', 'F'. These values can be character values or numeric values, but not a combination of character and numeric values (because formats themselves are either character or numeric).

When the specified values are character values, they must be enclosed in quotation marks and must match the case of the variable's values. The format's name must also start with a dollar sign ($). For example, the VALUE statement below defines the $COL format, which displays the character values as text labels.

```
proc format lib=formtlib;
   value $col
         'W' = 'Moon White'
         'B' = 'Sky Blue'
         'Y' = 'Sunburst Yellow'
         'G' = 'Rain Cloud Gray';
run;
```

When the specified values are numeric values, they are not enclosed in quotation marks, and the format's name should not begin with a dollar sign ($).

Specifying Value Ranges

You can specify a non-inclusive range of numeric values by using the less than symbol (<) to avoid any overlapping. In this example, the range of values from 0 to less than 13 is labeled as Child. The next range begins at 13, so the label Teenager would be assigned to the values 13 to 19.

```
proc format lib=formtlib;
   value agefmt
         0-<13='child'
         13-<20='teenager'
         20-<65='adult'
         65-100='senior citizen';
run;
```

You can also use the keywords LOW and HIGH to specify the lower and upper limits of a variable's value range. The keyword LOW does not include missing numeric values. The keyword OTHER can be used to label missing values as well as any values that are not specifically addressed in a range.

```
proc format lib=formtlib;
   value agefmt
         low-<13='child'
         13-<20='teenager'
         20-<65='adult'
         65-high='senior citizen'
         other='unknown';
run;
```

TIP If applied to a character format, the keyword LOW includes missing character values.

When specifying a label for displaying each range, remember to do the following:

- Enclose the label in quotation marks.
- Limit the label to 32,767 characters.
- Use two single quotation marks if you want an apostrophe to appear in the label:

```
000='employee''s jobtitle unknown';
```

To define several formats, you can use multiple VALUE statements in a single PROC FORMAT step. In this example, each VALUE statement defines a different format.

```
proc format;
   value gender
            1 = 'Male'
            2 = 'Female';
   value agegroup
           13 -< 20   = 'Teen'
           20 -< 65   = 'Adult'
           65 - HIGH = 'Senior';
   value $col
           'W' = 'Moon White'
           'B' = 'Sky Blue'
           'Y' = 'Sunburst Yellow'
           'G' = 'Rain Cloud Gray';
run;
```

The SAS log prints notes informing you that the formats have been created.

Log 12.1 *SAS Log*

```
146  proc format lib=formtlib;
147      value gender    1 = 'Male'
148                      2 = 'Female';
NOTE: Format GENDER is already on the library FORMTLIB.FORMATS.
NOTE: Format GENDER has been output.
149      value agegroup  13 -< 20   = 'Teen'
150                      20 -< 65   = 'Adult'
151                      65 - HIGH = 'Senior';
NOTE: Format AGEGROUP is already on the library FORMTLIB.FORMATS.
NOTE: Format AGEGROUP has been output.
152      value $col      'W' = 'Moon White'
153                      'B' = 'Sky Blue'
154                      'Y' = 'Sunburst Yellow'
155                      'G' = 'Rain Cloud Gray';
NOTE: Format $COL is already on the library FORMTLIB.FORMATS.
NOTE: Format $COL has been output.
```

Associating User-Defined Formats with Variables

How SAS Finds Format Catalogs

To use the GENDER, AGEGROUP, and $COL formats in a subsequent SAS session, you must assign the libref Formtlib again.

```
libname formtlib 'C:\Users\Student1\formats\lib';
```

SAS searches for the formats GENDER, AGEGROUP, and $COL in two libraries, in this order:

- the temporary library referenced by the libref Work
- a permanent library referenced by the libref Formtlib

SAS uses the first instance of a specified format that it finds.

TIP You can delete formats using PROC CATALOG.

Assigning Formats to Variables

Just as with SAS formats, you associate a user-defined format with a variable in a FORMAT statement.

```
data work.carsurvey;
  set cert.cars;
  format Sex gender. Age agegroup. Color $col. Income Dollar8.;
run;
```

Remember, you can place the FORMAT statement in either a DATA step or a PROC step. By placing the FORMAT statement in a DATA step, you permanently associate a format with a variable. Note that you do not have to specify a width value when using a user-defined format.

When you submit the PRINT procedure, the output for Work.CarSurvey now shows descriptive labels instead of the values for Age, Sex, Income, and Color.

```
proc print data=work.carsurvey;
run;
```

Output 12.1 *Work.CarSuvery Data Set with Formatted Values*

Obs	Age	Sex	Income	Color
1	Teen	Male	$14,000	Sunburst Yellow
2	Adult	Male	$65,000	Rain Cloud Gray
3	Adult	Female	$35,000	Moon White
4	Adult	Male	$44,000	Sunburst Yellow
5	Adult	Female	$83,000	Moon White
6	Senior	Male	$44,000	Sky Blue
7	Teen	Female	$15,000	Rain Cloud Gray
8	Senior	Female	$33,000	Sky Blue

When associating a format with a variable, remember to do the following:

- Use the same format name in the FORMAT statement that you specified in the VALUE statement.
- Place a period at the end of the format name when it is used in the FORMAT statement.

If you do not format all of a variable's values, then those that are not listed in the VALUE statement are printed as they appear in the SAS data set. In the example below, the value of 2 was not defined in the VALUE statement for GENDER as shown in observation 3, 5, 7, and 8.

```
libname formtlib 'C:\Users\Student1\formats\lib';
proc format lib=formtlib;
   value gender
           1 = 'Male';
   value agegroup
          13 -< 20  = 'Teen'
          20 -< 65  = 'Adult'
```

```
            65 - HIGH = 'Senior';
   value $col
            'W' = 'Moon White'
            'B' = 'Sky Blue'
            'Y' = 'Sunburst Yellow'
            'G' = 'Rain Cloud Gray';
run;
data work.carsurvey;
  set cert.cars;
  format Sex gender. Age agegroup.Color $col. Income Dollar8.;
run;
proc print data=work.carsurvey;
run;
```

Output 12.2 *Work.Carsurvey Data Set with Missing Formatted Values*

Obs	Age	Sex	Income	Color
1	Teen	Male	$14,000	Sunburst Yellow
2	Adult	Male	$65,000	Rain Cloud Gray
3	Adult	2	$35,000	Moon White
4	Adult	Male	$44,000	Sunburst Yellow
5	Adult	2	$83,000	Moon White
6	Senior	Male	$44,000	Sky Blue
7	Teen	2	$15,000	Rain Cloud Gray
8	Senior	2	$33,000	Sky Blue

Displaying User-Defined Formats

When you build a large catalog of permanent formats, it can be easy to forget the exact spelling of a specific format name or its range of values. Adding the keyword FMTLIB to the PROC FORMAT statement displays a list of all the formats in your catalog, along with descriptions of their values.

```
libname formtlib 'c:\sas\formats\lib';
proc format library=formtlib fmtlib;
run;
```

When you submit this PROC step, a description of each format in your permanent catalog is displayed as output.

Output 12.3 *Output of the Formtlib Catalog*

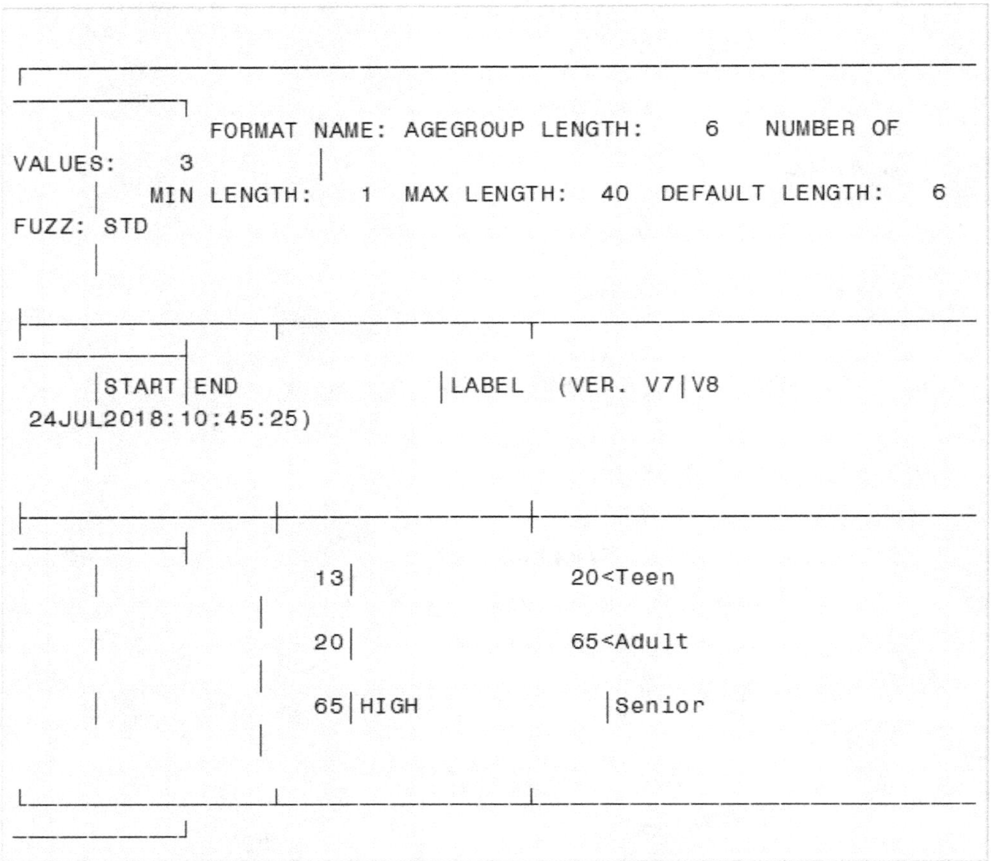

```
FORMAT NAME: AGEGROUP LENGTH:    6   NUMBER OF VALUES:    3
MIN LENGTH:   1  MAX LENGTH:  40  DEFAULT LENGTH:   6  FUZZ: STD

START |END          |LABEL  (VER. V7|V8 24JUL2018:10:45:25)

        13|         20<Teen
        20|         65<Adult
        65|HIGH       |Senior
```

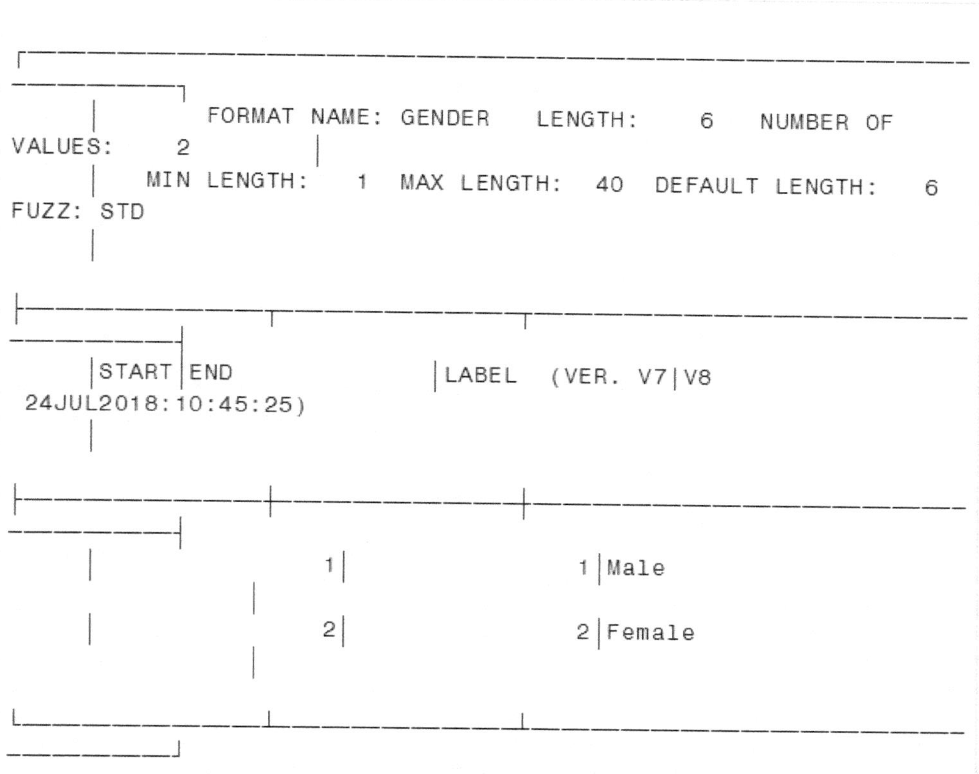

```
FORMAT NAME: GENDER   LENGTH:    6   NUMBER OF VALUES:    2
MIN LENGTH:   1  MAX LENGTH:  40  DEFAULT LENGTH:   6  FUZZ: STD

|START |END          |LABEL  (VER. V7|V8 24JUL2018:10:45:25)

            1|            1|Male
            2|            2|Female
```

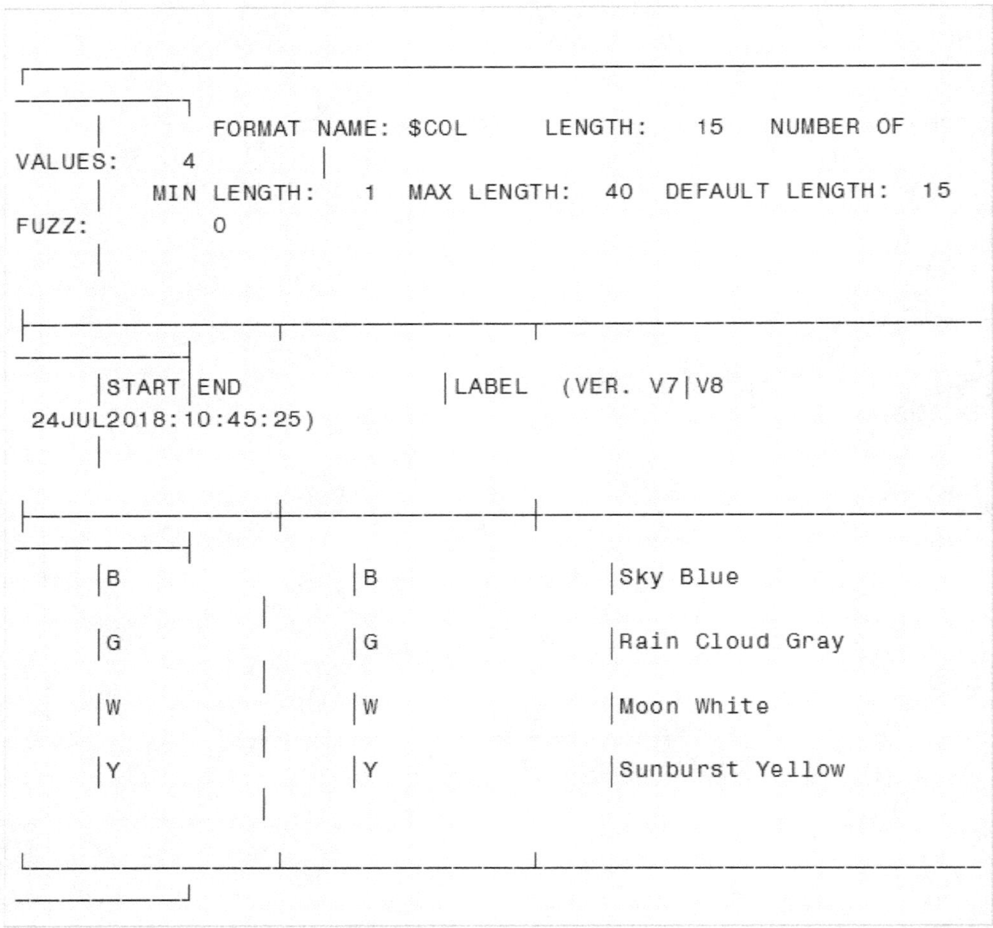

```
FORMAT NAME: $COL     LENGTH:   15   NUMBER OF VALUES:    4
MIN LENGTH:   1  MAX LENGTH:  40  DEFAULT LENGTH:  15  FUZZ:        0

START | END            | LABEL  (VER. V7|V8  24JUL2018:10:45:25)
B     | B              | Sky Blue
G     | G              | Rain Cloud Gray
W     | W              | Moon White
Y     | Y              | Sunburst Yellow
```

In addition to the name, range, and label, the format description includes the following details:

- length of the longest label
- number of values defined by this format
- version of SAS that was used to create the format
- date and time of creation

Chapter Quiz

Select the best answer for each question. Check your answers using the answer key in the appendix.

1. Suppose you do not specify the LIBRARY= option and your formats are stored in Work.Formats. How long do they exist?

   a. only for the current procedure

   b. only for the current DATA step

   c. only for the current SAS session

   d. permanently

2. Which of the following statements store your formats in a permanent catalog?

   a.
   ```
   libname formtlib 'C:\Users\Student1\sas\formats\lib';
   proc format lib=formtlib
      ...;
   ```

   b.
   ```
   libname formtlib 'C:\Users\Student1\sas\formats\lib';
   format lib=formtlib
      ...;
   ```

   c.
   ```
   formtlib='C:\Users\Student1\sas\formats\lib';
   proc format formtlib
      ...;
   ```

   d.
   ```
   formtlib='C:\Users\Student1\sas\formats\lib';
   proc formtlib
      ...;
   ```

3. When you create a format with the VALUE statement, the new format's name cannot end with a number, cannot end with a period, and cannot be the name of a SAS format. Which of the following is also true?

   a. The name cannot be the name of a data set variable.

   b. The name must be at least two characters long.

   c. The name must be at least eight characters long.

   d. The name must begin with a dollar sign ($) if used with a character variable.

4. Which of the following FORMAT procedures is written correctly?

   a.
   ```
   proc format lib=formtlib
      value colorfmt;
            1='Red'
            2='Green'
            3='Blue'
   run;
   ```

   b.
   ```
   proc format lib=formtlib;
      value colorfmt
            1='Red'
            2='Green'
            3='Blue';
   run;
   ```

   c.
   ```
   proc format lib=formtlib;
      value colorfmt;
            1='Red'
            2='Green'
            3='Blue'
   run;
   ```

   d.
   ```
   proc format lib=formtlib;
      value colorfmt
            1='Red';
            2='Green';
            3='Blue';
   run;
   ```

5. Which of these statements is false regarding what the ranges in the VALUE statement can specify?

   a. They can specify a single value, such as 24 or `'S'`.

b. a range of numeric values, such as 0-1500.

c. a range of character values, such as 'A'-'M'.

d. a list of numeric and character values separated by commas, such as 90,'B', 180,'D',270.

6. How many characters can be used in a label?

a. 96

b. 200

c. 256

d. 32,767

7. Which keyword can be used to label missing numeric values as well as any values that are not specified in a range?

a. LOW

b. MISS

c. MISSING

d. OTHER

8. You can place the FORMAT statement in either a DATA step or a PROC step. What happens when you place it in a DATA step?

a. You temporarily associate the formats with variables.

b. You permanently associate the formats with variables.

c. You replace the original data with the format labels.

d. You make the formats available to other data sets.

9. Suppose the format JOBFMT was created in a FORMAT procedure. Which FORMAT statement applies it to the variable JobTitle in the program output?

a. `format jobtitle jobfmt;`

b. `format jobtitle jobfmt.;`

c. `format jobtitle=jobfmt;`

d. `format jobtitle='jobfmt';`

10. Which keyword, when added to the PROC FORMAT statement, displays all the formats in your catalog?

a. CATALOG

b. LISTFMT

c. FMTCAT

d. FMTLIB

Chapter 13
SAS Date, Time, and Datetime Values

SAS Date and Time Values

Definitions

SAS date value
is a value that represents the number of days between January 1, 1960, and a specified date. SAS can perform calculations on dates ranging from 1582 C.E. to 19,900 C.E.. Dates before January 1, 1960, are negative numbers; dates after are positive numbers.

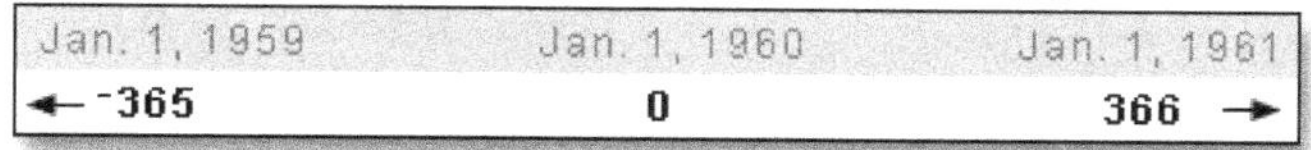

- SAS date values account for all leap year days, including the leap year day in the year 2000.

- SAS date values are based on the Gregorian calendar, and they are valid for the dates supplied above.

- Various SAS language elements handle SAS date values: functions, formats, and informats.

SAS time value
: is a value representing the number of seconds since midnight of the current day. SAS time values are between 0 and 86400.

SAS datetime value
: is a value representing the number of seconds between January 1, 1960, and an hour/minute/second within a specified date. SAS makes adjustments for leap years, but ignores leap seconds. SAS does not make adjustments for daylight saving time.

Example: Date and Time Values

SAS stores date values as numbers so that you can easily sort the values or perform arithmetic computations. You can use SAS date values as you use any other numeric values.

```
data work.test;
  set cert.temp;
  TotDay=enddate-startdate;
run;
proc print data=work.test;
run;
```

Output 13.1 *PROC PRINT Output of Work.Test (partial output)*

Obs	Address		Startdate	Enddate		TotDay
1	65 ELM DR		21142	21196		54
2	11 SUN DR		21108	21142		34
3	712 HARDWICK STREET	. . .	21145	21183	. . .	38
4	5372 WHITEBUD ROAD	more	21091	21102	more	11
5	11 TALYN COURT	variables	21125	21136	variables	11
6	101 HYNERIAN DR	. . .	21139	21188	. . .	49
7	11 RYGEL ROAD		20668	21048		380
8	121 E. MOYA STREET		21098	21102		4
9	1905 DOCK STREET		21108	21112		4
10	1304 CRESCENT AVE		20999	21122		123

Reading Dates and Times with Informats

Overview

SAS *date and time informats* read date and time expressions and convert them to SAS date and time values. Like other SAS informats, date and time informats have several parts:

- an informat name
- a field width
- a period delimiter

SAS informat names indicate the form of date expression that can be read using that particular informat. This chapter covers commonly used date and time informats such as these:

- DATE*w*.
- DATETIME*w*.
- MMDDYY*w*.
- TIME*w*.

There are several ways to represent a date. For example, all the following expressions represent the date October 15, 2017. Each of these common date expressions can be read using the appropriate SAS date informat.

Table 13.1 *Date Expressions and Corresponding SAS Date Informats*

Date Expression	SAS Date Informat
10/15/17	MMDDYY*w*.
15Oct17	DATE*w*.
15–10–17	DDMMYY*w*.
17/10/15	YYMMDD*w*.

The MMDDYYw. Informat

The informat MMDDYY*w*. reads date values in the form *mmddyy* or *mmddyyyy*.

Syntax, values read with MMDDYY*w*. informat:

mmddyy or *mmddyyyy*

- *mm* is an integer between 01 and 12, representing the month.
- *dd* is an integer between 01 and 31, representing the day.
- *yy* or *yyyy* is an integer that represents the year.

In the MMDDYY*w*. informat, the month, day, and year fields can be separated by blanks or delimiters such as - or /. If delimiters are present, they must occur between all fields in the values. Remember to specify a field width that includes not only the month, day, and year values, but any delimiters as well. Here are some date expressions that you can read using the MMDDYY*w*. informat:

Table 13.2 *Date Expressions and Corresponding SAS Date Informats*

Date Expression	SAS Date Informat
101517	`MMDDYY6.`
10/15/17	`MMDDYY8.`
10 15 17	`MMDDYY8.`
10-15-2017	`MMDDYY10.`

The DDMMYY*w*. informat and the YYMMDD*w*. informat are similar in that you can read the day, month, and year number with or without delimiters. The difference is the order of day, month, and year.

Example: Reading Dates with Formats and Informats

The following example illustrates reading a CSV file with dates in MMDDYY10. informat.

```
proc import datafile='C:\Users\Student1\cert\new_hires.csv'
  out=newhires
  dbms=csv
  replace;
  getnames=yes;
run;
proc print data=work.newhires;
run;
proc contents data=work.newhires;
run;
```

Output 13.2 *Partial Output of Work.NewHires*

Obs	Name	Hire_Date	Company	Country	Date_of_Birth
1	Gisela S. Santos	08/12/2017	Pede Nunc Sed Limited	Micronesia	08/21/1971
2	Maxwell L. Cooley	09/04/2017	A LLP	Somalia	04/30/1975
3	Thane P. Obrien	10/28/2017	Consectetuer Limited	Jamaica	04/23/1988
4	Minerva C. Conley	01/05/2018	Feugiat Tellus Lorem Institute	Fiji	02/18/1975
5	Kylee R. Finch	10/31/2017	Magna Incorporated	Myanmar	05/18/1973
			. . . *more observations* . . .		
95	Winifred K. Morales	04/24/2018	Fames Incorporated	Italy	11/25/1975
96	Thaddeus J. England	03/26/2018	Semper Auctor Corporation	Zambia	12/21/1996
97	Skyler O. George	05/16/2018	At Institute	Jamaica	06/02/1986
98	Kieran H. Tyler	09/21/2017	Vulputate Eu Ltd	Tuvalu	02/14/1971
99	Cairo F. Baldwin	05/24/2018	Amet LLP	Palau	08/02/1973
100	Robin U. Macias	10/09/2017	Elit Nulla LLP	Burkina Faso	05/14/1982

Output 13.3 *Partial Output of PROC CONTENTS Work.NewHires*

Alphabetic List of Variables and Attributes					
#	Variable	Type	Len	Format	Informat
3	Company	Char	30	$30.	$30.
4	Country	Char	31	$31.	$31.
5	Date_of_Birth	Num	8	MMDDYY10.	MMDDYY10.
2	Hire_Date	Num	8	MMDDYY10.	MMDDYY10.
1	Name	Char	20	$20.	$20.

The DATEw. Informat

The DATE*w*. informat reads date values in the form *ddmmmyy* or *ddmmmyyyy*.

Syntax, values read with DATE*w*. informat:

ddmmmyy or *ddmmmyyyy*

- *dd* is an integer from 01 to 31, representing the day.
- *mmm* is the first three letters of the month's name.
- *yy* or *yyyy* is an integer that represents the year.

Blanks or other special characters can appear between the day, month, and year, as long as you increase the width of the informat to include these delimiters. Here are some date expressions that you can read using the DATEw. informat:

Table 13.3 *Date Expressions and Corresponding SAS Date Informats*

Date Expression	SAS Date Informat
30May17	DATE7.
30May2017	DATE9.
30-May-2017	DATE11.

The TIMEw. Informat

The TIME*w*. informat reads values in the form *hh:mm:ss.ss*.

Syntax, values read with TIME*w*. informat:

hh:mm:ss.ss

- *hh* is an integer from 00 to 23, representing the hour.
- *mm* is an integer from 00 to 59, representing the minute.
- *ss.ss* is an optional field that represents seconds and hundredths of seconds.

If you do not enter a value for *ss.ss*, a value of zero is assumed. Here are some examples of time expressions that you can read using the TIME*w*. informat:

Table 13.4 *Time Expressions and Corresponding SAS Time Informats*

Time Expression	SAS Time Informat
17:00:01.34	TIME11.
17:00	TIME5.

Note: Five is the minimum acceptable field width for the TIME*w*. informat. If you specify a *w* value less than `5`, you will receive an error message in the SAS log.

The DATETIMEw. Informat

The DATETIME*w*. informat reads expressions that consist of two parts, a date value and a time value, in the form: *ddmmmyy hh:mm:ss.ss*.

Syntax, values read with DATETIME*w*. informat:

ddmmmyy hh:mm:ss.ss

- *ddmmmyy* is the date value, the same form as for the DATE*w*. informat
- The time value must be in the form *hh:mm:ss.ss*.
- *hh* is an integer from 00 to 23, representing the hour.
- *mm* is an integer from 00 to 59, representing the minute.
- *ss.ss* is an optional field that represents seconds and hundredths of seconds.
- The date value and time value are separated by a blank or other delimiter.

If you do not enter a value for *ss.ss*, a value of zero is assumed.

Note: In the time value, you must use delimiters to separate the values for hour, minutes, and seconds.

Table 13.5 *Date and Time Expressions and Corresponding SAS Datetime Informats*

Date and Time Expression	SAS Datetime Informat
30May2017:10:03:17.2	DATETIME20.
30May17 10:03:17.2	DATETIME18.
30May2017/10:03	DATETIME15.

Example: Using Dates and Times in Calculations

Suppose you work in the billing department of a small community hospital. In this example, you create a new SAS data set from the input data file that is referenced by the fileref Aprbills. A portion of the data file below shows the following patient data:

- last name
- date checked in
- date checked out
- daily room rate
- equipment cost

Output 13.4 *Unformatted Cert.AprBills Data Set*

	LastName	DateIn	DateOut	RoomRate	EquipCost
1	Akron	21277	21282	175	298.4
2	Brown	21284	21304	125	326.7
3	Carnes	21299	21302	125	174.2
4	Denison	21283	21285	175	87.41
5	Fields	21287	21295	175	378.9
6	Jamison	21288	21296	125	346.2

```
data work.aprhospitalbills;
  set cert.aprbills;
  Days=dateout-datein+1;                  /*#1*/
  RoomCharge=days*roomrate;               /*#2*/
  Total=roomcharge+equipcost;             /*#3*/
run;
proc print data=work.aprhospitalbills;
  format DateIn DateOut mmddyy8.;         /*#4*/
run;
```

1 Create a new variable named Days and calculate how many days each patient was hospitalized. Since DateIn and DateOut are numeric variables, you can simply subtract to find the difference. However, the dates should be inclusive because patients are charged for both the first and last days. Therefore, you must add 1 to the difference.

2 Create a new variable named RoomCharge by multiplying the number of Days by the RoomRate value.

3 To calculate the total cost for each patient, create a variable named Total whose value is the sum of RoomCharge and EquipCost.

4 Use the FORMAT statement to associate the format MMDDYY8. to the DateIn and DateOut variable.

Output 13.5 *PROC PRINT Output for Work.AprHospitalBills*

Obs	LastName	DateIn	DateOut	RoomRate	EquipCost	Days	RoomCharge	Total
1	Akron	04/03/18	04/08/18	175	298.40	5	875	1173.40
2	Brown	04/10/18	04/30/18	125	326.70	20	2500	2826.70
3	Carnes	04/25/18	04/28/18	125	174.20	3	375	549.20
4	Denison	04/09/18	04/11/18	175	87.41	2	350	437.41
5	Fields	04/13/18	04/21/18	175	378.90	8	1400	1778.90
6	Jamison	04/14/18	04/22/18	125	346.20	8	1000	1346.20

Displaying Date and Time Values with Formats

SAS stores date and time values as numeric values. You apply SAS formats to the data so that meaningful date and time values are displayed in reports.

The WEEKDATEw. Format

Use the WEEKDATE*w*. format to write date values in a format that displays the day of the week, month, day, and year.

Syntax, WEEKDATE*w*. format:

WEEKDATE*w*.

The WEEKDATE*w*. format writes date values in the form *day-of-week, month-name dd, yy* (or *yyyy*).

- *dd* is an integer between 01 and 31, representing the day.
- *yy* or *yyyy* is an integer that represents the year.

Note: If the *w* value is too small to write the complete day of the week and month, SAS abbreviates as needed.

```
proc print data=work.aprhospitalbills;
   format datein dateout weekdate17.;
run;
```

Output 13.6 *PROC PRINT Output for Work.AprHospitalBills*

Obs	LastName	DateIn	DateOut	RoomRate	EquipCost	Days	RoomCharge	Total
1	Akron	Tue, Apr 3, 2018	Sun, Apr 8, 2018	175	298.40	5	875	1173.40
2	Brown	Tue, Apr 10, 2018	Mon, Apr 30, 2018	125	326.70	20	2500	2826.70
3	Carnes	Wed, Apr 25, 2018	Sat, Apr 28, 2018	125	174.20	3	375	549.20
4	Denison	Mon, Apr 9, 2018	Wed, Apr 11, 2018	175	87.41	2	350	437.41
5	Fields	Fri, Apr 13, 2018	Sat, Apr 21, 2018	175	378.90	8	1400	1778.90
6	Jamison	Sat, Apr 14, 2018	Sun, Apr 22, 2018	125	346.20	8	1000	1346.20

You can vary the results by changing the *w* value in the format.

FORMAT Statement	Result
`format datein weekdate3.;`	Tue
`format datein weekdate10.;`	Tuesday
`format datein weekdate17.;`	Tue, Apr 3, 2018
`format datein weekdate31.;`	Tuesday, Apr 3, 2018

The WORDDATEw. Format

The WORDDATE*w*. format is similar to the WEEKDATE*w*. format, but it does not display the day of the week or the two-digit year values.

Syntax, WORDDATE*w*. format:

WORDDATE*w*.

The WORDDATE*w*. format writes date values in the form *month-name dd, yyyy*.

- *dd* is an integer between 01 and 31, representing the day.
- *yyyy* is an integer that represents the year.

Note: If the *w* value is too small to write the complete month, SAS abbreviates as needed.

```
proc print data=work.aprhospitalbills;
   format datein dateout worddate12.;
run;
```

***Output 13.7** PROC PRINT Output for Work.AprHospitalBills*

Obs	LastName	DateIn	DateOut	RoomRate	EquipCost	Days	RoomCharge	Total
1	Akron	Apr 3, 2018	Apr 8, 2018	175	298.40	5	875	1173.40
2	Brown	Apr 10, 2018	Apr 30, 2018	125	326.70	20	2500	2826.70
3	Carnes	Apr 25, 2018	Apr 28, 2018	125	174.20	3	375	549.20
4	Denison	Apr 9, 2018	Apr 11, 2018	175	87.41	2	350	437.41
5	Fields	Apr 13, 2018	Apr 21, 2018	175	378.90	8	1400	1778.90
6	Jamison	Apr 14, 2018	Apr 22, 2018	125	346.20	8	1000	1346.20

You can vary the results by changing the *w* value in the format.

***Table 13.6** FORMAT Statements and Corresponding Results*

FORMAT Statement	Result
`format datein worddate3.;`	Apr
`format datein worddate9.;`	April
`format datein worddate14.;`	April 3, 2018

You can permanently assign a format to variable values by including a FORMAT statement in the DATA step.

```
data work.aprhospitalbills;
  set cert.aprbills;
  Days=dateout-datein+1;
  RoomCharge=days*roomrate;
  Total=roomcharge+equipcost;
  format datein dateout worddate12.;
run;
proc print data=work.aprhospitalbills;
run;
```

Chapter Quiz

Select the best answer for each question. Check your answers using the answer key in the appendix.

1. SAS date values are the number of days since which date?
   a. January 1, 1900
   b. January 1, 1950
   c. January 1, 1960
   d. January 1, 1970
2. What is an advantage of storing dates and times as SAS numeric date and time values?
   a. They can easily be edited.
   b. They can easily be read and understood.
   c. They can be used in text strings like other character values.
   d. They can be used in calculations like other numeric values.
3. SAS does not automatically make adjustments for daylight saving time, but it does make adjustments for which one of the following?
   a. leap seconds
   b. leap years
   c. Julian dates
   d. time zones
4. An input data file has date expressions in the form 10222001. Which SAS informat should you use to read these dates?
   a. DATE6.
   b. DATE8.
   c. MMDDYY6.
   d. MMDDYY8.
5. What is the minimum width of the TIME*w*. informat?
   a. 4
   b. 5
   c. 6
   d. 7
6. Shown below are date and time expressions and corresponding SAS datetime informats. Which date and time expression cannot be read by the informat that is shown beside it?
   a. 30May2018:10:03:17.2 `DATETIME20.`
   b. 30May18 10:03:17.2 `DATETIME18.`
   c. 30May2018/10:03 `DATETIME15.`

d. 30May2018/1003 **DATETIME14.**

7. Suppose your program creates two variables from an input file. Both variables are stored as SAS date values: FirstDay records the start of a billing cycle, and LastDay records the end of that cycle. What would be the code for calculating the total number of days in the cycle?

   a. `TotDays=lastday-firstday;`

   b. `TotDays=lastday-firstday+1;`

   c. `TotDays=lastday/firstday;`

   d. You cannot use date values in calculations.

Chapter 14

Using Functions to Manipulate Data

The Basics of SAS Functions

Definition

SAS *functions* are pre-written routines that perform computations or system manipulations on arguments and return a value. Functions can return either numeric or character results. The value that is returned can be used in an assignment statement or elsewhere in expressions.

Uses of SAS Functions

You can use SAS functions in DATA step programming statements, in WHERE expressions, in macro language statements, in the REPORT procedure, and in Structured Query Language (SQL). They enable you to do the following:

- calculate sample statistics
- create SAS date values
- convert U.S. ZIP codes to state postal codes
- round values
- generate random numbers
- extract a portion of a character value
- convert data from one data type to another

SAS Functions Categories

SAS functions provide programming shortcuts. The following table shows you all of the SAS function categories. This book covers selected functions that convert data, manipulate SAS date values, and modify values of character variables.

Table 14.1 *SAS Function Categories*

Functions by Category			
Arithmetic	Descriptive Statistics*	Numeric*	State and ZIP code*
Array	Distance	Probability	Trigonometric
Bitwise Logical Operations	External Files	Quantile	Truncation*
CAS	External Routines	Random Number	Variable Control
Character*	Financial	SAS File I/O	Variable Information
Character String Matching	Hyperbolic	Search	Web Services
Combinatorial	Macro	Sort	Web Tools
Date and Time	Mathematical*	Special*	

* Denotes the functions that are covered in this chapter.

SAS Functions Syntax

Arguments and Variable Lists

To use a SAS function, specify the function name followed by the function arguments, which are enclosed in parentheses.

Syntax, SAS function:

function-name*(argument-1<,argument-n>)***;**

Each of the following are *arguments*:

- variables: mean(*x,y,z*)
- constants: mean(*456,502,612,498*)
- expressions: mean(37*2,192/5,*mean*(*22,34,56*))

Note: Even if the function does not require arguments, the function name must still be followed by parentheses (for example, *function-name()*).

When a function contains more than one argument, the arguments are usually separated by commas.

```
function-name(argument-1,argument-2,argument-n);
```

Example: Multiple Arguments

Here is an example of a function that contains multiple arguments. Notice that the arguments are separated by commas.

```
mean(x1,x2,x3)
```

The arguments for this function can also be written as a variable list.

```
mean(of x1-x3)
```

Target Variables

A target variable is the variable to which the result of a function is assigned. For example, in the statement below, the variable AvgScore is the target variable.

```
AvgScore=mean(exam1,exam2,exam3);
```

Unless the length of the target variable has been previously defined, a default length is assigned. The default length depends on the function; the default for character functions can be as long as 200.

TIP Default lengths can cause character variables to use more space than necessary in your data set. So, when using SAS functions, consider the appropriate length for any character target variables. If necessary, add a LENGTH statement to specify a length for the character target variable before the statement that creates the values of that variable.

Converting Data with Functions

A Word about Converting Data

The following code automatically converts the variable PayRate from character to numeric.

```
data work.newtemp;
  set cert.temp;
  Salary=payrate*hours;
run;
```

You can also use the INPUT function before performing a calculation. The INPUT function converts character data values to numeric values.

You can use the PUT function to convert numeric data values to character values.

Potential Problems of Omitting INPUT or PUT

If you skip INPUT or PUT function when converting data, SAS detects the mismatched variables and tries an automatic character-to-numeric or numeric-to-character conversion. However, this action is not always successful. Suppose each value of PayRate begins with a dollar sign ($). When SAS tries to automatically convert the values of PayRate to numeric values, the dollar sign blocks the process. The values cannot be converted to numeric values. Similar problems can occur with automatic numeric-to-character conversion.

Therefore, it is a recommended best practice to include INPUT and PUT functions in your programs to avoid data type mismatches and automatic conversion.

Automatic Character-to-Numeric Conversion

By default, if you reference a character variable in a numeric context such as an arithmetic operation, SAS tries to convert the variable values to numeric. For example, in the DATA step below, the character variable PayRate appears in a numeric context. It is multiplied by the numeric variable Hours to create a new variable named Salary.

```
data work.newtemp;
  set cert.temp;
  Salary=payrate*hours;
run;
```

When this step executes, SAS automatically attempts to convert the character values of PayRate to numeric values so that the calculation can occur. This conversion is completed by creating a temporary numeric value for each character value of PayRate. This temporary value is used in the calculation. The character values of PayRate are not replaced by numeric values.

Whenever data is automatically converted, a message is written to the SAS log stating that the conversion has occurred.

Log 14.1 *SAS Log*

```
9246  data work.temp;
9247  set cert.temp;
9248  salary=payrate*hours;
9249  run;

NOTE: Character values have been converted to numeric values at the places given
by:
      (Line):(Column).
      9248:8
NOTE: There were 10 observations read from the data set CERT.TEMP.
NOTE: The data set WORK.TEMP has 10 observations and 16 variables.
NOTE: DATA statement used (Total process time):
      real time           0.00 seconds
      cpu time            0.00 seconds
```

When Automatic Conversion Occurs

Automatic character-to-numeric conversion occurs in the following circumstances:

- A character value is assigned to a previously defined numeric variable, such as the numeric variable Rate.

  ```
  Rate=payrate;
  ```

- A character value is used in an arithmetic operation.

  ```
  Salary=payrate*hours;
  ```

- A character value is compared to a numeric value, using a comparison operator.

  ```
  if payrate>=rate;
  ```

- A character value is specified in a function that requires numeric arguments.

  ```
  NewRate=sum(payrate,raise);
  ```

The following statements are true about automatic conversion.

- It uses the *w.* informat, where *w* is the width of the character value that is being converted.
- It produces a numeric missing value from any character value that does not conform to standard numeric notation (digits with an optional decimal point, leading sign, or scientific notation).

Table 14.2 *Automatic Conversion of Character Variables*

Character Value	Automatic Conversion	Numeric Value
`12.47`	→	12.47
`-8.96`	→	-8.96
`1.243E1`	→	12.43
`1,742.64`	→	.

Restriction for WHERE Expressions

The WHERE statement does not perform automatic conversions in comparisons. The simple program below demonstrates what happens when a WHERE expression encounters the wrong data type. The variable Number contains a numeric value, and the variable Character contains a character value, but the two WHERE statements specify the wrong data type.

```
data work.convtest;
  Number=4;
  Character='4';
run;
proc print data=work.convtest;
  where character=4;
run;
proc print data=work.convtest;
  where number='4';
run;
```

This mismatch of character and numeric variables and values prevents the program from processing the WHERE statements. Automatic conversion is not performed. Instead, the program stops, and error messages are written to the SAS log.

Log 14.2 *SAS Log*

```
9254 data work.convtest;
9255   Number=4;
9256   Character='4';
9257 run;

NOTE: The data set WORK.CONVTEST has 1 observations and 2 variables.
NOTE: DATA statement used (Total process time):
      real time           0.01 seconds
      cpu time            0.01 seconds

9258 proc print data=work.convtest;
9259   where character=4;
ERROR: WHERE clause operator requires compatible variables.
9260 run;

NOTE: The SAS System stopped processing this step because of errors.
NOTE: PROCEDURE PRINT used (Total process time):
      real time           0.00 seconds
      cpu time            0.00 seconds

9261 proc print data=work.convtest;
9262   where number='4';
ERROR: WHERE clause operator requires compatible variables.
9263 run;

NOTE: The SAS System stopped processing this step because of errors.
```

Explicit Character-to-Numeric Conversion

Using the INPUT Function

Use the INPUT function to convert character data values to numeric values. You can explicitly convert the character values of PayRate to numeric values by using the INPUT function.

Syntax, INPUT function:

INPUT(*source, informat***)**

- *source* indicates the character variable, constant, or expression to be converted to a numeric value.
- a numeric *informat* must also be specified, as in this example:

```
input(payrate,2.)
```

When choosing the informat, be sure to select a numeric informat that can read the form of the values.

Table 14.3 *Character Values and Associated Informats*

Character Value	Informat
2115233	7.
2,115,233	COMMA9.

Example: INPUT Function

The function uses the numeric informat COMMA9. to read the values of the character variable SaleTest. Then the resulting numeric values are stored in the variable Test. Here is an example of the INPUT function:

```
Test=input(saletest,comma9.);
```

You can use the INPUT function to convert the character values of PayRate to numeric values.

Because PayRate has a length of 2, the numeric informat 2. is used to read the values of the variable.

```
input(payrate,2.)
```

In the following program, the function is added to the assignment statement in the DATA step.

```
data work.newtemp;
  set cert.temp;
  Salary=input(payrate,2.)*hours;
run;
```

After the DATA step is executed, the new data set, which contains the variable Salary, is created. Notice that no conversion messages appear in the SAS log when the INPUT function is used.

Log 14.3 *SAS Log*

```
9272 data work.newtemp;
9273   set cert.temp;
9274   Salary=input(payrate,2.)*hours;
9275 run;

NOTE: There were 10 observations read from the data set CERT.TEMP.
```

Output 14.1 *PROC PRINT Output of Work.NewTemp (partial output)*

Obs	Address		Startdate	Enddate	Payrate	Days	Hours		Dept	Site	Salary
1	65 ELM DR		19NOV2017	12JAN2018	10	11	88		DP	26	880
2	11 SUN DR		16OCT2017	19NOV2017	8	25	200		PURH	57	1600
3	712 HARDWICK STREET	. . .	22NOV2017	30DEC2017	40	26	208	. . .	PERS	34	8320
4	5372 WHITEBUD ROAD	*more*	29SEP2017	10OCT2017	15	10	80	*more*	BK	57	1200
5	11 TALYN COURT	*variables*	02NOV2017	13NOV2017	12	9	72	*variables*	DP	95	864
6	101 HYNERIAN DR	. . .	16NOV2017	04JAN2018	15	7	64	. . .	BK	44	960
7	11 RYGEL ROAD		02AUG2016	17AUG2017	12	12	96		DP	59	1152
8	121 E. MOYA STREET		06OCT2017	10OCT2017	10	5	40		PUB	38	400
9	1905 DOCK STREET		16OCT2017	20OCT2017	10	5	30		DP	44	300
10	1304 CRESCENT AVE		29JUN2017	30OCT2017	15	5	25		DP	90	375

The syntax of the INPUT function is very similar to the syntax of the PUT function (which performs numeric-to-character conversions).

INPUT(*source, informat***)**

PUT(*source, format)***)**

However, note that the INPUT function requires an informat, whereas the PUT function requires a format. To remember which function requires a format versus an informat, note that the INPUT function requires an informat.

Automatic Numeric-to-Character Conversion

The automatic conversion of numeric data to character data is very similar to character-to-numeric conversion. Numeric data values are converted to character values whenever they are used in a character context.

For example, the numeric values of the variable Site are converted to character values if you do the following:

- assign the numeric value to a previously defined character variable, such as the character variable SiteCode: SiteCode=site;
- use the numeric value with an operator that requires a character value, such as the concatenation operator: SiteCode=site||dept;
- specify the numeric value in a function that requires character arguments, such as the SUBSTR function: Region=substr(site,1,4);

Specifically, SAS writes the numeric value with the BEST12. format, and the resulting character value is right-aligned. This conversion occurs before the value is assigned or used with any operator or function. However, automatic numeric-to-character conversion can cause unexpected results. For example, suppose the original numeric value has fewer than 12 digits. The resulting character value has leading blanks, which might cause problems when you perform an operation or function.

Automatic numeric-to-character conversion also causes a message to be written to the SAS log indicating that the conversion has occurred.

Explicit Numeric-to-Character Conversion

Use the PUT function to explicitly convert numeric data values to character data values.

Suppose you want to create a new character variable named Assignment that concatenates the values of the numeric variable Site and the character variable Dept. The new variable values must contain the value of Site followed by a slash (/) and then the value of Dept (for example, `26/DP`).

Figure 14.1 *SAS Data Set Cert.Temp (partial data set)*

. . . more variables . . .

Dept	Site	Salary	Assignment
DP	26	880	26/DP
PURH	57	1600	57/PURH
PERS	34	8320	34/PERS
BK	57	1200	57/BK
DP	95	864	95/DP
BK	44	960	44/BK
DP	59	1152	59/DP
PUB	38	400	38/PUB
DP	44	300	44/DP
DP	90	375	90/DP

Here is an assignment statement that contains the concatenation operator (||) to indicate that Site should be concatenated with Dept, using a slash as a separator.

```
data work.newtemp;
```

```
  set cert.temp;
  Assignment=site||'/'||dept;
run;
```

Note: The slash is enclosed in quotation marks. All character constants must be enclosed in quotation marks.

Submitting this DATA step causes SAS to automatically convert the numeric values of Site to character values because Site is used in a character context. The variable Site appears with the concatenation operator, which requires character values. To explicitly convert the numeric values of Site to character values, you must add the PUT function to your assignment statement.

Syntax, PUT function:

PUT(*source, format*)

- *source* indicates the numeric variable, constant, or expression to be converted to a character value
- a *format* matching the data type of the source must also be specified, as in this example:

```
put(site,2.)
```

Here are several facts about the PUT function.

- The PUT function always returns a character string.
- The PUT function returns the source written with a format.
- The format must agree with the source in type.
- Numeric formats right-align the result; character formats left-align the result.
- When you use the PUT function to create a variable that has not been previously identified, it creates a character variable whose length is equal to the format width.

When you use a numeric variable as the source, you must specify a numeric format.

To explicitly convert the numeric values of Site to character values, use the PUT function in an assignment statement, where Site is the source variable. Because Site has a length of 2, choose 2. as the numeric format. The DATA step adds the new variable from the assignment statement to the data set.

```
data work.newtemp;
  set cert.temp;
  Assignment=put(site,2.)||'/'||dept;
run;
proc print data=work.newtemp;
run;
```

Output 14.2 *PROC PRINT Output of Work.NewTemp (partial output)*

Obs	Address	*. . . more variables . . .*	Startdate	Enddate	Payrate	Days	Hours	*. . . more variables . . .*	Dept	Site	Salary	Assignment
1	65 ELM DR		19NOV2017	12JAN2018	10	11	88		DP	26	880	26/DP
2	11 SUN DR		16OCT2017	19NOV2017	8	25	200		PURH	57	1600	57/PURH
3	712 HARDWICK STREET		22NOV2017	30DEC2017	40	26	208		PERS	34	8320	34/PERS
4	5372 WHITEBUD ROAD		29SEP2017	10OCT2017	15	10	80		BK	57	1200	57/BK
5	11 TALYN COURT		02NOV2017	13NOV2017	12	9	72		DP	95	864	95/DP
6	101 HYNERIAN DR		16NOV2017	04JAN2018	15	7	64		BK	44	960	44/BK
7	11 RYGEL ROAD		02AUG2016	17AUG2017	12	12	96		DP	59	1152	59/DP
8	121 E. MOYA STREET		06OCT2017	10OCT2017	10	5	40		PUB	38	400	38/PUB
9	1905 DOCK STREET		16OCT2017	20OCT2017	10	5	30		DP	44	300	44/DP
10	1304 CRESCENT AVE		29JUN2017	30OCT2017	15	5	25		DP	90	375	90/DP

Notice that no conversion messages appear in the SAS log when you use the PUT function.

Log 14.4 *SAS Log*

```
9355 data work.newtemp;
9356  set cert.temp;
9357  Assignment=put(site,2.)||'/'||dept;
9358  run;

NOTE: There were 10 observations read from the data set CERT.TEMP.
NOTE: The data set WORK.NEWTEMP has 10 observations and 17 variables.
```

Manipulating SAS Date Values with Functions

SAS Date Functions

SAS stores date, time, and datetime values as numeric values. You can use several functions to create these values. For more information about datetime values, see Chapter 13, "SAS Date, Time, and Datetime Values," on page 241.

Table 14.4 *Typical Use of SAS Date Functions*

Function	Example Code	Result
MDY	`date=mdy(mon,day,yr);`	SAS date
TODAYDATE	`now=today();` `now=date();`	today's date as a SAS date
TIME	`curtime=time();`	current time as a SAS time

Use other functions to extract months, quarters, days, and years from SAS date values.

Table 14.5 Selected Functions to Use with SAS Date Values

Function	Example Code	Result
DAY	`day=day(date);`	day of month (1-31)
QTR	`quarter=qtr(date);`	quarter (1-4)
WEEKDAY	`wkday=weekday(date);`	day of week (1-7)
MONTH	`month=month(date);`	month (1-12)
YEAR	`yr=year(date);`	year (4 digits)

INTCK	`x=intck('day',d1,d2);`
	`x=intck('week',d1,d2);`
	`x=intck('month',d1,d2);`
	`x=intck('qtr',d1,d2);`
	`x=intck('year',d1,d2);`
		days from D1 to D2
		weeks from D1 to D2
		months from D1 to D2
		quarters from D1 to D2
		years from D1 to D2

INTNX	`x=intnx('interval', start-from,increment);`	date, time, or datetime value
DATDIF YRDIF	`x=datdif(date1,date2,'ACT/ACT');` `x=yrdif(date1,date2,'ACT/ACT');`	days between date1 and date2 years between date1 and date2

YEAR, QTR, MONTH, and DAY Functions

Overview of YEAR, QTR, MONTH, and DAY Functions

Every SAS date value can be queried for the values of its year, quarter, month, and day. You extract these values by using the functions YEAR, QTR, MONTH, and DAY. They each work the same way.

Syntax, YEAR, QTR, MONTH, and DAY functions:

YEAR(*date*)

QTR(*date*)

MONTH(*date*)

DAY(*date*)

date is a SAS date value that is specified either as a variable or as a SAS date constant.

The YEAR function returns a four-digit numeric value that represents the year (for example, 2018). The QTR function returns a value of 1, 2, 3, or 4 from a SAS date value to indicate the quarter of the year in which a date value falls. The MONTH function returns a numeric value that ranges from 1 to 12, representing the month of the year. The value 1 represents January, 2 represents February, and so on. The DAY function returns a numeric value from 1 to 31, representing the day of the month.

Table 14.6 Selected Date Functions and Their Uses

Function	Description	Form	Sample Value
YEAR	Extracts the year value from a SAS date value.	YEAR*(date)*	`2018`
QTR	Extracts the quarter value from a SAS date value	QTR*(date)*	`1`
MONTH	Extracts the month value from a SAS date value.	MONTH*(date)*	`12`
DAY	Extracts the day value from a SAS date value	DAY*(date)*	`5`

Example: Finding the Year and Month

Suppose you want to create a subset of the data set Cert.Temp that contains information about all temporary employees who were hired in November 2017. The data set Cert.Temp contains the beginning and ending dates for staff employment, but there are no month or year variables in the data set. To determine the year in which employees were hired, you can apply the YEAR function to the variable that contains the employee start date, StartDate. Here is a way to write the YEAR function:

```
year(startdate)
```

Likewise, to determine the month in which employees were hired, you apply the MONTH function to StartDate.

```
month(startdate)
```

To create the new data set, you include these functions in a subsetting IF statement within a DATA step. The subsetting IF statement specifies the new data set include only the observations where the YEAR function extracts a value of 2017 and the MONTH function extracts a value of 11. The value of 11 stands for November.

```
data work.nov17;
  set cert.temp;
  if year(startdate)=2017 and month(startdate)=11;
run;
```

When you add a PROC PRINT step to the program, you can view the new data set.

```
proc print data=work.nov17;
  format startdate enddate birthdate date9.;
run;
```

The new data set contains information about only those employees who were hired in November 2017.

Output 14.3 *PROC PRINT Output of Work.Nov17 (partial output)*

Obs	Address		Startdate	Enddate	
1	65 ELM DR	. . .	19NOV2017	12JAN2018	. . .
2	712 HARDWICK STREET	more	22NOV2017	30DEC2017	more
3	11 TALYN COURT	variables	02NOV2017	13NOV2017	variables
4	101 HYNERIAN DR	. . .	16NOV2017	04JAN2018	. . .

Example: Finding the Year

Suppose you want to create a subset of the data set Cert.Temp that contains information about all temporary employees who were hired during a specific year, such as 2016. Cert.Temp contains the dates on which employees began work with the company and their ending dates, but there is no year variable.

To determine the year in which employees were hired, you can apply the YEAR function to the variable that contains the employee start date, StartDate. You write the YEAR function as follows:

```
year(startdate)
```

To create the new data set, you include this function in a subsetting IF statement within a DATA step. This subsetting IF statement specifies that only observations in which the YEAR function extracts a value of **`2016`** are placed in the new data set.

```
data work.temp16;
  set cert.temp;
  if year(startdate)=2016;
run;
```

When you add a PROC PRINT step to the program, you can view the new data set.

```
data work.temp16;
  set cert.temp;
  where year(startdate)=2016;
run;
proc print data=work.temp16;
  format startdate enddate birthdate date9.;
run;
```

The new data set contains information for only those employees who were hired in 2016.

Output 14.4 *PROC PRINT Output of Work.Temp16 (partial output)*

Obs	Address	City	State	Zip	Phone	Startdate	Enddate	
1	11 RYGEL ROAD	CHAPEL HILL	NC	27514	9972070	02AUG2016	17AUG2017	...more variables...

WEEKDAY Function

Overview of the WEEKDAY Function

The WEEKDAY function enables you to extract the day of the week from a SAS date value.

Syntax, WEEKDAY function:

WEEKDAY(*date*)

date is a SAS date value that is specified either as a variable or as a SAS date constant.

The WEEKDAY function returns a numeric value from 1 to 7. The values represent the days of the week.

Table 14.7 *Values for the WEEKDAY Function*

Value	Equals	Day of the Week
1	=	Sunday
2	=	Monday
3	=	Tuesday
4	=	Wednesday
5	=	Thursday
6	=	Friday
7	=	Saturday

Example: WEEKDAY Function

For example, suppose the data set Cert.Sch contains a broadcast schedule. The variable AirDate contains SAS date values. To create a data set that contains only weekend broadcasts, you use the WEEKDAY function in a subsetting IF statement. You include only observations in which the value of AirDate corresponds to a Saturday or Sunday.

```
data work.schwkend;
  set cert.sch;
  if weekday(airdate)in(1,7);
run;
proc print data=work.schwkend;
run;
```

Output 14.5 *PROC PRINT Output of Weekday Function*

Obs	Program	Producer	AirDate
1	River to River	NPR	04/01/2000
2	World Cafe	WXPN	04/08/2000
3	Classical Music	NPR	04/08/2000
4	Symphony Live	NPR	04/01/2000
5	Symphony Live	NPR	04/16/2000
6	World Cafe	WXPN	04/08/2000

Note: In the example above, the statement **`if weekday(airdate) in (1,7);`** is the same as **`if weekday(airdate)=7 or weekday(airdate)=1;`**

MDY Function

Overview of the MDY Function

The MDY function returns a SAS date value from month, day, and year values.

Syntax, MDY function:

MDY (month, day, year)

- *month* specifies a numeric constant, variable, or expression that represents an integer from 1 through 12.
- *day* specifies a numeric constant, variable, or expression that represents an integer from 1 through 31.
- *year* specifies a numeric constant, variable, or expression with a value of a two-digit or four-digit integer that represents that year.

Example: MDY Function

In the data set Cert.Dates, the values for month, day, and year are stored in the numeric variables Month, Day, and Year. It is possible to write the following MDY function to create the SAS date values:

```
mdy(month,day,year)
```

To create a new variable to contain the SAS date values, place this function in an assignment statement.

```
data work.datestemp;
  set cert.dates;
  Date=mdy(month,day,year);
run;
proc print data=work.datestemp;
  format date mmddyy10.;
run;
```

Output 14.6 *PROC PRINT Output of Work.Datestemp*

Obs	year	month	day	date
1	2018	1	22	01/22/2018
2	2018	2	9	02/09/2018
3	2018	3	5	03/05/2018
4	2018	4	27	04/27/2018
5	2018	5	10	05/10/2018
6	2018	6	6	06/06/2018
7	2018	7	23	07/23/2018
8	2018	8	11	08/11/2018
9	2018	9	3	09/03/2018
10	2018	10	5	10/05/2018
11	2018	11	23	11/23/2018
12	2018	12	13	12/13/2018

The MDY function can also add the same SAS date to every observation. This might be useful if you want to compare a fixed beginning date with different end dates. Just use numbers instead of data set variables when providing values to the MDY function.

```
data work.datestemp;
  set cert.dates;
  DateCons=mdy(6,17,2018);
run;
proc print data=work.datestemp;
  format DateCons mmddyy10.;
run;
```

Output 14.7 *PROC PRINT Output of Work.Datestemp*

Obs	year	month	day	DateCons
1	2018	1	22	06/17/2018
2	2018	2	9	06/17/2018
3	2018	3	5	06/17/2018
4	2018	4	27	06/17/2018
5	2018	5	10	06/17/2018
6	2018	6	6	06/17/2018
7	2018	7	23	06/17/2018
8	2018	8	11	06/17/2018
9	2018	9	3	06/17/2018
10	2018	10	5	06/17/2018
11	2018	11	23	06/17/2018
12	2018	12	13	06/17/2018

To display the years clearly, format SAS dates with the DATE9. format. This forces the year to appear with four digits, as shown above in the Date and DateCons variables of the Work.DatesTenp output.

Example: Finding the Date

The data set Cert.Review2018 contains a variable named Day. This variable contains the day of the month for each employee's performance appraisal. The appraisals were all completed in December of 2018.

The following DATA step uses the MDY function to create a new variable named ReviewDate. This variable contains the SAS date value for the date of each performance appraisal.

```
data work.review2018 (drop=Day);
  set cert.review2018;
  ReviewDate=mdy(12,day,2018);
run;
proc print data=work.review2018;
  format ReviewDate mmddyy10.;
run;
```

Output 14.8 *PROC PRINT Output of Work.Review2018*

Obs	Name	Rate	Site	ReviewDate
1	Mitchell, K.	A2	Westin	12/12/2018
2	Worton, M.	A5	Stockton	12/03/2018
3	Smith, A.	B1	Center City	12/17/2018
4	Kales, H.	A3	Stockton	12/04/2018
5	Khalesh, P.	A1	Stockton	12/07/2018
6	Samuel, P.	B4	Center City	12/05/2018
7	Daniels, B.	C1	Westin	12/07/2018
8	Mahes, K.	B2	Center City	12/04/2018
9	Hunter, D.	B2	Westin	12/10/2018
10	Moon, D.	A2	Stockton	12/05/2018
11	Crane, N.	B1	Stockton	12/03/2018

Note: If you specify an invalid date in the MDY function, SAS assigns a missing value to the target variable.

```
data work.review2018 (drop=Day);
  set cert.review2018;
  ReviewDate=mdy(15,day,2018);
run;
proc print data=work.review2018;
  format ReviewDate mmddyy10.;
run;
```

DATE and TODAY Functions

Overview of the DATE Function

The DATE function returns the current date as a numeric SAS date value.

Note: If the value of the TIMEZONE= system option is set to a time zone name or time zone ID, the return values for date and time are determined by the time zone.

Syntax, DATE function:

DATE ()

The DATE function does not require any arguments, but it must be followed by parentheses.

The DATE function produces the current date in the form of a SAS date value, which is the number of days since January 1, 1960.

Overview of the TODAY Function

The TODAY function returns the current date as a numeric SAS date value.

Note: If the value of the TIMEZONE= system option is set to a time zone name or time zone ID, the return values for date and time are determined by the time zone.

Syntax, TODAY function:

TODAY ()

The TODAY function does not require any arguments, but it must be followed by parentheses.

The TODAY function produces the current date in the form of a SAS date value, which is the number of days since January 1, 1960.

Example: The DATE and TODAY Functions

The DATE and TODAY functions have the same form and can be used interchangeably. To add a new variable, which contains the current date, to the data set Cert.Temp. To create this variable, write an assignment statement such as the following:

```
EditDate=date();
```

After this statement is added to a DATA step and the step is submitted, the data set that contains EditDate is created. To display these SAS date values in a different form, you can associate a SAS format with the values. For example, the FORMAT statement below associates the DATE9. format with the variable EditDate. The output that is created by this PROC PRINT step appears below.

Note: For this example, the SAS date values shown below were created by submitting this program on July 20, 2018.

```
data work.tempdate;
  set cert.dates;
  EditDate=date();
run;
proc print data=work.tempdate;
  format EditDate date9.;
run;
```

Output 14.9 *PROC PRINT Output of Work.TempDate*

Obs	year	month	day	EditDate
1	2018	1	22	20JUL2018
2	2018	2	9	20JUL2018
3	2018	3	5	20JUL2018
4	2018	4	27	20JUL2018
5	2018	5	10	20JUL2018
6	2018	6	6	20JUL2018
7	2018	7	23	20JUL2018
8	2018	8	11	20JUL2018
9	2018	9	3	20JUL2018
10	2018	10	5	20JUL2018
11	2018	11	23	20JUL2018
12	2018	12	13	20JUL2018

INTCK Function

Overview of the INTCK Function

The INTCK function returns the number of interval boundaries of a given kind that lie between two dates, times, or datetime values. You can use it to count the passage of days, weeks, months, and so on.

Syntax, INTCK function:

INTCK (*'interval'* , *from*, *to*)

- *'interval'* specifies a character constant or a variable. Interval can appear in uppercase or lowercase. The value can be one of the following:
  - DAY
  - WEEKDAY
  - WEEK
  - TENDAY
  - SEMIMONTH
  - MONTH
  - QTR
  - SEMIYEAR
  - YEAR
- *from* specifies a SAS date, time, or datetime value that identifies the beginning of the time span.
- *to* specifies a SAS date, time, or datetime value that identifies the end of the time span.

Note: The type of interval (date, time, or datetime) must match the type of value in *from*.

Details

The INTCK function counts intervals from fixed interval beginnings, not in multiples of an interval unit from the *from* value. Partial intervals are not counted. For example, WEEK intervals are counted by Sundays rather than seven-day multiples from the *from* argument. MONTH intervals are counted by day 1 of each month, and YEAR intervals are counted from 01JAN, not in 365-day multiples.

Consider the results in the following table. The values that are assigned to the variables Weeks, Months, and Years are based on consecutive days.

Table 14.8 *Examples of SAS Statements and Their Values*

Example Code	Value
`Weeks=intck('week','31dec2017'd,'01jan2018'd);`	0
`Months=intck('month','31dec2017'd,'01jan2018'd);`	1
`Years=intck('year','31dec2017'd,'01jan2018'd);`	1

Because December 31, 2017, is a Sunday, no WEEK interval is crossed between that day and January 1, 2018. However, both MONTH and YEAR intervals are crossed.

Examples: INTCK Function

The following statement creates the variable Years and assigns it a value of `2`. The INTCK function determines that two years have elapsed between June 15, 2016, and June 15, 2018.

```
Years=intck('year','15jun2016'd,'15jun2018'd);
```

Note: As shown here, the *from* and *to* dates are often specified as date constants.

Likewise, the following statement assigns the value 24 to the variable Months.

```
Months=intck('month','15jun2016'd,'15jun2018'd);
```

However, the following statement assigns 0 to the variable Years, even though 364 days have elapsed. In this case, the YEAR boundary (01JAN) is not crossed.

```
Years=intck('year','01jan2018'd,'31dec2018'd);
```

Example: The INTCK Function and Periodic Events

A common use of the INTCK function is to identify periodic events such as due dates and anniversaries.

The following program identifies mechanics whose 20th year of employment occurs in the current month. It uses the INTCK function to compare the value of the variable Hired to the date on which the program is run.

```
data work.anniversary;
  set cert.mechanics(keep=id lastname firstname hired);
  Years=intck('year',hired,today());
  if years=20 and month(hired)=month(today());
run;
proc print data=work.anniversary;
  title '20-Year Anniversaries';
run;
```

The following output is created when the program is run in July 2018.

Output 14.10 *PROC PRINT Output of Work.Anniversary*

20 Year Anniversaries This Month

Obs	ID	LastName	FirstName	Hired	years
1	1499	BAREFOOT	JOSEPH	23JUL98	20
2	1065	CHAPMAN	NEIL	23JUL98	20
3	1406	FOSTER	GERALD	10JUL98	20
4	1423	OSWALD	LESLIE	16JUL98	20

INTNX Function

Overview of the INTNX Function

The INTNX function is similar to the INTCK function. The INTNX function applies multiples of a given interval to a date, time, or datetime value and returns the resulting value. You can use the INTNX function to identify past or future days, weeks, months, and so on.

Syntax, INTNX function:

INTNX(*'interval',start-from,increment*, <*'alignment'*>**)**

- *'interval'* specifies a character constant or variable.
- *start-from* specifies a starting SAS date, time, or datetime value.
- *increment* specifies a negative or positive integer that represents time intervals toward the past or future.
- *'alignment'* (optional) forces the alignment of the returned date to the beginning, middle, or end of the interval.

Note: The type of interval (date, time, or datetime) must match the type of value in *start-from* and *increment*.

Details

When you specify date intervals, the value of the character constant or variable that is used in *interval* can be one of the following:

- DATETIME
- DAY
- QTR
- MONTH
- SEMIMONTH
- SEMIYEAR
- TENDAY
- TIME
- WEEK

- WEEKDAY
- YEAR

Example: INTNX Function

For example, the following statement creates the variable TargetYear and assigns it a SAS date value of **22281**, which corresponds to January 1, 2021.

```
TargetYear=intnx('year','20Jul18'd,3);
```

Likewise, the following statement assigns the value for the date July 1, 2018, to the variable TargetMonth.

```
TargetMonth=intnx('semiyear','01Jan18'd,1);
```

SAS date values are based on the number of days since January 1, 1960. Yet the INTNX function can use intervals of weeks, months, years, and so on.

The purpose of the optional alignment argument is to specify whether the returned value should be at the beginning, middle, or end of the interval. When specifying date alignment in the INTNX function, use the following values or their corresponding aliases:

- BEGINNING Alias: B
- MIDDLE Alias: M
- END Alias: E
- SAME Alias: SAMEDAY or S

The best way to understand the alignment argument is to see its effect on identical statements. The following table shows the results of three INTNX statements that differ only in the value of alignment.

Table 14.9 *Alignment Values for the INTNX Function*

Example Code	Date Value
`MonthX=intnx('month','01jan2018'd,5,'b');`	**21336** (June 1, 2018)
`MonthX=intnx('month','01jan2018'd,5,'m');`	**21350** (June 15, 2018)
`MonthX=intnx('month','01jan2018'd,5,'e');`	**21365** (June 30, 2018)

These INTNX statements count five months from January, but the returned value depends on whether alignment specifies the beginning, middle, or end day of the resulting month. If alignment is not specified, the beginning day is returned by default.

DATDIF and YRDIF Functions

The DATDIF and YRDIF functions calculate the difference in days and years between two SAS dates, respectively. Both functions accept start dates and end dates that are specified as SAS date values. Also, both functions use a basis argument that describes how SAS calculates the date difference.

Syntax, DATDIF, and YRDIF functions:

DATDIF(*start_date,end_date,basis)***)**

YRDIF(*start_date,end_date,basis)***)**

- *start_date* specifies the starting date as a SAS date value.
- *end_date* specifies the ending date as a SAS date value.
- *basis* specifies a character constant or variable that describes how SAS calculates the date difference.

There are two character strings that are valid for basis in the DATDIF function, and four character strings that are valid for basis in the YRDIF function. These character strings and their meanings are listed in the table below.

Table 14.10 *Character Strings in the DATDIF Function*

Character String	Meaning	Valid in DATDIF	Valid in YRDIF
`'30/360'`	specifies a 30-day month and a 360-day year	yes	yes
`'ACT/ACT'`	uses the actual number of days or years between dates	yes	yes
`'ACT/360'`	uses the actual number of days between dates in calculating the number of years (calculated by the number of days divided by 360)	no	yes
`'ACT/365'`	uses the actual number of days between dates in calculating the number of years (calculated by the number of days divided by 365)	no	yes

The best way to understand the different options for the basis argument is to see the different effects that they have on the value that the function returns. The table below lists four YRDIF functions that use the same start date and end date. Each function uses one of the possible values for basis, and each one returns a different value.

Table 14.11 *Examples of the YRDIF Function*

Example Code	Returned Value

`data _null_;`
`  x=yrdif('16feb2016'd,'16jun2018'd,'30/360');`
`  put x;`
`run;`
	2.3333333333

`data _null_;`
`  x=yrdif('16feb2016'd, '16jun2018'd, 'ACT/ACT');`
`  put x;`
`run;`
	2.3291114604

Example Code	Returned Value
`data _null_; x=yrdif('16feb2016'd, '16jun2018'd, 'ACT/360'); put x; run;`	2.3638888889
`data _null_; x=yrdif('16feb2016'd, '16jun2018'd, 'ACT/365'); put x; run;`	2.3315068493

Modifying Character Values with Functions

SCAN Function

Overview of the SCAN Function

The SCAN function returns the *n*th word from a character string. The SCAN function enables you to separate a character value into words and to return a specified word.

Figure 14.2 *SCAN Function*

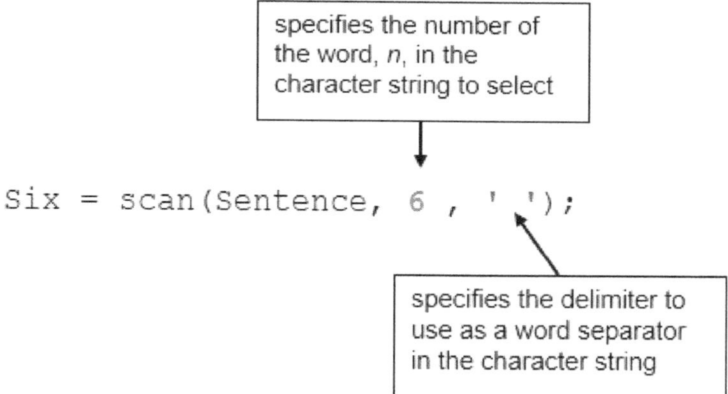

Note: In SAS 9.4 or later, if the variable has not yet been given a length, then the SCAN function returns the value and assigns the variable the given length of the first argument. In SAS 9.3 or earlier, by default, the variable is assigned a length of 200.

Syntax, SCAN function:

SCAN(*argument,n<,<delimiters>>***)**

- *argument* specifies the character variable or expression to scan.
- *n* specifies which word to return.
- *delimiters* are special characters that must be enclosed in single quotation marks (' '). If you do not specify *delimiters*, default delimiters are used.

Details

- Leading delimiters before the first word in the character string do not affect the SCAN function.
- If there are two or more contiguous delimiters, the SCAN function treats them as one.
- If *n* is greater than the number of words in the character string, the SCAN function returns a blank value.
- If *n* is negative, the SCAN function selects the word in the character string starting from the end of the string.

Example: Create New Name Variables

Use the SCAN function to create your new name variables for Cert.Staff. First, examine the values of the existing Name variable to determine which characters separate the names in the values.

```
LastName=scan(name,1);
```

Notice that blanks and commas appear between the names and that the employee's last name appears first, then the first name, and then the middle name.

To create the LastName variable to store the employee's last name, you write an assignment statement that contains the following SCAN function:

```
LastName=scan(name,1,' ,');
```

Note that a blank and a comma are specified as delimiters. You can also write the function without listing delimiters, because the blank and comma are default delimiters.

```
LastName=scan(name,1);
```

Here is the complete DATA step that is needed to create LastName, FirstName, and MiddleName. Notice that the original Name variable is dropped from the new data set.

```
data work.newnames(drop=name);
  set cert.staff;
  LastName=scan(name,1);
  FirstName=scan(name,2);
run;
```

Specifying Delimiters

The SCAN function uses delimiters to separate a character string into words. Delimiters are characters that are specified as word separators. For example, if you are working with the character string below and you specify the comma as a delimiter, the SCAN function separates the string into three words.

Then the function returns the word that you specify. In this example, if you specify the third word, the SCAN function returns the word HIGH.

Here is another example that uses the comma as a delimiter, and specifies that the third word be returned.

```
209 RADCLIFFE ROAD, CENTER CITY, NY, 92716
```

In this example, if you specify the third word, the word returned by the SCAN function is NY (NY contains a leading blank).

Specifying Multiple Delimiters

When using the SCAN function, you can specify as many delimiters as needed to correctly separate the character expression. When you specify multiple delimiters, SAS uses any of the delimiters, singly or in any combination, as word separators. For example, if you specify both the slash and the hyphen as delimiters, the SCAN function separates the following text string into three words:

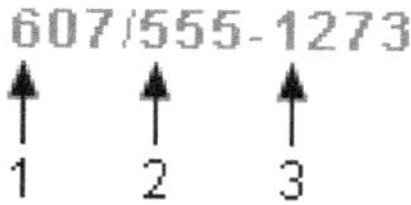

The SCAN function treats two or more contiguous delimiters, such as the parenthesis and slash below, as one delimiter. Also, leading delimiters have no effect.

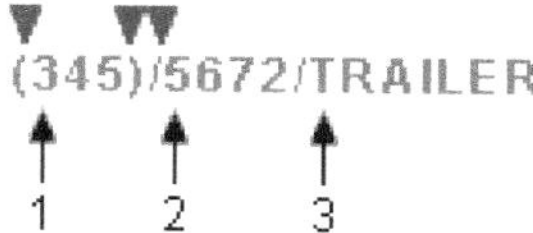

Default Delimiters

If you do not specify delimiters when using the SCAN function, default delimiters are used. Here are the default delimiters:

```
blank . < ( + | & ! $ * ) ; ^ - / , %
```

Specifying Variable Length

If a variable is not assigned a length before it is specified in the SCAN function, the variable is given the length of the first argument. This length could be too small or too large for the remaining variables.

You can add a LENGTH statement to the DATA step, and specify an appropriate length for all three variables. The LENGTH statement is placed before the assignment statement that contains the SCAN function so that SAS can specify the length the first time it encounters the variable.

```
data work.newnames(drop=name);
  set cert.staff;
  length LastName FirstName $ 12;
  LastName=scan(name,1);
  FirstName=scan(name,2);
  MiddleInitial=scan(name,3);
run;
proc print data=newnames;
run;
```

Output 14.11 *PROC PRINT Output of Work.NewNames (partial output)*

Obs	ID	DOB	WageCategory	WageRate	Bonus	LastName	FirstName	Middle_Initial
1	1351	-4685	S	3392.50	1187.38	Farr	Sue	
2	161	-5114	S	5093.75	1782.81	Cox	Kay	B
3	212	-2415	S	1813.30	634.65	Moore	Ron	
4	2512	-2819	S	1572.50	550.37	Ruth	G	H
5	2532	-780	H	13.48	500.00	Hobbs	Roy	

. . . *more observations*. . .

Obs	ID	DOB	WageCategory	WageRate	Bonus	LastName	FirstName	Middle_Initial
21	5002	-832	S	5910.75	2068.76	Welch	W	B
22	5112	-4146	S	4045.85	1416.05	Delgado	Ed	
23	511	-822	S	4480.50	1568.18	Vega	Julie	
24	5132	-3129	S	6855.90	2399.57	Overby	Phil	
25	5151	-10209	S	3163.00	1107.05	Coxe	Susan	
26	1351	-4685	S	3392.50	1187.38	Farr	Sue	

SUBSTR Function

Overview of the SUBSTR Function

The SUBSTR function extracts a substring from an argument, starting at a specific position in the string.

Figure 14.3 *SUBSTR Function*

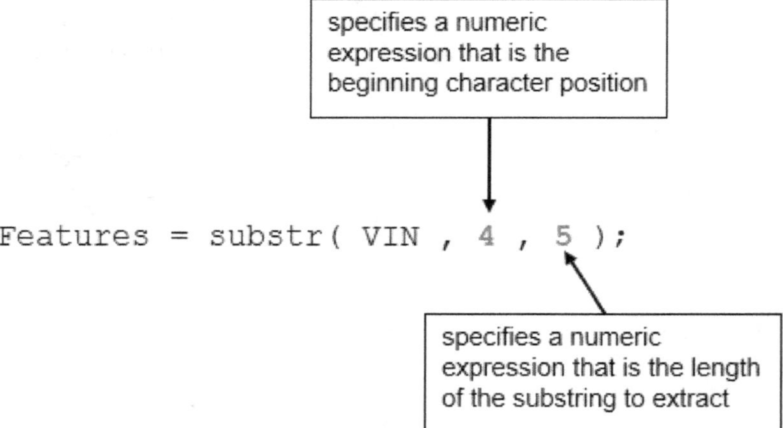

The SUBSTR function can be used on either the right or left of the equal sign to replace character value constants.

Syntax, SUBSTR function:

SUBSTR(*argument, position* <,n>)

- *argument* specifies the character variable or expression to scan.
- *position* is the character position to start from.
- *n* specifies the number of characters to extract. If *n* is omitted, all remaining characters are included in the substring.

Example: SUBSTR Function

This example begins with the task of extracting a portion of a value. In the data set Cert.AgencyEmp, the names of temporary employees are stored in three name variables: LastName, FirstName, and MiddleName.

Obs	Agency	ID	LastName	FirstName	MiddleName
1	Adminstrative Support, Inc.	F274	CICHOCK	ELIZABETH	MARIE
2	Adminstrative Support, Inc.	F101	BENINCASA	HANNAH	LEE
3	OD Consulting, Inc.	F054	SHERE	BRIAN	THOMAS
4	New Time Temps Agency	F077	HODNOFF	RICHARD	LEE

However, suppose you want to modify the data set to store only the middle initial instead of the full middle name. To do so, you must extract the first letter of the middle name values and assign these values to the new variable MiddleInitial.

Obs	Agency	ID	LastName	FirstName	MiddleInitial
1	Adminstrative Support, Inc.	F274	CICHOCK	ELIZABETH	M
2	Adminstrative Support, Inc.	F101	BENINCASA	HANNAH	L
3	OD Consulting, Inc.	F054	SHERE	BRIAN	T
4	New Time Temps Agency	F077	HODNOFF	RICHARD	L

Using the SUBSTR function, you can extract the first letter of the MiddleName value to create the new variable MiddleInitial.

You write the SUBSTR function as the following:

```
substr(middlename,1,1)
```

This function extracts a character string from the value of MiddleName. The string to be extracted begins in position 1 and contains one character. This function is placed in an assignment statement in the DATA step.

```
data work.agencyemp(drop=middlename);
  set cert.agencyemp;
  length MiddleInitial $ 1;
  MiddleInitial=substr(middlename,1,1);
run;
proc print data=work.agencyemp;
run;
```

The new MiddleInitial variable is given the same length as MiddleName. The MiddleName variable is then dropped from the new data set.

Obs	Agency	ID	LastName	FirstName	MiddleInitial
1	Adminstrative Support, Inc.	F274	CICHOCK	ELIZABETH	M
2	Adminstrative Support, Inc.	F101	BENINCASA	HANNAH	L
3	OD Consulting, Inc.	F054	SHERE	BRIAN	T
4	New Time Temps Agency	F077	HODNOFF	RICHARD	L

You can use the SUBSTR function to extract a substring from any character value if you know the position of the value.

Replacing Text Using SUBSTR

There is a second use for the SUBSTR function. This function can also be used to replace the contents of a character variable. For example, suppose the local phone exchange `622` was replaced by the exchange `433`. You need to update the character variable Phone in Cert.Temp to reflect this change.

Obs	Address	. . . *more variables* . . .	Phone	. . . *more variables* . . .
1	65 ELM DR		6224549	
2	11 SUN DR		6223251	
3	712 HARDWICK STREET		9974749	
4	5372 WHITEBUD ROAD		6970540	
5	11 TALYN COURT		3633618	

. . . *more observations* . . .

You can use the SUBSTR function to complete this modification. The syntax of the SUBSTR function, when used to replace a variable's values, is identical to the syntax for extracting a substring.

SUBSTR(*argument*,*position*,*n*)

However, in this case, note the following:

- The first argument specifies the character variable whose values are to be modified.
- The second argument specifies the position at which the replacement is to begin.
- The third argument specifies the number of characters to replace. If *n* is omitted, all remaining characters are replaced.

Positioning the SUBSTR Function

SAS uses the SUBSTR function to extract a substring or to modify a variable's values, depending on the position of the function in the assignment statement.

When the function is on the right side of an assignment statement, the function returns the requested string.

```
MiddleInitial=substr(middlename,1,1);
```

But if you place the SUBSTR function on the left side of an assignment statement, the function is used to modify variable values.

```
substr(region,1,3)='NNW';
```

When the SUBSTR function modifies variable values, the right side of the assignment statement must specify the value to place into the variable. For example, to replace the fourth and fifth characters of a variable named Test with the value `92`, you write the following assignment statement:

```
substr(test,4,2)='92';
```

Test		Test
S7381K2	→	S7392K2
S7381K7	→	S7392K7

It is possible to use the SUBSTR function to replace the `622` exchange in the variable Phone. This assignment statement specifies that the new exchange `433` should be placed in the variable Phone, starting at character position 1 and replacing three characters.

```
data work.temp2;
  set cert.temp;
  substr(phone,1,3)='433';
run;
proc print data=work.temp2;
run;
```

However, executing this DATA step places the value `433` into all values of Phone.

Obs	Address		Phone	
1	65 ELM DR		4334549	
2	11 SUN DR		4333251	
3	712 HARDWICK STREET		4334749	
4	5372 WHITEBUD ROAD	...more variables ...	4330540	...more variables ...
5	11 TALYN COURT		4333618	
6	101 HYNERIAN DR		4336732	
7	11 RYGEL ROAD		4332070	
8	121 E. MOYA STREET		4333020	
9	1905 DOCK STREET		4335303	
10	1304 CRESCENT AVE		4331557	

You need to replace only the values of Phone that contain the **622** exchange. To extract the exchange from Phone, add an assignment statement to the DATA step. Notice that the SUBSTR function is used on the right side of the assignment statement.

```
data work.temp2(drop=exchange);
  set cert.temp;
  Exchange=substr(phone,1,3);
  substr(phone,1,3)='433';
run;
proc print data=work.temp2;
run;
```

Now the DATA step needs an IF-THEN statement to verify the value of the variable Exchange. If the exchange is **622**, the assignment statement executes to replace the value of Phone.

```
data work.temp2(drop=exchange);
  set cert.temp;
  Exchange=substr(phone,1,3);
  if exchange='622' then substr(phone,1,3)='433';
run;
proc print data=work.temp2;
run;
```

After the DATA step is executed, the appropriate values of Phone contain the new exchange.

Figure 14.4 PROC PRINT Output of Work.Temp2 (partial output)

Obs	Address		Phone	
1	65 ELM DR		4334549	
2	11 SUN DR		4333251	
3	712 HARDWICK STREET	...more variables ...	9974749	...more variables ...
4	5372 WHITEBUD ROAD		6970540	
5	11 TALYN COURT		3633618	
6	101 HYNERIAN DR		9976732	
7	11 RYGEL ROAD		9972070	
8	121 E. MOYA STREET		3633020	
9	1905 DOCK STREET		6565303	
10	1304 CRESCENT AVE		4341557	

To summarize, when the SUBSTR function is on the right side of an assignment statement, the function extracts a substring.

```
MiddleInitial=substr(middlename,1,1);
```

When the SUBSTR function is on the left side of an assignment statement, the function replaces the contents of a character variable.

```
substr(region,1,3)='NNW';
```

SCAN versus SUBSTR Functions

The SUBSTR function is similar to the SCAN function. Here is a brief comparison. Both the SCAN and SUBSTR functions can extract a substring from a character value:

- SCAN extracts words within a value that is marked by delimiters.
- SUBSTR extracts a portion of a value by starting at a specified location.

The SUBSTR function is best used when you know the exact position of the string that you want to extract from the character value. It is unnecessary to mark the string by delimiters. For example, the first two characters of the variable ID identify the class level of college students. The position of these characters does not vary within the values of ID.

The SUBSTR function is the best choice to extract class level information from ID. By contrast, the SCAN function is best used during the following actions:

- You know the order of the words in the character value.
- The starting position of the words varies.
- The words are marked by some delimiter.

LEFT and RIGHT Functions

Overview of the LEFT and RIGHT Functions

- The LEFT function left-aligns a character expression.

  LEFT returns an argument with leading blanks moved to the end of the value.
- The RIGHT function right-aligns a character expression.

  RIGHT returns an argument with trailing blanks moved to the start of the value.

Syntax, LEFT and RIGHT function:

LEFT(*argument*)

RIGHT(*argument*)

argument specifies a character constant, variable, or expression.

Example: LEFT Function

The following example uses the LEFT function to left-align character expressions.

```
data _null_;
  a='DUE DATE';
  b='   DUE DATE';
  c=left(a);
  d=left(b);
  put c $8.;
  put d $12.;
run;
```

The following is displayed in the SAS log. The LEFT function returns the argument with leading blanks moved to the end of the value. In the example, b has three leading blanks and, in the output, the leading blanks are moved to the end of DUE DATE. DUE DATE is left-aligned.

```
DUE DATE
DUE DATE
```

Example: RIGHT Function

The following example uses the RIGHT function to right-align character expressions.

```
data _null_;
  a='DUE DATE';
  b='DUE DATE   ';
  c=right(a);
  d=right(b);
  put c $8.;
```

```
  put d $12.;
run;
```

The following is displayed in the SAS log. The RIGHT function returns the argument with leading blanks moved to the front of the value. In the example, b has three trailing blanks and, in the output, the trailing blanks are moved before DUE DATE. DUE DATE is right-aligned.

```
DUE DATE
   DUE DATE
```

Concatenation Operator

The concatenation operator concatenates character values. The operator can be expressed as || (two vertical bars), ¦¦ (two broken vertical bars), or !!(two exclamation points).

```
FullName = First || Middle || Last;
```

The length of the resulting variable is the sum of the lengths of each variable or constant in the concatenation operation. You can also use a LENGTH statement to specify a different length for the new variable.

The concatenation operator does not trim leading or trailing blanks. If variables are padded with trailing blanks, use the TRIM function to trim trailing blanks from values before concatenating them.

TRIM Function

Overview of the TRIM Function

The TRIM function removes trailing blanks from character expressions and returns one blank if the expression contains missing values.

```
FullName = trim(First) || trim(Middle) || Last;
```

The TRIM function is useful for concatenating because the concatenation operator does not remove trailing blanks.

If the TRIM function returns a value to a variable that was not yet assigned a length, by default, the variable length is determined by the length of the argument.

Syntax, TRIM function:

TRIM(*argument*)

argument can be any character expression. Here are examples:

- a character variable: trim(address)
- another character function: trim(left(id))

Example: TRIM Function

```
data work.nametrim;
  length Name $ 20 First Middle Last $ 10;
  Name= 'Jones, Mary Ann, Sue';
  First = left(scan(Name, 2, ','));
  Middle = left(scan(Name, 3, ','));
```

```
    Last = scan(name, 1, ',');
    FullName = trim(First) || trim(Middle) ||Last;
    drop Name;
  run;

  proc print data=work.nametrim;
  run;
```

Figure 14.5 *TRIM Function*

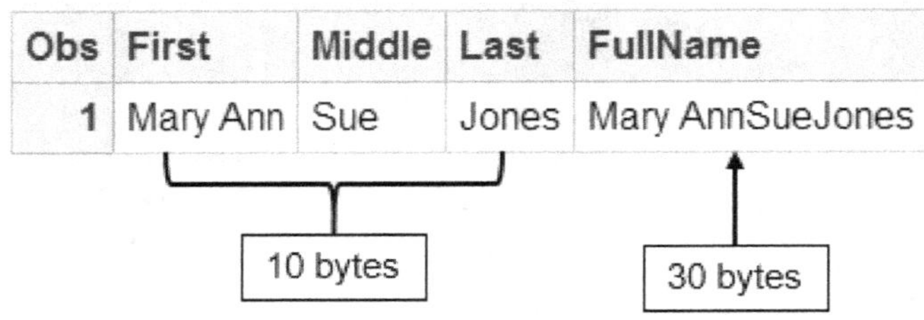

Obs	First	Middle	Last	FullName
1	Mary Ann	Sue	Jones	Mary AnnSueJones

CATX Function

Overview of the CATX Function

The CATX function enables you to concatenate character strings, remove leading and trailing blanks, and insert separators. The CATX function returns a value to a variable, or returns a value to a temporary buffer. The results of the CATX function are usually equivalent to those that are produced by a combination of the concatenation operator and the TRIM and LEFT functions.

In the DATA step, if the CATX function returns a value to a variable that has not previously been assigned a length, then the variable is given the length of 200. To save storage space, you can add a LENGTH statement to your DATA step, and specify an appropriate length for your variable. The LENGTH statement is placed before the assignment statement that contains the CATX function so that SAS can specify the length the first time it encounters the variable.

If the variable has not previously been assigned a length, the concatenation operator (||) returns a value to a variable. The variable's given length is the sum of the length of the values that are being concatenated. Otherwise, you can use the LENGTH statement before the assignment statement containing the TRIM function to assign a length.

Recall that you can use the TRIM function with the concatenation operator to create one address variable. The address variable contains the values of the three variables Address, City, and Zip. To remove extra blanks from the new values, use the DATA step shown below:

```
data work.newaddress(drop=address city state zip);
  set cert.temp;
  NewAddress=trim(address)||', '||trim(city)||', '||zip;
run;
```

You can accomplish the same concatenation using only the CATX function.

Syntax, CATX function:

CATX(*separator,string-1* <,...*string-n*>**)**

- *separator* specifies the character string that is used as a separator between concatenated strings
- *string* specifies a SAS character string.

Example: Create New Variable Using CATX Function

You want to create the new variable NewAddress by concatenating the values of the Address, City, and Zip variables from the data set Cert.Temp. You want to strip excess blanks from the old variable's values and separate the variable values with a comma and a space. The DATA step below uses the CATX function to create NewAddress.

```
data work.newaddress(drop=address city state zip);
  set cert.temp;
  NewAddress=catx(', ',address,city,zip);
run;
proc print data=work.newaddress;
run;
```

The revised DATA step creates the values that you would expect for NewAddress.

Output 14.12 *SAS Data Set Work.NewAddress (partial output)*

Obs	Phone	. . . more variables . . .	NewAddress
1	6224549		65 ELM DR, CARY, NC, 27513
2	6223251		11 SUN DR, CARY, NC, 27513
3	9974749		712 HARDWICK STREET, CHAPEL HILL, NC, 27514
4	6970540		5372 WHITEBUD ROAD, RALEIGH, NC, 27612
5	3633618		11 TALYN COURT, DURHAM, NC, 27713
6	9976732		101 HYNERIAN DR, CARRBORO, NC, 27510
7	9972070		11 RYGEL ROAD, CHAPEL HILL, NC, 27514
8	3633020		121 E. MOYA STREET, DURHAM, NC, 27713
9	6565303		1905 DOCK STREET, CARY, NC, 27513
10	4341557		1304 CRESCENT AVE, RALEIGH, NC, 27612

INDEX Function

Overview of the INDEX Function

The INDEX function enables you to search a character value for a specified string. The INDEX function searches values from left to right, looking for the first occurrence of the string. It returns the position of the string's first character. If the string is not found, it returns a value of 0.

Syntax, INDEX function:

INDEX(*source, excerpt***)**

- *source* specifies the character variable or expression to search.
- *excerpt* specifies a character string that is enclosed in quotation marks (").

Example: Search for Occurrences of a Phrase

Suppose you want to search the values of the variable Job, which lists job skills. You want to create a data set that contains the names of all temporary employees who have word processing experience. The following figure shows a partial output of the Cert.Temp data set.

Figure 14.6 *Cert.Temp (partial output)*

Obs	Address	. . . more variables . . .	Job	. . . more variables . . .
1	65 ELM DR		word processing	
2	11 SUN DR		Filing Admin.Duties	
3	712 HARDWICK STREET		Organizational Dev. Specialis	
4	5372 WHITEBUD ROAD		Bookkeeping word processing	
5	11 TALYN COURT		word processing sec. work	
6	101 HYNERIAN DR		Bookkeeping word processing	
7	11 RYGEL ROAD		word processing	
8	121 E. MOYA STREET		word processing sec. work	
9	1905 DOCK STREET		word processing	
10	1304 CRESCENT AVE		word processing	

To search for the occurrences of the phrase “word processing” in the values of the variable Job, you write the INDEX function as shown below. Note that the character string is enclosed in quotation marks.

```
index(job,'word processing')
```

To create the new data set, include the INDEX function in a subsetting IF statement. Only those observations in which the function locates the string and returns a value greater than 0 are written to the data set.

```
data work.datapool;
  set cert.temp;
  where index(job,'word processing') > 0;
run;
proc print data=work.datapool;
run;
```

Here is the data set that shows the temporary employees who have word processing experience. The program processed all of the observations in the Cert.Temp data set.

Output 14.13 *Work.DataPool (partial output)*

Obs	Address
1	65 ELM DR
2	5372 WHITEBUD ROAD
3	11 TALYN COURT
4	101 HYNERIAN DR
5	11 RYGEL ROAD
6	121 E. MOYA STREET
7	1905 DOCK STREET
8	1304 CRESCENT AVE

. . . *more variables* . . .

Job
word processing
Bookkeeping word processing
word processing sec. work
Bookkeeping word processing
word processing
word processing sec. work
word processing
word processing

. . . *more variables* . . .

Note that the INDEX function is case sensitive, so the character string that you search for must be specified exactly as it is recorded in the data set. For example, the INDEX function shown below would not locate any employees who have word-processing experience.

```
index(job,'WORD PROCESSING')
```

Finding a String Regardless of Case

To ensure that all occurrences of a character string are found, you can use the UPCASE or LOWCASE function with the INDEX function. The UPCASE and LOWCASE functions enable you to convert variable values to uppercase or lowercase letters. You can then specify the character string in the INDEX function accordingly.

```
index(upcase(job),'WORD PROCESSING')

index(lowcase(job),'word processing')
```

FIND Function

Overview of the FIND Function

The FIND function enables you to search for a specific substring of characters within a specified character string.

- The FIND function searches the string, from left to right, for the first occurrence of the substring, and returns the position in the string of the substring's first character.
- If the substring is not found in the string, the FIND function returns a value of 0.
- If there are multiple occurrences of the substring, the FIND function returns only the position of the first occurrence.

Syntax, FIND function:

FIND(*string,substring<,modifiers><,startpos>* **)**

- *string* specifies a character constant, variable, or expression that is searched for substrings.
- *substring* is a character constant, variable, or expression that specifies the substring of characters to search for in *string*.
- *modifiers* is a character constant, variable, or expression that specifies one or more modifiers.
- *startpos* is an integer that specifies the position at which the search should start and the direction of the search. The default value for *startpos* is 1.

Note: If *string* or *substring* is a character literal, you must enclose it in quotation marks.

Details

The modifiers argument enables you to specify one or more modifiers for the function, as listed below.

- The modifier i causes the FIND function to ignore character case during the search. If this modifier is not specified, FIND searches for character substrings with the same case as the characters in substring.
- The modifier t trims trailing blanks from string and substring.

Here are several facts about modifiers and constants.

- If the modifier is a constant, enclose it in quotation marks.
- Specify multiple constants in a single set of quotation marks.
- Modifier values are not case sensitive.

If startpos is not specified, FIND starts the search at the beginning of the string and searches the string from left to right. If startpos is specified, the absolute value of startpos determines the position at which to start the search. The sign of startpos determines the direction of the search. That is, when startpos is positive, FIND searches from startpos to the right, When startpos is negative, FIND searches from startpos to the left.

Example: Find Word Processing Jobs in a Data Set

The values of the variable Job are all lowercase. Therefore, to search for the occurrence of word processing in the values of the variable Job, you write the FIND function as shown below. Note that the character substring is enclosed in quotation marks.

```
find(job,'word processing')
```

To create the new data set, include the FIND function in a subsetting IF statement. Only those observations in which the function locates the string and returns a value greater than 0 are written to the data set.

```
data work.datapool;
  set cert.temp;
  where find(job,'word processing') > 0;
run;
proc print data=work.datapool;
run;
```

Output 14.14 *Work.DataPool (partial output)*

Obs	Address
1	65 ELM DR
2	5372 WHITEBUD ROAD
3	11 TALYN COURT
4	101 HYNERIAN DR
5	11 RYGEL ROAD
6	121 E. MOYA STREET
7	1905 DOCK STREET
8	1304 CRESCENT AVE

. . . *more variables* . . .

Job
word processing
Bookkeeping word processing
word processing sec. work
Bookkeeping word processing
word processing
word processing sec. work
word processing
word processing

. . . *more variables* . . .

UPCASE Function

The UPCASE function converts all letters in a character expression to uppercase.

Syntax, UPCASE function:

UPCASE(*argument***)**

argument can be any SAS character expression, such as a character variable or constant.

In this example, the function is placed in an assignment statement in a DATA step. You can change the values of the variable Job in place.

```
data work.upcasejob;
  set cert.temp;
  Job=upcase(job);
run;
proc print data=work.upcasejob;
run;
```

The new data set contains the converted values of Job.

Output 14.15 *Work.UpcaseJob (partial output)*

Obs	Address
1	65 ELM DR
2	11 SUN DR
3	712 HARDWICK STREET
4	5372 WHITEBUD ROAD
5	11 TALYN COURT
6	101 HYNERIAN DR
7	11 RYGEL ROAD
8	121 E. MOYA STREET
9	1905 DOCK STREET
10	1304 CRESCENT AVE

. . . *more variables* . . .

Job
WORD PROCESSING
FILING ADMIN.DUTIES
ORGANIZATIONAL DEV. SPECIALIS
BOOKKEEPING WORD PROCESSING
WORD PROCESSING SEC. WORK
BOOKKEEPING WORD PROCESSING
WORD PROCESSING
WORD PROCESSING SEC. WORK
WORD PROCESSING
WORD PROCESSING

. . . *more variables* . . .

LOWCASE Function

The LOWCASE function converts all letters in a character expression to lowercase.

Syntax, LOWCASE function:

LOWCASE(*argument*)

argument can be any SAS character expression, such as a character variable or constant.

In this example, the function converts the values of the variable Contact to lowercase letters.

```
data work.lowcasecontact;
  set cert.temp;
  Contact=lowcase(contact);
run;
proc print data=work.lowcasecontact;
run;
```

Output 14.16 *Work.LowcaseContact (partial output)*

Obs	Address		Contact	
1	65 ELM DR		word processor	
2	11 SUN DR		admin. asst.	
3	712 HARDWICK STREET		consultant	
4	5372 WHITEBUD ROAD	...more variables ...	bookkeeper asst.	...more variables ...
5	11 TALYN COURT		word processor	
6	101 HYNERIAN DR		bookkeeper asst.	
7	11 RYGEL ROAD		word processor	
8	121 E. MOYA STREET		word processor	
9	1905 DOCK STREET		word processor	
10	1304 CRESCENT AVE		word processor	

PROPCASE Function

The PROPCASE function converts all words in an argument to proper case (so that the first letter in each word is capitalized).

Syntax, PROPCASE function:

PROPCASE(*argument*<,*delimiter(s)*>)

- *argument* can be any SAS expression, such as a character variable or constant.
- *delimiter(s)* specifies one or more delimiters that are enclosed in quotation marks. The default delimiters are blank, forward slash, hyphen, open parenthesis, period, and tab.

Note: If you specify *delimiter(s)*, then the default delimiters are no longer in effect.

- The PROPCASE function first converts all letters to lowercase letters and then converts the first character of words to uppercase.

- The first character of a word is the first letter of a string or any letter preceded by a default list of delimiters.

  Default delimiter List: blank / — (. tab

TIP Delimiters can be specified as a second argument, instead of using the default list.

In this example, the function converts the values of the variable named Contact to proper case and uses the default delimiters.

```
data work.propcasecontact;
  set cert.temp;
  Contact=propcase(contact);
run;
proc print data=work.propcasecontact;
run;
```

After the DATA step executes, the new data set is created.

Output 14.17 *Work.PropcaseContact (partial output)*

Obs	Address	. . . more variables . . .	Contact	. . . more variables . . .
1	65 ELM DR		Word Processor	
2	11 SUN DR		Admin. Asst.	
3	712 HARDWICK STREET		Consultant	
4	5372 WHITEBUD ROAD		Bookkeeper Asst.	
5	11 TALYN COURT		Word Processor	
6	101 HYNERIAN DR		Bookkeeper Asst.	
7	11 RYGEL ROAD		Word Processor	
8	121 E. MOYA STREET		Word Processor	
9	1905 DOCK STREET		Word Processor	
10	1304 CRESCENT AVE		Word Processor	

TRANWRD Function

Overview of the TRANWRD Function

The TRANWRD function replaces or removes all occurrences of a word in a character string. The translated characters can be located anywhere in the string.

Figure 14.7 *TRANWRD Function*

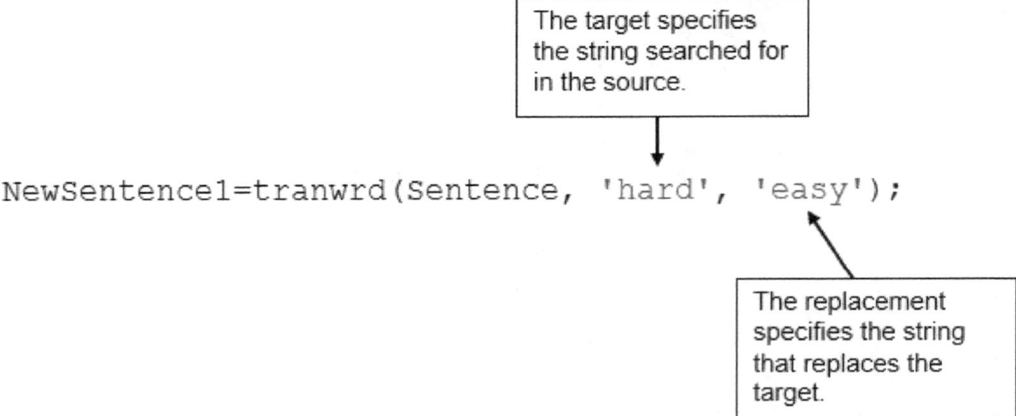

Syntax, TRANWRD function:

TRANWRD(*source,target,replacement***)**

- *source* specifies the source string that you want to translate.
- *target* specifies the string that SAS searches for in *source*.
- *replacement* specifies the string that replaces *target*.

Note: *target* and *replacement* can be specified as variables or as character strings. If you specify character strings, be sure to enclose the strings in quotation marks (' ' or " ").

In a DATA step, if the TRANWRD function returns a value to a variable that has not previously been assigned a length, then that variable is given a length of 200 bytes. To save storage space, you can add a LENGTH statement to the DATA step and specify an appropriate length for the variable. SAS sets the length of a new character variable the first time it is encountered in the DATA step. Be sure to place the LENGTH statement before the assignment statements that contain the TRANWRD function.

Example: Update Variables in Place Using TRANWRD Function

You can use TRANWRD function to update variables in place. In this example, the function updates the values of Name by changing every occurrence of the string Monroe to Manson.

```
name=tranwrd(name,'Monroe','Manson')
```

Another example of the TRANWRD function is shown below. In this case, two assignment statements use the TRANWRD function to change all occurrences of Miss or Mrs. to Ms.

```
data work.after;
  set cert.before;
  name=tranwrd(name,'Miss','Ms.');
  name=tranwrd(name,'Mrs.','Ms.');
run;
proc print data=work.after;
run;
```

The new data set is created. The TRANWRD function changes all occurrences of Miss or Mrs. to Ms.

Figure 14.8 PROC PRINT Output of the TRANWRD Function

Obs	Name
1	Ms. Millicent Garrett Fawcett
2	Ms. Charlotte Despard
3	Ms. Emmeline Pankhurst
4	Ms. Sylvia Pankhurst

COMPBL Function

The COMPBL function removes multiple blanks from a character string by translating each occurrence of two or more consecutive blanks into a single blank.

Syntax, COMPBL function:

COMPBL(*source*)

- *source* specifies a character constant, variable, or expression to compress.

If a variable is not assigned a length before the COMPBL function returns a value to the variable, then the variable is given the length of the first argument.

The following SAS statements produce these results:

SAS Statement	Result
	`----+----1----+---2--`

`data _null_;`
`  string='Hey`
`   Diddle  Diddle';`
`  string=compbl(string);`
`  put string;`
`run;`
	`Hey Diddle Diddle`

`data _null_;`
`  string='125    E Main St';`
`  length address $10;`
`  address=compbl(string);`
`  put address;`
`run;`
	`125 E Main`

COMPRESS Function

Overview of the COMPRESS Function

The COMPRESS function returns a character string with specified characters removed from the original string. Null arguments are allowed and treated as a string with a length of zero.

Syntax, COMPRESS function:

COMPRESS(*source***<,** *characters***> <,** *modifier(s)***>)**

- *source* specifies a character constant, variable, or expression from which specified characters are removed.
- *characters* specifies a character constant, variable, or expression that initializes a list of characters.

  By default, the characters in this list are removed from the source argument. If you specify the K modifier in the third argument, then only the characters in this list are kept in the result.

  Note: You can add more characters to this list by using other modifiers in the third argument. Enclose a literal string of characters in quotation marks.

- *modifier* specifies a character constant, variable, or expression in which each non-blank character modifies the action of the COMPRESS function. Blanks are ignored.

  a or A
  : Adds alphabetic characters to the list of characters.

  c or C
  : Adds control characters to the list of characters.

  d or D
  : Adds digits to the list of characters.

  f or F
  : Adds the underscore character and English letters to the list of characters.

  g or G
  : Adds graphic characters to the list of characters.

  h or H
  : Adds a horizontal tab to the list of characters.

  i or I
  : Ignores the case of the characters to be kept or removed.

  k or K
  : Keeps the characters in the list instead of removing them.

  l or L
  : Adds lowercase letters to the list of characters.

  n or N
  : Adds digits, the underscore character, and English letters to the list of characters.

  o or O
  : Processes the second and third arguments once rather than every time the COMPRESS function is called. You can use the O modifier to make the COMPRESS function more efficient when you call it in a loop, where the second and third arguments do not change.

  p or P
  : Adds punctuation marks to the list of characters

  s or S
  : Adds space characters (blank, horizontal tab, vertical tab, carriage return, line feed, and form feed) to the list of characters.

  t or T
  : Trims trailing blanks from the first and second arguments.

  u or U
  : Adds uppercase letters to the list of characters.

  w or W
  : Adds printable characters to the list of characters.

  x or X
  : Adds hexadecimal characters to the list of characters.

TIP If the *modifier* is a constant, enclose it in quotation marks. Specify multiple constants in a single set of quotation marks. *Modifier* can also be expressed as a variable or an expression.

Based on the number of arguments, the COMPRESS functions works as follows:

Number of Arguments	Result
only the first argument, *source*	All blanks have been removed from the argument. If the argument is completely blank, then the result is a string with a length of zero. If you assign the result to a character variable with a fixed length, then the value of that variable is padded with blanks to fill its defined length.
the first two arguments, *source* and *chars*	All characters that appear in the second argument are removed from the result.
three arguments, *source*, *chars*, and *modifier(s)*	The K modifier (specified in the third argument) determines whether the characters in the second argument are kept or removed from the result.

The COMPRESS function compiles a list of characters to keep or remove, comprising the characters in the second argument plus any types of characters that are specified by the modifiers. For example, the D modifier specifies digits. Both of the following function calls remove digits from the result:

```
compress(source, "1234567890");
compress(source, , "d");
```

To remove digits and plus or minus signs, you can use either of the following function calls:

```
compress(source, "1234567890+-");
compress(source, "+-", "d");
```

Example: Compress a Character String

```
data _null_;
  a='A B C D';
  b=compress(a);
  put b=;
run;
```

Log 14.5 *SAS Log*

```
b=ABCD
```

Example: Compress a Character String Using a Modifier

The following example uses the I modifier to ignore the case of the characters to remove.

```
data _null_;
  x='919-000-000 nc  610-000-000 pa     719-000-000 CO  419-000-000 Oh';
  y=compress(x, 'ACHONP', 'i');
```

```
put y=;
run;
```

The following is printed to the SAS log.

Log 14.6 *SAS Log*

```
y=919-000-000  610-000-000      719-000-000  419-000-000
```

Modifying Numeric Values with Functions

SAS provides additional functions to create or modify numeric values. These include arithmetic, financial, and probability functions. This book covers the following selected functions.

CEIL and FLOOR Functions

To return integers that are greater than or equal to the argument, use these functions:

- The CEIL function returns the smallest integer that is greater than or equal to the argument.
- The FLOOR function returns the largest integer that is less than or equal to the argument.

Syntax, CEIL and FLOOR function:

CEIL(*argument*)

FLOOR(*argument*)

argument is a numeric variable, constant, or expression.

If the argument is within 1E-12 of an integer, the function returns that integer.

The following SAS statements produce this result:

Table 14.12 *CEIL and FLOOR Functions*

SAS Statement	Result
CEIL Function Examples	

`data _null_;`
`  var1=2.1;`
`  var2=-2.1;`
`  a=ceil(var1);`
`  b=ceil(var2);`
`  put "a=" a;`
`  put "b=" b;`
`run;`
	`a=3`
	`b=-2`

SAS Statement	Result

`data _null_;`
`  c=ceil(1+1.e-11);`
`  d=ceil(-1+1e-11);`
`  e=ceil(1+1.e-13)`
`  put "c=" c;`
`  put "d=" d;`
`  put "e=" e;`
`run;`
	c=2
	d=0
	e=1

`data _null_;`
`  f=ceil(223.456);`
`  g=ceil(763);`
`  h=ceil(-223.456);`
`  put "f=" f;`
`  put "g=" g;`
`  put "h=" h;`
`run;`
	f=224
	g=763
	h=-223

FLOOR Function Examples	

`data _null_;`
`  var1=2.1;`
`  var2=-2.1;`
`  a=floor(var1);`
`  b=floor(var2);`
`  put "a=" a;`
`  put "b=" b;`
`run;`
	a=2
	b=-3

`data _null_;`
`  c=floor(1+1.e-11);`
`  d=floor(-1+1e-11);`
`  e=floor(1+1.e-13)`
`  put "c=" c;`
`  put "d=" d;`
`  put "e=" e;`
`run;`
	c=1
	d=-1
	e=1

`data _null_;`
`  f=floor(223.456);`
`  g=floor(763);`
`  h=floor(-223.456);`
`  put "f=" f;`
`  put "g=" g;`
`  put "h=" h;`
`run;`
	f=223
	g=763
	h=-224

INT Function

To return the integer portion of a numeric value, use the INT function. Any decimal portion of the INT function argument is discarded.

Syntax, INT function:

INT(*argument*)

argument is a numeric variable, constant, or expression.

The two data sets shown below give before-and-after views of values that are truncated by the INT function.

```
data work.creditx;
  set cert.credit;
  Transaction=int(transaction);
run;
proc print data=work.creditx;
run;
```

Output 14.18 *INT Function Comparison*

Data Set Cert.Credit
(Before INT Function)

Obs	Account	Name	Type	Transaction
1	1118	ART CONTUCK	D	57.69
2	2287	MICHAEL WINSTONE	D	145.89
3	6201	MARY WATERS	C	45.00
4	7821	MICHELLE STANTON	A	304.45
5	6621	WALTER LUND	C	234.76
6	1086	KATHERINE MORRY	A	64.98
7	0556	LEE McDONALD	D	70.82
8	7821	ELIZABETH WESTIN	C	188.23
9	0265	JEFFREY DONALDSON	C	78.90
10	1010	MARTIN LYNN	D	150.55

Data Set Work.CreditX
(After INT Function)

Obs	Account	Name	Type	Transaction
1	1118	ART CONTUCK	D	57
2	2287	MICHAEL WINSTONE	D	145
3	6201	MARY WATERS	C	45
4	7821	MICHELLE STANTON	A	304
5	6621	WALTER LUND	C	234
6	1086	KATHERINE MORRY	A	64
7	0556	LEE McDONALD	D	70
8	7821	ELIZABETH WESTIN	C	188
9	0265	JEFFREY DONALDSON	C	78
10	1010	MARTIN LYNN	D	150

ROUND Function

To round values to the nearest specified unit, use the ROUND function.

Syntax, ROUND function:

ROUND(*argument,round-off-unit*)

- *argument* is a numeric variable, constant, or expression.
- *round-off-unit* is numeric and nonnegative.

If a rounding unit is not provided, a default value of 1 is used, and the argument is rounded to the nearest integer. The two data sets shown below give before-and-after views of values that are modified by the ROUND function. The first ROUND function rounds the variable AccountBalance to the nearest integer. The second ROUND function rounds the variable InvoicedAmount to the nearest tenth decimal place. The third ROUND function rounds the variable AmountRemaining to the nearest hundredth decimal place.

```
data work.rounders;
```

```
  set cert.rounders;
  AccountBalance=round(AccountBalance, 1);
  InvoicedAmount=round(InvoicedAmount, 0.1);
  AmountRemaining=round(AmountRemaining, 0.02);
  format AccountBalance InvoicedAmount PaymentReceived AmountRemaining dollar9.2;
run;
proc print data=work.rounders;
run;
```

Output 14.19 *Before and After ROUND Function*

Data Set Cert.Rounders, before the ROUND function

Obs	Account	AccountBalance	InvoicedAmount	PaymentReceived	AmountRemaining
1	1118	6246.34	967.84	1214.18	2214.18
2	2287	3687.14	607.30	4294.44	0.00
3	6201	1607.93	137.41	700.00	1045.34
4	7821	7391.62	1069.37	5000.00	3460.99
5	6621	7017.50	9334.08	8351.58	8000.00
6	1086	556.36	1537.28	1300.28	793.36
7	2556	6388.10	3577.82	6900.82	3065.10
8	7821	10872.96	3885.08	10872.96	3885.08
9	5265	1057.46	637.42	1200.00	494.88
10	1010	6387.13	0.00	3193.57	3193.56

Data Set Work.Rounders, after the ROUND function

Obs	Account	AccountBalance	InvoicedAmount	PaymentReceived	AmountRemaining
1	1118	$6,246.00	$967.80	$1,214.18	$2,214.18
2	2287	$3,687.00	$607.30	$4,294.44	$0.00
3	6201	$1,608.00	$137.40	$700.00	$1,045.34
4	7821	$7,392.00	$1,069.40	$5,000.00	$3,461.00
5	6621	$7,018.00	$9,334.10	$8,351.58	$8,000.00
6	1086	$556.00	$1,537.30	$1,300.28	$793.36
7	2556	$6,388.00	$3,577.80	$6,900.82	$3,065.10
8	7821	$10873.00	$3,885.10	$10872.96	$3,885.08
9	5265	$1,057.00	$637.40	$1,200.00	$494.88
10	1010	$6,387.00	$0.00	$3,193.57	$3,193.56

Nesting SAS Functions

To write more efficient programs you can nest functions as appropriate. You can nest any functions as long as the function that is used as the argument meets the requirements for the argument. For example, you can nest the SCAN function within the SUBSTR function in an assignment statement to compute the value for MiddleInitial:

```
MiddleInitial=substr(scan(name,3),1,1);
```

This example of nested numeric functions determines the number of years between June 15, 2018, and today:

```
Years=intck('year','15jun2018'd,today());
```

Chapter Quiz

Select the best answer for each question. Check your answers using the answer key in the appendix.

1. Within the data set Cert.Temp, PayRate is a character variable and Hours is a numeric variable. What happens when the following program is run?

   ```
   data work.temp;
      set cert.temp;
      Salary=payrate*hours;
   run;
   ```

   a. SAS converts the values of PayRate to numeric values. No message is written to the log.

   b. SAS converts the values of PayRate to numeric values. A message is written to the log.

   c. SAS converts the values of Hours to character values. No message is written to the log.

   d. SAS converts the values of Hours to character values. A message is written to the log.

2. A typical value for the character variable Target is **123,456**. Which statement correctly converts the values of Target to numeric values when creating the variable TargetNo?

   a. `TargetNo=input(target,comma6.);`

   b. `TargetNo=input(target,comma7.);`

   c. `TargetNo=put(target,comma6.);`

   d. `TargetNo=put(target,comma7.)`

3. A typical value for the numeric variable SiteNum is 12.3. Which statement correctly converts the values of SiteNum to character values when creating the variable Location?

   a. `Location=dept||'/'||input(sitenum,3.1);`

   b. `Location=dept||'/'||input(sitenum,4.1);`

   c. `Location=dept||'/'||put(sitenum,3.1);`

   d. `Location=dept||'/'||put(sitenum,4.1);`

4. The variable Address2 contains values such as **Piscataway, NJ**. How do you assign the two-letter state abbreviations to a new variable named State?

   a. `State=scan(address2,2);`

b. `State=scan(address2,13,2);`

c. `State=substr(address2,2);`

d. `State=substr(address2,13,2);`

5. The variable IDCode contains values such as **123FA** and **321MB**. The fourth character identifies sex. How do you assign these character codes to a new variable named Sex?

a. `Sex=scan(idcode,4);`

b. `Sex=scan(idcode,4,1);`

c. `Sex=substr(idcode,4);`

d. `Sex=substr(idcode,4,1);`

6. Because of the growth within the 919 area code, the telephone exchange 555 is being reassigned to the 920 area code. The data set Clients.Piedmont includes the variable Phone, which contains telephone numbers in the form **919-555-1234**. Which of the following programs correctly changes the values of Phone?

a.
```
data work.piedmont(drop=areacode exchange);
   set cert.piedmont;
   Areacode=substr(phone,1,3);
   Exchange=substr(phone,5,3);
   if areacode='919' and exchange='555'
     then scan(phone,1,3)='920';
run;
```

b.
```
data work.piedmont(drop=areacode exchange);
   set cert.piedmont;
   Areacode=substr(phone,1,3);
   Exchange=substr(phone,5,3);
   if areacode='919' and exchange='555'
     then phone=scan('920',1,3);
run;
```

c.
```
data work.piedmont(drop=areacode exchange);
   set cert.piedmont;
   Areacode=substr(phone,1,3);
   Exchange=substr(phone,5,3);
   if areacode='919' and exchange='555'
     then substr(phone,1,3)='920';
run;
```

d.
```
data work.piedmont(drop=areacode exchange);
   set cert.piedmont;
   Areacode=substr(phone,1,3);
   Exchange=substr(phone,5,3);
   if areacode='919' and exchange='555'
     then phone=substr('920',1,3);
run;
```

7. Suppose you need to create the variable FullName by concatenating the values of FirstName, which contains first names, and LastName, which contains last names. What is the best way to remove extra blanks between first names and last names?

a.
```
data work.maillist;
   set cert.maillist;
   length FullName $ 40;
   fullname=trim firstname||' '||lastname;
```

```
run;
```

b.
```
data work.maillist;
   set cert.maillist;
   length FullName $ 40;
   fullname=trim(firstname)||' '||lastname;
run;
```

c.
```
data work.maillist;
   set cert.maillist;
   length FullName $ 40;
   fullname=trim(firstname)||' '||trim(lastname);
run;
```

d.
```
data work.maillist;
   set cert.maillist;
   length FullName $ 40;
   fullname=trim(firstname||' '||lastname);
run;
```

8. Within the data set Cert.Bookcase, the variable Finish contains values such as **`ash, cherry, teak, matte-black`**. Which of the following creates a subset of the data in which the values of Finish contain the string **`walnut`**? Make the search for the string case-insensitive.

a.
```
data work.bookcase;
   set cert.bookcase;
   if index(finish,walnut) = 0;
run;
```

b.
```
data work.bookcase;
   set cert.bookcase;
   if index(finish,'walnut') > 0;
run;
```

c.
```
data work.bookcase;
   set cert.bookcase;
   if index(lowcase(finish),walnut) = 0;
run;
```

d.
```
data work.bookcase;
   set cert.bookcase;
   if index(lowcase(finish),'walnut') > 0;
run;
```

Chapter 15
Producing Descriptive Statistics

The MEANS Procedure

What Does the MEANS Procedure Do?

The MEANS procedure provides data summarization tools to compute descriptive statistics for variables across all observations and within groups of observations. For example, PROC MEANS does the following:

- calculates descriptive statistics based on moments

- estimates quantiles, which includes the median
- calculates confidence limits for the mean
- identifies extreme values
- performs a *t* test

By default, PROC MEANS displays output.

MEANS Procedure Syntax

The MEANS procedure can include many statements and options for specifying statistics.

Syntax, MEANS procedure:

PROC MEANS <DATA=*SAS-data-set*>
<*statistic-keyword(s)*> <*option(s)*>;

RUN;

- *SAS-data-set* is the name of the data set to be analyzed.
- *statistic-keyword(s)* specify the statistics to compute.
- *option(s)* control the content, analysis, and appearance of output.

Example: Default PROC MEANS Output

In its simplest form, PROC MEANS prints the *n*-count (number of non missing values), the mean, the standard deviation, and the minimum and maximum values of every numeric variable in a data set.

```
proc means data=cert.survey;
run;
```

Output 15.1 *PROC MEANS Output of Cert.Survey*

The MEANS Procedure

Variable	N	Mean	Std Dev	Minimum	Maximum
Item1	4	3.7500000	1.2583057	2.0000000	5.0000000
Item2	4	3.0000000	1.6329932	1.0000000	5.0000000
Item3	4	4.2500000	0.5000000	4.0000000	5.0000000
Item4	4	3.5000000	1.2909944	2.0000000	5.0000000
Item5	4	3.0000000	1.6329932	1.0000000	5.0000000
Item6	4	3.7500000	1.2583057	2.0000000	5.0000000
Item7	4	3.0000000	1.8257419	1.0000000	5.0000000
Item8	4	2.7500000	1.5000000	1.0000000	4.0000000
Item9	4	3.0000000	1.4142136	2.0000000	5.0000000
Item10	4	3.2500000	1.2583057	2.0000000	5.0000000
Item11	4	3.0000000	1.8257419	1.0000000	5.0000000
Item12	4	2.7500000	0.5000000	2.0000000	3.0000000
Item13	4	2.7500000	1.5000000	1.0000000	4.0000000
Item14	4	3.0000000	1.4142136	2.0000000	5.0000000
Item15	4	3.0000000	1.6329932	1.0000000	5.0000000
Item16	4	2.5000000	1.9148542	1.0000000	5.0000000
Item17	4	3.0000000	1.1547005	2.0000000	4.0000000
Item18	4	3.2500000	1.2583057	2.0000000	5.0000000

Specifying Descriptive Statistics Keywords

The default statistics in the MEANS procedure are *n*-count (number of nonmissing values), the mean, the standard deviation, and the minimum and maximum values of every numeric variable in a data set. However, you might need to compute a different statistic such as median or range of the values. Use the statistic keyword option in the PROC MEANS statement to specify one or more statistics to display in the output.

Here are the available keywords in the PROC statement:

Table 15.1 *Descriptive Statistics Keywords*

Keyword	Description
CLM	The two-sided confidence limit for the mean.
CSS	The sum of squares corrected for the mean.
CV	The percent coefficient of variation.
KURTOSIS | KURT	Measures the heaviness of tails.
LCLM	The one-sided confidence limit below the mean.
MAX	The maximum value.
MEAN	The arithmetic mean or average of all the values.
MIN	The minimum value.

Keyword	Description
MODE	The value that occurs most frequently.
N	The number of observations with nonmissing values.
NMISS	The number of observations with missing values.
RANGE	Calculated as the difference between the maximum value and the minimum value.
SKEWNESS | SKEW	Measures the tendency of the deviations to be larger in one direction than in the other.
STDDEV | STD	Is the standard deviation s and is computed as the square root of the variance.
STDERR | STDMEAN	The standard error of the mean.
SUM	Sum
SUMWGT	The sum of the weights.
UCLM	The one-sided confidence limit above the mean
USS	The value of the uncorrected sum of squares.
VAR	Variance.

Table 15.2 *Quantile Statistic Keywords*

Keyword	Description
MEDIAN | P50	The middle value or the 50th percentile.
P1	1st percentile.
P5	5th percentile.
P10	10th percentile.
Q1 | P25	The lower quartile or 25th percentile.
Q3 | P75	The upper quartile or 75th percentile.
P90	90th percentile.
P95	95th percentile.

Keyword	Description
P99	99th percentile.
QRANGE	The interquartile range and is calculated as the difference between the upper and lower quartile, Q3 — Q1.

Table 15.3 Hypothesis Testing Keywords

Keyword	Description
PROBT | PRT	The two-tailed *p*-value for Student's *t* statistic, T, with $n - 1$ degrees of freedom. This value is the probability under the null hypothesis of obtaining a more extreme value of T than is observed in this sample.
T	The Student's *t* statistic to test the null hypothesis that the population mean is equal to μ_0 and is calculated as $\frac{\overline{X} - \mu_0}{8/\sqrt{\sum w_i}}$

Example: Specifying Statistic Keywords

To determine the median and range of Cert.Survey numeric values, add the MEDIAN and RANGE keywords as options.

```
proc means data=cert.survey median range;
run;
```

Output 15.2 *PROC MEANS Output of Cert.Survey Displays Only Median and Range*

Variable	Median	Range
Item1	4.0000000	3.0000000
Item2	3.0000000	4.0000000
Item3	4.0000000	1.0000000
Item4	3.5000000	3.0000000
Item5	3.0000000	4.0000000
Item6	4.0000000	3.0000000
Item7	3.0000000	4.0000000
Item8	3.0000000	3.0000000
Item9	2.5000000	3.0000000
Item10	3.0000000	3.0000000
Item11	3.0000000	4.0000000
Item12	3.0000000	1.0000000
Item13	3.0000000	3.0000000
Item14	2.5000000	3.0000000
Item15	3.0000000	4.0000000
Item16	2.0000000	4.0000000
Item17	3.0000000	2.0000000
Item18	3.0000000	3.0000000

Limiting Decimal Places with MAXDEC= Option

By default, PROC MEANS uses the BEST*w*. format to display numeric values in the report.

When there is no format specification, SAS chooses the format that provides the most information about the value according to the available field width. At times, this can result in unnecessary decimal places, making your output hard to read. To limit decimal places, use the MAXDEC= option in the PROC MEANS statement, and set it equal to the length that you prefer.

Syntax, PROC MEANS statement with MAXDEC= option:

PROC MEANS <DATA=*SAS-data-set*>
    <*statistic-keyword(s)*> **MAXDEC=*n*;**

n specifies the maximum number of decimal places.

```
proc means data=cert.diabetes min max maxdec=0;
run;
```

Output 15.3 *PROC MEANS Output of Cert.Diabetes with the MAXDEC= Option*

Variable	Minimum	Maximum
ID	1128	9723
Age	15	63
Height	61	75
Weight	102	240
Pulse	65	100
FastGluc	152	568
PostGluc	206	625

Specifying Variables Using the VAR Statement

By default, the MEANS procedure generates statistics for every numeric variable in a data set. But the typical focus is on just a few variables, particularly if the data set is large. It also makes sense to exclude certain types of variables. The values of a numeric identifier variable ID, for example, are unlikely to yield useful statistics.

To specify the variables that PROC MEANS analyzes, add a VAR statement and list the variable names.

Syntax, VAR statement:

VAR *variable(s)*;

variable(s) lists numeric variables for which to calculate statistics.

```
proc means data=cert.diabetes min max maxdec=0;
  var age height weight;
run;
```

Output 15.4 *Specifying Variables in the PROC MEANS Output of Cert.Diabetes*

Variable	Minimum	Maximum
Age	15	63
Height	61	75
Weight	102	240

In addition to listing variables separately, you can use a numbered range of variables.

```
proc means data=cert.survey mean stderr maxdec=2;
  var item1-item5;
run;
```

Output 15.5 *PROC MEANS Output of Cert.Survey with Variable Range*

Variable	Mean	Std Error
Item1	3.75	0.63
Item2	3.00	0.82
Item3	4.25	0.25
Item4	3.50	0.65
Item5	3.00	0.82

Group Processing Using the CLASS Statement

You often want statistics for groups of observations, rather than for the entire data set. For example, census numbers are more useful when grouped by region than when viewed as a national total. To produce separate analyses of grouped observations, add a CLASS statement to the MEANS procedure.

Syntax, CLASS statement:

CLASS *variable(s)*;

variable(s) specifies category variables for group processing.

CLASS variables are used to categorize data. CLASS variables can be either character or numeric, but they should contain a limited number of discrete values that represent meaningful groupings. If a CLASS statement is used, then the N Obs statistic is calculated. The N Obs statistic is based on the CLASS variables, as shown in the output below.

The output of the program shown below is grouped by values of the variables Survive and Sex. The order of the variables in the CLASS statement determines their order in the output table.

```
proc means data=cert.heart maxdec=1;
  var arterial heart cardiac urinary;
  class survive sex;
run;
```

Output 15.6 *PROC MEANS Output Grouped by Values of Variables*

Survive	Sex	N Obs	Variable	N	Mean	Std Dev	Minimum	Maximum
DIED	1	4	Arterial	4	92.5	10.5	83.0	103.0
			Heart	4	111.0	53.4	54.0	183.0
			Cardiac	4	176.8	75.2	95.0	260.0
			Urinary	4	98.0	186.1	0.0	377.0
	2	6	Arterial	6	94.2	27.3	72.0	145.0
			Heart	6	103.7	16.7	81.0	130.0
			Cardiac	6	318.3	102.6	156.0	424.0
			Urinary	6	100.3	155.7	0.0	405.0
SURV	1	5	Arterial	5	77.2	12.2	61.0	88.0
			Heart	5	109.0	32.0	77.0	149.0
			Cardiac	5	298.0	139.8	66.0	410.0
			Urinary	5	100.8	60.2	44.0	200.0
	2	5	Arterial	5	78.8	6.8	72.0	87.0
			Heart	5	100.0	13.4	84.0	111.0
			Cardiac	5	330.2	87.0	256.0	471.0
			Urinary	5	111.2	152.4	12.0	377.0

Group Processing Using the BY Statement

Like the CLASS statement, the BY statement specifies variables to use for categorizing observations.

Syntax, BY statement:

BY *variable(s)*;

variable(s) specifies category variables for group processing.

But BY and CLASS differ in two key ways:

- Unlike CLASS processing, BY-group processing requires that your data already be sorted or indexed in the order of the BY variables. Unless data set observations are already sorted, you must run the SORT procedure before using PROC MEANS with any BY group.

  CAUTION:

  If you do not specify an output data set by using the OUT= option, PROC SORT overwrites the initial data set with newly sorted observations.

- The layout of BY-group results differs from the layout of CLASS group results. Note that the BY statement in the program below creates four small tables; a CLASS statement would produce a single large table.

```
proc sort data=cert.heart out=work.heartsort;
  by survive sex;
run;
proc means data=work.heartsort maxdec=1;
  var arterial heart cardiac urinary;
  by survive sex;
run;
```

Figure 15.1 *BY Groups Created by PROC MEANS*

Survive=DIED Sex=1

Variable	N	Mean	Std Dev	Minimum	Maximum
Arterial	4	92.5	10.5	83.0	103.0
Heart	4	111.0	53.4	54.0	183.0
Cardiac	4	176.8	75.2	95.0	260.0
Urinary	4	98.0	186.1	0.0	377.0

Survive=DIED Sex=2

Variable	N	Mean	Std Dev	Minimum	Maximum
Arterial	6	94.2	27.3	72.0	145.0
Heart	6	103.7	16.7	81.0	130.0
Cardiac	6	318.3	102.6	156.0	424.0
Urinary	6	100.3	155.7	0.0	405.0

Survive=SURV Sex=1

Variable	N	Mean	Std Dev	Minimum	Maximum
Arterial	5	77.2	12.2	61.0	88.0
Heart	5	109.0	32.0	77.0	149.0
Cardiac	5	298.0	139.8	66.0	410.0
Urinary	5	100.8	60.2	44.0	200.0

Survive=SURV Sex=2

Variable	N	Mean	Std Dev	Minimum	Maximum
Arterial	5	78.8	6.8	72.0	87.0
Heart	5	100.0	13.4	84.0	111.0
Cardiac	5	330.2	87.0	256.0	471.0
Urinary	5	111.2	152.4	12.0	377.0

TIP The CLASS statement is easier to use than the BY statement because it does not require a sorting step. However, BY-group processing can be more efficient when your categories might contain many levels.

Creating a Summarized Data Set Using the OUTPUT Statement

To write summary statistics to a new data set, use the OUTPUT statement in the MEANS procedure.

Syntax, OUTPUT statement:

OUTPUT OUT=*SAS-data-set statistic=variable(s)***;**

- OUT= specifies the name of the output data set.
- *statistic=* specifies which statistic to store in the output data set.
- *variable(s)* specifies the names of the variables to create. These variables represent the statistics for the analysis variables that are listed in the VAR statement.

Tip: You can use multiple OUTPUT statements to create several OUT= data sets.

The OUTPUT statement writes statistics to a new SAS data set. By default, the default summary statistics are produced for all numeric variables or for the variables specified in the VAR statement. To specify specific statistics to be produced in the new SAS data set, specify *output-statistic-specification= variable-name* in the OUTPUT statement.

The following example creates a PROC MEANS report.

```
proc means data=cert.diabetes;
  var age height weight;                                    /*#1*/
  class sex;                                                /*#2*/
  output out=work.diabetes_by_gender                        /*#3*/
    mean=AvgAge AvgHeight AvgWeight
    min=MinAge MinHeight MinWeight;
run;
proc print data=work.diabetes_by_gender noobs;              /*#4*/
  title1 'Diabetes Results by Gender';
run;
```

1 Specify the analysis variables. The VAR statement specifies that PROC MEANS calculate the default statistics on the Age, Height, and Weight variables.

2 Specify subgroups for the analysis. The CLASS statement separates the analysis by the values of Sex.

3 Specify the output data set options. The OUTPUT statement creates the Work.Diabetes_By_Gender data set and writes the mean value to the new variables AvgAge, AvgHeight, and AvgWeight. The statement also writes the min value to the new variables, MinAge, MinHeight, and MinWeight.

4 Print the output data set Work.Diabetes_By_Gender. The NOOBS option suppresses the observation numbers.

The following output is of Cert.Diabetes from the MEANS procedure.

Output 15.7 *PROC MEANS Output of Cert.Diabetes*

Sex	N Obs	Variable	N	Mean	Std Dev	Minimum	Maximum
F	11	Age	11	48.9090909	13.3075508	16.0000000	63.0000000
		Height	11	63.9090909	2.1191765	61.0000000	68.0000000
		Weight	11	150.4545455	18.4464828	102.0000000	168.0000000
M	9	Age	9	44.0000000	12.3895117	15.0000000	54.0000000
		Height	9	70.6666667	2.6457513	66.0000000	75.0000000
		Weight	9	204.2222222	30.2893454	140.0000000	240.0000000

In addition to the variables that you specify, PROC MEANS adds the following variables to the output set.

FREQ
: contains the number of observations that a given output level represents.

STAT
: contains the names of the default statistics if you omit statistic keywords.

TYPE
: contains information about the class variables. By default _TYPE_ is a numeric variable. If you specify CHARTYPE in the PROC statement, then _TYPE_ is a character variable. When you use more than 32 class variables, _TYPE_ is automatically a character variable.

The following output is of Work.Diabetes_By_Gender from the PRINT procedure.

Output 15.8 *PROC PRINT Output of Work.Diabetes_By_Gender*

Diabetes Results By Gender

Sex	_TYPE_	_FREQ_	AvgAge	AvgHeight	AvgWeight	MinAge	MinHeight	MinWeight
	0	20	46.7000	66.9500	174.650	15	61	102
F	1	11	48.9091	63.9091	150.455	16	61	102
M	1	9	44.0000	70.6667	204.222	15	66	140

TIP You can use the NOPRINT option in the PROC MEANS statement to suppress the default report.

The FREQ Procedure

What Does the FREQ Procedure Do?

PROC FREQ is a procedure that is used give descriptive statistics about a SAS data set. The procedure creates one-way, two-way, and *n*-way frequency tables. It also describes data by reporting the distribution of variable values. The FREQ procedure creates crosstabulation tables to summarize data for two or more categorical values by displaying the number of observations for each combination of variable values.

TIP It is a best practice that you use the TABLES statement with PROC FREQ.

FREQ Procedure Syntax

The FREQ procedure can include many statements and options for controlling frequency output.

Syntax, FREQ procedure:

PROC FREQ *<options>*;
RUN;

The following table lists the options that are available in the PROC FREQ statement.

Table 15.4 *PROC FREQ Statement Options*

Option	Description
COMPRESS	Begins the display of the next one-way frequency table on the same page as the preceding one-way table if there is enough space to begin the table. By default, the next one-way table begins on the current page only if the entire table fits on that page. *Note:* The COMPRESS option is not valid with the PAGE option.
DATA=*SAS-data-set*	Names the *SAS-data-set* to be analyzed by PROC FREQ. If you omit the DATA= option, the procedure uses the most recently created SAS data set.

Option	Description
FORMCHAR(1,2,7)='*formchar-string*'	Defines the characters to be used for constructing the outlines and dividers for the cells of crosstabulation table displays. The *formchar-string* should be three characters long. The characters are used to draw the vertical separators (position 1), the horizontal separators (position 2), and the vertical-horizontal intersections (position 7). If you do not specify the FORMCHAR= option, PROC FREQ uses FORMCHAR(1,2,7)='|-+' by default. Position 1 Default: | The characters are used to draw vertical separators. Position 2 Default: — The characters are used to draw horizontal separators. Position 7 Default: + The characters are used to draw intersections of vertical and horizontal separators. Specifying all blanks for *formchar-string* produces crosstabulation tables with no outlines or dividers—for example, FORMCHAR(1,2,7)=' '. You can use any character in *formchar-string*, including hexadecimal characters. If you use hexadecimal characters, you must put an x after the closing quotation mark.
NLEVELS	Displays the "Number of Variable Levels" table, which provides the number of levels for each variable named in the TABLES statements.
NOPRINT	Suppresses the display of all output. You can use the NOPRINT option when you want to create only an output data set.

Option	Description
<ORDER=DATA | FORMATTED | FREQ | INTERNAL>=	Specifies the order of the variable levels in the frequency and crosstabulation tables, which you request in the TABLES statement. The ORDER= option can take the following values: DATA order of appearance in the input data set FORMATTED external formatted value, except for numeric variables with no explicit format, which are sorted by their unformatted (internal) value FREQ descending frequency count; levels with the most observations come first in the order INTERNAL unformatted value *Note:* The ORDER= option does not apply to missing values, which are always ordered first.
PAGE	Displays only one table per page. Otherwise, PROC FREQ displays multiple tables per page as space permits. *Note:* The PAGE option is not valid with the COMPRESS option.

Example: Creating a One-Way Frequency Table (Default)

By default, the FREQ procedure creates a one-way table that contains the frequency, percent, cumulative frequency, and cumulative percent of every value of every variable in the input data set. In the following example, the FREQ procedure creates crosstabulation tables for each of the variables.

```
proc freq data=cert.usa;
run;
```

Output 15.9 *PROC FREQ Output of Cert.Usa*

Dept	Frequency	Percent	Cumulative Frequency	Cumulative Percent
ADM10	5	33.33	5	33.33
ADM20	4	26.67	9	60.00
ADM30	2	13.33	11	73.33
CAM10	3	20.00	14	93.33
CAM20	1	6.67	15	100.00

WageCat	Frequency	Percent	Cumulative Frequency	Cumulative Percent
H	1	6.67	1	6.67
S	14	93.33	15	100.00

WageRate	Frequency	Percent	Cumulative Frequency	Cumulative Percent
13.65	1	6.67	1	6.67
1572.5	1	6.67	2	13.33
1813.3	1	6.67	3	20.00
2960	1	6.67	4	26.67
3392.5	1	6.67	5	33.33
3420	1	6.67	6	40.00
3819.2	1	6.67	7	46.67
4045.8	1	6.67	8	53.33
4480.5	1	6.67	9	60.00
4522.5	1	6.67	10	66.67
5260	1	6.67	11	73.33
5910.8	1	6.67	12	80.00
6855.9	1	6.67	13	86.67
6862.5	1	6.67	14	93.33
9073.8	1	6.67	15	100.00

Manager	Frequency	Percent	Cumulative Frequency	Cumulative Percent
Coxe	5	33.33	5	33.33
Delgado	5	33.33	10	66.67
Overby	5	33.33	15	100.00

JobType	Frequency	Percent	Cumulative Frequency	Cumulative Percent
1	1	6.67	1	6.67
3	1	6.67	2	13.33
5	1	6.67	3	20.00
10	1	6.67	4	26.67
20	2	13.33	6	40.00
50	2	13.33	8	53.33
240	4	26.67	12	80.00
420	2	13.33	14	93.33
440	1	6.67	15	100.00

Specifying Variables Using the TABLES Statement

By default, the FREQ procedure creates frequency tables for every variable in a data set. But this is not always what you want. A variable that has continuous numeric values (such as DateTime) can result in a lengthy and meaningless table. Likewise, a variable that has a unique value for each observation (such as FullName) is unsuitable for PROC FREQ processing. Frequency distributions work best with variables whose values are categorical, and whose values are better summarized by counts rather than by averages.

To specify the variables to be processed by the FREQ procedure, include a TABLES statement.

Syntax, TABLES statement:

TABLES *variable(s)*;

variable(s) lists the variables to include.

Example: Creating a One-Way Table for One Variable

The TABLES statement tells SAS the specific frequency tables that you want to create. The following example creates only one frequency table for the variable Sex as specified in the TABLES statement. The other variables are suppressed.

```
proc freq data=cert.diabetes;
  tables sex;
run;
```

Output 15.10 *One-Way Table for the Variable Sex*

Sex	Frequency	Percent	Cumulative Frequency	Cumulative Percent
F	11	55.00	11	55.00
M	9	45.00	20	100.00

Example: Determining the Report Layout

The order in which the variables appear in the TABLES statement determines the order in which they are listed in the PROC FREQ report.

Consider the SAS data set Cert.Loans. The variables Rate and Months are categorical variables, so they are the best choices for frequency tables.

```
proc freq data=cert.loans;
  tables rate months;
run;
```

Output 15.11 *Frequency Tables for Rate and Months*

Rate	Frequency	Percent	Cumulative Frequency	Cumulative Percent
9.50%	2	22.22	2	22.22
9.75%	1	11.11	3	33.33
10.00%	2	22.22	5	55.56
10.50%	4	44.44	9	100.00

Months	Frequency	Percent	Cumulative Frequency	Cumulative Percent
12	1	11.11	1	11.11
24	1	11.11	2	22.22
36	1	11.11	3	33.33
48	1	11.11	4	44.44
60	2	22.22	6	66.67
360	3	33.33	9	100.00

In addition to listing variables separately, you can use a numbered range of variables.

```
proc freq data=cert.survey;
  tables item1-item3;
run;
```

Output 15.12 *Frequency Tables for Item1–Item3*

Item1	Frequency	Percent	Cumulative Frequency	Cumulative Percent
2	1	25.00	1	25.00
4	2	50.00	3	75.00
5	1	25.00	4	100.00

Item2	Frequency	Percent	Cumulative Frequency	Cumulative Percent
1	1	25.00	1	25.00
3	2	50.00	3	75.00
5	1	25.00	4	100.00

Item3	Frequency	Percent	Cumulative Frequency	Cumulative Percent
4	3	75.00	3	75.00
5	1	25.00	4	100.00

TIP To suppress the display of cumulative frequencies and cumulative percentages in one-way frequency tables and in list output, add the NOCUM option to your TABLES statement. Here is the syntax:

TABLES *variable(s)* / **NOCUM**;

Create Two-Way and N-Way Tables

The simplest crosstabulation is a two-way table. To create a two-way table or *n*-way table, join the variables with an asterisk (*) in the TABLES statement in a PROC FREQ step. For a two-way table, one table is created. For *n*-way tables, a series of tables are produced with a table for each level of the variables.

Syntax, TABLES statement for crosstabulation:

TABLES *variable-1* **variable-2* <* *... variable-n*>;

Here are the options for two-way tables:

- *variable-1* specifies table rows.
- *variable-2* specifies table columns.

Tip: You can include up to 50 variables in a single multi-way table request.

When crosstabulations are specified, PROC FREQ produces tables with cells that contain the following frequencies:

- cell frequency
- cell percentage of total frequency
- cell percentage of row frequency
- cell percentage of column frequency

Example: Creating Two-Way Tables

In the following example, you can create a two-way table to see the frequency of fasting glucose levels for each value for the variable Sex.

```
proc freq data=cert.diabetes;
  tables sex*fastgluc;
run;
```

Output 15.13 *Two-Way Table Output Cert.Diabetes (partial output)*

Frequency Percent Row Pct Col Pct	Table of Sex by FastGluc											
		FastGluc										
	Sex	152	155	156	166	177	193		447	486	492	568	Total
	F	1 5.00 9.09 100.00	1 5.00 9.09 100.00	0 0.00 0.00 0.00	1 5.00 9.09 100.00	1 5.00 9.09 100.00	1 5.00 9.09 100.00	. . . *more*	0 0.00 0.00 0.00	0 0.00 0.00 0.00	0 0.00 0.00 0.00	1 5.00 9.09 100.00	11 55.00
	M	0 0.00 0.00 0.00	0 0.00 0.00 0.00	1 5.00 11.11 100.00	0 0.00 0.00 0.00	0 0.00 0.00 0.00	0 0.00 0.00 0.00	*variables* . . .	1 5.00 11.11 100.00	1 5.00 11.11 100.00	1 5.00 11.11 100.00	0 0.00 0.00 0.00	9 45.00
	Total	1 5.00	1 5.00	1 5.00	1 5.00	1 5.00	1 5.00		1 5.00	1 5.00	1 5.00	1 5.00	20 100.00

Note that the first variable, Sex, forms the table rows, and the second variable, FastGluc, forms the columns. Reversing the order of the variables in the TABLES statement would reverse their positions in the table. Note also that the statistics are listed in the legend box.

Examples: Creating N-Way Tables

The following example creates a series of two-way tables with a table for each level of the other variables. The variables WhiteCells and AG are the rows and columns that are crosstabulated by the variable Survived.

```
proc format;
  value Survive 0='Dead'
                1='Alive';
run;
proc freq data=cert.leukemia;
  tables Survived*AG*WhiteCells;
  format Survived survive.;
run;
```

Output 15.14 *N-Way Tables (partial output)*

Frequency
Percent
Row Pct
Col Pct

Table 1 of AG by WhiteCells

Controlling for Survived=Dead

AG	WhiteCells 750	1500	2300	2600	3000		31000	32000	35000	52000	79000	1000000	Total
Absent	0	1	0	0	0		1	0	0	0	0	1	12
	0.00	5.56	0.00	0.00	0.00		5.56	0.00	0.00	0.00	0.00	5.56	66.67
	0.00	8.33	0.00	0.00	0.00	. . .	8.33	0.00	0.00	0.00	0.00	8.33	
	.	100.00	.	.	.	more	100.00	.	0.00	0.00	.	33.33	
Present	0	0	0	0	0	variables	0	0	1	1	0	2	6
	0.00	0.00	0.00	0.00	0.00	. . .	0.00	0.00	5.56	5.56	0.00	11.11	33.33
	0.00	0.00	0.00	0.00	0.00		0.00	0.00	16.67	16.67	0.00	33.33	
	.	0.00	.	.	.		0.00	.	100.00	100.00	.	66.67	
Total	0	1	0	0	0		1	0	1	1	0	3	18
	0.00	5.56	0.00	0.00	0.00		5.56	0.00	5.56	5.56	0.00	16.67	100.00

Frequency
Percent
Row Pct
Col Pct

Table 2 of AG by WhiteCells

Controlling for Survived=Alive

AG	WhiteCells 750	1500	2300	2600	3000		31000	32000	35000	52000	79000	1000000	Total
Absent	0	0	0	0	1		0	0	0	0	1	1	4
	0.00	0.00	0.00	0.00	6.67		0.00	0.00	0.00	0.00	6.67	6.67	26.67
	0.00	0.00	0.00	0.00	25.00	. . .	0.00	0.00	0.00	0.00	25.00	25.00	
	0.00	.	0.00	0.00	100.00	more	.	0.00	.	.	100.00	50.00	
Present	1	0	1	1	0	variables	0	1	0	0	0	1	11
	6.67	0.00	6.67	6.67	0.00	. . .	0.00	6.67	0.00	0.00	0.00	6.67	73.33
	9.09	0.00	9.09	9.09	0.00		0.00	9.09	0.00	0.00	0.00	9.09	
	100.00	.	100.00	100.00	0.00		.	100.00	.	.	0.00	50.00	
Total	1	0	1	1	1		0	1	0	0	1	2	15
	6.67	0.00	6.67	6.67	6.67		0.00	6.67	0.00	0.00	6.67	13.33	100.00

Creating Tables Using the LIST Option

When three or more variables are specified, the multiple levels of *n*-way tables can produce considerable output. Such bulky, often complex crosstabulations are often easier to read when they are arranged as a continuous list. Although this arrangement eliminates row and column frequencies and percentages, the results are compact and clear.

TIP The LIST option is not available when you also specify statistical options.

To generate list output for crosstabulations, add a slash (/) and the LIST option to the TABLES statement in your PROC FREQ step.

Syntax, TABLES statement:

TABLES *variable-1* **variable-2* <* ... *variable-n*> / **LIST;**

Here are the options for two-way tables:

- *variable-1* specifies table rows.
- *variable-2* specifies table columns.

Tip: You can include up to 50 variables in a single multi-way table request.

Example: Using the LIST Option

As in the previous example, the following example creates a series of two-way tables with a table for each level of the other variables. The variables WhiteCells and AG are the rows and columns that are crosstabulated by the variable Survived. Use the LIST option in the TABLES statement to make the PROC FREQ output easier to read. The output is generated in a continuous list.

```
proc format;
  value survive 0='Dead'
                1='Alive';
run;
proc freq data=cert.leukemia;
  tables Survived*AG*WhiteCells / list;
  format Survived survive.;
run;
```

Output 15.15 *PROC FREQ Output in List Format (partial output)*

Survived	AG	WhiteCells	Frequency	Percent	Cumulative Frequency	Cumulative Percent
Dead	Absent	1500	1	3.03	1	3.03
Dead	Absent	4000	1	3.03	2	6.06
Dead	Absent	5300	1	3.03	3	9.09
Dead	Absent	9000	1	3.03	4	12.12
Dead	Absent	10000	1	3.03	5	15.15

. . . *more observations*. . .

Survived	AG	WhiteCells	Frequency	Percent	Cumulative Frequency	Cumulative Percent
Alive	Present	9400	1	3.03	29	87.88
Alive	Present	10000	1	3.03	30	90.91
Alive	Present	10500	1	3.03	31	93.94
Alive	Present	32000	1	3.03	32	96.97
Alive	Present	1000000	1	3.03	33	100.00

Example: Using the CROSSLIST Option

The CROSSLIST option displays crosstabulation tables in ODS column format instead of the default crosstabulation cell format. In a CROSSLIST table display, the rows correspond to the crosstabulation table cells, and the columns correspond to descriptive statistics such as Frequency and Percent. The CROSSLIST table displays the same information as the default crosstabulation table, but uses an ODS column format instead of the table cell format

```
proc format;
  value survive 0='Dead'
                1='Alive';
run;
proc freq data=cert.leukemia;
  tables Survived*AG*whitecells / crosslist;
  format Survived survive.;
run;
```

Output 15.16 *Table Created by the CROSSLIST Option Survived=Dead (partial output)*

Table of AG by WhiteCells					
Controlling for Survived=Dead					
AG	WhiteCells	Frequency	Percent	Row Percent	Column Percent
Absent	750	0	0.00	0.00	.
	1500	1	5.56	8.33	100.00
	2300	0	0.00	0.00	.
	2600	0	0.00	0.00	.
	3000	0	0.00	0.00	.

. . . *more observations*. . .

AG	WhiteCells	Frequency	Percent	Row Percent	Column Percent
	Total	12	66.67	100.00	
Present	750	0	0.00	0.00	.
	1500	0	0.00	0.00	0.00
	2300	0	0.00	0.00	.
	2600	0	0.00	0.00	.
	3000	0	0.00	0.00	.

. . . *more observations*. . .

AG	WhiteCells	Frequency	Percent	Row Percent	Column Percent
	Total	6	33.33	100.00	
Total	750	0	0.00		.
	1500	1	5.56		100.00
	2300	0	0.00		.
	2600	0	0.00		.
	3000	0	0.00		.

. . . *more observations*. . .

AG	WhiteCells	Frequency	Percent	Row Percent	Column Percent
	35000	1	5.56		100.00
	52000	1	5.56		100.00
	79000	0	0.00		.
	1000000	3	16.67		100.00
	Total	18	100.00		

Output 15.17 *Table Created by the CROSSLIST Option Survived=Alive (partial output)*

Table of AG by WhiteCells					
Controlling for Survived=Alive					
AG	**WhiteCells**	**Frequency**	**Percent**	**Row Percent**	**Column Percent**
Absent	750	0	0.00	0.00	0.00
	1500	0	0.00	0.00	.
	2300	0	0.00	0.00	0.00
	2600	0	0.00	0.00	0.00
	3000	1	6.67	25.00	100.00
	. . . *more observations*. . .				
	Total	4	26.67	100.00	
Present	750	1	6.67	9.09	100.00
	1500	0	0.00	0.00	.
	2300	1	6.67	9.09	100.00
	2600	1	6.67	9.09	100.00
	3000	0	0.00	0.00	0.00
	. . . *more observations*. . .				
	Total	11	73.33	100.00	
Total	750	1	6.67		100.00
	1500	0	0.00		.
	2300	1	6.67		100.00
	2600	1	6.67		100.00
	3000	1	6.67		100.00
	. . . *more observations*. . .				
	35000	0	0.00		.
	52000	0	0.00		.
	79000	1	6.67		100.00
	1000000	2	13.33		100.00
	Total	15	100.00		

Suppressing Table Information

Another way to control the format of crosstabulations is to limit the output of the FREQ procedure to a few specific statistics. Remember that when crosstabulations are run, PROC FREQ produces tables with cells that contain these frequencies:

- cell frequency
- cell percentage of total frequency

- cell percentage of row frequency
- cell percentage of column frequency

You can use options to suppress any of these statistics. To control the depth of crosstabulation results, add any combination of the following options to the TABLES statement:

- NOFREQ suppresses cell frequencies
- NOPERCENT suppresses cell percentages
- NOROW suppresses row percentages
- NOCOL suppresses column percentages

Example: Suppressing Percentages

You can suppress frequency counts, rows, and column percentages by using the NOFREQ, NOROW, and NOCOL options in the TABLES statement.

```
proc format;
  value survive  0='Dead'
                 1='Alive';
run;
proc freq data=cert.leukemia;
  tables Survived*AG*whitecells / nofreq norow nocol;
  format Survived survive.;
run;
```

Output 15.18 *Suppressing Percentage Information (partial output)*

Percent	Table 1 of AG by WhiteCells												
	Controlling for Survived=Dead												
	WhiteCells												
AG	750	1500	2300	2600	3000		31000	32000	35000	52000	79000	1000000	Total
Absent	0.00	5.56	0.00	0.00	0.00	. . .	5.56	0.00	0.00	0.00	0.00	5.56	66.67
Present	0.00	0.00	0.00	0.00	0.00	*more variables*	0.00	0.00	5.56	5.56	0.00	11.11	33.33
Total	0 0.00	1 5.56	0 0.00	0 0.00	0 0.00	. . .	1 5.56	0 0.00	1 5.56	1 5.56	0 0.00	3 16.67	18 100.00

Percent	Table 2 of AG by WhiteCells												
	Controlling for Survived=Alive												
	WhiteCells												
AG	750	1500	2300	2600	3000		31000	32000	35000	52000	79000	1000000	Total
Absent	0.00	0.00	0.00	0.00	6.67	. . .	0.00	0.00	0.00	0.00	6.67	6.67	26.67
Present	6.67	0.00	6.67	6.67	0.00	*more variables*	0.00	6.67	0.00	0.00	0.00	6.67	73.33
Total	1 6.67	0 0.00	1 6.67	1 6.67	1 6.67	. . .	0 0.00	1 6.67	0 0.00	0 0.00	1 6.67	2 13.33	15 100.00

Chapter Quiz

Select the best answer for each question. Check your answers using the answer key in the appendix.

1. The default statistics produced by the MEANS procedure are *n*-count, mean, minimum, maximum, and which one of the following statistics:

   a. median

   b. range

   c. standard deviation

   d. standard error of the mean

2. Which statement limits a PROC MEANS analysis to the variables Boarded, Transfer, and Deplane?

   a. `by boarded transfer deplane;`

   b. `class boarded transfer deplane;`

   c. `output boarded transfer deplane;`

   d. `var boarded transfer deplane;`

3. The data set Cert.Health includes the following numeric variables. Which is a poor candidate for PROC MEANS analysis?

   a. `IDnum`

   b. `Age`

   c. `Height`

   d. `Weight`

4. Which of the following statements is true regarding BY-group processing?

   a. BY variables must be either indexed or sorted.

   b. Summary statistics are computed for BY variables.

   c. BY-group processing is preferred when you are categorizing data that contains few variables.

   d. BY-group processing overwrites your data set with the newly grouped observations.

5. Which group processing statement produced the PROC MEANS output shown below?

The MEANS Procedure

Survive	Sex	N Obs	Variable	N	Mean	Std Dev	Minimum	Maximum
DIED	1	4	Arterial	4	92.5000000	10.4721854	83.0000000	103.0000000
			Heart	4	111.0000000	53.4103610	54.0000000	183.0000000
			Cardiac	4	176.7500000	75.2257713	95.0000000	260.0000000
			Urinary	4	98.0000000	186.1343601	0	377.0000000
	2	6	Arterial	6	94.1666667	27.3160514	72.0000000	145.0000000
			Heart	6	103.6666667	16.6573307	81.0000000	130.0000000
			Cardiac	6	318.3333333	102.6034437	156.0000000	424.0000000
			Urinary	6	100.3333333	155.7134120	0	405.0000000
SURV	1	5	Arterial	5	77.2000000	12.1942609	61.0000000	88.0000000
			Heart	5	109.0000000	31.9687347	77.0000000	149.0000000
			Cardiac	5	298.0000000	139.8499196	66.0000000	410.0000000
			Urinary	5	100.8000000	60.1722527	44.0000000	200.0000000
	2	5	Arterial	5	78.8000000	6.8337398	72.0000000	87.0000000
			Heart	5	100.0000000	13.3790882	84.0000000	111.0000000
			Cardiac	5	330.2000000	86.9839066	256.0000000	471.0000000
			Urinary	5	111.2000000	152.4096454	12.0000000	377.0000000

a. `class sex survive;`

b. `class survive sex;`

c. `by sex survive;`

d. `by survive sex;`

6. Which program can be used to create the following output?

Sex	N Obs	Variable	N	Mean	Std Dev	Minimum	Maximum
F	11	Age	11	48.9090909	13.3075508	16.0000000	63.0000000
		Height	11	63.9090909	2.1191765	61.0000000	68.0000000
		Weight	11	150.4545455	18.4464828	102.0000000	168.0000000
M	9	Age	9	44.0000000	12.3895117	15.0000000	54.0000000
		Height	9	70.6666667	2.6457513	66.0000000	75.0000000
		Weight	9	204.2222222	30.2893454	140.0000000	240.0000000

a.
```
proc means data=cert.diabetes;
   var age height weight;
   class sex;
   output out=work.sum_gender
      mean=AvgAge AvgHeight AvgWeight;
run;
```

b.
```
proc freq data=cert.diabetes;
   tables height weight sex;
run;
```

c.
```
proc means data=cert.diabetes noprint;
   var age height weight;
   class sex;
   output out=work.sum_gender
      mean=AvgAge AvgHeight AvgWeight;
run;
```

d. Both a and b.

7. By default, PROC FREQ creates a table of frequencies and percentages for which data set variables?

   a. character variables

   b. numeric variables

   c. both character and numeric variables

   d. none: variables must always be specified

8. Frequency distributions work best with variables that contain which types of values?

   a. continuous values

   b. numeric values

   c. categorical values

   d. unique values

9. Which PROC FREQ step produced this two-way table?

The FREQ Procedure

Frequency Percent Row Pct Col Pct	Table of Weight by Height			
	Height			
Weight	< 5'5"	5'5-10"	> 5'10"	Total
< 140	2 10.00 100.00 28.57	0 0.00 0.00 0.00	0 0.00 0.00 0.00	2 10.00
140-180	5 25.00 50.00 71.43	5 25.00 50.00 62.50	0 0.00 0.00 0.00	10 50.00
> 180	0 0.00 0.00 0.00	3 15.00 37.50 37.50	5 25.00 62.50 100.00	8 40.00
Total	7 35.00	8 40.00	5 25.00	20 100.00

a.
```
proc freq data=cert.diabetes;
   tables height weight;
   format height htfmt. weight wtfmt.;
run;
```

b.
```
proc freq data=cert.diabetes;
   tables weight height;
   format weight wtfmt. height htfmt.;
run;
```

c.
```
proc freq data=cert.diabetes;
   tables height*weight;
   format height htfmt. weight wtfmt.;
run;
```

d.
```
proc freq data=cert.diabetes;
   tables weight*height;
   format weight wtfmt. height htfmt.;
run;
```

10. Which PROC FREQ step produced this table?

The FREQ Procedure

Percent	Table of Sex by Weight			
	Weight			
Sex	< 140	140-180	> 180	Total
F	10.00	45.00	0.00	55.00
M	0.00	5.00	40.00	45.00
Total	2 10.00	10 50.00	8 40.00	20 100.00

a.
```
proc freq data=cert.diabetes;
   tables sex weight / list;
   format weight wtfmt.;
run;
```

b.
```
proc freq data=cert.diabetes;
   tables sex*weight / nocol;
   format weight wtfmt.;
run;
```

c.
```
proc freq data=cert.diabetes;
   tables sex weight / norow nocol;
   format weight wtfmt.;
run;
```

d.
```
proc freq data=cert.diabetes;
   tables sex*weight / nofreq norow nocol;
   format weight wtfmt.;
run;
```

Chapter 16
Creating Output

The Output Delivery System (ODS)

Overview of ODS

The SAS Output Delivery System (ODS) gives you flexibility in generating, storing, and reproducing SAS procedure and DATA step output along with a wide range of formatting options.

ODS enables you to create reports for popular software applications. For example, use the ODS PDF statement to create PDF files for viewing with Adobe Acrobat or for printing. With ODS, you easily create output in a variety of formats, including Microsoft Excel and Power Point, HTML, PDF, and RTF.

Opening and Closing ODS Destinations

You use ODS statements to specify destinations for your output. Each destination creates a specific type of formatted output. The following table lists some of the ODS destinations that are currently supported.

Destination	Result
Document	a hierarchy of output objects that enables you to render multiple ODS output without rerunning procedures.
EXCEL	writes Excel spreadsheet files that are compatible with Microsoft Office 2010 and later versions.
HTML	output that is formatted in Hypertext Markup Language (HTML). You do not have to specify the ODS HTML statement to produce basic HTML output.
Markup Languages Family	output that is formatted using markup languages such as Extensible Markup Language (XML).
Output	SAS data sets.
Printer Family (PDF, and so on)	output that is formatted for a high-resolution printer such as PostScript (PS), Portable Document Format (PDF), or Printer Control Language (PCL) files.
RTF	Rich Text Format output.

This book covers the EXCEL, HTML, PDF, and RTF destinations.

Note: SAS Studio has user interface controls to create and save HTML, PDF, and RTF ODS output.

Using Statements to Open and Close ODS Destinations

Syntax

For each type of formatted output that you want to create, you use an ODS statement to open the destination. At the end of your program, you use another ODS statement to close the destination so that you can access your output.

Syntax, ODS statement to open and close destinations:

ODS *open-destination*;

ODS *close-destination* **CLOSE;**

- *open-destination* is a keyword, and any required options for the type of output that you want to create. Here are examples:
  - HTML FILE=*'html-file-pathname'*
  - LISTING
- *close-destination* is a keyword for the type of output.

You can issue ODS statements in any order, depending on whether you need to open or close the destination. Most ODS destinations are closed by default. You open them at the beginning of your program and close them at the end. The exception is the HTML destination, which is open by default.

Figure 16.1 *Default ODS Destination*

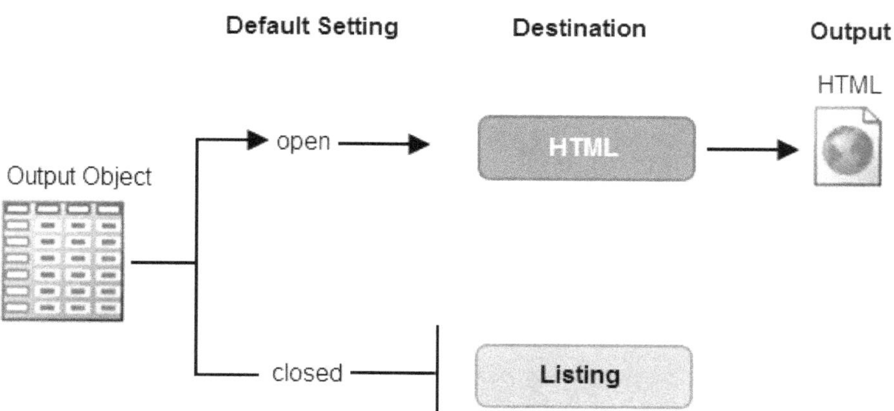

Closing Multiple ODS Destinations at Once

You can produce output in multiple formats at once by opening each ODS destination at the beginning of the program.

When you have more than one open ODS destination, you can use the keyword _ALL_ in the ODS CLOSE statement to close all open destinations at once.

Closing the HTML Destination

Because open destinations use system resources, it is a good idea to close the HTML destination at the beginning of your program if you do not want to produce HTML output. Here is an example:

```
ods html close;
```

The HTML destination remains closed until you end your current SAS session or until you re-open the destination. It is good programming practice to reset the ODS destination to HTML output (the default setting) at the end of your programs.

```
ods html path="%qsysfunc(pathname(work))";
```

Creating HTML Output with ODS

The ODS HTML Statement

To create simple HTML output files in the default location using the default file-naming conventions, you do not have to specify the ODS HTML statement. However, to create HTML output with options specified, you open the HTML destination using the ODS HTML statement.

Note: You do not have to specify the ODS HTML statement to produce basic HTML output unless the HTML destination is closed.

Syntax, ODS HTML statement:

ODS HTML BODY =*file-specification*;

ODS HTML CLOSE ;

- *file-specification* identifies the file that contains the HTML output. The specification can be any of the following:
  - a quoted string that contains the HTML filename (use only the filename to write the file to your current working directory, such as **C:\Users\Student1\Documents and Settings*username*\My Documents\My SAS Files**). Example: **ODS HTML BODY=** "*myreport.html*";
  - a quoted string that contains the complete directory path and HTML filename (include the complete pathname if you want to save the HTML file to a specific location other than your working directory). Example: **ODS HTML BODY=** "*c:\Users \Student1\reportdir\myreport.html*";
  - a fileref (unquoted file shortcut) that has been assigned to an HTML file using the FILENAME statement. Example: **FILENAME MYHTML** "*c:\reportdir\myreport.html*"; **ODS HTML BODY=MYHTML**;
  - a SAS catalog entry in the form *entry-name*.html. Note that the catalog name is specified in the PATH= option and the *entry-name*.html value for the BODY= option is unquoted. Example: **ODS HTML PATH=***work.mycat* **BODY=***myentry* **BODY=bodyfile.html**;

TIP FILE= can also be used to specify the file that contains the HTML output. FILE= is an alias for BODY=.

TIP You can also use the PATH= option to explicitly specify a directory path for your file.

Example: Creating Output with PROC PRINT

The following program creates PROC PRINT output in an HTML file. The ODS HTML BODY= option specifies the file **`C:\Users\Student1\cert\admit.html`** in the Windows operating environment as the file that contains the PROC PRINT results.

```
ods html body='C:\Users\Student1\cert\admit.html';
proc print data=cert.admit label;
  var sex age height weight actlevel;
  label actlevel='Activity Level';
run;
ods html close;
ods html path="%qsysfunc(pathname(work))";
```

The HTML file admit.html contains the results of all procedure steps between the ODS HTML statement and ODS HTML CLOSE statement.

Output 16.1 *HTML Output*

Obs	Sex	Age	Height	Weight	Activity Level
1	M	27	72	168	HIGH
2	F	34	66	152	HIGH
3	F	31	61	123	LOW
4	F	43	63	137	MOD
5	M	51	71	158	LOW
6	M	29	76	193	HIGH
7	F	32	67	151	MOD
8	M	35	70	173	MOD
9	M	34	73	154	LOW
10	F	49	64	172	LOW
11	F	44	66	140	HIGH
12	F	28	62	118	LOW
13	M	30	69	147	MOD
14	F	40	69	163	HIGH
15	M	47	72	173	MOD
16	M	60	71	191	LOW
17	F	43	65	123	MOD
18	M	25	75	188	HIGH
19	F	22	63	139	LOW
20	F	41	67	141	HIGH
21	M	54	71	183	MOD

Creating HTML Output with a Table of Contents

Overview

The BODY= specification is one way to create an HTML file containing procedure output. To create an HTML file that has a table of contents with links to the output of each specific procedure, specify additional files in the ODS HTML statement.

Syntax, ODS HTML statement to create a linked table of contents:

ODS HTML

BODY=*body-file-specification*

CONTENTS=*contents-file-specification*

FRAME=*frame-file-specification*;

ODS HTML CLOSE;

- *body-file-specification* is the name of an HTML file that contains the procedure output.
- *contents-file-specification* is the name of an HTML file that contains a table of contents with links to the procedure output.
- *frame-file-specification* is the name of an HTML file that integrates the table of contents and the body file. If you specify FRAME=, you must also specify CONTENTS=.

TIP To direct the HTML output to a specific storage location, specify the complete pathname of the HTML file in the *file-specification*.

Here is an example that does the following:

- The BODY= specification creates the file data.html in **C:\Users\Student1\cert** directory. The body file contains the results of the two procedures.
- The CONTENTS= specification creates the file toc.html in the **C:\Users\Student1\cert** directory. The table of contents file has links to each procedure output in the body file.
- The FRAME= specification creates the file frame.html in the **C:\Users\Student1\cert** directory. The frame file integrates the table of contents and the body file.

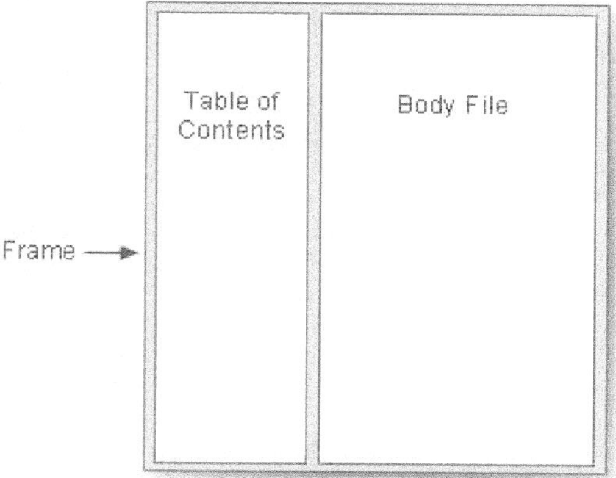


```
ods html body='C:\Users\Student1\cert\data.html'
  contents='C:\Users\Student1\cert\toc.html'
  frame='C:\Users\Student1\cert\frame.html';
proc print data=cert.admit (obs=10) label;
  var id sex age height weight actlevel;
  label actlevel='Activity Level';
run;
proc print data=cert.stress2 (obs=10);
  var id resthr maxhr rechr;
run;
ods html close;
```

```
ods html path="%qsysfunc(pathname(work))";
```

Viewing Frame Files

The Results window does not display links to frame files. In the Windows environment, only the body file automatically appears in the internal browser or your preferred web browser.

To view the frame file that integrates the body file and the table of contents, select **File** ⇨ **Open** from within the internal browser or your preferred web browser. Then open the frame file that you specified using FRAME=. In the example above, this file is frame.html, which is stored in the Cert directory in the Windows environment.

The frame file, frame.html, is shown below.

Figure 16.2 Frame File, frame.html (partial output)

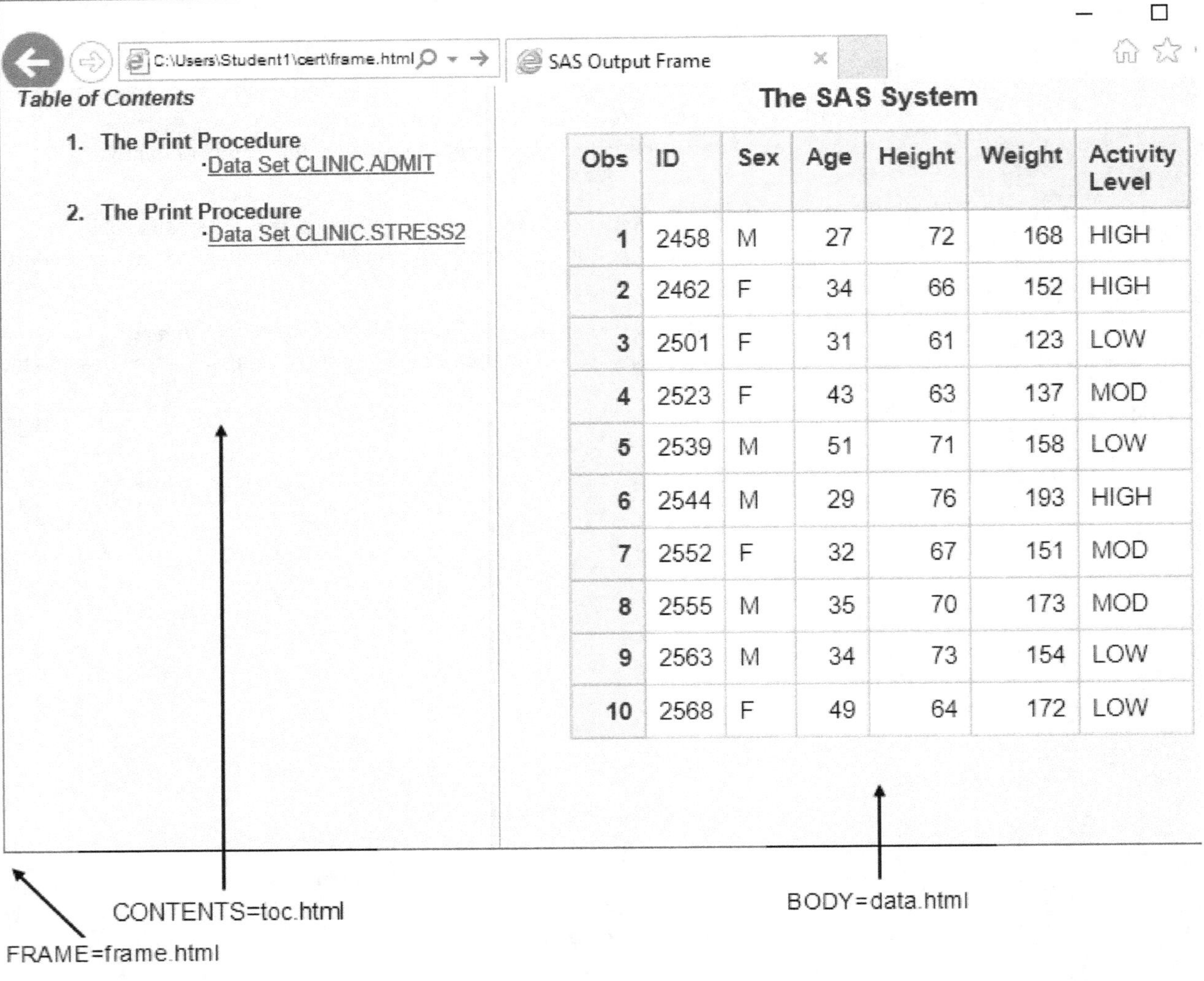

Obs	ID	Sex	Age	Height	Weight	Activity Level
1	2458	M	27	72	168	HIGH
2	2462	F	34	66	152	HIGH
3	2501	F	31	61	123	LOW
4	2523	F	43	63	137	MOD
5	2539	M	51	71	158	LOW
6	2544	M	29	76	193	HIGH
7	2552	F	32	67	151	MOD
8	2555	M	35	70	173	MOD
9	2563	M	34	73	154	LOW
10	2568	F	49	64	172	LOW

Using the Table of Contents

The table of contents that was created by the CONTENTS= option contains a numbered heading for each procedure that creates output. Below each heading is a link to the output for that procedure.

TIP On some browsers, you can select a heading to contract or expand the table of contents.

Figure 16.3 Table of Contents

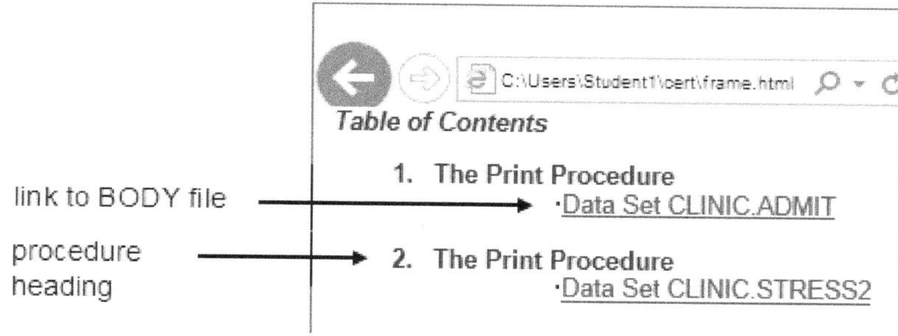

Using Options to Specify Links and Paths

Overview

When ODS generates HTML files for the body, contents, and frame, it also generates links between the files using HTML filenames that you specify in the ODS HTML statement. If you specify complete pathnames, ODS uses those pathnames in the links that it generates.

The following ODS statement creates a frame file that links to **C:\Users\Student1\cert\toc.html** and **C:\Users\Student1\cert\data.html**, and a contents file that has links to **C:\Users\Student1\cert\data.html**.

```
ods html body='C:\Users\Student1\cert\data.html'
         contents='C:\Users\Student1\cert\toc.html'
         frame='C:\Users\Student1\cert\frame.html';
```

A portion of the source code for the HTML file frame.html is shown below. Notice that the links have the complete pathnames from the file specifications for the contents and body files.

Example Code 1 *Source Code for the HTML File Frame.html*

```
<FRAME MARGINWIDTH="4" MARGINHEIGHT="0" SRC="C:\Users\Student1\cert\toc.html"
    NAME="contents" SCROLLING=auto>
<FRAME MARGINWIDTH="9" MARGINHEIGHT="0" SRC="C:\Users\Student1\cert\data.html"
    NAME="body" SCROLLING=auto>
```

These links work when you are viewing the HTML files locally. If you want to place these files on a web server so that others can access them, then the link needs to include either the complete URL for an absolute link or the HTML filename for a relative link.

The URL= Suboption

To provide a URL that ODS uses in all the links that it creates to the file, specify the URL= suboption in the BODY= or CONTENTS= file specification. You can use the URL= suboption in any ODS file specification except FRAME= (because no ODS file references the frame file).

Syntax, URL= suboption in a file specification:

(URL= "*Uniform-Resource-Locator*";

- *Uniform-Resource-Locator* is the name of an HTML file or the full URL of an HTML file. ODS uses this URL instead of the file specification in all the links and references that it creates that point to the file.

TIP The URL= suboption is useful for building HTML files that might be moved from one location to another. If the links from the contents and page files are constructed with a simple URL (one name), they work as long as the contents, page, and body files are all in the same location.

Example: Relative URLs

In this ODS HTML statement, the URL= suboption specifies only the HTML filename. This is the most common style of linking between files because maintenance is easier. The files can be moved as long as they all remain in the same directory or storage location.

```
ods html body='C:\Users\Student1\cert\data.html' (url='data.html')
  contents='C:\Users\Student1\cert\toc.html' (url='toc.html')
  frame='C:\Users\Student1\cert\frame.html';
```

The source code for frame.html has only the HTML filename as specified in the URL= suboptions for the body and contents files.

Example Code 2 *Source Code for the HTML File Frame.html*

```
<FRAME MARGINWIDTH="4" MARGINHEIGHT="0" SRC="toc.html"
    NAME="contents" SCROLLING=auto>
<FRAME MARGINWIDTH="9" MARGINHEIGHT="0" SRC="data.html"
    NAME="body" SCROLLING=auto>
```

Example: Absolute URLs

Alternatively, in this ODS HTML statement, the URL= suboptions specify complete URLs using HTTP. These files can be stored in the same or different locations.

```
ods html body='C:\Users\Student1\cert\data.html'
        (url='http://mysite.com/cert/data.html')
        contents='C:\Users\Student1\cert\toc.html'
        (url='http://mysite.com/cert/toc.html')
        frame='C:\Users\Student1\cert\frame.html';
```

As you would expect, the source code for Frame.html has the entire HTTP addresses that you specified in the URL= suboptions for the body and contents file.

Example Code 3 *Source Code for the HTML File Frame.html*

```
<FRAME MARGINWIDTH="4" MARGINHEIGHT="0" SRC="http://mysite.com/cert/data.html"
    NAME="contents" SCROLLING=auto>
<FRAME MARGINWIDTH="9" MARGINHEIGHT="0" SRC="http://mysite.com/cert/toc.html"
    NAME="body" SCROLLING=auto>
```

TIP When you use the URL= suboption to specify a complete URL, you might need to move your files to that location before you can view them.

The PATH= Option

Use the PATH= option to specify the location of the files.

Syntax, PATH= option with the URL= suboption:

PATH=*file-location-specification*<(URL=NONE | "*Uniform-Resource-Locator*">

- *file-location-specification* identifies the location where you want HTML files to be saved. It can be one of the following:
  - the complete pathname to an aggregate storage location, such as a directory or partitioned data set
  - a fileref (file shortcut) that has been assigned to a storage location
  - a SAS catalog (*libname.catalog*)
- *Uniform-Resource-Locator* provides a URL for links in the HTML files that ODS generates. If you specify the keyword NONE, no information from the PATH= option appears in the links or references.

  If you do not use the URL= suboption, information from the PATH= option is added to links and references in the files that are created.

Note: In the z/OS operating environment, if you store your HTML files as members in a partitioned data set, the PATH=value must be a PDSE, not a PDS. You can allocate a PDSE within SAS as shown in this example:

```
filename pdsehtml '.example.htm'
    dsntype=library dsorg=po
    disp=(new, catlg, delete);
```

You should specify valid member names for the HTML files (without extensions).

Example: PATH= Option with URL=NONE

In the following program, the PATH= option directs the files data.html, toc.html, and frame.html to the **C:\Users\Student1\cert** directory in the Windows operating environment. The links from the frame file to the body and contents files contain only the HTML filenames data.html and toc.html.

```
ods html path='C:\Users\Student1\cert\' (url=none)
  body='data.html'
  contents='toc.html'
  frame='frame.html';
proc print data=cert.admit;
run;
proc print data=cert.stress2;
run;
ods html close;
ods html path="%qsysfunc(pathname(work))";
```

This program generates the same files and links as the previous example in which you learned how to use the URL= suboption with the BODY= and CONTENTS= file specifications. However, it is simpler to specify the path once in the PATH= option and to specify URL=NONE.

TIP If you plan to move your HTML files, you should specify URL=NONE with the PATH= option to prevent information from the PATH= option from creating URLs that are invalid or incorrect.

Example: PATH= Option without the URL= Suboption

In the following program, the PATH= option directs the files data.html, toc.html, and frame.html to the **C:\Users\Student1\cert** directory in the Windows operating environment. The links from the frame file to the body and contents files contain the complete pathnames, **C:\Users\Student1\cert\data.html** and **C:\Users\Student1\cert\toc.html**:

```
ods html path='C:\Users\Student1\cert\'
  body='data.html'
  contents='toc.html'
  frame='frame.html';
proc print data=cert.admit;
run;
proc print data=cert.stress2;
run;
ods html close;
ods html path="%qsysfunc(pathname(work))";
```

Example: PATH= Option with a Specified URL

In the following program, the PATH= option directs the files data.html, toc.html, and frame.html to the **C:\Users\Student1\cert** directory in the Windows operating environment. The links from the frame file to the body and contents files contain the specified URLs, http://mysite.com/cert/data.html, and http://mysite.com/cert/toc.html:

```
ods html path='C:\Users\Student1\cert\ (url='http://mysite.com/cert/')
  body='data.html'
  contents='toc.html'
  frame='frame.html';
proc print data=cert.admit;
run;
proc print data=cert.stress2;
run;
ods html close;
ods html path="%qsysfunc(pathname(work))";
```

Changing the Appearance of HTML Output

Style Templates

You can change the appearance of your HTML output by specifying a style in the STYLE= option in the ODS HTML statement. Here are some of the style templates that are currently available:

- Banker
- BarrettsBlue
- Default
- HTMLblue
- Minimal
- Statistical

TIP To see a list of styles that SAS supplies, submit the following code:

```
proc template;
```

```
  list styles/store=sashelp.tmplmst;
run;
```

Syntax, STYLE= option:

STYLE=*style-name*;

- *style-name* is the name of a valid SAS or user-defined style template.

TIP Do not enclose *style-name* in quotation marks.

Example: The STYLE= Option (Banker Style)

In the following program, the STYLE= option applies the Banker style to the output for the PROC PRINT step:

```
ods html body='C:\Users\Student1\cert\data.html'
  style=banker;
proc print data=cert.admit label;
  var sex age height weight actlevel;
run;
ods html close;
ods html path="%qsysfunc(pathname(work))";
```

Figure 16.4 PROC PRINT Output with Banker Style Applied (partial output)

Obs	Sex	Age	Height	Weight	ActLevel
1	M	27	72	168	HIGH
2	F	34	66	152	HIGH
3	F	31	61	123	LOW
4	F	43	63	137	MOD
5	M	51	71	158	LOW
6	M	29	76	193	HIGH

Note: Your site might have its own, customized, style templates.

Creating PDF Output with ODS

The ODS PDF Statement

To open, manage, or close the PDF destinations that produce PDF output, use the ODS PDF statement:

Syntax, ODS PDF statement:

ODS PDF <(<ID=>*identifier*)> <*action*>;

- (<ID=>*identifier*) enables you to open multiple instances of the same destination at the same time. Each instance can have different options.
  - *identifier* can be numeric or can be a series of characters that begin with a letter or an underscore. Subsequent characters can include letters, underscores, and numerals.
- *action* can be one of the following:
  - CLOSE action closes the destination and any files that are associated with it.
  - EXCLUDE *exclusions*| ALL | NONE action excludes one or more output objects from the destination.

  Note: The default is NONE. A destination must be open for this action to take effect.
  - SELECT *selections*| ALL | NONE action selects output objects for the specified destination.

  Note: The default is ALL. A destination must be open for this action to take effect.
  - SHOW action writes the current selection list or exclusion list for the destination to the SAS log.

  Note: If the selection or exclusion list is the default list (SELECT ALL), then SHOW also writes the entire selection or exclusion list. The destination must be open for this action to take effect.

In SAS Studio, the PDF destination is open by default. In SAS Studio, you must use the ODS PDF statement with at least one action or option. When you do this, it opens another instance of a PDF destination and creates PDF output.

The ODS Printer Family of Statements

The ODS PDF statement is part of the ODS printer family of statements. Statements in the printer family open the PCL, PDF, PRINTER, or PS destination, producing output that is suitable for a high-resolution printer. The ODS PCL, ODS PRINTER, and ODS PS statements are also members of the ODS printer family of statements.

Opening and Closing the PDF Destination

You can modify an open PDF destination with many ODS PDF options. However, the FILE= and SAS options perform the following actions on an open PDF destination:

- close the open destination referred to in the ODS PDF statement
- close any files associated with the open PDF destination
- open a new instance of the PDF destination

Note: If you use one of these actions, you should explicitly close the destination yourself.

Working with the Table of Contents

The ODS PDF destination provides the following navigation tools:

- The default table of contents (TOC), which is a clickable bookmark tree that is not printed.

Figure 16.5 PDF Output Default Bookmark Tree

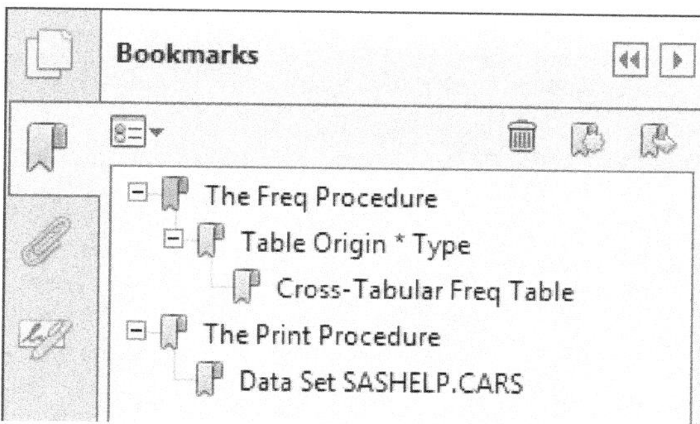

- A printable table of contents, which is generated using the CONTENTS=YES option in the ODS PDF FILE= statement. The output that is created this way is static and does not count toward the page count of the PDF file. The text "Table of Contents" is customizable using PROC TEMPLATE, and the text of each of the entries is customizable with the ODS PROCLABEL statement and CONTENTS= options in some of the PROC statements.

Figure 16.6 PDF Output Default Table of Contents Page

Table of Contents

The Freq Procedure 1
Table Origin * Type 1
Cross-Tabular Freq Table 1
The Print Procedure 2
Data Set SASHELP.CARS 2

The text displayed by the nodes of each tool is controlled with the following:

- the ODS PROCLABEL statement
- the CONTENTS=, the DESCRIPTION=, and the OBJECTLABEL= options
- the DOCUMENT destination and procedure
- the TEMPLATE procedure

Example: Creating PDF Output Using the FILE= Option

This example opens an instance of the PDF destination to create PDF output. The FILE= option specifies the PDF filename.

```
ods html close;
ods pdf file="SamplePDF";
proc freq data=sashelp.cars;
  tables origin*type;
run;
ods pdf close;
```

***Figure 16.7** PDF Output of FREQ Procedure*

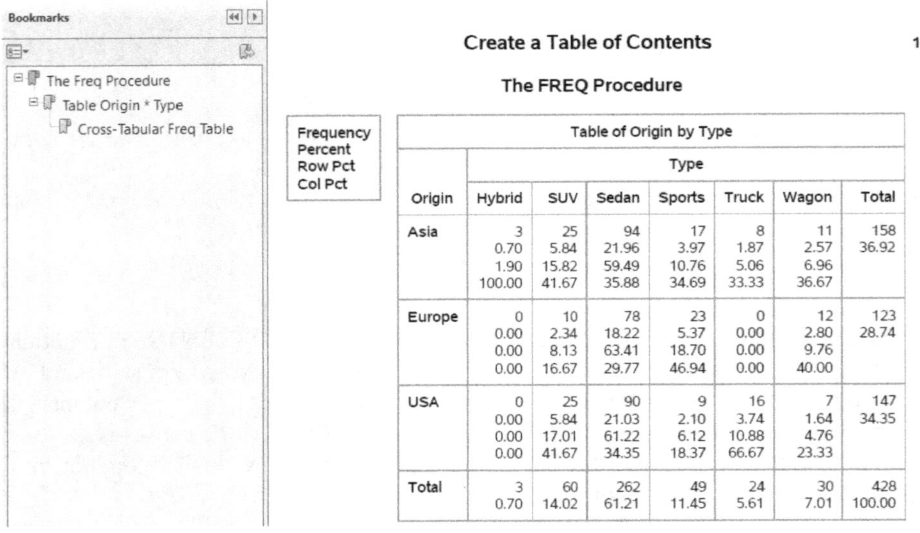

Create a Table of Contents 1

The FREQ Procedure

Frequency
Percent
Row Pct
Col Pct

Table of Origin by Type							
	Type						
Origin	Hybrid	SUV	Sedan	Sports	Truck	Wagon	Total
Asia	3 0.70 1.90 100.00	25 5.84 15.82 41.67	94 21.96 59.49 35.88	17 3.97 10.76 34.69	8 1.87 5.06 33.33	11 2.57 6.96 36.67	158 36.92
Europe	0 0.00 0.00 0.00	10 2.34 8.13 16.67	78 18.22 63.41 29.77	23 5.37 18.70 46.94	0 0.00 0.00 0.00	12 2.80 9.76 40.00	123 28.74
USA	0 0.00 0.00 0.00	25 5.84 17.01 41.67	90 21.03 61.22 34.35	9 2.10 6.12 18.37	16 3.74 10.88 66.67	7 1.64 4.76 23.33	147 34.35
Total	3 0.70	60 14.02	262 61.21	49 11.45	24 5.61	30 7.01	428 100.00

Example: Creating a Printable Table of Contents

By default, ODS PDF does not create a printable table of contents, only a click-able bookmark tree. This example shows you how to create a printable table of contents.

```
ods html close;
title "Create a Table of Contents";
options nodate;
ods pdf file="MyDefaultToc.pdf" contents=yes bookmarklist=hide;
proc freq data=sashelp.cars;
  tables origin*type;
run;
proc print data=sashelp.cars (obs=15);
run;
ods pdf close;
ods html path="%qsysfunc(pathname(work))";
```

The ODS PDF statement uses the following options:

- The FILE= option specifies the PDF filename.
- The CONTENTS=YES option specifies that a table of contents is created.
- The BOOKMARKLIST=HIDE option specifies that a bookmark tree is created, but hidden.

***Figure 16.8** Printable Table of Contents for PDF Output*

Table of Contents

The Freq Procedure 1
  Table Origin * Type 1
    Cross-Tabular Freq Table 1
The Print Procedure 2
  Data Set SASHELP.CARS 2

Changing the Appearance of PDF Output

Style Templates

You can change the appearance of your PDF output by specifying a style in the STYLE= option in the ODS PDF statement. The default style for PDF output is Pearl. Here are the style templates that are currently available:

- FancyPrinter
- FestivalPrinter
- GrayscalePrinter
- Journal
- MeadowPrinter
- MonoChromePrinter
- Monospace
- NormalPrinter
- Pearl
- Printer
- Sapphire
- SasDocPrinter
- SeasidePrinter

Example: The STYLE= Option (FestivalPrinter Style)

In the following program, the STYLE= option applies the FestivalPrinter style to the output for the ODS PDF statement:

```
ods html close;
ods pdf file="SamplePDF" style=FestivalPrinter;
proc freq data=sashelp.cars;
  tables origin*type;
run;
ods pdf close;
```

Figure 16.9 *ODS PDF Output with the FestivalPrinter Style Applied*

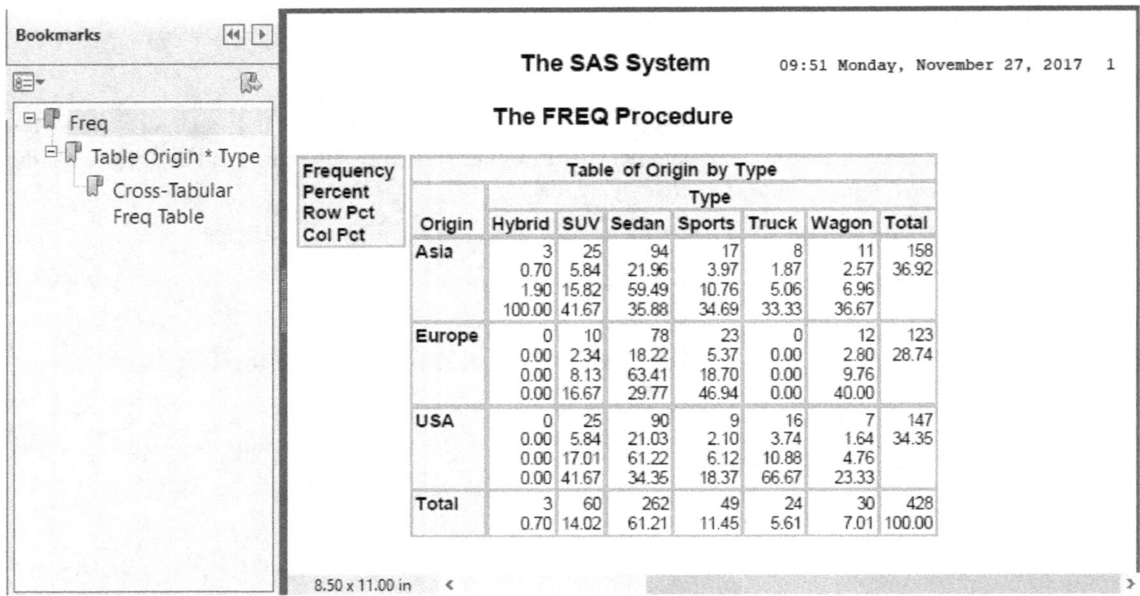

Frequency Percent Row Pct Col Pct	Table of Origin by Type						
	Type						
Origin	Hybrid	SUV	Sedan	Sports	Truck	Wagon	Total
Asia	3 0.70 1.90 100.00	25 5.84 15.82 41.67	94 21.96 59.49 35.88	17 3.97 10.76 34.69	8 1.87 5.06 33.33	11 2.57 6.96 36.67	158 36.92
Europe	0 0.00 0.00 0.00	10 2.34 8.13 16.67	78 18.22 63.41 29.77	23 5.37 18.70 46.94	0 0.00 0.00 0.00	12 2.80 9.76 40.00	123 28.74
USA	0 0.00 0.00 0.00	25 5.84 17.01 41.67	90 21.03 61.22 34.35	9 2.10 6.12 18.37	16 3.74 10.88 66.67	7 1.64 4.76 23.33	147 34.35
Total	3 0.70	60 14.02	262 61.21	49 11.45	24 5.61	30 7.01	428 100.00

Creating RTF Output with ODS

The ODS RTF Statement

To open, manage, or close the RTF destinations that produces output that is written in Rich Text Format for use with Microsoft Word, use the ODS RTF statement:

Syntax, ODS RTF statement:

ODS RTF <(<ID=>*identifier*)> <*action*>;

- (<ID=>*identifier*) enables you to open multiple instances of the same destination at the same time. Each instance can have different options.
  - *identifier* can be numeric or can be a series of characters that begin with a letter or an underscore. Subsequent characters can include letters, underscores, and numerals.
- *action* can be one of the following:
  - CLOSE action closes the destination and any files that are associated with it.
  - EXCLUDE *exclusions*| ALL | NONE action excludes one or more output objects from the destination.

  Note: The default is NONE. A destination must be open for this action to take effect.

  - SELECT *selections*| ALL | NONE action selects output objects for the specified destination.

  Note: The default is ALL. A destination must be open for this action to take effect.

  - SHOW action writes the current selection list or exclusion list for the destination to the SAS log.

  Note: If the selection or exclusion list is the default list (SELECT ALL), then SHOW also writes the entire selection or exclusion list. The destination must be open for this action to take effect.

Opening and Closing the RTF Destination

You can modify an open RTF destination with many ODS RTF options. However, the FILE= option performs the following actions on an open RTF destination:

- close the open destination referred to in the ODS RTF statement
- close any files associated with the open RTF destination
- open a new instance of the RTF destination

TIP If you use the FILE= option, you should explicitly close the destination yourself.

Understanding How RTF Formats Output

RTF produces output for Microsoft Word. Although other applications can read RTF files, the RTF output might not work successfully with the other applications.

The RTF destination enables you to view and edit the RTF output. ODS does not define the vertical measurement, which means that SAS does not determine the optimal place to position each item on the page. For example, page breaks are not always fixed because you do not want your RTF output tables to split at inappropriate places when you edit your text. Your tables remain intact on one page, or they break where you specify.

However, Microsoft Word requires the widths of table columns, and Microsoft Word cannot adjust tables if they are too wide for the page. Therefore, ODS measures the width of the text and tables (horizontal measurement). All of the column widths can be set properly by SAS, and the table can be divided into panels if it is too wide to fit on a single page.

In short, when producing RTF output for input to Microsoft Word, SAS determines the horizontal measurement, and Microsoft Word controls the vertical measurement. Because Microsoft Word can determine how much room there is on the page, your tables are displayed consistently even after you modify your RTF file.

Note: Complex tables that contain a large number of observations can reduce system efficiencies and take longer to process.

ODS RTF and Graphics

ODS RTF produces output in rich text format, which supports three formats for graphics that Microsoft Word can read.

Format for Graphics	**Corresponding SAS Graphics Driver**
emfblips	EMF
pngblips	PNG
jpegblips	JPEG

When you do not specify a target device, the default target is EMF.

Example: Using the STYLE= Option (FestivalPrinter Style)

In the following program, the STYLE= option applies the FestivalPrinter style to the output for the ODS RTF statement:

```
ods html close;
ods rtf file="SampleRTF" style=FestivalPrinter;
proc freq data=sashelp.cars;
  tables origin*type;
run;
ods rtf close;
```

Figure 16.10 *ODS RTF Output with the FestivalPrinter Style Applied*

01:41 Friday, December 01, 2017 1

The SAS System

The FREQ Procedure

Table of Origin by Type							
Origin	Type						
Frequency Percent Row Pct Col Pct	Hybrid	SUV	Sedan	Sports	Truck	Wagon	Total
Asia	3 0.70 1.90 100.00	25 5.84 15.82 41.67	94 21.96 59.49 35.88	17 3.97 10.76 34.69	8 1.87 5.06 33.33	11 2.57 6.96 36.67	158 36.92
Europe	0 0.00 0.00 0.00	10 2.34 8.13 16.67	78 18.22 63.41 29.77	23 5.37 18.70 46.94	0 0.00 0.00 0.00	12 2.80 9.76 40.00	123 28.74
USA	0 0.00 0.00 0.00	25 5.84 17.01 41.67	90 21.03 61.22 34.35	9 2.10 6.12 18.37	16 3.74 10.88 66.67	7 1.64 4.76 23.33	147 34.35
Total	3 0.70	60 14.02	262 61.21	49 11.45	24 5.61	30 7.01	428 100.00

Creating EXCEL Output with ODS

The ODS EXCEL Statement

To open, manage, or close the Excel destinations that produce Excel spreadsheet files that are compatible with Microsoft 2010 and later versions, use the ODS EXCEL statement:

Syntax, ODS EXCEL statement:

ODS EXCEL <(<ID=>*identifier*)> <*action*>;

ODS EXCEL <(<ID=>*identifier*)> <*option(s)*>;

- (<ID=>*identifier*) enables you to open multiple instances of the same destination at the same time. Each instance can have different options.
  - *identifier* can be numeric or can be a series of characters that begin with a letter or an underscore. Subsequent characters can include letters, underscores, and numerals.
- *action* can be one of the following:
  - CLOSE action closes the destination and any files that are associated with it.
  - EXCLUDE *exclusions*| ALL | NONE action excludes one or more output objects from the destination.

  Note: The default is NONE. A destination must be open for this action to take effect.
  - SELECT *selections*| ALL | NONE action selects output objects for the specified destination.

  Note: The default is ALL. A destination must be open for this action to take effect.
  - SHOW action writes the current selection list or exclusion list for the destination to the SAS log.

  Note: If the selection or exclusion list is the default list (SELECT ALL), then SHOW also writes the entire selection or exclusion list. The destination must be open for this action to take effect.

Details about the Excel ODS Destination

The ODS destination for Excel uses Microsoft Open Office XML Format for Office 2010 and later. This statement produces XML and represents a way to define and format data for easy exchange.

The ODS destination for Excel creates Microsoft spreadsheet in ML XML. Each table is placed in its own worksheet within a workbook. This destination supports ODS styles, trafficlighting, and custom formats. Numbers, currency, and percentages are correctly detected and displayed. Style override, a TAGATTR= style attribute, can be used to create custom formats for the data. By default, titles and footnotes are included in the worksheet, but they are part of the header and footer of the worksheet.

Portrait is the default printing orientation. The orientation can be changed to landscape.

Example: Customizing Your Excel Output

The following example illustrates a customized Excel workbook that contains PROC MEANS output.

```
ods excel file='multitablefinal.xlsx'   /*#1*/
  options (sheet_interval="bygroup"          /*#2*/
    suppress_bylines='yes'                   /*#3*/
    sheet_label='country'                    /*#4*/
    embedded_titles='yes');                  /*#5*/
title 'Wage Rates By Manager';
proc means data=cert.usa;
  by manager;
  var wagerate;
run;
```

```
ods excel close;                                 /*#6*/
```

1 The ODS EXCEL statement opens an instance of an Excel workbook and creates a new Excel workbook called Multitablefinal.xlsx.

2 The SHEET_INTERVAL= option creates a new worksheet for each BY group.

3 The SUPPRESS_BYLINES= option suppresses the BY lines for each BY group.

4 The SHEET_LABEL= option customizes the worksheet label.

5 The EMBEDDED_TITLES= option embeds the title that is created by the TITLE statement in the output.

6 THE ODS CLOSE statement closes the destination and any associated files.

Figure 16.11 *Customized Excel Output*

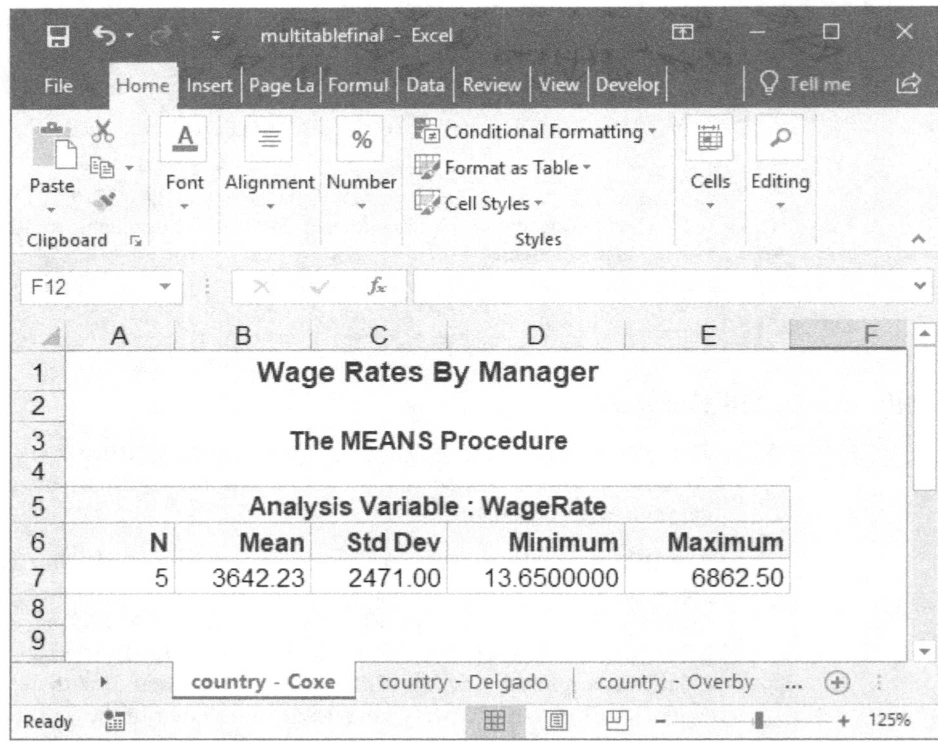

The EXPORT Procedure

The Basics of PROC EXPORT

Note: The EXPORT procedure is available for Windows, UNIX, or LINUX operating environments.

The EXPORT procedure reads data from a SAS data set and writes it to an external data source. In Base SAS 9.4, external data sources include delimited files and JMP files. In delimited files, a delimiter can be a blank, comma, or tab that separates columns of data values. If you have a license for SAS/ACCESS Interface to PC Files, you can also export to additional file formats, such as to a Microsoft Access database, Microsoft Excel workbook, DBF file, and Lotus spreadsheets.

The EXPORT procedure uses one of these methods to export data:

- generated DATA step code
- generated SAS/ACCESS code

PROC EXPORT Syntax

You control the results with options and statements that are specific to the output data source. The EXPORT procedure generates the specified output file and writes information about the export to the SAS log. The log displays the DATA step or the SAS/ACCESS code that the EXPORT procedure generates.

Syntax, PROC EXPORT statement:

PROC EXPORT DATA=<*libref.*>*SAS-data-set*
OUTFILE= "*filename*"
<DBMS=*identifier*>**;**
<REPLACE>**;**

- *libref.SAS-data-set* identifies the input SAS data set with either a one- or two-level SAS name (library and member name). If you specify a one-level name, by default, the EXPORT procedure uses either the USER library (if assigned) or the WORK library.

  Default: If you do not specify a SAS data set to export, the EXPORT procedure uses the most recently created SAS data set. SAS keeps track of the data sets with the system variable _LAST_. To be certain that the EXPORT procedure uses the correct data set, you should identify the SAS data set.
- *filename* specifies the complete path and filename or a fileref for the output PC file, spreadsheet, or delimited external file.

  If you specify a fileref, or if the complete path and filename do not include special characters (such as the backslash in a path), lowercase characters, or spaces, you can omit the quotation marks.
- *identifier* specifies the type of data to export. To export to a DBMS table, you must specify the DBMS option by using a valid database identifier. For DBMS=DLM, the default delimiter character is a space. However, you can use DELIMITER='*char*' statement within the EXPORT procedure to define a specific delimiter character.
- REPLACE overwrites an existing file. If you do not specify REPLACE, the EXPORT procedure does not overwrite an existing file.

The following values are valid for the DBMS identifier:

Table 16.1 *DBMS Identifiers Supported in Base SAS*

Identifier	Output Data Source	Extension
CSV	Delimited file (comma-separated values)	.csv
DLM	Delimited file (default delimiter is a space)	

JMP	JMP files, Version 7 or later format	.jmp
TAB	Delimited file (tab-delimited values)	.txt

The availability of an output external data source depends on these conditions:

- the operating environment and, in some cases, the platform as specified in the previous table.
- whether your site has a license for SAS/ACCESS Interface to PC Files. If you do not have a license, only delimited and JMP files are available.

Example: Exporting a Subset of Observation to a CSV File

This example exports the SAS data set Cert.Leukemia to a delimited file.

```
proc export data=cert.leukemia (where=(survived=1))   /*#1*/
  outfile="C:\cert\leukemia_surv.csv"                 /*#2*/
  dbms=csv                                            /*#3*/
  replace;                                            /*#4*/
run;
```

1 The DATA= option specifies the input file. The WHERE option requests a subset of the observations.

2 The OUTFILE= option specifies the output file.

3 The DBMS= option specifies that the output file is a CSV file

4 The REPLACE option overwrites an existing file.

The EXPORT procedure produces this external CSV file:

Output 16.2 *CSV File*

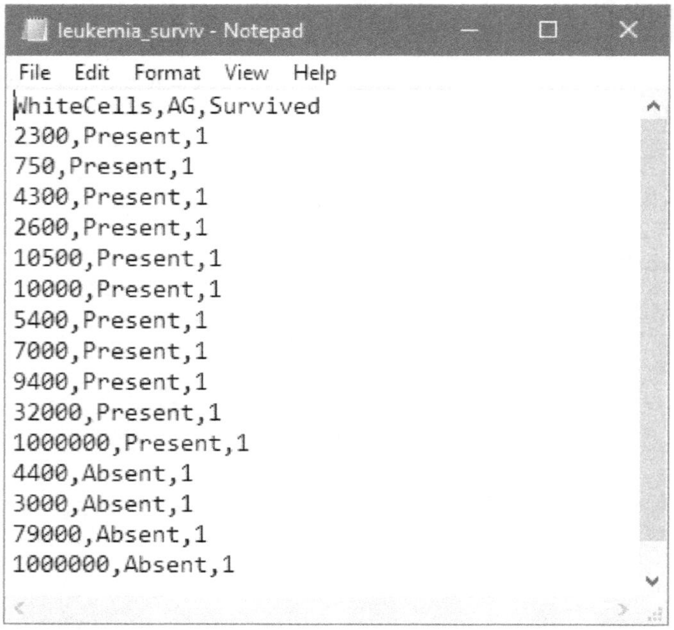

```
leukemia_surviv - Notepad
File Edit Format View Help
WhiteCells,AG,Survived
2300,Present,1
750,Present,1
4300,Present,1
2600,Present,1
10500,Present,1
10000,Present,1
5400,Present,1
7000,Present,1
9400,Present,1
32000,Present,1
1000000,Present,1
4400,Absent,1
3000,Absent,1
79000,Absent,1
1000000,Absent,1
```

Chapter Quiz

Select the best answer for each question. Check your answers using the answer key in the appendix.

1. Using ODS statements, how many types of output can you generate at once?
   a. 1
   b. 2
   c. 3
   d. as many as you want

2. If ODS is set to its default settings, what types of output are created by the following code?

```
ods html file='c:\myhtml.htm';
ods pdf file='c:\mypdf.pdf';
```

   a. HTML and PDF
   b. PDF only
   c. HTML, PDF, and EXCEL
   d. No output is created because ODS is closed by default.

3. What is the purpose of closing the HTML destination in the following code?

```
ods HTML close;
ods pdf ... ;
```

   a. It conserves system resources.
   b. It simplifies your program.
   c. It makes your program compatible with other hardware platforms.
   d. It makes your program compatible with previous versions of SAS.

4. When the following code runs, what does the file D:\Output\body.html contain?

```
ods html body='d:\output\body.html';
proc print data=work.alpha;
run;
proc print data=work.beta;
run;
ods html close;
```

   a. The PROC PRINT output for Work.Alpha.
   b. The PROC PRINT output for Work.Beta.
   c. The PROC PRINT output for both Work.Alpha and Work.Beta.
   d. Nothing. No output is written to D:\Output\body.html.

5. When the following code runs, what file is loaded by the links in D:\Output \contents.html?

```
ods html body='d:\output\body.html'
  contents='d:\output\contents.html'
  frame='d:\output\frame.html';
```

a. D:\Output\body.html

b. D:\Output\contents.html

c. D:\Output\frame.html

d. There are no links from the file D:\Output\contents.html.

6. The table of contents that was created by the CONTENTS= option contains a numbered heading for which of the following?

a. each procedure

b. each procedure that creates output

c. each procedure and DATA step

d. each HTML file created by your program

7. When the following code runs, what will the file D:\Output\frame.html display?

```
ods html body='d:\output\body.html'
  contents='d:\output\contents.html'
  frame='d:\output\frame.html';
```

a. The file D:\Output\contents.html .

b. The file D:\Output\frame.html.

c. The files D:\Output\contents.html and D:\Output\body.html.

d. It displays no other files.

8. What is the purpose of the following URL= suboptions?

```
ods html body='d:\output\body.html' (url='body.html')
  contents='d:\output\contents.html'
  (url='contents.html')
  frame='d:\output\frame.html';
```

a. To create absolute link addresses for loading the files from a server.

b. To create relative link addresses for loading the files from a server.

c. To allow HTML files to be loaded from a local drive.

d. To send HTML output to two locations.

9. Which ODS HTML option was used in creating the following table?

Obs	Sex	Age	Height	Weight	ActLevel
1	M	27	72	168	HIGH
2	F	34	66	152	HIGH
3	F	31	61	123	LOW

a. `format=MeadowPrinter`

b. `format='MedowPrinter'`

c. `style=MeadowPrinter`

d. `style='MeadowPrinter'`

10. What is the purpose of the PATH= option?

```
ods html path='d:\output' (url=none)
  body='body.html'
  contents='contents.html'
  frame='frame.html';
```

a. It creates absolute link addresses for loading HTML files from a server.

b. It creates relative link addresses for loading HTML files from a server.

c. It allows HTML files to be loaded from a local drive.

d. It specifies the location of HTML file output.

Part 2

Workbook

Chapter 17

Practice Programming Scenarios

Scenario 1

Directions

This scenario uses the Cert.Patients and Cert.Measure data sets. Write a SAS program to do the following:

- Sort Cert.Patients and Cert.Measure by ID.
- Use the match-merging technique to combine Cert.Patients and Cert.Measure to create a new temporary data set named Work.Merge.
- Select observations for the patients under the age of 50.
- Sort the new data set, Work.Merge, by Age in descending order.
- Save the sorted data set as Work.Sortpatients.

Test Your Code

1. What the value of the Age variable for observation 6 in Work.Sortpatients?
2. What is the value of the Weight variable for observation 3 in Work.Sortpatients?

Objectives Accomplished

- Combine SAS data sets using match-merging.
- Use a DATA step to create a SAS data set from an existing SAS data set.
- Use the IF/THEN-ELSE statements to process data conditionally.
- Use the SORT procedure to re-order observations in place or write them out to a new data set.

Scenario 2

Directions

This scenario uses the Cert.Stress data set. Write a SAS program to do the following:

- Create a new temporary SAS data set that uses Cert.Stress and store the results in Work.Stress1.
- Remove observations with RestHR values that are greater than or equal to 70.
- Create a new variable called TotalTime. The value of TotalTime is the value of TimeMin multiplied by 60, plus the value of TimeSec.

- Remove TotalTime values that are less than 600.

Test Your Code

1. How many observations are in Work.Stress1?
2. What is the value of TotalTime for observation 5 in Work.Stress1?

Objectives Accomplished

- Use a DATA step to create a SAS data set from an existing SAS data set.
- Control which observations and variables in a SAS data set are processed and written out to a new data set.
- Use assignment statements in the DATA step.
- Use IF/THEN-ELSE statements to process data conditionally.

Scenario 3

Directions

This scenario uses the Cert.Staff data set. Write a SAS program to do the following:

- Create a new temporary SAS data set that uses Cert.Staff and store the results in Work.StaffReports.
- Select observations where WageCategory is not equal to H.
- Format the variable DOB as mmddyy10.
- Create a new variable named Raise whose value is WageRate multiplied by 3%.
- Determine the grand total of Raise for the entire data set.

Test Your Code

1. For observation 5, what is the value of DOB?
2. For observation 15, what is the value of Raise? Round your answer to 2 decimal places.
3. What is the grand total of Raise for the entire data set?

Objectives Accomplished

- Use a DATA step to create a SAS data set from an existing SAS data set.
- Use SAS date and time formats to specify how the values are displayed.
- Control which observations and variables in a SAS data set are processed and written out to a new data set.
- Use assignment statements in the DATA step.

- Use the SUM statement to accumulate subtotals and totals.

Scenario 4

Directions

This scenario uses the Cert.Laguardia data set. Write a SAS program to do the following:

- Print the data set Cert.Laguardia sorted and grouped by Dest. Save your sorted data set as a temporary data set, Work.Laguardia.
- Store the results, grouped by the variable Dest, in a PDF file named "LGA Airport.pdf" using the FestivalPrinter style with a report title, "Laguardia Flights".

Test Your Code

1. What is the file size of the LGA Airport.pdf file?
2. What is the value of Boarded in observation 13?
3. What is the destination value in observation 42?

Objectives Accomplished

- Enhance reports system with user-defined formats, titles, footnotes, and SAS System reporting options.
- Generate reports using ODS statements:
  - Identify the ODS destinations.
  - Create HTML, PDF, and RTF files with ODS statements.
  - Use the STYLE= option to specify a style template.

Scenario 5

Directions

Open the ehs01 program from the EHS folder and correct the errors in the program. For instructions, see the commented code in the program that is marked by a slash (/) and an asterisk (*).

Example Code 1 *ehs01 Program: Fix the Errors*

```
data work.aprilbills drop=Total, EquipCost;                  /*#1*/
   set cert.aprbills;
   if Days > 7 then Discount=(RoomCharge)*20% else 0;        /*#2*/
   TotalDue=Total-Discount;                                  /*#3*/
   format DateIn DateOut date9;                              /*#4*/
   format RoomRate RoomCharge Discount TotalDue dollar10.;   /*#5*/
```

```
proc print data=work.aprilbills;                                    /* #6 */
```

Here are instructions that are commented in the program, ehs01.

1 Drop the variables Total and EquipCost.

2 If the Days variable is greater than 7, then Discount is the value of RoomCharge multiplied by 20 %. If the Days variable is less than or equal to 7, then Discount is set to 0.

3 Create a new variable, TotalDue, with a value of Total minus Discount.

4 Format DateIn and DateOut to appear as 05APR2009.

5 Format the variables RoomRate, RoomCharge, Discount, and TotalDue to appear as $100.00.

6 Print your results.

Test Your Code

1. What is the value of the variable TotalDue in observation 4?
2. What is the value of the variable Discount in observation 5?

Objectives Accomplished

- Identify the characteristics of SAS statements.
- Define SAS syntax rules and identify syntax errors such as misspelled keywords, unmatched quotation marks, missing semicolons, and invalid options.
- Use the log to help diagnose syntax errors in a given program.

Scenario 6

Directions

This scenario uses the Excel file heart.xlsx. Write a SAS program to do the following and store the results in the data set Work.Heart.

- Import the Excel file heart.xlsx.
- Drop the AgeAtDeath and DeathCause variables from the Work.Heart data set.
- Include only the observations where Status=Alive in the Work.Heart data set.
- If the AgeCHDdiag variable has a missing value (.), then do not include the value in Work.Heart.
- Create a new variable Smoking_Status, set its length to 17 characters, and use the following criteria:
  - If the value of Smoking is between 0 and less than 6, then Smoking_Status is "None (0–5)".
  - If the value of Smoking is between 6 and 15 inclusively, then Smoking_Status is "Moderate (6–15)".

- If the value of Smoking is between 16 and 25 inclusively, then Smoking_Status is "Heavy (16–25)".
- If the value of Smoking is greater than 25, then Smoking_Status is "Very Heavy (>25)".

- If there are any other values for the variable Smoking, set Smoking_Status to "Error".
- Create a two-way frequency table using variables AgeCHDdiag and Smoking_Status and suppress column percentage, row percentage, and cell percentage.

Test Your Code

1. What is the total number of Heavy Smokers (16–25)?
2. What is the frequency value of Very Heavy (>25) smokers for AgeCHDDiag 48?
3. What is the frequency value of Smoking_Status = "Error"?

Objectives Accomplished

- Access SAS data sets with the SET statement.
- Use a DATA step to create a SAS data set from an existing SAS data set.
- Use IF-THEN/ELSE statements to process data conditionally.
- Use assignment statement to create new variables and assign a value in the DATA step.
- Define the length of a variable using the LENGTH statement.
- Generate summary reports and frequency tables using Base SAS procedures.

Scenario 7

Directions

This scenario uses the Cert.Temp18 data set. Write a SAS program to do the following:

- Create a temporary SAS data set that uses Cert.Temp18 and store the results as Work.Scenario7.
- Format the Day variable so that the date appears as 01JAN2018.
- Use a function to create a variable named Month that is equal to the numeric value of the month of the Day variable. For example, if the month is January, Month=1, if the month is February, Month=2, and so on.
- Create a one-way frequency table using the variable HighTemp.
- Use PROC MEANS to calculate the mean and standard deviation for the variables AvgHighTemp and AvgLowTemp by the new Month variable.

Test Your Code

1. What is the frequency for a HighTemp of 63?
2. What is the HighTemp on January 12, 2018?
3. What is the mean for AvgLowTemp for Month=1? (Round your answer to the nearest integer.)
4. What is the standard deviation (std) for AvgHighTemp for Month=3? (Round your answer to two decimal places.)

Objectives Accomplished

- Use a DATA step to create a SAS data set from an existing SAS data set.
- Use SAS date and time formats to specify how the values are displayed.
- Use assignment statements to create new variables and assign a value in the DATA step.
- Use SAS functions to manipulate character data, numeric data, and SAS date values.
- Generate summary reports and frequency tables using Base SAS procedures.

Scenario 8

Directions

This scenario uses the Cert.Addresses data set. Write a SAS program to do the following:

- Create a temporary SAS data set that uses Cert.Addresses and store the results in Work.Scenario8.
- Extract the 5-digit ZIP codes from the State variable and store them in the ZipCode variable.
- Extract the two letters from the State variable and store them in the State variable.
- Create a one-way frequency table using the variable State.

Test Your Code

1. What is the frequency for the state of NY?
2. Which observation contains ZipCode 85069?
3. How many states have the frequency number of 4?

Objectives Accomplished

- Use a DATA step to create a SAS data set from an existing SAS data set.

- Use assignment statements to create new variables and assign a value in the DATA step.
- Use SAS functions such as SUBSTR to search a character value and extract a portion of the value.
- Generate frequency tables using Base SAS procedures.

Scenario 9

Directions

This scenario uses the Cert.Empdata, Cert.Empdatu, and Cert.Empdatu2 data sets. Write a SAS program to do the following:

- Concatenate Cert.Empdata, Cert.Empdatu, and Cert.Empdatu2 to create Work.FlightEmpData.
- Create a macro variable named &Location and set the value of this macro variable to USA.
- Include only the observations whose value for Country is the value of the macro variable.
- Keep only observations whose salary is $30,000 or greater.
- Sort the data by variable Salary in descending order.
- Use PROC EXPORT to export the data to a CSV file and save it as flightempdata.csv.

Test Your Code

1. What is the value of Salary in observation 4?
2. What is the size (in bytes) of the CSV file that you exported?

Objectives Accomplished

- Use a DATA step to create a SAS data set from an existing SAS data set.
- Create a simple raw data file by using the EXPORT procedure as an alternative to the DATA step.
- Use the WHERE statement in the DATA step to select observations to be processed.
- Use the SORT procedure to re-order observations in place or write them out to a new data set.
- Create macro variables with the %LET statement.

Scenario 10

Directions

Open the ehs02 program from the EHS folder and correct the errors in the program below.

Example Code 2 *ehs02 Program: Fix the Errors*

```
work.mycars;
   set sashelp.cars;
   AvgMPG=mean(mpg_city, mpg_highway);
run;
title 'Cars With Average MPG Over 40';
proc print data=work.mycars
   var make model type avgmpg;
   where AvgMPG>40;
run;
title 'Average MPG by Car Type';
proc means data=work.mycars avg min max maxdec=1;
   var avgmpg;
   class type;
run;
title;
```

Test Your Code

1. What is the number of observations where the variable Type is Sedan?
2. How many observations are printed to the report titled, “Cars With Average MPG Over 40”?

Objectives Accomplished

- Identify the characteristics of SAS statements.
- Define SAS syntax rules and identify common syntax errors such as misspelled keywords, unmatched quotation marks, missing semicolons, and invalid options.
- Use the log to help diagnose syntax errors in a given program.

Part 3

Quiz Answer Keys and Scenario Solutions

Appendix 1
Chapter Quiz Answer Keys

Chapter 2: Basic Concepts

1. Correct answer: c

   Rows in the data set are called observations, and columns are called variables. Missing values do not affect the structure of the data set.

2. Correct answer: a

   When it encounters a DATA, PROC, or RUN statement, SAS stops reading statements and executes the previous step in the program. This program contains one DATA step and two PROC steps, for a total of three program steps.

3. Correct answer: b

   It must be a character variable, because the values contain letters and underscores, which are not valid characters for numeric values.

4. Correct answer: a

   It must be a numeric variable, because the missing value is indicated by a period rather than by a blank. Missing values in numeric variables are indicated by a period while character values are indicated by a blank. Numeric values are also right justified while character values are left justified.

5. Correct answer: d

   If you use VALIDVARNAME=ANY, the name can begin with or contain any characters, including blanks, national characters, special characters, and multi-byte characters. The name can be up to 32 bytes long. The name must contain at least one character, and the variable name can contain mixed-case letters.

6. Correct answer: d

   To store a file permanently in a SAS data library, you assign it a libref. For example, by assigning the libref Cert to a SAS data library, you specify that files within the library are to be stored until you delete them. Therefore, SAS files in the Cert and Certxl libraries are permanent files.

7. Correct answer: d

   To reference a temporary SAS file in a DATA step or PROC step, you can specify the one-level name of the file (for example, Forecast) or the two-level name using the libref Work (for example, Work.Forecast).

8. Correct answer: d

   The numeric variable Balance has a default length of 8. Numeric values (no matter how many digits they contain) are stored in 8 bytes of storage unless you specify a different length.

9. Correct answer: c

   The five statements are 1) the PROC PRINT statement (two lines long); 2) the VAR statement; 3) the WHERE statement (on the same line as the VAR statement); 4) the LABEL statement; and 5) the RUN statement (on the same line as the LABEL statement).

10. Correct answer: d

    Every SAS file is stored in a SAS library. A SAS library is a collection of SAS files, such as SAS data sets and catalogs. In some operating environments, a SAS library is a physical collection of files. In others, the files are only logically related. In the Windows and UNIX environments, a SAS library is typically a group of SAS files in the same folder or directory.

Chapter 3: Accessing Your Data

1. Correct answer: d

   Librefs remain in effect until the LIBNAME statement is changed, canceled, or until the SAS session ends.

2. Correct answer: b

   When you are using the default engine, you do not have to specify the engine name in the LIBNAME statement. However, you do have to specify the libref and the SAS data library name.

3. Correct answer: a

   A SAS engine is a set of internal instructions that SAS uses for writing to and reading from files in a SAS library. Each engine specifies the file format for files that are stored in the library, which in turn enables SAS to access files with a particular format. Some engines access SAS files, and other engines support access to other vendors' files.

4. Correct answer: a

   To print a summary of library contents with the CONTENTS procedure, use a period to append the _ALL_ option to the libref. Adding the NODS option suppresses detailed information about the files.

5. Correct answer: e

   All the programs listed violate the rules for assigning a libref. Librefs must be 1 to 8 characters long, must begin with a letter or underscore, and can contain only numbers, letters, or underscores. After you assign a libref, you specify it as the first level in the two-level name for a SAS file.

6. Correct answer: c

   The CONTENTS procedure creates a report that contains the contents of a library or the descriptor information for an individual SAS data set.

7. Correct answer: c

   The LIBNAME statement is global, which means that librefs stay in effect until changed or canceled, or until the SAS session ends. Therefore, the LIBNAME statement assigns the libref for the current SAS session only. You must assign a libref before accessing SAS files that are stored in a permanent SAS data library.

8. Correct answer: d

   The LIBNAME statement does not specify an engine. Therefore, it uses a default engine to create the States library.

Chapter 4: Creating SAS Data Sets

1. Correct answer: a

   You assign a fileref by using a FILENAME statement in the same way that you assign a libref by using a LIBNAME statement.

2. Correct answer: b

   By default, the IMPORT procedure reads delimited files as varying record-length files. If your external file has a fixed-length format, use the OPTIONS statement before the PROC IMPORT statement that includes the RECFM=F and LRECL= options.

3. Correct answer: a

   Use the OBS= option in the OPTIONS statement before the IMPORT procedure to limit the number of observations that SAS reads from the external file. When you use the OBS= option in the PROC PRINT statement, the whole file is imported but printing is limited to the number of observations specified. Use DELIMITER='.' to indicate that the delimiter is a period (.) and use GETNAMES=YES to read in the first line, which contains the variable names.

4. Correct answer: d

   To read an Excel workbook file, SAS must receive the following information in the DATA step: a libref to reference the Excel workbook to be read, the name and location (using another libref) of the new SAS data set, and the name of the Excel worksheet that is to be read.

5. Correct answer: d

   The GETNAMES statement specifies whether the IMPORT procedure generates SAS variable names from the data values in the first row in the input file. The default is GETNAMES=YES. NO specifies that the IMPORT procedure generates SAS variable names as VAR1, VAR2, and so on.

6. Correct answer: b

   When you associate a fileref with an individual external file, you specify the fileref in subsequent SAS statements and commands.

7. Correct answer: d

   The IMPORT procedure reads data from an external data source and writes it to a SAS data set. In delimited files, a delimiter (such as a blank, comma, or tab) separates columns of data values. You can also have a delimiter other than blanks, commas, or tabs. In those cases, PROC IMPORT reads the data from the external data source as well. You can have a delimiter such as an ampersand (&).

8. Correct answer: b

   Placing an explicit OUTPUT statement in a DATA step overrides the automatic output, so that observations are added to a data set only when the explicit OUTPUT statement is executed. The OUTPUT statement overrides the default behavior of the DATA step.

Chapter 5: Identifying and Correcting SAS Language Errors

1. Correct answer: a

   To correct errors in programs when you use the Editor window, you usually need to recall the submitted statements from the recall buffer to the Editor window. After correcting the errors, you can resubmit the revised program. However, before doing so, it is a good idea to clear the messages from the SAS log so that you do not confuse the old error messages with the new messages. Remember to check the SAS log again to verify that your program ran correctly.

2. Correct answer: d

   The missing quotation mark in the LABEL statement causes SAS to misinterpret the statements in the program. When you submit the program, SAS is unable to resolve the PROC step, and a `PROC PRINT running` message appears at the top of the active window.

3. Correct answer: c

   Syntax errors generally cause SAS to stop processing the step in which the error occurred. When a program that contains an error is submitted, messages regarding the problem also appear in the SAS log. When a syntax error is detected, the SAS log displays the word ERROR, identifies the possible location of the error, and gives an explanation of the error.

4. Correct answer: c

   Syntax errors occur because the program statements did not conform to the rules of the SAS language. Syntax errors, such as misspelled keywords, generally prevent SAS from executing the step in which the error occurred.

5. Correct answer: b

   When you submit a SAS statement that contains an invalid option, a log message notifies you that the option is not valid or not recognized. You should recall the program, remove or replace the invalid option, check your statement syntax as needed, and resubmit the corrected program.

6. Correct answer: b

   The DATA step contains a misspelled keyword (dat instead of data). However, this is such a common (and easily interpretable) error that SAS produces only a warning message, not an error.

7. Correct answer: d

   The _N_ and _ERROR_ temporary variables can be helpful when debugging a DATA step. The _N_ variable displays debugging messages for a specified number of iterations of the DATA step. The _ERROR_ displays debugging messages when an error occurs.

8. Correct answer: d

   You can use the PUTLOG statement or the PUT statement to help identify errors and print messages in the SAS log. You can use the PUTLOG statement in a DATA step to write messages to the SAS log to help identify logic errors. You can also use temporary variables in the PUTLOG to assist in debugging. You can use the PUT statement to examine variables and print your own message to the SAS log.

9. Correct answer: c

   A logic error occurs when the program statements follow the rules and execute, but the results are not correct. You can use the PUTLOG statement in the DATA step to help identify logic errors.

Chapter 6: Creating Reports

1. Correct answer: c

   The DATA= option specifies the data set that you are listing, and the ID statement replaces the Obs column with the specified variable. The VAR statement specifies variables and controls the order in which they appear, and the WHERE statement selects rows based on a condition. The LABEL option in the PROC PRINT statement causes the labels that are specified in the LABEL statement to be displayed.

2. Correct answer: a

   You use the DATA= option to specify the data set to be printed. The LABEL option specifies that variable labels appear in output instead of in variable names.

3. Correct answer: d

In the WHERE statement, the IN operator enables you to select observations based on several values. You specify values in parentheses and separated by spaces or commas. Character values must be enclosed in quotation marks and must be in the same case as in the data set.

4. Correct answer: c

   In a PROC SORT step, you specify the DATA= option to specify the data set to sort. The OUT= option specifies an output data set. The required BY statement specifies the variable or variables to use in sorting the data.

5. Correct answer: d

   You do not need to name the variables in a VAR statement if you specify them in the SUM statement, but you can. If you choose not to name the variables in the VAR statement as well, then the SUM statement determines their order in the output.

6. Correct answer: c

   The BY statement is required in PROC SORT. Without it, the PROC SORT step fails. However, the PROC PRINT step prints the original data set as requested.

7. Correct answer: a

   Column totals appear at the end of the report in the same format as the values of the variables, so b is incorrect. Work.Loans is sorted by Month and Amount, so c is incorrect. The program sums both Amount and Payment, so d is incorrect.

8. Correct answer: c

   To ensure that the compound expression is evaluated correctly, you can use parentheses to group the observations:

   ```
   account='101-1092' or rate eq 0.095
   ```

OBS	Account	Amount	Rate	Months	Payment
1	101-1092	$22,000	10.00%	60	$467.43
2	101-1731	$114,000	9.50%	360	$958.57
3	101-1289	$10,000	10.50%	36	$325.02
4	101-3144	$3,500	10.50%	12	$308.52
5	103-1135	$8,700	10.50%	24	$403.47
6	103-1994	$18,500	10.00%	60	$393.07
7	103-2335	$5,000	10.50%	48	$128.02
8	103-3864	$87,500	9.50%	360	$735.75
9	103-3891	$30,000	9.75%	360	$257.75

   For example, from the data set above, a and b select observations 2 and 8 (those that have a rate of 0.095); c selects no observations; and d selects observations 4 and 7 (those that have an amount less than or equal to 5000).

9. Correct answer: d

   By default, PROC PRINT prints all observations and variables. An Obs column is generated to identify the observation number, and variables and observations appear in the order in which they occur in the data set.

Chapter 7: Understanding DATA Step Processing

1. Correct answer: b

   During the compilation phase, the program data vector is created. The program data vector includes the two automatic variables _N_ and _ERROR_. The descriptor portion of the new SAS data set is created at the end of the compilation phase. The descriptor portion includes the name of the data set, the number of observations and variables, and the names and attributes of the variables. Observations are not written until the execution phase.

2. Correct answer: a

   Syntax checking can detect many common errors, but it cannot verify the values of variables or the correctness of formats.

3. Correct answer: c

   The DATA step executes once for each record in the input file, unless otherwise directed.

4. Correct answer: d

   The remaining variables are initialized to missing. Missing numeric values are represented by periods, and missing character values are represented by blanks.

5. Correct answer: b

   The default value of _ERROR_ is 0, which means there is no data error. When an error occurs, whether one error or multiple errors, the value is set to 1.

6. Correct answer: d

   By default, at the end of the DATA step, the values in the program data vector are written to the data set as an observation. Then, control returns to the top of the DATA step, the value of the automatic variable _N_ is incremented by one, and the values of variables that were created in programming statements are reset to missing. The automatic variable _ERROR_ is reset to 0 if necessary.

7. Correct answer: a

   The order in which variables are defined in the DATA step determines the order in which the variables are stored in the data set.

8. Correct answer: c

   When SAS cannot detect syntax errors, the DATA step compiles, but it does not execute.

9. Correct answer: d

   The variable type for Bonus is incorrect. When there is an incorrect variable type, SAS attempts to automatically convert to the correct variable type. If it cannot, SAS continues processing and produces output with missing values.

10. Correct answer: c

    The FREQ procedure detects invalid character and numeric values by looking at distinct values. You can use PROC FREQ to identify any variables that were not given an expected value.

11. Correct answer: d

At the bottom of the DATA step, the compilation phase is complete, and the descriptor portion of the new SAS data set is created. There are no observations because the DATA step has not yet executed.

Chapter 8: BY-Group Processing

1. Correct answer: d

   When you use the BY statement with the SET statement, the DATA step creates the temporary variables FIRST. and LAST. They are not stored in the data set.

2. Correct answer: d

   Before you can perform BY-group processing, your data must follow a pattern. If your data is not ordered or grouped in some pattern, BY-group processing results in an error.

3. Correct answer: a

   In the DATA step, during BY-group processing only, the temporary variables FIRST.*variable* and LAST.*variable* are available for DATA step programming, but they do not appear in the output data set.

4. Correct answer: c

   The SORT procedure sorts the data Cert.Credit by the variable Type in ascending order. You do not have to specify the order in the BY statement in PROC SORT unless you are sorting in DESCENDING order.

5. Correct answer: b

   A BY group includes all observations with the same BY value. If you use more than one variable in a BY statement, a BY group is a group of observations with the same combination of values for these variables. Each BY group has a unique combination of values for the variables.

6. Correct answer: c

   SAS determines FIRST.*variable* by looking at each observation. When an observation is the first in a BY group, SAS sets the value of the FIRST.*variable* to 1. This happens when the value of the variable changed from the previous observation. For all other observations in the BY group, the value of FIRST.*variable* is 0.

7. Correct answer: a

   The SORT procedure sorts the data Cert.Choices by the variable Day first, then Flavor in ascending order, and finally writes the sorted data set to Work.Choices.

Chapter 9: Creating and Managing Variables

1. Correct answer: c

   Program c correctly deletes the observation in which the value of Finish is `oak` and the value of Price is less than 200. It also creates TotalPrice by summing the variable Price down observations, and then drops Price by using the DROP statement in the DATA step.

2. Correct answer: c

   Logical comparisons that are enclosed in parentheses are evaluated as true or false before they are compared to other expressions. In the example, the AND comparison within the nested parentheses is evaluated before being compared to the OR comparison.

3. Correct answer: b

   You must enclose character values in quotation marks, and you must specify them in the same case in which they appear in the data set. The value `OK` is not identical to `Ok`, so the value of Count is not changed by the IF-THEN statement.

4. Correct answer: d

   The length of a variable is determined by its first reference in the DATA step. When creating a new character variable, SAS allocates as many bytes of storage space as there are characters in the reference to that variable. The first reference to a new variable can also be made with a LENGTH statement or an assignment statement.

5. Correct answer: a

   You can write multiple ELSE statements to specify a series of mutually exclusive conditions. The ELSE statement must immediately follow the IF-THEN statement in your program. An ELSE statement executes only if the previous IF-THEN/ELSE statement is false.

6. Correct answer: a

   The length of a new variable is determined by the first reference in the DATA step, not by data values. In this case, the length of Type is determined by the value `Fixed`. The LENGTH statement is in the wrong place; it must occur before any other reference to the variable in the DATA step. You can run PROC CONTENTS on the data set to see the length of each variable.

7. Correct answer: b

   To select variables, you can use a DROP or KEEP statement in any DATA step. You can also use the DROP= or KEEP= data set options following a data set name in any DATA or PROC step. However, you cannot use DROP or KEEP statements in PROC steps.

8. Correct answer: b

   The variables Age, Weight, and Group are specified using the KEEP= option in the SET statement. When Cert.Fitness is being read, Age, Weight, and Group are the variables that create Work.Cardiac. The variables Age and Group are specified in the DROP= option in the DATA statement. Age and Group are dropped from Work.Cardiac.

9. Correct answer: c

   You specify the data set to be created in the DATA statement. The DROP= data set option prevents variables from being written to the data set. Because you use the variable OrdrTime when processing your data, you cannot drop OrdrTime in the SET statement. If you use the KEEP= option in the SET statement, then you must list OrdrTime as one of the variables to be kept.

Chapter 10: Combining SAS Data Sets

1. Correct answer: a

   This example is a case of one-to-one matching, which requires multiple SET statements. Where same-named variables occur, values that are read from the second data set replace those that are read from the first data set. Also, the number of observations in the new data set is the number of observations in the smallest original data set.

2. Correct answer: b

   This is a case of concatenation, which requires a list of data set names in the SET statement and one or more BY variables in the BY statement. Notice that observations in each BY group are read sequentially, in the order in which the data sets and BY variables are listed. The new data set contains all the variables from all the input data sets, as well as the total number of records from all input data sets.

3. Correct answer: a

   Concatenating appends the observations from one data set to another data set. The new data set contains the total number of records from all input data sets, so b is incorrect. All the variables from all the input data sets appear in the new data set, so c is incorrect.

4. Correct answer: a

   The concatenated data sets are read sequentially, in the order in which they are listed in the SET statement. The second observation in Work.Reps does not contain a value for Sale, so a missing value appears for this variable. (Note that if you merge the data sets, the value of Sale for the second observation is `$30,000`.)

5. Correct answer: b

   If you have variables with the same name in more than one input data set, values of the same-named variable in the first data set in which it appears are overwritten by values of the same-named variable in subsequent data sets.

6. Correct answer: a

   The DATA step uses the IN= data set option, and the subsetting IF statement excludes unmatched observations from the output data set. So, answers a and b, which contain unmatched observations, are incorrect.

7. Correct answer: d

   Match-merging overwrites same-named variables in the first data set with same-named variables in subsequent data sets. To prevent overwriting, rename variables by using the RENAME= data set option in the MERGE statement.

8. Correct answer: c

   The two input data sets are not sorted by values of the BY variable, so the DATA step produces errors and stops processing.

9. Correct answer: c

   In this example, the new data set contains one observation for each unique value of ID. The new data set is shown below.

Obs	ID	Name	Dept	Project	Hours
1	000	Miguel	A12	Document	.
2	111	Fred	B45	Survey	35
3	222	Diana	B45	Document	40
4	777	Steve			0
5	888	Monique	A12	Document	37
6	999	Vien	D03	Survey	.

10. Correct answer: a

    In the new data set, the third observation is the second observation for ID number 2 (Kelly Windsor). The value for Bonus is retained from the previous observation because the BY variable value did not change. The new data set is shown below.

Obs	ID	Name	Sale	Bonus
1	1	Nay Rong	$28,000	$2,000
2	2	Kelly Windsor	$30,000	$4,000
3	2	Kelly Windsor	$40,000	$4,000
4	3	Julio Meraz	$15,000	$3,000
5	3	Julio Meraz	$20,000	$3,000
6	3	Julio Meraz	$20,000	$3,000
7	3	Julio Meraz	$25,000	$3,000
8	4	Richard Krabill	$35,000	$2,500

Chapter 11: Processing Data with DO Loops

1. Correct answer: c

   DO loops are DATA step statements and cannot be used in conjunction with PROC steps.

2. Correct answer: c

   The number of iterations is determined by the DO statement's stop value, which in this case is 12.

3. Correct answer: a

   Use a DO loop to perform repetitive calculations starting at 1 and looping 15 times.

4. Correct answer: d

   At the end of the 15th iteration of the DO loop, the value for Year is incremented to 2005. Because this value exceeds the stop value, the DO loop ends. At the bottom of the DATA step, the current values are written to the data set.

5. Correct answer: b

The OUTPUT statement overrides the automatic output at the end of the DATA step. On the last iteration of the DO loop, the value of Year, 2004, is written to the data set.

6. Correct answer: d

   The number of observations is based on the number of times the OUTPUT statement executes. The new data set has 20 observations, one for each iteration of the DO loop.

7. Correct answer: b

   Place the monthly calculation in a DO loop within a DO loop that iterates once for each year. The DO WHILE and DO UNTIL statements are not used here because the number of required iterations is fixed. A non-iterative DO group would not be useful.

8. Correct answer: a

   The DO UNTIL condition is evaluated at the bottom of the loop, so the enclosed statements are always executed at least once.

9. Correct answer: c

   Because the DO WHILE loop is evaluated at the top of the loop, you specify the condition that must exist in order to execute the enclosed statements.

10. Correct answer: a

    The WHILE expression causes the DO loop to stop executing when the value of Distance becomes equal to or greater than 250.

Chapter 12: SAS Formats and Informats

1. Correct answer: c

   If you do not specify the LIBRARY= option, formats are stored in a default format catalog named Work.Formats. The libref Work signifies that any format that is stored in Work.Formats is a temporary format; it exists only for the current SAS session.

2. Correct answer: a

   To store formats in a permanent catalog, you first write a LIBNAME statement to associate the libref with the SAS data library in which the catalog will be stored. Then add the LIB= (or LIBRARY=) option to the PROC FORMAT statement, specifying the name of the catalog.

3. Correct answer: d

   The name of a format that is created with a VALUE statement must begin with a dollar sign ($) if it applies to a character variable.

4. Correct answer: b

   A semicolon is needed after the PROC FORMAT statement. The VALUE statement begins with the keyword VALUE and ends with a semicolon after all the labels have been defined.

5. Correct answer: d

   You can list values separated by commas, but the list must contain either all numeric values or all character values. Data set variables are either numeric or character.

6. Correct answer: d

   When specifying a label, enclose it in quotation marks and limit the label to 32,767 characters.

7. Correct answer: d

   MISS and MISSING are invalid keywords, and LOW does not include missing numeric values. The keyword OTHER can be used in the VALUE statement to label missing values as well as any values that are not specifically included in a range.

8. Correct answer: b

   By placing the FORMAT statement in a DATA step, you permanently associate the defined format with variables.

9. Correct answer: b

   To associate a user-defined format with a variable, place a period at the end of the format name when it is used in the FORMAT statement.

10. Correct answer: d

    Adding the keyword FMTLIB to the PROC FORMAT statement displays a list of all the formats in your catalog, along with descriptions of their values.

Chapter 13: SAS Date, Time, and Datetime Values

1. Correct answer: c

   A SAS date value is the number of days from January 1, 1960, to the given date.

2. Correct answer: d

   In addition to tracking time intervals, SAS date and time values can be used in calculations like other numeric values. This lets you calculate values that involve dates much more easily than in other programming languages.

3. Correct answer: b

   SAS automatically makes adjustments for leap years.

4. Correct answer: d

   The SAS informat MMDDYY*w*. reads dates such as 10222001, 10/22/01, or 10-22-01. In this case, the field width is eight.

5. Correct answer: b

   The minimum acceptable field width for the TIME*w*. informat is five. If you specify a *w* value less than five, you receive an error message in the SAS log.

6. Correct answer: d

   In the time value of a date and time expression, you must use delimiters to separate the values for hour, minutes, and seconds.

7. Correct answer: b

   To find the number of days spanned by two dates, subtract the first day from the last day and add one. Because SAS date values are numeric values, they can easily be used in calculations.

Chapter 14: Using Functions to Manipulate Data

1. Correct answer: b

   When this DATA step is executed, SAS automatically converts the character values of PayRate to numeric values so that the calculation can occur. Whenever data is automatically converted, a message is written to the SAS log stating that the conversion has occurred.

2. Correct answer: b

   You explicitly convert character values to numeric values by using the INPUT function. Be sure to select an informat that can read the form of the values.

3. Correct answer: d

   You explicitly convert numeric values to character values by using the PUT function. Be sure to select a format that can read the form of the values.

4. Correct answer: a

   The SCAN function is used to extract words from a character value when you know the order of the words, when their position varies, and when the words are marked by some delimiter. In this case, you do not need to specify delimiters, because the blank and the comma are default delimiters.

5. Correct answer: d

   The SUBSTR function is best used when you know the exact position of the substring to extract from the character value. You specify the position to start from and the number of characters to extract.

6. Correct answer: c

   The SUBSTR function replaces variable values if it is placed on the left side of an assignment statement. When placed on the right side (as in Question 5), the function extracts a substring.

7. Correct answer: b

   The TRIM function removes trailing blanks from character values. In this case, extra blanks must be removed from the values of FirstName. Although answer c also works, the extra TRIM function for the variable LastName is unnecessary. Because of the LENGTH statement, all values of FullName are padded to 40 characters.

8. Correct answer: d

   Use the INDEX function in a subsetting IF statement, enclosing the character string in quotation marks. Only those observations in which the function locates the string and returns a value greater than 0 are written to the data set.

Chapter 15: Producing Descriptive Statistics

1. Correct answer: c

By default, the MEANS procedure produces the n, mean, minimum, maximum, and standard deviation.

2. Correct answer: d

   To specify the variables that PROC MEANS analyzes, add a VAR statement and list the variable names.

3. Correct answer: a

   Unlike Age, Height, or Weight, the values of IDnum are unlikely to yield any useful statistics.

4. Correct answer: a

   Unlike CLASS processing, BY-group processing requires that your data already be indexed or sorted in the order of the BY variables. You might need to run the SORT procedure before using PROC MEANS with a BY group.

5. Correct answer: b

   A CLASS statement produces a single large table, whereas BY-group processing creates a series of small tables. The order of the variables in the CLASS statement determines their order in the output table.

6. Correct answer: a

   You can use PROC MEANS to create the table. The MEANS procedure provides data summarization tools to compute descriptive statistics for the variables Age, Height, and Weight for each Sex group.

7. Correct answer: c

   By default, PROC FREQ creates a table for all variables in a data set.

8. Correct answer: c

   Both continuous values and unique values can result in lengthy, meaningless tables. Frequency distributions work best with categorical values.

9. Correct answer: d

   An asterisk is used to join the variables in a two-way TABLES statement. The first variable forms the table rows. The second variable forms the table columns.

10. Correct answer: d

    An asterisk is used to join the variables in crosstabulation tables. The only results shown in this table are cell percentages. The NOFREQ option suppresses cell frequencies, the NOROW option suppresses row percentages, and the NOCOL option suppresses column percentages.

Chapter 16: Creating Output

1. Correct answer: d

   You can generate any number of output types as long as you open the ODS destination for each type of output you want to create.

2. Correct answer: a

HTML output is created by default in the SAS windowing environment for the Windows operating environment and UNIX, so these statements create HTML and PDF output.

3. Correct answer: a

   By default, in the SAS windowing environment for the Windows operating environment and UNIX, SAS programs produce HTML output. If you want only RTF output, it is a good idea to close the HTML destination before creating RTF output, as an open destination uses system resources.

4. Correct answer: c

   When multiple procedures are run while HTML output is open, procedure output is appended to the same body file.

5. Correct answer: a

   The CONTENTS= option creates a table of contents containing links to the body file, `D:\Output\body.html`.

6. Correct answer: b

   The table of contents contains a numbered heading for each procedure that creates output.

7. Correct answer: c

   The FRAME= option creates an HTML file that integrates the table of contents and the body file.

8. Correct answer: b

   Specifying the URL= suboption in the file specification provides a URL that ODS uses in the links that it creates. Specifying a simple (one name) URL creates a relative link address to the file.

9. Correct answer: c

   You can change the appearance of HTML output by using the STYLE= option in the ODS HTML statement. The style name doe not need quotation marks.

10. Correct answer: d

    You use the PATH= option to specify the location for HTML files to be stored. When you use the PATH= option, you do not need to specify the full path name for the body, contents, or frame files.

Appendix 2

Programming Scenario Solutions

Scenario 1

Code Solution

The solution listed below is one example of a program that could be used to accomplish each task within each scenario. Your code can be different, so long as it results in the same answers.

```
proc sort data=cert.patients out=work.patients;    /*#1*/
  by id;
run;
proc sort data=cert.measure out=work.measure;
  by id;
run;
data work.merge;                                   /*#2*/
  merge work.patients work.measure;                /*#3*/
  by id;                                           /*#4*/
  if age<50;                                       /*#5*/
run;
proc sort data=work.merge out=work.sortpatients;   /*#6*/
  by descending Age;
run;
proc print data=work.sortpatients;                 /*#7*/
run;
```

1 Sort Cert.Patients and Cert.Measure by ID. You specify the DATA= option to specify the data set to sort. The OUT= option specifies an output data set. The required BY statement specifies the variable or variables to use in sorting the data.

2 The DATA step creates a new temporary data set named Work.Merge.

3 The MERGE statement combines observations from Work.Patients and Work.Measure into a single observation in a new data set, Work.Merge, according to the values of a common variable.

4 The BY statement identifies the variable that the MERGE statement uses to combine observations. During match-merging, SAS sequentially checks each observation of each data set to see whether the BY values match and then writes the combined observation to the new data set.

5 The IF statement specifies that only patients under the age of 50 are read into Work.Merge.

6 Sort Work.Merge by Age in descending order. You specify the DATA= option to specify the data set to sort. The OUT= option specifies an output data set. The required BY statement specifies the variable or variables to use in sorting the data. The DESCENDING option precedes the variable name.

7 The PROC PRINT step enables you to view the contents of the sorted data set, Work.Sortpatients.

Output A2.1 *PROC PRINT Output of Work.Sortpatients*

Obs	ID	Sex	Age	Height	Weight
1	1129	F	48	61	137
2	5438	F	42	62	168
3	8045	M	40	72	200
4	8125	M	39	70	176
5	9012	F	39	63	157
6	2304	F	16	61	102

Test Your Code Solution

1. Correct Answer: 16
2. Correct Answer: 200

If your answers are not correct, verify that you have sorted your data in descending order and that you used the PRINT procedure to print Work.Sortpatients.

Scenario 2

Code Solution

The solution listed below is one example of a program that could be used to accomplish each task within each scenario. Your code can be different, so long as it results in the same answers.

```
data work.stress1;                     /*#1*/
  set cert.stress;                     /*#2*/
  where RestHR <=70;                   /*#3*/
  TotalTime=(timemin*60)+timesec;      /*#4*/
  if TotalTime<600 then delete;        /*#5*/
run;
proc print data=work.stress1;          /*#6*
run;
```

1 The DATA step creates a new, temporary data set named, Work.Stress1.

2 The SET statement specifies the SAS data set that you want to read from. To create Work.Stress1, you read from Cert.Stress.

3 The WHERE statement selects only the observations where the values of RestHR are greater than or equal to 70.

4 The assignment statement creates the TotalTime variable by multiplying the value of TimeMin by 60 and adding the value of TimeSec. The values of TotalTime are assigned to each observation.

5 The IF-THEN and DELETE statements subset the data by omitting observations that have a TotalTime variable value less than 600.

6 The PROC PRINT step enables you to view the contents of the new data set, Work.Stress1.

Output A2.2 *PROC PRINT Output of Work.Stress1*

Obs	ID	Name	RestHR	MaxHR	RecHR	TimeMin	TimeSec	Tolerance	TotalTime
1	2462	Almers, C	68	171	133	10	5	I	605
2	2552	Reberson, P	69	158	139	15	41	D	941
3	2555	King, E	70	167	122	13	13	I	793
4	2571	Nunnelly, A	65	181	141	15	2	I	902
5	2586	Derber, B	68	176	119	17	35	N	1055
6	2588	Ivan, H	70	182	126	15	41	N	941

Test Your Code Solution

1. Correct Answer: 6
2. Correct Answer: 1055

If your answers are not correct, verify that you omitted the observations from the Work.Stress1 data set.

Scenario 3

Code Solution

The solution listed below is one example of a program that could be used to accomplish each task within each scenario. Your code can be different, so long as it results in the same answers.

```
data work.staffreports;                /*#1*/
  set cert.staff;                      /*#2*/
  where WageCategory ne'H';            /*#3*/
  format DOB mmddyy10.;                /*#4*/
  Raise=WageRate*0.03;                 /*#5*/
run;
proc print data=work.staffreports;     /*#6*/
  sum Raise;                           /*#7*/
run;
```

1 The DATA step creates a new data set named Work.Staffreports.

2 The SET statement specifies the SAS data set that you want to read from. To create Work.Staffreports, you read from Cert.Staff.

3 The WHERE statement selects only the observations for the values of WageCategory that do not equal H.

4 The FORMAT statement formats the DOB variable in the mmddyy10. format.

5 The assignment statement creates the Raise variable. The values for Raise are assigned for each observation by multiplying the value of WageRate by 3%.

6 The PROC PRINT step enables you to view the contents of the new data set, Work.Staffreports.

7 The SUM statement generates a grand total for the Raise variable.

Output A2.3 *PROC PRINT Output of Work.Staffreports*

Obs	ID	Name	DOB	WageCategory	WageRate	Bonus	Raise
1	1351	Farr, Sue	03/05/1947	S	3392.50	1187.38	101.78
2	161	Cox, Kay B	12/31/1945	S	5093.75	1782.81	152.81
3	212	Moore, Ron	05/22/1953	S	1813.30	634.65	54.40
4	2512	Ruth, G H	04/13/1952	S	1572.50	550.37	47.18
5	282	Shaw, Rick	07/17/1951	S	2192.25	767.29	65.77
6	3782	Bond, Jim S	12/04/1948	S	2247.50	786.63	67.43
7	381	Smith, Anna	06/09/1950	S	2082.75	728.96	62.48
8	3922	Dow, Tony	10/04/1947	S	2960.00	1036.00	88.80
9	412	Star, Burt	02/19/1956	S	2300.00	805.00	69.00
10	442	Lewis, Ed D	03/04/1950	S	3420.00	1197.00	102.60
11	452	Fox, Jim E	11/09/1945	S	3902.35	1365.82	117.07
12	4551	Wong, Kim P	06/12/1942	S	3442.50	1204.88	103.28
13	472	Hall, Joe B	07/17/1961	S	2262.50	791.88	67.88
14	482	Chin, Mike	12/02/1952	S	2938.00	1028.30	88.14
15	5002	Welch, W B	09/21/1957	S	5910.75	2068.76	177.32
16	5112	Delgado, Ed	08/25/1948	S	4045.85	1416.05	121.38
17	511	Vega, Julie	10/01/1957	S	4480.50	1568.18	134.42
18	5132	Overby, Phil	06/08/1951	S	6855.90	2399.57	205.68
19	5151	Coxe, Susan	01/19/1932	S	3163.00	1107.05	94.89
20	1351	Farr, Sue	03/05/1947	S	3392.50	1187.38	101.78
							2024.05

Test Your Code Solution

1. Correct Answer: 07/17/1951
2. Correct Answer: 177.32
3. Correct Answer: 2024.05

If your answers are not correct, verify that you have observations from the Work.Staffreports data set.

Scenario 4

Code Solution

The solution listed below is one example of a program that could be used to accomplish each task within the scenario. Your code can be different, as long as it results in the same answers.

```
proc sort data=cert.laguardia out=work.laguardia;     /*#1*/
  by dest;
run;
title 'Laguardia Flights';                            /*#2*/
ods pdf file='LGA Airport' style=FestivalPrinter;     /*#3*/
proc print data=work.laguardia;                       /*#4*/
  by dest;                                            /*#5*/
run;
ods pdf close;                                        /*#6*/
```

1 When using the SORT procedure, the DATA= option specifies the input data set, and the OUT= option specifies the output data set. The required BY statement specifies the sorting variables.

2 The TITLE statement specifies title lines for SAS output. In this example, the TITLE statement titles the output Laguardia Flights.

3 The ODS PDF statement opens the PDF destination, which produces a PDF output. The PDF file is named LGA Airport, and FestivalPrinter is used as the style template with a .pdf extension.

4 The PROC PRINT statement prints the observations of Work.Laguardia using all of the variables. See Output A2.5 on page 400.

5 The BY statement in the PRINT procedure produces a separate section in the report for each BY group. As there are four destinations in Work.Laguardia, four separate sections are produced.

6 The ODS PDF CLOSE statement closes the PDF destination.

Output A2.4 *Partial Results: PROC PRINT Output of Work.Laguardia*

Obs	Flight	Date	Depart	Orig	Dest	Boarded	Transferred	Deplaned	Revenue
1	387	04MAR12	11:40	LGA	CPH	81	21	103	196540
2	387	05MAR12	11:40	LGA	CPH	142	8	152	134561
3	387	07MAR12	11:40	LGA	CPH	131	5	142	135632
4	387	08MAR12	11:40	LGA	CPH	150	9	162	128564
5	387	09MAR12	11:40	LGA	CPH	128	14	145	134523

...more observations...

Obs	Flight	Date	Depart	Orig	Dest	Boarded	Transferred	Deplaned	Revenue
42	271	05MAR12	13:17	LGA	PAR	177	22	203	128972
43	271	07MAR12	13:17	LGA	PAR	155	21	180	153423
44	271	08MAR12	13:17	LGA	PAR	152	20	176	133345
45	271	09MAR12	13:17	LGA	PAR	159	18	182	126543
46	271	10MAR12	13:17	LGA	PAR	182	9	198	134976

Output A2.5 *Partial Results: PROC PRINT Output of Work.Laguardia*

Laguardia Flights

Dest=CPH

Obs	Flight	Date	Depart	Orig	Boarded	Transferred	Deplaned	Revenue
1	387	04MAR12	11:40	LGA	81	21	103	196540
2	387	05MAR12	11:40	LGA	142	8	152	134561
3	387	07MAR12	11:40	LGA	131	5	142	135632
4	387	08MAR12	11:40	LGA	150	9	162	128564
5	387	09MAR12	11:40	LGA	128	14	145	134523
6	387	10MAR12	11:40	LGA	154	18	177	109885

...more observations...

Dest=PAR

Obs	Flight	Date	Depart	Orig	Boarded	Transferred	Deplaned	Revenue
34	271	04MAR12	11:40	LGA	146	8	163	156804
35	271	05MAR12	12:19	LGA	177	15	227	190098
36	271	07MAR12	9:31	LGA	155	18	172	166470
37	271	08MAR12	12:19	LGA	152	7	187	163248
38	271	09MAR12	13:17	LGA	159	15	191	170766
39	271	10MAR12	11:40	LGA	182	9	153	195468
40	271	03MAR12	13:17	LGA	147	29	183	123456
41	271	04MAR12	13:17	LGA	146	13	163	125632
42	271	05MAR12	13:17	LGA	177	22	203	128972
43	271	07MAR12	13:17	LGA	155	21	180	153423
44	271	08MAR12	13:17	LGA	152	20	176	133345
45	271	09MAR12	13:17	LGA	159	18	182	126543
46	271	10MAR12	13:17	LGA	182	9	198	134976

Output A2.6 *Partial Output: PDF Output: LGA Airport*

Laguardia Flights Friday, December 7,

Dest=CPH

Obs	Flight	Date	Depart	Orig	Boarded	Transferred	Deplaned	Revenue
1	387	04MAR12	11:40	LGA	81	21	103	196540
2	387	05MAR12	11:40	LGA	142	8	152	134561
3	387	07MAR12	11:40	LGA	131	5	142	135632
4	387	08MAR12	11:40	LGA	150	9	162	128564
5	387	09MAR12	11:40	LGA	128	14	145	134523
6	387	10MAR12	11:40	LGA	154	18	177	109885

Dest=FRA

Obs	Flight	Date	Depart	Orig	Boarded	Transferred	Deplaned	Revenue
7	622	03MAR12	12:19	LGA	180	16	200	187636
8	622	04MAR12	12:19	LGA	137	14	155	165456
9	622	05MAR12	12:19	LGA	185	11	199	125436
10	622	07MAR12	12:19	LGA	210	22	237	107865
11	622	08MAR12	12:19	LGA	176	5	187	178543
12	622	09MAR12	12:19	LGA	173	11	189	100987
13	622	10MAR12	12:19	LGA	129	12	147	134459

Dest=LON

Obs	Flight	Date	Depart	Orig	Boarded	Transferred	Deplaned	Revenue
14	219	04MAR12	9:31	LGA	232	18	250	189065
15	219	05MAR12	9:31	LGA	160	4	167	197456
16	219	06MAR12	9:31	LGA	163	14	183	162343
17	219	07MAR12	9:31	LGA	241	9	250	134520
18	219	08MAR12	9:31	LGA	183	11	197	106753
19	219	09MAR12	9:31	LGA	211	18	235	122766
20	219	10MAR12	9:31	LGA	167	7	181	198744

Test Your Code Solution

1. Correct Answer: 189KB – 199KB. You might get a slightly different answer, depending on your hardware, operating system, and software version. On the actual exam, all candidates work from the same cloned virtual machine, so the results will be consistent for grading.
2. Correct Answer: 129
3. Correct Answer: PAR

If your answers are not correct, verify that you used a BY statement in your PROC PRINT statement.

Scenario 5

Code Solution

The highlighted portions below illustrate the areas where corrections are required in order to make this program run and generate results.

```
data work.aprilbills (drop=Total EquipCost);
   set cert.aprbills;
   if Days>7 then Discount=(RoomCharge)*.20;
      else Discount=0;
   TotalDue=Total-Discount;
   format DateIn DateOut date9.;
   format RoomRate RoomCharge Discount TotalDue dollar10.2;
run;
proc print data=work.aprilbills;
run;
```

Output A2.7 *PROC PRINT Output of AprilBills*

Obs	LastName	DateIn	DateOut	RoomRate	Days	RoomCharge	Discount	TotalDue
1	Akron	05APR2009	09APR2009	$175.00	5	$875.00	$0.00	$1,173.45
2	Brown	12APR2009	01MAY2009	$125.00	20	$2,500.00	$500.00	$2,326.78
3	Carnes	27APR2009	29APR2009	$125.00	3	$375.00	$0.00	$549.24
4	Denison	11APR2009	12APR2009	$175.00	2	$350.00	$0.00	$437.41
5	Fields	15APR2009	22APR2009	$175.00	8	$1,400.00	$280.00	$1,498.96
6	Jamison	16APR2009	23APR2009	$125.00	8	$1,000.00	$200.00	$1,146.28

Test Your Code Solution

1. Correct Answer: $437.41
2. Correct Answer: $280.00

Scenario 6

Code Solution

The solution listed below is one example of a program that could be used to accomplish each task within the scenario. Your code can be different, as long as it results in the same answers.

```
libname certdata XLSX 'C:\Users\certdata\heart.xlsx';                  /*#1*/
data work.heart;                                                        /*#2*/
   set certdata.heart(drop=AgeAtDeath DeathCause);                      /*#3*/
   where Status='Alive';                                                /*#4*/
   if AgeCHDdiag=. then delete;                                         /*#5*/
   length Smoking_Status $17;                                           /*#6*/
   if 0<=Smoking<6 then Smoking_Status='Non-Smoker (0-5)';              /*#7*/
   else if 6<=Smoking<=15 then Smoking_Status='Moderate (6-15)';
   else if 16<=Smoking<=25 then Smoking_Status='Heavy (16-25)';
   else if Smoking>25 then Smoking_Status='Very Heavy (> 25)';
   else Smoking_Status='Error';                                         /*#8*/
run;
proc freq data=work.heart;                                              /*#9*/
   tables AgeCHDdiag*Smoking_Status/norow nocol nopercent;              /*#10*/
```

```
run;
```

1 The SAS/ACCESS LIBNAME statement creates the libref certdata, which points to the Excel workbook heart.xlsx.

2 The DATA step creates a new temporary data set named Work.Heart.

3 The SET statement indicates which worksheet in the Excel file to read. The SET statement specifies the libref (the reference to the Excel file) and the worksheet name as the input data. The DROP= data set option excludes the variables AgeAtDeath and DeathCause from being written to the data set. The DROP statement could also have been used.

4 The WHERE statement selects the observations where the value of the Status variable is Alive.

5 The IF statement causes the DATA step to continue processing only those observations that meet the condition of the expression specified in the IF statement. In the example, if the value of AgeCHDdiag is missing, then those observations are removed from the data set.

6 The LENGTH statement specifies that the length of Smoking_Status is set to 17 and is a character variable. This is used to avoid truncating values.

7 The IF/ELSE IF statements create values for the Smoking_Status variable by subsetting smoking values.

8 The ELSE statement gives an alternative action if all the other IF-THEN/ELSE statements are not executed.

9 The FREQ procedure creates a two-way frequency for Work.Heart.

10 The TABLES statement requests a two-way frequency table for the variables AgeCHDdiag and Smoking_Status. The options norow, nocol, and nopercent suppress row percentages, column percentages, and cell percentages.

Output A2.8 *Partial Results: PROC FREQ Results*

Frequency

Table of AgeCHDdiag by Smoking_Status

AgeCHDdiag(AgeCHDdiag)	Smoking_Status					
	Error	Heavy (16-25)	Moderate (6-15)	Non-Smoker (0-5)	Very Heavy (> 25)	Total
32	0	0	0	1	0	1
33	0	1	0	1	0	2
36	0	1	0	0	0	1
37	0	0	0	2	0	2
38	0	1	0	1	0	2
...more observations...						
84	0	0	2	2	0	4
85	0	1	0	2	0	3
86	0	0	0	3	0	3
87	0	0	0	1	0	1
88	0	0	0	2	0	2
Total	3	102	56	350	44	555

Test Your Code Solution

1. Correct Answer: 102
2. Correct Answer: 2
3. Correct Answer: 3

Scenario 7

Code Solution

The solution listed below is one example of a program that could be used to accomplish each task within the scenario. Your code can be different, as long as it results in the same answers.

```
data work.scenario7;                  /*#1*/
   set cert.temp18;                   /*#2*/
   format Day date9.;                 /*#3*/
   Month=month(day);                  /*#4*/
run;
proc freq data=work.scenario7;        /*#5*/
   tables HighTemp;                   /*#6*/
run;
proc means data=work.scenario7;       /*#7*/
   class month;                       /*#8*/
   var AvgLowTemp AvgHighTemp;        /*#9*/
run;
```

1 The DATA step creates a new temporary data set named Work.Scenario7.

2 The SET statement is used to read observations from one or more SAS data sets.

3 The FORMAT statement formats the Day variable in the date9. format.

4 The MONTH function returns the numeric value of the month within the Day variable.

5 The FREQ procedure creates one-way, two-way, and *n*-way tables. It also describes data by reporting the distribution of variable values.

6 The TABLES statement requests one-way to *n*-way frequency and crosstabulation tables and statistics. In this case, that is a one-way frequency with the default statistics for the variable HighTemp.

7 The MEANS procedure is used to compute descriptive statistics for the variables stated in the VAR statement.

8 The CLASS statement provides separate calculations for each value of the Month variable.

9 The VAR statement identifies the two variables, AvgLowTemp and AvgHighTemp, as the analysis variables, and also controls their order in the output.

Output A2.9 *PROC FREQ Results of High Temp*

HighTemp	Frequency	Percent	Cumulative Frequency	Cumulative Percent
21	2	2.22	2	2.22
23	1	1.11	3	3.33
26	2	2.22	5	5.56
27	1	1.11	6	6.67
28	1	1.11	7	7.78

...more observations...

HighTemp	Frequency	Percent	Cumulative Frequency	Cumulative Percent
68	2	2.22	85	94.44
74	1	1.11	86	95.56
77	1	1.11	87	96.67
78	2	2.22	89	98.89
82	1	1.11	90	100.00

Output A2.10 *PROC MEANS Results*

Month	N Obs	Variable	N	Mean	Std Dev	Minimum	Maximum
1	31	AvgLowTemp	31	28.6129032	0.4951376	28.0000000	29.0000000
		AvgHighTemp	31	43.1612903	1.7145801	35.0000000	47.0000000
2	28	AvgLowTemp	28	31.7500000	1.4813657	30.0000000	34.0000000
		AvgHighTemp	28	48.2857143	2.0880106	45.0000000	52.0000000
3	31	AvgLowTemp	31	37.6129032	2.5778210	34.0000000	42.0000000
		AvgHighTemp	31	55.8387097	3.1738176	51.0000000	61.0000000

Test Your Code Solution

1. Correct Answer: 2
2. Correct Answer: 64
3. Correct Answer: 29
4. Correct Answer: 3.17

Scenario 8

Code Solution

The solution listed below is one example of a program that could be used to accomplish each task within the scenario. Your code can be different, as long as it results in the same answers.

```
data work.scenario8;                          /*#1*/
```

```
   set cert.addresses;                          /*#2*/
   Zipcode=substr(State,3,5);                   /*#3*/
   State=substr(State,1,2);                     /*#4*/
run;
proc print data=work.scenario8;                 /*#5*/
   where zipcode='85069';
run;
proc freq data=work.scenario8 order=freq;       /*#6*/
   tables State;                                /*#7*/
run;
```

1 The DATA step creates a temporary data set named Work.Scenario8.

2 The SET statement reads observations from one or more SAS data sets.

3 The assignment statement creates a new variable, Zipcode, which uses the SUBSTR function to extract the last 5 characters of the values in the variable State, starting at and including character 3.

4 The assignment statement replaces the value of State and uses the SUBSTR function to extract 2 characters of the values in the variable State, starting at and including character 1.

5 The PRINT procedure enables you to view the contents of the new data set, Work.Scenario8 where Zipcode is equal to 85069.

6 The FREQ procedure creates one-way, two-way, and *n*-way tables. It also describes data by reporting the distribution of variable values. The ORDER=FREQ option orders the table by descending frequency.

7 The TABLES statement requests a one-way frequency with the default statistics for the variable State.

Output A2.11 *PROC PRINT Results*

Obs	Street	City	State	Tel	Zipcode
45	1861 Clarksburg Road	Harquala Valley	AZ	928-372-871	85069

Output A2.12 *PROC FREQ Results*

State	Frequency	Percent	Cumulative Frequency	Cumulative Percent
FL	4	6.56	4	6.56
NC	4	6.56	8	13.11
CA	3	4.92	11	18.03
NY	3	4.92	14	22.95
PA	3	4.92	17	27.87
...more observations...				
NJ	1	1.64	57	93.44
NM	1	1.64	58	95.08
UT	1	1.64	59	96.72
WA	1	1.64	60	98.36
WI	1	1.64	61	100.00

Test Your Code Solution

1. Correct Answer: 3
2. Correct Answer: 45
3. Correct Answer: 2

Scenario 9

Code Solution

The solution listed below is one example of a program that could be used to accomplish each task within the scenario. Your code can be different, as long as it results in the same answers.

```
%let Location=USA;                                        /*#1*/
data work.flightempdata;                                  /*#2*/
   set cert.empdata cert.empdatu cert.empdatu2;           /*#3*/
   where Country="&Location" and Salary >= 30000;         /*#4*/
run;
proc sort data=work.flightempdata;                        /*#5*/
   by descending Salary;
run;
proc export data=work.flightempdata                       /*#6*/
   outfile="C:\cert\flightempdata.csv"
   dbms=csv
   replace;
run;
```

1 The %LET statement creates a macro variable named Location that stores the character variable value of USA.

2 The DATA step creates a new temporary data set named Work.Flightempdata.

3 The SET statement reads and concatenates the observations from the Cert.Empdata, Cert.Empdatu, and Cert.Empdatu2 data sets in that order.

4 The WHERE statement selects observations from the SAS data sets Cert.Empdata, Cert.Empdatu, and Cert.Empdatu2 that have a value for Country that is equal to the value of the macro variable &location The statement also selects observations that have a value of Salary greater than or equal to $30,000.

5 The PROC SORT step sorts the SAS data set Work.Flightempdata by the values of the variable Salary in descending order.

6 PROC EXPORT exports the SAS data set Work.Flightempdata to a comma-separated value file. The DATA= option identifies the input SAS data set, and the OUTFILE= option specifies the complete path and filename for the delimited external file. The DBMS = option specifies the type of data to export (in this case CSV), and the REPLACE option overwrites an existing file.

Output A2.13 *PROC EXPORT Result: Flightempdata.csv*

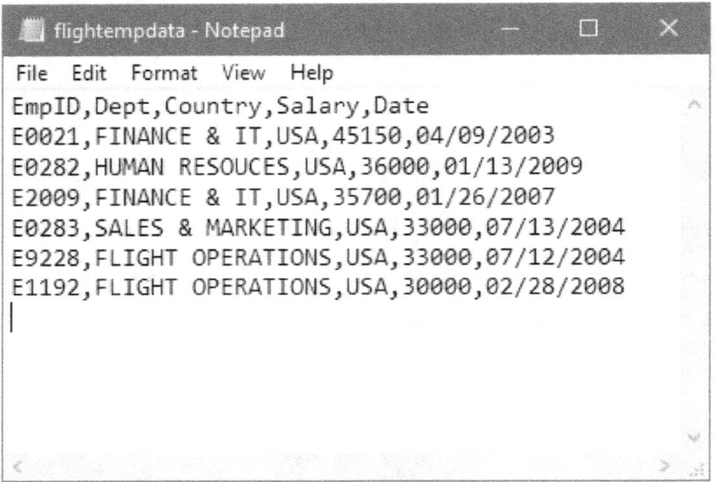

```
EmpID,Dept,Country,Salary,Date
E0021,FINANCE & IT,USA,45150,04/09/2003
E0282,HUMAN RESOUCES,USA,36000,01/13/2009
E2009,FINANCE & IT,USA,35700,01/26/2007
E0283,SALES & MARKETING,USA,33000,07/13/2004
E9228,FLIGHT OPERATIONS,USA,33000,07/12/2004
E1192,FLIGHT OPERATIONS,USA,30000,02/28/2008
```

Test Your Code Solution

1. Correct Answer: $33,000
2. Correct Answer: 290 – 300 bytes (any number within this range is an acceptable and correct answer)

Scenario 10

Code Solution

The highlighted portions below illustrate the areas where corrections are required in order to make this program run and generate results.

```
data work.mycars;
```

```
   set sashelp.cars;
   AvgMPG=mean(mpg_city, mpg_highway);
run;
title 'Cars With Average MPG Over 40';
proc print data=work.mycars;
   var make model type avgmpg;
   where AvgMPG>40;
run;
title 'Average MPG by Car Type';
proc means data=work.mycars mean min max maxdec=1;
   var avgmpg;
   class type;
run;
title;
```

Test Your Code Solution

1. Correct Answer: 262
2. Correct Answer: 4

Index

N

O

P

Q

CPSIA information can be obtained
at www.ICGtesting.com
Printed in the USA
BVHW011744100719
553080BV00012B/586/P

9 781642 951905